D0138931

STRAIGHTFORWARD STATISTICS

STRAIGHTFORWARD STATISTICS

Understanding the Tools of Research

Glenn Geher

AND

Sara Hall

OXFORD

UNIVERSITY PRESS

OXFORD

UNIVERSITY PRESS

Oxford University Press is a department of the University of Oxford.
It furthers the University's objective of excellence in research, scholarship,
and education by publishing worldwide.

Oxford   New York

Auckland   Cape Town   Dar es Salaam   Hong Kong   Karachi
Kuala Lumpur   Madrid   Melbourne   Mexico City   Nairobi
New Delhi   Shanghai   Taipei   Toronto

With offices in

Argentina   Austria   Brazil   Chile   Czech Republic   France   Greece
Guatemala   Hungary   Italy   Japan   Poland   Portugal   Singapore
South Korea   Switzerland   Thailand   Turkey   Ukraine   Vietnam

Oxford is a registered trademark of Oxford University Press
in the UK and certain other countries.

Published in the United States of America by
Oxford University Press
198 Madison Avenue, New York, NY 10016

© Oxford University Press 2014

All rights reserved. No part of this publication may be reproduced, stored in a
retrieval system, or transmitted, in any form or by any means, without the prior
permission in writing of Oxford University Press, or as expressly permitted by law,
by license, or under terms agreed with the appropriate reproduction rights organization.
Inquiries concerning reproduction outside the scope of the above should be sent to the
Rights Department, Oxford University Press, at the address above.

You must not circulate this work in any other form
and you must impose this same condition on any acquirer.

Library of Congress Cataloging-in-Publication Data
Geher, Glenn.
Straightforward statistics : understanding the tools of research / Glenn Geher, Sara Hall.
pages cm
Includes bibliographical references and index.
ISBN 978-0-19-975176-1
1. Psychometrics.   2. Psychology—Mathematical models.   3. Psychology—Research.
4. Statistics—Study and teaching (Higher)   I. Hall, Sara, 1979–   II. Title.
BF39.G427 2014
150.1'5195—dc23
2013035850

3 5 7 9 8 6 4 2
Printed in the United States of America
on acid-free paper

Glenn: For my dad, who has encouraged mathematical reasoning across my life. And for my mom, who has convinced me, always, that all stars are within reach.

Sara: To Benjamin, for everything, and to Jackson, Stella, Susanna, and Sailor, the best people I've ever met. Also to my parents, for giving me the confidence to live life fully and the ability to laugh about it.

CONTENTS

PREFACE

The trend in the production of academic textbooks in general—and psychological-statistics textbooks in particular—is toward incorporating ever more bells and whistles. Typical statistics textbooks are replete with boxes, figures, and illustrations. Further, the textbook itself (nowadays) is simply one element in a package—often including a study guide, a software workbook, and an accompanying website (for students) as well as multiple instructor's manuals, a separate accompanying website (for faculty), a testbank, and a fancy set of PowerPoint presentations—tailored to each chapter.

Another trend in statistics textbooks in psychology tends toward watering down the content. This trend is driven by a motivation to strike a balance between covering the concepts in sufficiently deep and broad detail and presenting the information in a way that is accessible to an often-resistant and anxious clientele: Undergraduate students who are afraid of math. While this trend toward watering the content down makes sense, we don't think it's necessary.

Straightforward Statistics: Understanding the Tools of Research was designed from the outset to be written so as to effectively strike that balance between sufficiently covering the important concepts that underlie psychological statistics and presenting the information in an accessible manner.

Why should you trust Glenn and Sara to be able to achieve this balance successfully? Good question. Let's start with Glenn. I took two different statistics courses as an undergraduate psychology major at the University of Connecticut. I then took four different advanced statistics classes at the University of New Hampshire as a PhD student. But it wasn't until Victor Benassi, who was chair of the UNH Psychology Department at the time, told me that I was set to teach Statistics—an essential part of our undergraduate major—in Spring of 1996–that I had to prove myself. I was a bit nervous. But why? I'd pretty much aced every stats class I'd taken. I'd implemented several advanced statistics in my research and was able to publish a high-quality research article in the journal *Intelligence* based on that work. Why would I balk at this?

For whatever reason, I did. And when I first got up there with those 35 or so bright undergraduate New Englanders looking me in the eyes on Day 1, I realized I had to teach these young people something. Something real. Something useful. Something that they could tell their parents about!

So I got a highly recommended textbook from the time, written by that famous couple out of Stonybrook, Art and Elaine Aron. And I read that book (the 1994 edition, which served as a significant inspiration for the current work) like I'd never read a book before. This one was for blood. This one mattered. My ability to teach this material to young minds that are mildly afraid of the content depended on me having a masterful understanding of the content. This is no small thing.

In other areas of psychology, you maybe can fake it. In talking about emotion research, for instance, you can make the case some emotional states only show up in some conditions using some measures…what you're studying is pretty much "real," but not like "really real." Welcome to teaching statistics—where "*real* is *really real.*" You better get it right! And that was the challenge to me in the Spring of1996. And given my tendency to take on pretty much any challenge that comes my way, I was up for it!

I taught the class—based loosely on Aron and Aron's textbook at the time. I loved it. And I think that the students tolerated it! My approach was sort of unique, because I didn't go in there feeling much above the students. My goal wasn't to show these people how smart I was or how smart they should be. Urgent message to college teachers—that's not the job! Rather, my goal has always been to best teach the content to the broadest number of learners. And to empower these individuals so that they want to learn and so that they feel they can move forward in life able to apply what we've taught them in all domains. When I first started teaching statistics, I worked really hard with this objective in mind. And this objective characterizes my teaching to this day. This book has that philosophy of teaching and learning entrenched on every page. The material progresses slowly and clearly—always connected to content that came before or that is on the horizon. And repetition rears its head throughout this book—based on the premise that the more repetition, the better with this kind of complex material.

When I first met Sara Hall (then Sara Hubbard), she was a 17-year-old college student who grew up in the middle of the farms of Oregon. The paper she wrote for my introductory psychology class was about 10 times longer than any of the other papers—and about 100 times better. The second I met her, this kid had arrived. At 17, she was fully able to discuss material at a PhD level—and was able to take an active role in research to help uncover important questions of human personality and development. She was like nothing I'd ever seen! After she transferred from Western Oregon University (where we met) to Southern Oregon University, she worked with a faculty member interested in the psychology of statistics—and, together, they presented research on this topic at several research meetings. Sara was shaping up to be an expert on the details of undergraduate education related to statistics. When it came time for me to look for a coauthor for this book—someone whom I could trust 100% to do a stellar job—Sara immediately came to mind.

From the outset, our goal has been to create an accessible, accurate, coherent, and engaging presentation of statistics that can stand alone in one's education if needed. We are pretty down-to-earth, and we very much hope that this fact trickled down to the words we use.

What Makes Our Approach to Teaching Statistics Unique?

1. A Narrative, Accessible Voice

People are prepared to follow coherent information—narratives, stories. Technical information is best presented in a way that's accessible and that is part of a broader story. Statistics includes lots of technical information—and to help convey this information, we take every bit of it and work to integrate this information into narrative, meaningful passages designed to get students to really understand the point of the material.

2. Conceptual

In our experience, every statistics teacher in the world says that his or her approach is the conceptual approach. We're no different! Of course, we truly believe that our approach is highly conceptual in nature.

Every technical term and idea (e.g., the "sum of the squared deviation scores") is put into context: What is this term? Why do we compute it? What does it tell us? Well, it turns out that the sum of the squared deviation scores is one index of how much scores in a sample of scores tend to vary from one another—and the way that this is computed totally maps onto this fact. If scores vary a lot from each other in a sample, the sum of the squared deviation scores will be a high number. If they do not vary much from one another, this number will be relatively low. All the formulas and technical ideas in this class are explicated in such conceptual language—in terms of what these things actually mean!

3. Content

This book is also comprehensive for an undergraduate course in statistics. It includes 13 chapters addressing the basic topics that are used in modern behavioral statistics, along with appendices that help provide additional content related to advanced statistics and a special appendix that provides step-by-step instructions and guidance regarding how to use SPSS, the state-of-the-art software in our field, to compute many of the statistics that are presented in this class.

4. Current Research

Each chapter includes a section related to current research that pertains to the statistic at hand. Thus, after learning about, for instance, statistical regression, students will read a summary of a statistical regression analysis from a recently published article in the journal *Evolutionary Psychology* to help them see how these statistics play out in real research.

5. No Frills

Despite the fact that we're not all that old and we're somewhat technologically savvy, we employed an extraordinarily no-frills approach in writing this book. To really understand statistics, a piece of chalk, a good textbook, and a chalkboard (and a calculator with a square root function!) are pretty much all that are needed.

This no-frills approach goes beyond my "only chalk needed here" method. In my (GG's) 15+ years of teaching this class, I've never relied on "ancillary" materials such as test banks provided by the publisher, PowerPoint slides, and the like. If you're the teacher, then you should make the test. And you should make the materials that you present to the students. This philosophy ensures that the teacher is right in the trenches with the students.

Our primary rationale for such a no-frills approach is straightforward: A good statistics textbook—roughly having between 10-20 chapters of high-level academic material—is, if anything, *too much* information. And college students don't do well with too much.

If a good, solid statistics textbook alone is too much information, then a textbook plus the typical ancillary materials (e.g., PowerPoint slides, separate study book, etc.) may be more than too much! And if students don't do well with "too much information," they're likely to do worse with "more than too much."

Statistics tends to be so daunting and abstract for undergraduate students such that the bells and whistles don't necessarily help—rather, they may make things more complex and, ultimately, more difficult. The no-frills approach is designed to really encourage students and instructors to engage primarily with the material itself.

REFERENCE

Aron, A., & Aron, E.N. (1994). Statistics for Psychology. Upper Saddle River, NJ: Prentice-Hall.

ACKNOWLEDGEMENTS

The folks at Oxford University Press fully live up their reputation! We initially signed with Oxford when Lori Handelman was the editor. Her warmth and insight helped shape this book along a very positive trajectory. We were fortunate to have this book picked up by our fearless editor, Abby Gross, who represents the best of the publishing world. From the start, this book has been in great hands! In addition, the follow-up by the folks at Oxford, including amazing editorial assistance by Elina Carmona, Joanna Ng, Marc Schneider, and Suzanne Walker, has been huge. And thanks to long-term collaborator, Scott Barry Kaufman, for suggesting Oxford as a venue for this book!

And huge thanks to our statistics teachers—particularly Rebecca Warner of the University of New Hampshire (statistician sine quo non)—whose brilliance lies in the fact that she can make any complex idea simple to understand for pretty much anyone. And many thanks to the wonderful Teaching Assistants that I (GG) have had at SUNY New Paltz—several of whom have seen and commented on earlier drafts of this book. In particular, Lisa Schimski has been a tour de force in providing detailed feedback and comments on this book—and has been hugely helpful in presenting an early version of this book to our statistics students at New Paltz. Thanks Lisa—you're awesome!

And many thanks to the folks who have made time in our lives so that we had time to create this book. This mostly includes our spouses! Ben is an all-star whose helpful and supportive nature fully allowed Sara to make time for this project. And Kathy, who learned statistics side-by-side with me (GG) at UNH back in the day when we used a "mainframe" computer—has been hugely helpful on this project from forever. And thanks to our kids—who are our ultimate motivators—for Sara, there are four—Jackson, Stella, Susanna, and Sailor—and Glenn's fortunate to have Andrew and Megan. We hope and trust that all six of these kids come to love statistics as much as we do some day!

STRAIGHTFORWARD STATISTICS

PRELUDE: WHY DO I NEED TO LEARN STATISTICS?

"I went into psychology because I want to help people—not to learn a bunch of scientific math stuff."

"I majored in psych to avoid classes like this one…"

"I'm not good at math."

"I'm scared of this course."

"What does statistics have to do with psychology, anyway?"

n my 15+ years of teaching psychological statistics to undergraduate students, I find that these kinds of comments are typical when students first walk into the classroom. Teaching psychological statistics to undergraduates is particularly challenging given the facts that:

A. Students do not want to learn the material.

B. Students do not perceive the material as relevant to their interests.

and

C. Students are often downright scared of the course.

No other course in a typical undergraduate curriculum has such attitudinal barriers from the outset.

No problem. Each of these issues can be addressed in the teaching of this course. In fact, as this course progresses, students will see that the ideas from this class have the capacity to expand students' understanding of the world more so than most other classes in the psychology curriculum.

The content of other classes changes with time. What is considered a fact about human personality in 2013 may, from the perspective of textbooks to be published in 2028, eventually be deemed a strange, erroneous, and outdated belief resulting from the use of rudimentary methods. The same goes for the other content areas of psychology—from developmental psychology to social psychology to cognitive neuroscience. Statistics, on the other hand, has a universal and timeless quality to it. Many of the statistical procedures presented in this book—such as Pearson's correlation coefficient, the within-groups t-test, or the one-way analysis of variance—have stood the test of time. This fact alone suggests that there is something useful about the ideas included in this course.

Let's consider the three barriers described here in turn. First, think about Barrier-to-Teaching-Statistics #1: Students do not want to learn the material. This barrier suggests that there is something uninteresting about the content of the course. It's perceived as boring and lifeless. This perception simply need not be true. There is no other course in the typical psychology curriculum that is so filled with right answers. Being able to arrive at right answers is, as you will see through this course, downright fun.

Further, the material in this course follows a coherent, logical pattern that simply does not typify any other course in psychology. For students who pay attention and stay on top of their work, the logic that underlies this course is sure to be rewarding.

But is it relevant? Consider Barrier-to-Teaching-Statistics #2: Students do not perceive the material as relevant to their interests. The good news is that, yes, statistics is extremely relevant to your interests! All people, to some extent, are psychologists—trying to understand the behavior of themselves and of the people around them (Kelley, 1967). Consider these kinds of questions that we ask ourselves on a regular basis:

"Was that smile an expression of interest in me, or just friendliness? I wonder if there's a good way to tell such smiles apart."

"Why is that guy so popular—I think he's such a jerk. Does being a jerk somehow make him popular?"

"What should I do to make sure I study enough for the exams in this class? What are the best studying strategies to succeed in a stats course?"

"I can't believe she just said that! What is it about some people that makes them say whatever they think while others are more reserved?"

In analyzing these kinds of questions in our day-to-day lives, we are, in effect, using statistical reasoning. For instance, consider the question of whether popular guys are jerks. In thinking about this hypothesis, you may go through the different men in your social circle—thinking about which ones are jerks and which aren't. You may even discuss these things with your friends—trying to come up with an answer to the question at hand. In an informal way, you are actually engaging in statistical reasoning. In this case, the reasoning may reflect what we call inferential statistics—designed to allow us to infer if some pattern we see in a small sample (e.g., the sample of guys in our social circle) may map onto some general aspect of the population at large (guys in general).

In short, we use statistical reasoning *all the time*. Understanding the elements of statistical procedures—and developing the language to express statistical concepts—will surely prove helpful in your attempts to understand the world in your future, regardless of your career path.

While statistics are useful in understanding the nature of our worlds in general, they are particularly useful in the scientific study of behavior—i.e., in Psychology. Nearly all the ideas you learn about in your other psychology classes are based on statistics. Consider social psychology. In this course, students typically learn the following *facts*:

A.   People tend to be more giving toward members of their own group than members of other groups—even if group designations are based on non-meaningful groupings (Tajfel & Billig, 1981).

B.   People tend to ignore situational factors that cause the behavior of others (Ross, 1977).

C. Symmetrical faces are perceived as more attractive than non-symmetrical faces (Langlois & Roggman, 1991).

Each of these facts—or summaries of findings from published studies in social psychology—is based on statistics. Thus, to understand where these findings come from, you must understand the nature of statistics. Further, to be able to effectively critique these findings, you must understand the nature of statistics. Lastly, to be able to produce similar findings by conducting your own research—on your own research questions—you must understand the nature of statistics. In short, understanding statistics is essential to your education in psychology. That's why we make you take this class.

Finally, consider Barrier-to-Teaching-Statistics #3: Students are scared of this course. Is there any reason to be scared of this course? Hogwash! Put simply: If you got into college, you can handle the content of this course. The math's not that hard. In fact, typically, the math involved in the statistics you'll be working with consists of nothing more complex than basic algebra—a topic regularly taught to 8th graders. If ever there were a course in which diligence pays off—it's this one. Come to class, do your homework, ask questions of your instructor, stay on top of things, and there's an incredibly good chance that you will excel.

THE NATURE OF FINDINGS AND FACTS IN THE BEHAVIORAL SCIENCES

In terms of your education in psychology, this course in statistics serves to help you interpret, understand, and question the many findings and facts that you come across. Consider, for example, the finding that men tend to be more bothered by infidelity of a sexual nature compared with women—and that women tend to be more bothered by emotional infidelity (i.e., their partner falling in love with someone else) than men. In the original study on this phenomenon, David Buss and his colleagues (Buss, Larsen, & Semmelworth, 1992) found that men show a bigger increase in heart rate when thinking about sexual infidelity than do women. Specifically, Buss et al. report that male pulse rate increased 4.76 beats per minute when they were presented with thoughts of sexual infidelity, while females' pulse rates increased by 2.25 beats per minute in response to those same thoughts. On the other hand, males' pulse rates increased 3.00 beats per minute to the emotional infidelity thoughts, while females' pulse rates increased by 2.57 beats per minute in this emotional-thought condition.

Since the publication of this article in 1992, many researchers have conducted follow-up research to address whether Buss et al.'s findings are valid. Some of these researchers clearly support Buss et al.—others don't. Are males more jealous in instances of sexual infidelity compared with females? To address this question seriously means looking at the scientific literature on this topic. In order to do that, for better or worse, you absolutely need to understand statistics. Otherwise, you're stuck in the position of just taking others' word. And a bright, educated individual should make a habit of avoiding that.

Let's take a look at Buss et al.'s finding. The presentation of average increases in pulse rate means that both males and females increased in pulse rates (from baseline) when thinking about sexual infidelity. On average, males' pulse rates increased more. In fact, males' pulse rate increased 2.51 beats per minute more than females. Further, males' increase to the sexual image was 1.57 beats per minute more than the comparable female difference (for females, their pulse rate was .32 beats per minute higher for the emotional thought sample compared with the sexual one). Here are some questions that we ultimately can answer with the understanding of statistics presented in this course:

Is the difference between males' pulse rate in response to sexual and emotional thoughts (1.57 beats per minute) large?
Is this difference bigger than we could expect by chance?
How likely is it that adult males and females who were not in that study—from all reaches of the globe—would respond in the same ways as the subjects in that study?
Did all males show an increase in pulse rate when presented with the sexual infidelity thoughts?
Did all females show an increase in pulse rate when presented with the sexual infidelity thoughts?
How much did the males in the sample vary from one another in terms of heart-rate increases?
How much did the females in the sample vary from one another in terms of heart-rate increases?
Is the amount of variability across the male and female samples equivalent—and, if not, what would that imply about the findings?

In one simple sentence in that article, Buss et al. address many of these questions. They write, "Men showed a substantial increase in PR (pulse rate) to both images (emotional and sexual), but significantly more so in response to the sexual infidelity image (t(31) = 2.29, p < .05)." These researchers also submit the standard deviations for males and females in their presentation of the results. As we'll see in this course, the standard deviation is a useful and straightforward index of how much scores in a sample vary from one another. The educated student of statistics can take all this information—the presentation of means, standard deviation, and the t-test— and come up with good answers to all the aforementioned questions.

But that's not all. The educated statistics student can also read the many articles that came after Buss et al.'s first publication on this topic and interpret the findings from those articles, ultimately developing for him or herself a very sophisticated and informed understanding of the nature of sex differences in responses to infidelity that typify humans. Yes, you can do that after you successfully complete this course. Not bad.

STATISTICAL SIGNIFICANCE AND EFFECT SIZE

Let's start with a totally inane research premise: I doubt very much that 1st-grade girls who happen to have curly hair differ from 1st-grade girls who happen to have straight hair in terms of the average number of Little Ponies they own. To try to address this hypothesis, I randomly go into the schools and find 100 curly-haired girls and 100 straight-haired girls, and count their Ponies. In statistics, we're generally trying to take data (pieces of information that are quantified in some way) collected from a sample of some population of interest in an attempt to deter-mine if there are some meaningful trends, patterns, and/or differences between groups that are noteworthy. In the current example, the researcher is asking whether curly-haired 1st-grade girls differ from straight-haired 1st-grade girls in the number of Little Ponies they have—on average. Importantly, given the nature of this research question, we're not interested in these

200 little girls in particular. Rather, we're interested in whether there are differences between the general populations of straight-haired and curly-haired 1st-grade girls in terms of the number of Little Ponies owned. For practical reasons, we can't count the number of Ponies of all the 1st-grade girls in the world; thus, we will collect data from samples representing the two types (curly-haired and straight-haired) and use statistics to try to generalize our findings to the bigger populations of interest.

We implement this ridiculous research by systematically counting the number of Little Ponies of 100 randomly selected girls with straight hair and another 100 randomly selected girls with curly hair (all 1st graders in the same school). Let's consider two scenarios:

SCENARIO A:
Your statistical test (that you carry out effectively due to your having aced this course) tells you that curly-haired girls have significantly more Little Ponies compared to their straight-haired counterparts. However, the effect size estimate that you compute tells you that the effect is actually quite small.

OR

SCENARIO B:
Your statistical test tells you that curly-haired girls have significantly more Little Ponies compared to their straight-haired counterparts AND the effect size estimate that you compute tells you that the effect is actually quite large.

What do you make of all this? Well, this thought-exercise is designed to get you to understand—in a simple way—the distinction between statistical significance and effect size. If a statistical test comes out as indicating statistical significance, then you have found an effect that:

Is unlikely to have come about by chance alone and, further, that is likely to be an accurate representation of patterns of data at the level of the populations of interest.

Let's dissect that: If the finding is unlikely to come about by chance, then the pattern found in your sample (in this case, the difference between the average amount of Ponies owned by curly-haired versus straight-haired little girls) is probably not just due to the fact that different samples taken from the same population tend be slightly different from one another. If the finding is statistically significant, then it is unlikely that differences between the means of the samples are just due to chance, in which case you can be reasonably sure that the pattern you found in your samples accurately reflects how things are at the population levels. In other words, you can say that it is most likely the case that the average number of Ponies owned by all the curly-haired 1st-grade girls in the world is higher than the average number for all the straight-haired 1st-grade girls.

Reread all of that if you feel you need to, since what it means for something to be statistically significant is not particularly intuitive, but, rather, involves a convoluted set of abstract steps. At the same time, the issue of statistical significance is absolutely central to this course. Much of the latter part of this book is dedicated to the underlying logic and mathematical nature of this process.

On the other hand, for something to have a big effect size is a bit simpler. Effect size indices are used to tell us whether an effect we obtain in our statistics is, simply, big—is it worth talking about? Should we call our neighbors to check out this particular effect size?

The interesting thing about all this is as follows: Statistical significance and effect size are not identical to one another. Thus, you can have an outcome that is statistically significant but that does not have a big effect size—and vice versa (you can fail to obtain statistical significance even with a great big effect size). Throughout this course, you will study different ways to assess both statistical significance and effect sizes. Learning about both these concepts hand-in-hand will very much allow you to think critically about how to compute and interpret statistics.

Consider our hypothetical examples. In SCENARIO A, the curly-haired girls have significantly more Ponies than the straight-haired girls, but the effect size is small. That means that the population average for the curly-haired girls is probably bigger than the average for the straight-haired girls, but only a little bit—probably not enough to matter in a practical sense. If this scenario were the case, you'd probably have a hard time predicting the number of Ponies a little girl had from the curliness of her hair. In SCENARIO B, there is both statistical significance *and* a large effect size. In this kind of scenario, you can infer both that (a) the average number of Ponies for the entire population of curly-haired 1st-grade girls is greater than the average number for the entire population of straight-haired girls *and* (b) the difference is likely big and meaningful (e.g., an average number of Ponies owned of 32 for curly-haired girls versus an average number of Ponies owned of 17 for straight-haired girls).

Statistical significance is important—but it's not enough. Understanding both statistical significance and effect size in both intuitive and computationally sophisticated ways can be useful in many analytical problems you encounter in your future—inside the classroom and out.

DESCRIPTIVE AND INFERENTIAL STATISTICS

For this course, statistical procedures will be categorized into two broad domains: descriptive statistics and inferential statistics. In the end, you'll see that there is actually quite a bit of overlap between the different statistics that are pigeonholed in this manner—but this organization is useful in understanding basic statistical issues.

Descriptive statistics are exactly that—statistics that describe. Such statistics either describe the pattern of data in a single variable *or* they describe the nature of the relationships among multiple variables. For instance, the mean is the arithmetic average of a group of numbers. Suppose that you are interested in describing the general nature of how students scored on the first examination in a statistics class. To describe this variable, you would likely compute the mean score on the examination for all students. If the mean is 95, for instance, you could conclude that the students generally did very well. If the mean is 18, one might think that the instructor should change his or her teaching style—and maybe adopt a better textbook! As we'll see throughout this course, there are several methods used to describe data from a single variable.

Descriptive statistics that address multiple variables concurrently generally are rooted in statistics we refer to as correlational in nature. Correlational statistics address whether multiple variables are related to one another. For instance, is there a relationship between how close students sit to the front of the room and scores on examinations? This question is descriptive in nature—and it addresses this multiple-variable sort of descriptive statistic (it is concerned with describing the relationship between two variables (in this case, proximity to the front of the room (variable 1) and score on the exam (variable 2)). There are several issues to consider in understanding descriptive statistics that examine the relationship among multiple variables—and much of this course is dedicated to understanding these issues.

Inferential statistics pertain to the issue of statistical significance (as described in a prior section in this chapter). The *inferential* part of inferential statistics corresponds to our ability to make inferences about populations from samples. These statistics are probability-based—their general purpose is to allow us to demonstrate that it is very likely the case that a pattern found among a sample is representative of a pattern in the population at large. The Little Ponies example described prior speaks to this kind of question. The test that would be used to address if curly-haired little girls and straight-haired little girls differed significantly from one another in terms of number of Little Ponies owned would be a specific kind of inferential statistical procedure (in this case, called a between-groups t-test). The specific question addressed by this kind of statistic is essentially this: Is a pattern found using samples (e.g., the samples of curly-haired and straight-haired little girls) likely to hold at the population level? That is, is the pattern found in the data (in this case, this pattern corresponds to the fact that the mean number of Little Ponies for the curly-haired girl sample was greater than the mean number for the straight-haired sample) likely to be representative of the pattern found at the population level? If so, the mean number of Ponies owned by all the curly-haired 1st-grade girls in the world is greater than the mean number of Ponies owned by all the straight-haired 1st-grade girls.

These statistics are inferential because of the inference we make about populations based on data from samples. Using a basic understanding of probability theory and some interesting logic that comprises statistical hypothesis testing, inferential statistics are very useful in allowing us to understand the world.

A CONCEPTUAL APPROACH TO TEACHING AND LEARNING STATISTICS

This book is designed to foster a conceptual approach to the understanding of statistics. With that said, students should realize that nearly every professor who teaches statistics (or writes a statistics textbook) claims to be presenting a conceptual approach! But the approach here really is conceptual in nature!

What does a conceptual approach mean? First off, it means the focus in presenting the information is on the ideas—not the computation. It used to be that there were not computers to do all the statistics for psychologists who conduct research. Back then, researchers needed to compute statistics by hand—perhaps with calculators. This work was tedious—prone to error—and time-consuming. Back then, it was extremely important to learn the most efficient means for computing statistics by hand. As a function of that environment, there was a movement to figure out formulas that were not particularly intuitive—but that were mathematically equivalent to their conceptual/intuitive counterparts—and that were simply fastest for getting answers.

Times have changed. We now have computers and great statistical software to allow researchers to conduct analyses in seconds that would have taken weeks back in the day. This fact poses a challenge to someone teaching statistics. If you just teach students how to use the software and get answers, students cannot possibly understand what it is that they are doing. Such an approach seems lacking. You need to know the concepts—you need to know what you're doing.

The approach taken in this text encourages a conceptual understanding by (a) presenting the concepts in a clear, detailed manner, (b) teaching conceptually based formulas for computing statistics, and (c) providing an appendix on using statistical software (SPSS) that walks students through the process of computing and interpreting several common statistics. The confluence of these three elements (clear presentation of concepts, presentation of conceptually based formulas, and a straightforward presentation of statistical software) should allow the serious student to walk away with a deep, thorough, and practical education in statistics.

THE NATURE OF THIS BOOK

The defining features of this book address both its organization and its underlying philosophy. The organization of this book progresses from simple descriptive statistics (in a section titled Describing Single Variables) to complex descriptive statistics (in a section titled Describing Patterns of Relationships Among Two Variables). After a solid grounding in descriptive statistics is achieved, the book moves on to inferential statistics—starting with several chapters in a section titled Conceptual Ingredients of Inferential Statistics, then progressing to a final section titled Inferential Statistics in the Real World.

Chapters 2 through 13 follow a basic algorithm. Concepts, formulas, and examples of problems being worked out are presented in turn. Further, each chapter will conclude with a list of key terms and a set of homework problems. For half the homework problems (Set A), the answers are worked out in the back of this book. These problems—with their corresponding answers—should allow you to practice and help you really learn how to do the work. For the other half (Set B), students will not have access to the answers. However, the Set B problems will be no more challenging than the Set A problems—thus, if you can master the Set A problems, you should be able to master the Set B problems—and you should be able to master any examination on this material that is thrown your way.

The philosophy of this book is captured in the subtitle: the phrase. We've already addressed how this book is designed to be highly conceptual. Let's turn to the no-frills idea. News-Flash: Mastering an undergraduate statistics course is no easy feat. Accordingly, there has been a movement in the creation of textbooks and corresponding materials to make this as easy as possible for students. However, it seems that the use of technology to enhance statistics textbooks has drawbacks. These days, a typical statistics textbook has many ancillaries (i.e., supplemental things to go with the textbook). These ancillaries often include a special CD with additional information, an accompanying website, a separate workbook, and so on.

Reading, understanding, and mastering a single statistics textbook in one semester is plenty. The no-frills approach taken here follows this line of thought. There are no extras. The textbook is designed to be altogether sufficient for the purposes of learning this material. Time spent looking at the accompanying CD, going to the accompanying website, or reviewing the accompanying workbook is time spent away from mastering the textbook. Anything you'll need to develop a strong and thorough undergraduate-level understanding of statistics for psychology *is in here*. No bells and whistles—no frills.

HOW TO APPROACH THIS CLASS AND WHAT YOU SHOULD GET OUT OF IT

Nearly all college students should be able to master this class. If you had what it takes to *get into college*, then you have what it takes to understand the concepts you'll find in this book! However, note that there are a lot of ideas—and all the information is cumulative. That is, content from one chapter nearly always relates to content from earlier chapters. There is no way you can understand how to interpret a score in a normal distribution (chapter 7), for instance, if you don't completely understand how to compute and interpret a standardized score (chapter 4).

The successful student in this class is the one who does not miss a beat. Attend all classes — do all the homework. Don't ever hesitate to ask your instructor (or teaching assistant) for help. We get paid to educate you—that's our job.

The student who takes this class seriously and is steadfast in his or her work will reap many rewards. In addition to the academic success that is nearly sure to follow that student's diligence and effort, the student's mastery of the material will allow him or her to understand things that happen in this world in a new light. Once you master this material, you can ask questions that you never could ask before. Further, you will have the intellectual toolbox to allow you to answer and interpret these questions.

Importantly, the questions you'll be able to ask and answer after completing this course go well beyond psychology. Sure, you'll be able to ask and answer questions about human behavior (e.g., does playing violent videogames lead to feelings of anger and hostility?)—but you'll likely find yourself using the tools from this class to ask questions about many other things found in the world, possibly including:

The Weather: "It seems to be more likely to rain on the weekends compared with the weekdays—is there something to that?"
Plant Life: "Does this new organic lawn treatment reduce the number of dandelions in my yard?"
Technology: "This new operating system on my computer seems less able to handle Microsoft applications than my old operating system—is that a general problem with this operating system?"
Geology: "These granite boulders seem more prevalent in the high peaks of this state, but not of the high peaks of our neighboring state to the east. Is that right? If so, why the difference?"
Beer: "These two kegs came from the same beer store at the same time—but this one seems flatter. How can I figure out if it really is flatter?"
…and on and on and on.

If you take this class seriously, you'll walk away with tools for understanding the nature of things across all domains of your world. And you'll be well on your way to not only understanding research findings from psychology, but also to uncovering new truths about the world and our place in it. Welcome to Statistics!

KEY TERMS

Correlational statistics: Statistics that address whether multiple variables are related to one another
Data: Quantified pieces of information (plural of the little-used and little-know *datum*)
Descriptive statistics: Statistics that describe a pattern of data or the nature of the relationship among variables
Effect size: The magnitude of some statistical effect. It could correspond to the size of a relationship between variables, the size of a difference between means, or some other index of how *big* some statistical effect is
Inferential statistics: Probability-based statistics which allow inferences to be made about populations based on data collected from samples
Statistical significance: An indication that an effect found (based on data collected from samples) is unlikely to have come about by chance, and likely accurately represents the pattern of data in the population

HOMEWORK SET A

1. Each of the following presents a summary of a statistic that you might encounter in a psychological research article. For each, indicate if it is commenting on (a) just statistical significance, (b) just effect size, (c) both, or (d) neither. Further, explain each answer in a few sentences.

   i: In this research on whether males and females differ in terms of how happy they are with life, the difference between the means of the groups was minimal.

   ii: In our study, we found that dogs had more fleas than did cats. We can confidently infer that this pattern generalizes to the populations of dogs and cats at large.

   iii: Our research included one independent variable (whether participants were married or not) and three dependent variables (including self-esteem, income, and relationship satisfaction).

   iv: In this medical research, the relationship between weight and proclivity toward heart disease was significant.

   v: Not only did participants in the alcohol-consumption condition do considerably worse on the examination than members of the control group, but, further, this difference likely generalizes to populations beyond the samples studied here.

   vi: The heart rates of males who were exposed to images of young children who needed parental care actually increased much more from baseline compared with the heart rates of females in this same study.

2. In this chapter, you learned that a big effect size and statistical significance are not identical. Sometimes you have one, sometimes you have the other, sometimes you have both, sometimes you have neither. For this problem, create a hypothetical example for each of these four scenarios. Write out each answer in a paragraph or so.

   a. Describe a study that had a big effect size but NOT statistical significance.

   b. Describe a study that had statistical significance but NOT a big effect size.

   c. Describe a study that had a big effect size AND statistical significance.

   d. Describe a study that had neither a big effect size NOR statistical significance.

3. The distinction between descriptive and inferential statistics was presented here. In your answers, be sure to describe what it is about the study that makes it either descriptive or inferential in nature.

   a. Describe a hypothetical study that would be primarily designed to address a descriptive research question (and that would use descriptive statistics).

   b. Describe a hypothetical study that would be primarily designed to address an inferential research question (and that would use inferential statistics).

4. For this question, consider the following:

In a recent study on the effects of a woman's ovulatory cycle on mating desires, Haselton and Miller (2006) found that women in their peak fertility stage of ovulation report being more attracted to a highly creative male (who is not too successful) compared with a highly successful male (who is not too creative). This finding was statistically significant.

Based on the presentation of inferential statistics in this chapter, describe what it means that this finding is statistically significant. Be sure to make your explanation detailed and basic enough so that someone who never took a class in statistics would know what you were talking about.

HOMEWORK SET B

1. Consider the following scenario: A researcher reports that his findings indicate that 6-year-old boys enjoy climbing trees more so than do 6-year-old girls.
    a. If this finding is statistically significant, what does that mean?
    b. If this finding has a big effect size, what does that mean?
    c. If this finding has both statistical significance and a big effect size, what does that mean?
    d. If this finding has neither statistical significance nor a big effect size, what does that mean?
    e. If this finding has statistical significance, but not a big effect size, what does that mean?
    f. If this finding does not have statistical significance, but does have a big effect size, what does that mean?
2. Define the phrase "correlational statistics." In your definition, explain the point of these statistics to someone who is educated but knows nothing about statistics.
3. Consider the following hypothetical research reports, indicate whether the researchers are utilizing descriptive statistics or inferential statistics, and explain why. Also, if you decide that the particular example addresses descriptive statistics, indicate whether the study is correlational in nature. If so, discuss which variables are correlated with one another.
    a. Participants who preferred juice over water showed more signs of hyperactivity than participants who preferred water over juice.
    b. The mean age of people who chose to attend the matinee movie was 13 years.
    c. The dogs that slept outside weighed significantly less than the dogs that slept indoors.
    d. People who read more tend to score higher on tests of vocabulary and spelling.
    e. The finding that elderly people who have primary responsibility for an animal live longer than elderly people who do not have primary responsibility for an animal is significant, and generalizes to the population of elderly people beyond the participants of this research.

SET A ANSWERS

1. i. b. This summary comments on effect size because the difference between means is a measure of effect size. In this case, there is a small effect size due to the minimal difference between the groups.

    ii. a. This summary comments on statistical significance because the pattern was found to generalize to the larger population of dogs and cats. Although the summary indicates that dogs had more fleas than did cats, it does not state the size of this effect.

    iii. d. This summary does not give indication of effect size or statistical significance, but rather lists the variables in the study.

    iv. a. This summary comments on statistical significance, as it states that the relationship between the variables was significant. It does not indicate the size of the effect.

v. c. This summary comments on both effect size and statistical significance. The description of the effect size can be found in the statement that one group did "considerably worse" on the examination than the other group, and the effect is statistically significant because the results generalize to populations beyond the sample population.

vi. b. This summary comments on effect size, as it states that the increase in heart rates from baseline in one group was "much more" than the other group.

2. a. In a study aimed at determining if the amount of firewood available had an effect on the temperature of a home heated with a wood stove, results indicate that homes which had large quantities of firewood readily available did have higher temperatures than homes which did not have as much firewood available. However, the results did not generalize to the population beyond the study sample, and may have been due to chance.

b. In a study aimed at determining if the amount of firewood available had an effect on the temperature of a home heated with a wood stove, results indicate that homes which had large quantities of firewood readily available did have higher temperatures than homes which did not have as much firewood available, although the temperature difference between the two groups was very minimal. The results were statistically significant, indicating that among the population of homes heated with firewood, those with large quantities of available firewood do indeed have slightly higher temperatures than those with lesser amounts of firewood.

c. In a study aimed at determining if the amount of firewood available had an effect on the temperature of a home heated with a wood stove, results indicate that homes which had large quantities of firewood readily available did have higher temperatures than homes which did not have as much firewood available, and this difference in temperatures was very large. The results are statistically significant, meaning that in the population of homes with wood stoves beyond the study sample, homes with large amounts of available firewood are much warmer than homes with lesser amounts of firewood.

d. In a study aimed at determining if the amount of firewood available had an effect on the temperature of a home heated with a wood stove, results indicate that the difference in temperatures between the two homes was minimal, if there was any difference at all. The results were not statistically significant, meaning that they do not seem to apply to populations outside of the study sample.

3. a. The avian behavioral researchers of this study created a large red surface in a field. They then studied how many birds—of various species—landed on the surface during the day—for 10 straight days. Next, they recorded how frequently birds of these species landed on this surface and provided a graphical representation to show how inclined birds of different species were to land on this red surface.

b. This study addressed the question of whether men or women own more pairs of socks. A group of 100 men and 100 women were randomly selected, and their socks were counted. Statistics were preformed to determine which group owned more socks, and to determine whether the results generalize to the populations of men and women outside the study sample.

4. The finding that women who are at their peak fertility stage of ovulation are more attracted to highly creative males rather than highly successful males is statistically significant, meaning that women in general follow this pattern of attraction. If the entire population of women were tested, rather than just a sample of women, this pattern of attraction would still be found. Thus, these results strongly suggest that women during peak ovulation, in general, tend to be more attracted to indices of creativity than success.

REFERENCE

Haselton, M.G., & Miller, G. F. (2006). Women's fertility across the cycle increases the short-term attractiveness of creative intelligence compared to wealth. *Human Nature*, 17, 50–73.

DESCRIBING A SINGLE VARIABLE

Some things are constant—and some vary. Phenomena in the world are characterized by a host of attributes. In psychology, the phenomena we focus on are behavioral and psychological in nature. Organisms—humans included—demonstrate various behavioral attributes. For some attributes, there is little or no variability. People around the globe interpret smiles as reflecting happiness. People around the globe show a startle response if an unexpected loud noise is suddenly made in the environment. People around the globe seek food when they are hungry.

These are examples of constants. Attributes that do not vary.

Constants are not really all that interesting. Variability is what makes things interesting. In psychology, there are some behavioral attributes in which people show markedly different responses from one another. In other words, on such attributes, people *vary* from one another.

VARIABLES, VALUES, AND SCORES

You don't have to think too hard to come up with examples of attributes for which people vary from one another. It's a particularly easy task if you have roommates. Think for a second about any roommate you've ever had. How did you differ from one another? Here are some possibilities:

- You differ in terms of waking hours—perhaps she's a night owl and you're an early bird.
- You differ in terms of how much you like to go out—she's out partying every night while you're in the dorm room knitting.
- You differ in terms of how organized you keep your space—your stuff is labeled and put neatly in shelves and drawers—her stuff is collected in a pile that is deeply buried by another pile of stuff.
- She says "tom-AY-to" and you say "Tom-AH-to"...and so on.

All these prior examples correspond to attributes on which people vary—namely, in this case, differences in circadian rhythm, extraversion, conscientiousness, and linguistic dialect. As with people, situations also often vary from one another on a multitude of dimensions. Variability typifies the world.

A *variable* simply is some attribute (such as level of extraversion) for which there is some level of variability.

To best understand the idea of a *variable*, it's useful to grasp the related concepts of *value* and *score*.

Let's consider a classic psychological concept: extraversion—essentially, how outgoing someone is. We all know that people vary quite a bit on this dimension. Now imagine that you used a simple rating scale to measure the extraversion of 100 people for a study. You simply ask everyone in the study to rate themselves on a 10-point scale, reporting their own levels of extraversion. The scale (in this case a psychological rating scale, called a Likert scale) is anchored at 1 (very introverted) and 10 (very extraverted).

Now suppose that your roommate, Ashley, scored a 9 out of 10 on this scale. She's very extraverted. And suppose that you scored a 2 (remember, you like to knit!). Here are the basic concepts in terms of this example—the *variable* is extraversion—which is *operationalized* (mathematically measured) in terms of scores on this 1–10 scale. Each point on this scale (1, 2, 3,.... 10) is a *value*—a possible score on the variable. Ashley's actual *score* is 9; your actual *score* is 2 (see Table 2.1 for a summary).

Table 2.1: Distinguishing between *Variable, Value, and Score*

	Definition	Example
Variable	Some attribute that shows variability—there are multiple possible versions or values of the attribute.	The personality dimension of extraversion—people can vary considerably from one another in terms of how extraverted they are.
Value	A *possible* score on some measure of a variable.	On the 1–10 point extraversion scaled used for this research, *values* include each possible score (1, 2, 3, 4, 5, 6, 7, 8, 9, and 10)—with lower *values* corresponding to lower levels of extraversion and higher *values* corresponding to higher levels of extraversion.
Score	An actual data point on the measure of the variable; someone's actual score on the measure	Your extraverted friend Ashley's *score* on the extraversion scale was a 9 (out of a possible 10).

TYPES OF VARIABLES

The nature of the attribute in question that is being studied will determine the *type of variable* that you have on your hands. Some variables are *continuous variables*. These variables essentially include values that vary by degree.

For instance, high school GPA is a continuous variable. In many high schools, GPA varies from 0 to 100. Someone's GPA can be anywhere between (and including) these points. GPAs can be bad (e.g., 22.3), OK (e.g., 77.45), good (86.89), great (93.43), and so forth.

Importantly, with a true continuous variable, differences between the values spanning the entire range of scores have similar interpretations across the scale (the formal phrase for this kind of continuous variable is *interval-ratio variable*). With high school GPA, for instance, 95 is as much better than 90 compared with how much better 85 is than 80. In each case, the discrepancy is 5 points—and that gap of 5 points shares the same differential meaning regardless of the part of the range of scores in question.

Another kind of variable that you may remember from high school (unwittingly) is an *ordinal variable*. This kind of variable, which corresponds to ranks, represents simply where a score is in the order of a group of scores. You may be in first place, you may be in second, you may be in 15th, and so on.

High school rank corresponds to an ordinal variable. Interestingly, high school GPA and high school rank both set out to measure the same construct—academic achievement in high school—but they differ in the type of variable.

Finally, you can imagine a somewhat harsh high school in which the administration divides students into one of two categories—the college-track students and the non-college-track students. In this instance, there are only two "levels" of the variable—category one (college-track) or category two (non-college-track). Here, we are thinking about high school achievement as a *categorical variable*. A categorical variable simply has some number of categories—and someone "scores" by being in one category or another.

This lesson tells us that, often, a construct (i.e., concept) such as high school achievement may be operationally defined (i.e., measured) in terms of a number of different kinds of variables. Here, we have high school achievement differentially represented as a continuous variable (high school GPA), an ordinal variable (high school rank), and a categorical variable (college-track or not). See Table 2.2.

In conducting research, a primary goal is to come up with the best possible ways to measure our variables. Thinking here about high school achievement in terms of continuous, ordinal, and categorical variables, we see that the continuous version of the variable is more informative than the ordinal version, which is more informative than the categorical version. For this reason, all things considered, it is usually best to use a continuous conceptualization of a variable—followed by an ordinal conceptualization—then a categorical conceptualization.

To see how information is lost as we move from continuous, to ordinal, to categorical, consider a very small graduating class with three students. The two students at the top of the class have grades that are awesome, with GPAs of 99 and 98, respectively. Our third student is not doing quite as well—with a GPA of 80. Here's how the data would play out in terms of the continuous versus ordinal versus categorical measures that we've discussed. See Table 2.3.

Table 2.2: High School Achievement Represented by Different Types
of Variables for Joe the Imaginary Student

Variable Type	How variable is represented
Continuous Variable: High School GPA	84.45 (out of a possible 100)
Ordinal Variable: High School Rank	79th out of 233 students
Categorical: College-Track or Not	College-Track

Table 2.3: Comparison of Continuous, Ordinal, and Categorical Versions
of High School Achievement Variables

Student	GPA (continuous variable)	Rank (ordinal variable)	College-Track or Not (categorical variable)
Sarah	99	1	College-Track
Bob	98	2	College-Track
Emily	80	3	College-Track

Think about how different the information is depending on which version of the variable we're given. Based on just the categorical variable, we see that all these kids are defined as "on the college-track"—none seems to have achieved more academically than the others. This variable provides us with no information about the actual variability in high school achievement! The ordinal variable is OK—but not perfect. It tells us that Sarah did better than Bob and that Bob did better than Emily, but it leaves out a crucial point: Sarah only did a little better than Bob—and both Bob and Sarah did a lot better than Emily (who, we are sure, has lots of other good attributes!). An ordinal variable tells us only about the relative position of scores—it does not tell us about the magnitude of differences between scores. Continuous scores—such as GPA, here—tell us about both relative position of scores and the magnitude of differences between scores. As such, *all things equal, continuous versions of variables are the best to use for research purposes.*

All this said, you should note that with many variables, there are no options. Some variables, for instance, simply are categorical in nature. Differences between species are basically categorical. If you were going to do a study of dogs versus cats, species would be conceptualized in a categorical manner—and there's no getting around it. Similarly, if you were going to do a study of students who attend private versus public colleges, this would necessarily be a categorical variable. Often, whether a variable is to be measured as continuous, ordinal, or categorical is determined by the nature of the construct under study.

DESCRIBING SCORES FOR A SINGLE VARIABLE

Perhaps the most basic kind of actual *statistics* we compute pertain to describing the scores for a single variable. In describing scores for a single variable, we'll often want to know what kinds of scores were typical—a concept we refer to as the *central tendency* of the distribution of scores. We'll often also want to know the *pattern of variability* among the scores—how different were they from one another—and were there any noteworthy patterns in the nature of the ways that scores varied from each other?

INDICES OF CENTRAL TENDENCY

Suppose that after you graduate (with honors!), you realize how much you love statistics and decide to apply for a job as a researcher in your university's Office of Institutional Research (check it out—your school almost definitely has an office like this and people with strong statistical skills are sorely needed in these offices around the world!). Your first task involves a project dealing with the starting salaries of recent graduates. The main question being asked pertains to how much money recent graduates make as a function of their academic major. As a *pilot study* (small study done before a more formal, large-scale study), you find the starting salaries of five recent graduates from three different majors: Biology, Psychology, and Sociology. The data are as follows (see Table 2.4):

Table 2.4: Starting Salaries of Recent Graduates from Three Different Majors (in dollars per year)

Biology	Psychology	Sociology
35,000	22,000	8,000
30,000	19,000	19,000
25,000	30,000	15,000
25,000	24,000	10,000
34,000	25,000	2,000,000

You likely notice a few things off the bat. But one detail that sticks out like a sore thumb is found in your fifth sociology graduate—$2 million a year, wow! This example is based on a true story—several years ago, Christian Laettner was a Duke student and basketball star. He also was a sociology major—who got a huge salary in the NBA promptly upon graduating.

But this example provides us with something of a pickle regarding central tendency. Remember, central tendency refers to a typical kind of score in a *sample* of scores. Here, we have three samples—one for biology, one for psychology, and one for sociology. How can we best come up with a *typical* score in each case?

The most common index of central tendency is the *mean* (or arithmetic average). The mean makes intuitive sense and it takes several factors into account.

Here's the formula for the mean: $M = \dfrac{\Sigma X}{N}$.

In this case, M means "mean," Σ means "the sum of all that follows this expression," and N means "the number of scores in the sample." Thus, as you may have already anticipated, the mean = all the scores in the sample added up, then divided by the number of scores.

For example, for the biology graduates, to compute the mean, we'll get the sum of all five of these scores (i.e., the sum of 35,000, 30,000, 25,000, 25,000, and 34,000), which is 149,000. We'll then divide this sum by the number of scores (5) to get the mean of 29,800. The mean—or in this case, average starting salary—for the Bio grads is $29,800. This seems about right for what we expect for a typical score in the sample, looking over the raw scores. Usually, the mean is our best index of central tendency in that it simply best captures the "central tendency" of the distribution of scores in the sample (or it best captures what a typical score in the sample is like).

Another index of central tendency that is often used is the *median*. When you're driving on a highway, the median is that bit that's right in the middle. And that's what *median* refers to. In a sample of scores, the median is the *score that is in the middle of all other scores (when scores are arranged sequentially)*. This parenthetical is pretty important—the median is not the middle score per se, it's the middle score of a set of numbers when the numbers are arranged in

Table 2.5: Means, Medians, and Modes for Starting Salaries of Recent
Graduates from Three Different Majors (in dollars per year)

Biology	Psychology	Sociology
35,000	22,000	8,000
30,000	19,000	19,000
25,000	30,000	15,000
25,000	24,000	10,000
34,000	25,000	2,000,000
$M = 29,800$	$M = 24,000$	$M = 410,400$
Median = 30,000	Median = 24,000	Median = 15,000
Mode = 25,000	Mode = No Mode Exists	Mode = No Mode Exists

order. Note that if you have an even number of scores, you'll get "two medians." In this case, it's appropriate to take the average of these two numbers and represent this result as your median. Thus, to get the median for the biology salaries, we need to first arrange the scores sequentially, as such: 25,000, 25,000, 30,000, 34,000, 35,000. The median, or score in the middle, is 30,000. Thus, the *median* starting salary for the Bio grads is $30,000. Pretty close to the mean, huh? This happens often—the median is frequently considered a decent index of central tendency.

The final index of central tendency that's often used is the *mode*—which is the single most common score in the sample. Sometimes there is more than one mode (if there are two scores that are equally as common as one another). The mode is pretty simple. For the Bio grads, two people have starting salaries of $25,000—no other score is represented more than once. The mode is therefore $25,000. Here, you can see that the mode doesn't seem to capture a typical score, as 25,000 may be the mode, but is also the very bottom of the entire *range* of scores (with the *range* being all the values between the lowest and highest scores in the distribution—in this case, 25,000 to 35,000). The mode is usually considered the least valid index of central tendency.

Table 2.5 includes the means, medians, and modes for our three samples.

As stated prior, the mean is *usually* the most representative and reliable index of central tendency. But what's up with sociology? The mean starting salary in this example is $410,400. That's a bit misleading! If you were going to advertise sociology as "the major that gets you the big bucks," you may well have a lawsuit on your hands and some very angry parents at some point! For sociology, the median, at $15,000, is actually much more representative of typical scores in the sample.

Here's the lesson: Given how the mean is calculated, it is *very sensitive to outliers*. An *outlier* is a score that is just off the scale—and is way higher than the other scores or way way lower (yes, we've used the word *way* twice to underscore the concept!). Given the manner in which the mean is computed, it has no way of compensating for outliers. One way that researchers deal with this issue is to delete outliers from data sets—simply to make the mean a more reliable index of central tendency. An alternative that is sometimes feasible (but, as we'll see with more advanced statistics, not always feasible) is to use the median, which is relatively insensitive to outliers.

A practical use of the median is found in your weekly newspaper's real estate section. This section often includes the housing prices in various contexts (e.g., the price of recent sales—the prices of sales of this year compared with last year at this time, etc.). Take a good look next time—odds are that the central tendency is presented as the median—not as the mean. For instance, it might say "the median sale price for July was $232,000." Why is this? Well, if you live in the United States of America, you know that this country prides itself on equality for all—but it is also "the land of opportunity." That partly translates into the fact that the very wealthy people in this country are actually *very, very* wealthy. Wealth is not distributed equally—and while most people live in regular houses, the people at the top of the economic scale live in outrageously fancy houses, with prices that are, for the rest of us, off the scale. All it takes is one very rich person to have a $10 million house in the hills on the outside of town (it's gated, so you can't see it!), and the mean becomes a poor marker of central tendency for real estate prices.

INDICES OF VARIABILITY (AND THE SHEER BEAUTY OF STANDARD DEVIATION!)

With a sample of scores on a variable (interchangeably referred to as a *distribution of scores*), we are often interested in central tendency—what typical scores are like—but that's not the whole story. Often, much of the story of the data resides in the nature of how scores vary from one another within the distribution of scores—a characteristic of data that we refer to, broadly, as *variability*.

To put a face to the concept of variability, let's set up a simple example. Suppose two basketball teams played last night—and the score ended as a tie: 100 to 100. Each team has five players (no one's on the bench!). Knowing these facts alone, you might think that the teams are very even. Based on just this information, your best guess might be that they are very similar teams with similar kinds of players—who are generally matched in ability. You would be wrong. Here are the scoring breakdowns for each team (see Table 2.6):

Table 2.6: Scoring Breakdowns for Two Hypothetical Basketball Teams

Player #	Team A (Points scored per player)	Team B (Points scored per player)
1	20	50
2	20	0
3	20	0
4	20	0
5	20	50
Mean	20	20
Median	20	0
Mode	20	0

These teams are actually pretty different from one another when we look closely at the patterns of scoring! Let's see what our markers of central tendency tell us. Each team has a mean of 20—the average number of points scored is 20 for both Teams A and B. But the median for Team A is 20 while the median for Team B is 0! Similarly, the mode for Team A is 20 and the mode for Team B is 0.

What's going on here is this: The teams vary from each other in terms of the patterns of variability! This example works well to explicate variability in the most literal terms. Look at the scores for Team A. How much do the scores vary from one another? Well, everyone got 20. So no score varied from any other score. So there is ZERO variability.

Just as we came up with different indices of central tendency, we will come up with different indices of variability. Importantly, each index of variability should come up with an answer for Team A's variability which means ZERO. If there is zero variability, then an index of the variability should say so!

Similarly, the scores for Team B vary somewhat from one another. For Team B, it looks like there are two stars and three duds! Stars vary from duds—and this point is reflected in the variability between the scores of the different players from one another. So indices of variability for Team B should all essentially say "there is some variability" and "there is more variability between scores for Team B than there is for Team A."

That said, let's get into the nuts and bolts of computing indices of variability. First, let's walk through the process for Team A.

This example includes several indices of variability. First, it includes *deviation scores*— each deviation score reflects how much any particular score (or X—referring to a particular real (or *raw*) score) deviates from the mean of the sample. Because the mean is the average of all the raw scores, the average of the deviation scores will always be zero (based on the fact that each deviation score is the raw score minus the mean). For this reason, the sum or average of the deviation scores cannot be used as a summary index of variability, because it will always be zero!

Due to this "deviation scores always sum to zero" issue, we need to determine a mechanism by which we can come up with a summary statistic to mark variability that is devoid of this "sum to zero" issue. The process by which statisticians have come to address this issue is by squaring deviation scores. Thus, we run into the column of squared deviation scores (signified by $(X-M)^2$). Squaring deviation scores has the liability of putting the scores on a different scale (a squared scale), but it has the benefit of ameliorating (getting rid of) all negative signs as (squared numbers are always positive). This fact makes it so that a sum of these numbers will not necessarily add to zero (see Table 2.7).

Table 2.7: Computing Indices of Variability for Team A

X	M	Deviation Score $(X–M)$	Squared Deviation Score $(X–M)^2$
20	20	0	0
20	20	0	0
20	20	0	0
20	20	0	0
20	20	0	0
$\Sigma = 100$;			$\Sigma (X–M)^2 = 0$
$N = 5$			
$M = 20$			$SD^2 = \dfrac{(X-M)^2}{N} = 0$
			$SD = \sqrt{(SD)^2} = 0$

So far we have met two indices of variability: (a) a deviation score (X–M), representing how much each individual score deviates from the mean and (b) a squared deviation score $(X–M)^2$, representing the deviation score squared.

But when we talk about statistics that reflect variability, we are not talking about an individual score. Rather, we are talking about a summary of the pattern of variability for the entire sample (or distribution) of scores. In other words, we're not interested if X is very different from another score in the sample—we're interested in whether the scores tend to vary a lot from one another *overall*.

Let's now discuss three indices of this *overall* variability.

First, we can sum the squared deviation scores. In terms of symbols, this concept is represented as follows: $\Sigma(X–M)^2$ (it's simply the sum symbol (Σ) preceding the expression for an individual squared deviation score. So we add those up! This concept, the *sum of the squared deviation scores*, is also represented by SS (in other words, SS = Σ (X–M)^2).

The sum of the squared deviation scores is important—and we like it because it is our first overall index of variability for a distribution of scores! But it's not perfect. SS makes no correction for N (or the number of scores). Thus, if we have a sample of scores and we know that SS = 20, we don't actually know all that much! We also need to know the scale the raw scores are on (is this number based on college GPA, ranging from 0 to 4, household annual income, ranging from $0 to $100 million, or what?). In addition, we need to know how many scores this is based on. Is this based on five scores or five million scores? SS is a nice start, but it doesn't really have an easy interpretation in summarizing the *variability* of scores on a variable.

Our second overall index of variability is the *variance* (represented by SD^2). The variance is essentially the average of the squared deviation scores. It is computed simply as follows: $SD^2 = \dfrac{SS}{N}$ (or, equivalently), $SD^2 = \dfrac{\Sigma(X-M)^2}{N}$. This formula solves one problem of the SS as a summary statistic—it corrects for the N. It essentially says, "there is this much variability in terms of sums of squared deviation scores *on average*." This is an improvement. At least compared with SS, SD^2 produces a result that is sensitive to the number of scores in the distribution.

However, SD^2 is also imperfect! Recall that due to the "deviation scores always summing to zero" issue, we squared our deviation scores (to get rid of the negative signs—a very practical maneuver). The second we did that, we put all our scores on a squared scale. So suddenly, we're not dealing with the units of interest—we're dealing with squared units of interest, which are likely not very interpretable. After all, they're not on the scale that the variable is on.

The solution to this problem is actually remarkably simple: We'll now take the square root of SD^2, and we'll have a summary of the variability of the scores that (a) is corrected for N and (b) is on the same scale as the raw scores. The reasoning is that we put everything in squared units—so now, we're going to step back to non-squared units. Meet Standard Deviation (SD); the gold standard in summarizing variability of a distribution of scores. And, as you can see, we're already set up to know the equation for SD: $SD = \sqrt{(SD)^2}$. In fact, SD is so much more useful than the variance in summarizing variability that the variance is actually labeled in terms of SD! (Insert mild sadness regarding the variance's existence right about here.)

Note that standard deviation is actually not equal to the average amount that the scores vary from one another (for technical reasons). It is, however, *roughly* this same concept. Thus, we can think of standard deviation as more or less the average amount that scores in a distribution vary from one another.

With all this said, let's look at the special case of scores for Team A. Remember, Team A is an egalitarian team—everyone scored 20 points. There is no variability between the scores of the players. As a result, each and every index of variability should mathematically reflect this idea of zero variability.

Check out Table 2.7 to see how this works. First, note that each deviation score (X–M) = 0. That's because each score deviates ZERO from the mean! Next, note that each squared deviation score ((X–M)²) = 0, also indicating that the scores vary ZERO from one another. Now let's look at our three summary indices of variability: SS, SD², and SD. SS is the sum of the squared deviation scores. These are all zero. So their sum is zero. SS = 0, indicating that the scores do not vary from one another at all. SD², or the variance, is the average of SS. SD² = 0, again, signaling that scores do not vary from one another. Finally, SD = 0. In light of our conceptual definition of standard deviation (provided earlier in this section), then, the scores on average (roughly) vary zero from one another.

Introducing variability with an example with zero variability has the advantage of making the concept of *zero variability* very tangible in terms of each marker of variability. However, you might find it a bit unchallenging! OK, Hotshot! Let's take a look at all these same indices of variability using Team B. Recall that for Team B, the total amount scored was 100, just as it was for Team A. However, on this team, two players scored 50 each and no one else scored at all. See Table 2.8.

Aha—now we've got some variability. In thinking about the data from Team A and Team B concurrently, the idea of variability should be very obvious. For Team A, the scores do not vary from one another at all. And each index of variability, for Team A, shows this point. For Team B, the scores are not all identical to one another—some variability exists. Further, more variability exists for Team B than for Team A. Therefore, the mathematical indices of variability for Team B should all demonstrate this point. Let's see if this is so.

First, the deviation scores for Team B are all different from zero. Each score in this sample deviates from the mean. Next, the squared deviation scores also differ from zero. Again, this point shows that the scores vary from the mean. SS, or the sum of the squared deviation scores, is 3,000. That's a lot more than the 0 we found for Team A! The variance for Team B is 600. Also a lot more than the 0 we found for Team A! Finally, the standard deviation for Team B is 24.49.

Table 2.8: Computing Indices of Variability for Team B

X	M	Deviation Score (X–M)	Squared Deviation Score (X–M)²
50	20	30	900
0	20	–20	400
0	20	–20	400
0	20	–20	400
50	20	30	900
$\Sigma = 100$;			$\Sigma (X–M)^2 = 3,000$
$N = 5$			
$M = 20$			$SD^2 = \dfrac{\Sigma(X-M)^2}{N} = 600$
			$SD = \sqrt{(SD)^2} = 24.49$

Recall that SD is interpretable in terms of the scale of the actual scores. So we can think of 24.49 in terms of actual number of points scored by players in the game. For Team B, scores varied on average from one another roughly by 24.49.

At this point, you can easily imagine creating scores for another five-player team with even more variability. And if you created the numbers so that the scores varied even more from one another, then the markers of variability (including, most importantly, standard deviation) would all increase as well.

Before moving on, it's useful to think about how to interpret standard deviation. Given the intuitive nature of standard deviation (as roughly the average amount that scores in a distribution vary from one another), it is often used for various purposes. Often, one standard deviation is used as a cutoff for defining an *extreme* or *noteworthy* score. As we'll see in later chapters that deal with probability, scores in most distributions that are more than a standard deviation from the mean are relatively rare (just *how rare* will be the subject of future chapters—stay tuned!). So if, for an example, you know that the mean GPA at your school is 2.5 and the standard deviation is .5, then a score of 3.0 is one standard deviation above the mean (simply, 3.0 is .5 higher than 2.5). Thus, if your GPA is 3.11, you can say, accurately, that your GPA is *more than a standard deviation above the mean*. This would be a good thing! If, on the other hand, your GPA were 1.9, that would be bad news, as one standard deviation below the mean would be 2.5-0.5, or 2.0. In this scenario, your score would be more than one standard deviation *below* the mean. And so forth. It's a little rough-around-the-edges (as we'll see in later chapters), but being more than a standard deviation from the mean is often a useful way to define whether a score is *extremely* different from the mean.

ROUNDING

This is probably a good time to raise the issue of rounding. To stay on the same page, it's useful if we are all using the same algorithm (or system) to round numbers, especially if doing calculations by hand. Since psychology writing is generally guided by the *Publication Manual of the American Psychology Association (APA)*—a book utilized by psychology (and related) journals worldwide, which provides detailed direction on how to write psychological research reports— we adhere to the APA's guidelines on rounding numbers. The APA advises that numbers be rounded to two decimal places. Thus, a very simple and standard rule to help keep consistency is that if the number in the third decimal place is 5 or greater, round up; otherwise, round down. See Table 2.9 for examples.

Table 2.9: Examples of Rounding to Two Decimal Places

This number rounds to...	this...
3.221033	3.22
3.225001	3.23
109.999	110.00
109.22000	109.22 (no change)

DESCRIBING FREQUENCIES OF VALUES FOR A SINGLE VARIABLE

When we have a set of raw data for a single variable, in addition to presenting information regarding the central tendency (mean, median, and/or mode) and variability (usually represented by standard deviation), it is often helpful to simply present the raw data in tabular (or table) format so the reader can just look at the data in an organized fashion.

In doing so, we can create a *frequency table*. A frequency table is probably something you've been making since 3rd-grade math class—it just has some specific aspects that we like to use to standardize the process a bit. To help us think about this, let's imagine a very simple scenario. Suppose that you're conducting a study to examine the relationship between extraversion and physical strength. To measure physical strength, you count how many pull-ups five of your friends can do. The numbers come out as follows: 3, 1, 10, 3, 5. Table 2.10 includes a frequency table for these data.

This table shows all the possible values in the range—and how frequent each value was in the actual data. *10* happened once. *9* happened zero times....*3* happened twice...and so on. A frequency table, then, is simply a record of how frequently each possible value emerged.

Here are the formal steps to making a frequency table:

1. **Create a column for the possible values** based on either the actual range (in this example, 1 to 10) or the possible range (here, 0 to 10; we included 0 as it's possible that someone could not do a pull-up!). These values (i.e., possible scores on the variable) are arranged from highest to lowest—and this list of values should include all values in the range (even if no one scored at a particular value (e.g., no one did 6 pull-ups, but 6 is included as it's a value in the range)).
2. **Create a column for *tick marks*.** These are just marks that count frequency. You'll have one mark for each time someone scored for a particular value. If two scores emerge for that value, put a second tick mark. Once you get five, you take the four prior ones and put a slash through it (ⱦ), then you start with new tick marks for 6, 7, 8, and 9; for the tenth, you put a slash through the prior four, and so on. See Table 2.10 for an example.

Table 2.10: Frequency Table for Pull-Up Data

Value	Tick Marks	Frequency
10	|	1
9		0
8		0
7		0
6		0
5	|	1
4		0
3	||	2
2		0
1	|	1
0		0

3. **Create a column labeled** *Frequency*.
4. **Look at each piece of raw data and cross each one out**, one at a time. When you cross it out, **put a tick mark for the value** in the tick mark column. Do this process one-by-one for each piece of raw data.
5. When you've recorded tick marks for all data, **write the appropriate numbers in the frequency column**. Each number simply represents how frequent each value is (it's a sum of the tick marks for that value—if there are zero tick marks, write *0*).

If you want, you can put the finished product on the fridge!

Here's another example to work with. Suppose you wanted to conduct a study to see if the number of pets someone has is related to his or her scores on a measure of happiness. You collect data from 13 people—here are the raw scores for the *number of pets* variable: 0, 5, 0, 3, 0, 1, 2, 5, 0, 0, 3, 0, 4. See results in Table 2.11.

Table 2.11: Frequency Table for *Number of Pets*

Value	Tick Marks	Frequency
5	||	2
4	|	1
3	||	2
2	|	1
1	|	1
0	⊪⊬ |	6

Note that you can also make a *grouped frequency table*—which is especially useful if you have a lot of different values in a range. For instance, if you were going to describe the SAT scores of 10 students, you might get many different values—600, 610, 620…1,790, 1,800…and all values in between. This would make for a pretty messy table!

A grouped frequency table is just like a frequency table with one exception: Along the X-axis, instead of representing each individual value, you'll use *intervals* (or clusters of values). If you were going to represent data on SAT scores, for instance, you would perhaps want to include intervals of 200 points—such as found in the example data in Table 2.12:

A grouped-frequency table has advantages over an individual frequency table, as it makes the data much more easily interpretable and coherent. Many of the details of a grouped-frequency table are negotiable—such as the number of intervals, the size of the intervals, and so forth. Since the point of a grouped-frequency table is to increase coherence, you would usually work these details out as part of the process to best match a particular data set.

Here are the formal steps to making a grouped frequency table:

1. **Create a column for the intervals, representing groups of values** based on either the actual range or the possible range. These values (i.e., possible scores on the variable) are arranged from highest to lowest—and this list of intervals should include all values in the range (even if no one scored at a particular value).
2. **Create a column for** *tick marks*. Just as with an individual frequency table, these are just marks that count frequency—they pertain to how frequently each interval was represented.

Table 2.12: Grouped Frequency Table for SAT
Scores for 10 Students

Interval	Tick Marks	Frequency
600–799	|	1
800–999	|||	3
1,000–1,199		0
1,200–1,399	|||	3
1,400–1,599	|	1
1,600–1,800	||	2

3. **Create a column labeled** *Frequency*.
4. **Look at each piece of raw data and cross each one out**, one at a time. When you cross it out, **put a tick mark for the interval** in the appropriate tick mark column. Do this process one-by-one for each piece of raw data.
5. When you've recorded tick marks for all data, **write the appropriate numbers in the frequency column**. Each number simply represents how frequent each interval is (it's a sum of the tick marks for that value—if there are zero tick marks, write *0*).

REPRESENTING FREQUENCY DATA GRAPHICALLY

A standard bar graph or line graph can be created to help us get a more coherent picture of our data. Converting information from a frequency table to a visual or graphical format is relatively easy.

A bar graph used to represent frequency data is referred to as a *histogram* (or a *frequency histogram*). A histogram has the range of values across the X-axis and the possible frequencies (usually starting with zero) for the Y-axis. Figure 2.1 shows a *frequency histogram* for the *number of pets* variable.

The steps for converting information from a frequency table into a frequency histogram are as follows:

1. **Create an X-axis that includes the entire range of values (lower numbers to the left, higher numbers to the right).** Importantly, add a value below the lowest value in the range and add a value above the highest value in the range. Thus, if the lowest possible value on your X-axis is 0, put –1. If the highest possible value is 6, put 7. You'll soon see why we do this!
2. **Create a Y-axis that includes all the possible frequencies, typically starting at zero.** (With the *number of pets* example, the most frequent value (of zero) occurs 6 times; so the Y-axis should go from *0* (for any values that did not have any frequency) to *6*).
3. **Create a bar for each value that represents the frequency for that value (with the *number of pets* example, the bar for the value of zero should go up to a frequency of 6, the bar for the value of 5 should have a frequency of 2, etc.).** Note that the bars for adjacent values should be touching each other (it is standard to not have spaces between the bars).

The other standard way to represent information from a frequency table graphically is via a *frequency polygon*. This is a fancy term for a line graph. A frequency polygon is very similar

Frequency Histogram for # of Pets

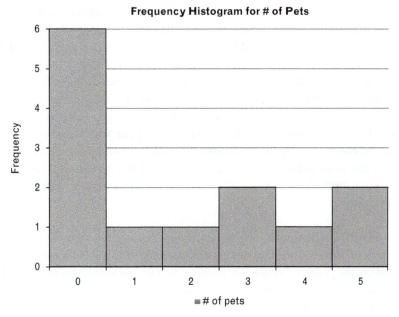

FIGURE 2.1: Frequency Histogram for *Number of Pets.*

to a frequency histogram. Along the X-axis are values of the variable, and along the Y-axis are frequencies corresponding to how frequent each value is in the distribution.

Figure 2.2 shows a frequency polygon for the *number of pets* data.

The steps for converting information from a frequency table into a frequency polygon are very similar to the steps in creating a histogram. These are as follows:

1. **Create an X-axis that includes the entire range of values** (lower numbers to the left, higher numbers to the right). Importantly, add a value below the lowest value in the range and add a value above the highest value in the range. Thus, if the lowest possible value on your X-axis is 0, put −1. If the highest possible value is 6, put 7. You'll soon see why we do this!

Frequency Polygon for # of Pets

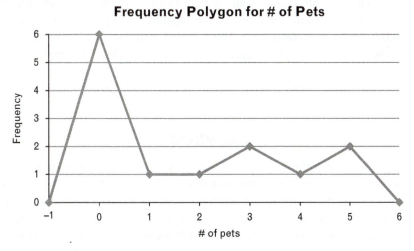

FIGURE 2.2: Frequency Polygon for # of Pets.

2. **Create a Y-axis that includes all the possible frequencies**, typically starting at zero. With the *number of pets* example, the most frequent value (of zero) occurs 6 times; so the Y-axis should go from *0* (for any values that did not have any frequency) to 6.
3. **For each value, make a point in the space that corresponds to the frequency**. For the values that you put which are below the lowest value in the range and above the highest value in the range, put a dot at the Y-axis (corresponding to a frequency of 0).
4. **Starting with the dot at 0 for the lowest value on your X-axis, make a straight line to the dot corresponding to the frequency for the next value**. Then make a straight line from that point to the next point, and so on, until you have made a straight line from the point for the highest value of the range to the X-axis for the value that is above the highest value.

You now have the skills needed to make a frequency polygon to describe how the frequencies in a sample of data are distributed across the values. We can now make some nice summary statements about the patterns found in the frequencies. First, we notice that the *modal* (i.e., most common) value is 0. Most people in the sample have no pets. We also notice that there are some *bumps* for the values of 3 and 5.

A frequency polygon gives you an immediate sense of the nature of both the central tendency and variability of a variable. In looking over a frequency polygon, we can assess several parameters of the nature of the distribution of scores. Specifically, we can address the following:

MODALITY

Modality, which speaks to the central tendency of scores in a distribution, corresponds to the concept of *mode*, or most common score in a distribution. Modality is a slightly broader concept than *mode* in that it pertains to *relatively frequent clusters of values* (as opposed to the single most frequent score). So you might have, for instance, a distribution in which a particular value in the middle is most common—we would refer to this as a *unimodal* distribution (based on our assessment of the frequency polygon). Or we might have two *peaks* in the frequency polygon (two relatively common clusters of values)—in which case we would refer to the distribution as *bimodal* or *multimodal*. See Figure 2.3 for visual examples of unimodal and bimodal distributions.

SKEWNESS

Skewness can also be gleaned from a frequency polygon—corresponding to the pattern of variability in a distribution. Sometimes scores in a distribution are clustered to the positive side of the X-axis (i.e., the right) or toward the negative side of the X-axis (i.e., the left). If scores are clustered to the right, there are fewer scores on the negative side, so we refer to this as *negatively skewed*. If there are fewer scores on the positive side, we refer to the distribution as *positively*

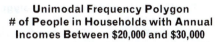

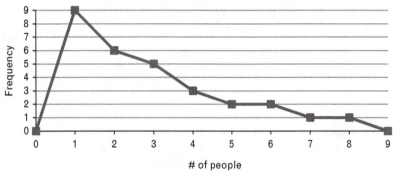

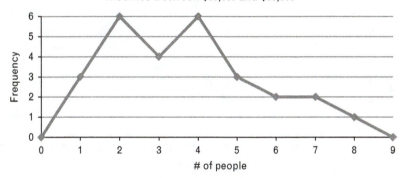

FIGURE 2.3: Frequency Polygons and Modality of a Distribution of Scores.

skewed. See Figure 2.4 for examples of frequency polygons that are negatively and positively skewed.

KURTOSIS

A final detail that can be extrapolated from a frequency polygon refers to *kurtosis*—or *how peaked or flat the primary peak of a distribution is.* In cases of a distribution being either particularly peaked or particularly flat, we refer to the distribution as *kurtotic.* This concept, by the way, is actually conceived of in a manner that is relative to a *normal distribution,* which is a special, mathematically derived distribution—a symmetrical, bell-shaped curve with a peak that is, really, *just so.* See Figure 2.5 for a glimpse at a normal distribution. A distribution that is *kurtotic,* then, is a distribution with a peak that is more peaked or more flat than the peak found in this special distribution. For example, suppose you had a very egalitarian team of basketball players (as in our prior example in which everyone scored 20 on one team). The frequency polygon for such a distribution would be very, very peaked! As such, it would be *kurtotic* (in this case, unnaturally kurtotic!).

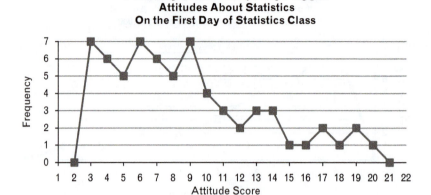

FIGURE 2.4: Frequency Polygons and Skewness.

DESCRIBING DATA FOR A CATEGORICAL VARIABLE

So far, we have talked about describing data from a continuous variable. But sometimes we have to describe data from a categorical variable. For instance, it is very common in psychological research to ask participants for their gender—and to code them into male or female (sometimes, to address transgender issues, additional categories are included).

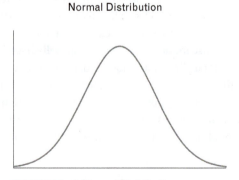

FIGURE 2.5: A Normal Distribution.

Table 2.13: Frequency Table for *Categorical Variable of Gender in Study of 200 College Students*

Value (Category)	Tick Marks	Frequency	Percentage
Male	JHT JHT JHT JHT JHT JHT JHT JHT JHT JHT JHT JHT JHT JHT JHT JHT JHT JHT	90	45%
Female	JHT JHT JHT JHT JHT JHT JHT JHT JHT JHT JHT JHT JHT JHT JHT JHT JHT JHT JHT JHT JHT	110	55%

Suppose you conducted a study of 200 college students and you wanted to describe the pattern of gender among your participants—supposing, further, that everyone in your study self-identified as either male or female. The way to do this is truly simple—you would count the number of males and the number of females—and you would simply report these numbers (e.g., 90 males and 110 females). Formally, this description would actually be a representation of the frequency of different values. Here, your two categorical values for the variable of gender would be male and female. They are not on a continuum together—they are qualitatively different values. We could represent these data using a frequency table—by employing the same algorithm that we utilized for a frequency table for a continuous variable but having our values simply reflect the values of the categorical variable. To create a frequency table for a categorical variable, you would do the following:

1. **Create a column for the possible values (or categories)**. In the case of counting the number of males versus females, you would simply have two categories (male and female). And it would not matter which you placed first.
2. **Create a column for *tick marks***. These are just marks that count frequency for each value. See Table 2.13 for an example.
3. **Create a column labeled *Frequency***.
4. **Create a column labeled Percentage**. (With a categorical variable, it is common to present this information to give the reader a quick sense of the relative frequency of the value within the distribution).
5. **Look at each piece of raw data and cross each one out**, one at a time. When you cross it out, **put a tick mark for the value** in the tick mark column. Do this process one-by-one for each piece of raw data.
6. When you've recorded tick marks for all data, **write the appropriate numbers in the frequency column**. Each number simply represents how frequent each value (or category) is. See Table 2.13.

To graphically represent the data from a frequency table for a categorical variable, a frequency histogram is typically used (and a frequency polygon actually does not make sense for this kind of data!). See Figure 2.6 for a frequency histogram of the gender data used in this example.

A REAL RESEARCH EXAMPLE

In a study on the nature of qualities that young adults advertise in personal ads, Gallant, Williams, Fisher, and Cox (2011) had participants make judgments about personal ads collected

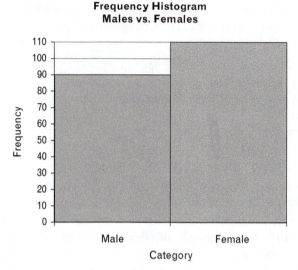

FIGURE 2.6: Frequency Histogram Representing Frequency of Males versus Females.

from 300 people (who had posted ads on a dating website). In describing the individuals from the photographs, these authors use several of the descriptive statistics included in this chapter to provide a snapshot of the individuals included in these photographs. Specifically, the authors write:

> A total of 150 male and 150 female photographs were analyzed. The photographs were collected according to the type of relationship each individual sought. Thus, we collected photographs of 50 men and 50 women who were seeking an intimate relationship, 50 men and 50 women who were seeking a dating relationship, and 50 men and 50 women who were seeking a long-term relationship, for a total of 300 photographs. Any individual who cross-posted their advertisement to more than one relationship category was excluded. All individuals had an advertised age that ranged between 18 and 35 (men's age in years: $M = 29.36$, $SD = 3.53$, women's age: $M = 27.23$, $SD = 4.36$). With respect to ethnicity, 66.7% of advertisers identified themselves as White, 1.0% as Black, 6.3% as Asian, 8.6% selected "Other" (e.g., Arabic, Indigenous/First Nations, Hispanic/Latino), and 17.4% chose not to answer the question (p. 112).

Several of the statistics described in this chapter are addressed here. Regarding the age of the participants, the authors present the *range* (18 to 35). Note that age is a continuous variable. They also provide the mean and standard deviation for this variable—separately for males and females. Additionally, these authors describe a categorical variable: ethnicity. In doing so, they provide the percentage of individuals from the photographs who represent four different categories of ethnicity.

With skills you have obtained from this chapter, if you wanted to, you could expand this section of their results! For instance, if you had the raw data, you could create a frequency table—or a grouped frequency table—for age. You could follow this up with a frequency histogram or polygon. And you could then analyze your graphs and comment on the modality, skewness, and kurtosis of this variable. And more!

SUMMARY

The descriptive statistics presented in this chapter are foundational to all advanced statistics. Before you can describe statistical relationships among multiple variables, you first need to be able to describe the nature of a single variable. In this chapter, we learned about different kinds of variables and how to describe them. In describing variables, we learned about the important concepts of central tendency and variability—as well as how to describe both continuous and categorical variables in tabular and graphical format. You are now ready to tackle one of the most useful statistics going—standardized scores!

KEY TERMS

Bimodal distribution: A distribution in which two particular values are common

Categorical variable: A variable that has some number of categories, and someone "scores" by being in one category or another

Central tendency: The typical score in a sample of scores

Constants: Attributes that do not vary

Continuous variables: Variables that include values that vary by degree

Deviation score: How much any particular score deviates from the mean of the sample

Distribution of scores: A sample of scores

Frequency histogram: A bar graph used to represent frequency data, with a range of values across the x-axis and possible frequencies along the y-axis

Frequency polygon: A line graph used to represent frequency data, with values of the variable along the x-axis and frequencies of values along the y-axis

Frequency table: A table that shows all the possible values in a range and how frequent each value is in the actual data

Grouped frequency table: A frequency table that uses intervals of values, rather than individual values

Interval-ratio variable: A true continuous variable, with differences between the values across the entire range of scores having similar interpretation across the scale

Kurtosis: The extent that the primary peak of a distribution is peaked or flat

Kurtotic: A distribution that has a particularly peaked or particularly flat primary peak, as compared to a normal distribution

Operationalized: Mathematically measured

Ordinal variable: A variable which corresponds to ranks, representing where a score is in the order of a sample of scores

Mean: Arithmetic average $M = \sum X/N$

Median: The score that is in the middle of all other scores when scores are arranged sequentially

Modality: Relatively frequent clusters of values

Mode: The single most common score in a sample

Multimodal distribution: A distribution in which more than one value is common

Negatively skewed distribution: A distribution with scores clustered on the right, or positive side of the distribution

Outlier: A score that is just off the scale, either much higher or much lower than other scores

Pattern of variability: The manner in which scores differ from one another within a distribution of scores

Pilot study: A small study done before a more formal, large-scale study

Positively skewed distribution: A distribution with scores clustered on the left, or negative side of the distribution

Range of scores: All the values between the lowest and highest scores in a distribution

Score: An actual data point on the measure of the variable; someone's actual score on the measure

Skewness: The pattern of variability in a distribution

SS: Sum of the squared deviation scores

Standard deviation (SD): The average amount that scores in a distribution vary from one another

Unimodal distribution: A distribution in which a particular value in the middle is most common.

Value: A possible score on some measure of a variable

Variability: How scores vary from one another within a distribution of scores

Variable: An attribute for which there is some level of variability

Variance: The average of the squared deviation scores

HOMEWORK SET A

1. Give two examples of each type of variable.
   a. Continuous variable
   b. Ordinal variable
   c. Categorical variable
2. Using APA format, round the following numbers:
   a. 6.173432
   b. 24.349651
   c. 101.95620
   d. 91.46879
   e. 67.011697
   f. 41. 99621
3. You are hired by three local businesses to determine the ages of their respective clients who are utilizing the facilities early in the mornings, information which will assist the businesses in advertising the availability of morning sessions to relevant populations. You collect data for a roller skating rink, a paintball arena, and a racquetball court. Your data is displayed in Table 2.14.
   a. Calculate the mean

Table 2.14: Homework Set A #3 Data

Ages of Clients: Roller Skating Rink	Ages of Clients: Paintball Arena	Ages of Clients: Racquetball Court
11	16	30
13	16	31
12	15	32
92	18	30
11	17	30
11	17	30
12	17	29
12	16	12
13	15	32
12	16	30

   b. Calculate the median
   c. Calculate the mode
   d. Indicate which index of central tendency is the most representative for each particular data set (roller skating rink, paintball arena, and racquetball court), or indicate if the mean, median, and mode are equally representative for the particular data set.
4. Due to your amazing statistical skills, you have been offered jobs with three different research groups. The three groups are equal in pay, workload, and all other factors you normally consider to help you decide which job offer to accept. Therefore, you decide to accept the offer from the group that is the most gregarious. After all, you might as well

work with friendly people! You administer a test of gregariousness to the five members of each group. The gregariousness scale is anchored at 1 (not gregarious) and 10 (very gregarious). Your data is displayed in Table 2.15. For each group, calculate a–f.

Table 2.15: Homework Set A #4 Data

Research Group A	Research Group B	Research Group C
2	9	10
3	8	2
4	8	3
3	7	9
1	8	5

   a. Deviation scores
   b. Squared deviation scores
   c. Sum of the squared deviation
   d. Variance
   e. Standard deviation
   f. What do the results of your statistical analyses tell you about the gregariousness of each group?

5. You are conducting a study to examine the relationship between personality type and the number of caffeinated beverages consumed in a day. You ask a sample of people with high-stress personality types how many caffeinated beverages they consumed that day, and you obtained these numbers:

2   4   3   4
4   5   3   4
3   2   3   5

   a. Create a frequency table
   b. Create a frequency histogram
   c. Create a frequency polygon
   d. Indicate whether the polygon is unimodal or bimodal
   e. Indicate the direction of skew, if any

6. You are considering taking a class that is rumored to require an extraordinary amount of study time to get a good grade. Knowing that you already have a full schedule and study time will be limited, you collect data from the students who just completed the course with an A or B regarding the amount of time they studied the day before the final exam, in minutes.

74   186   266   167
230   278   275   126
214   243   117   296

a. Create a grouped frequency table (using 30-minute intervals)

b. Create a grouped frequency histogram

c. Create a grouped frequency polygon

d. Indicate whether the polygon is unimodal or bimodal

e. Indicate the direction of skew, if any

7. A club on campus is debating whether to continue holding periodic informational meetings for members to discuss upcoming club activities and events. Half of the planning committee members theorize that most members of the club read the club website and are already aware of upcoming events, and come to the meetings simply for the refreshments provided. The other half of the planning committee members believe that the meetings are a valuable source of information for members, and the refreshments are simply a welcomed bonus. Figuring that everyone would claim to be attending the meeting for the information rather than the food, the committee decides to collect data by asking people as they enter the next informational meeting whether they are hungry. Here are the data:

Hungry	Hungry	Not hungry
Not hungry	Hungry	Hungry
Hungry	Hungry	Hungry
Hungry	Hungry	Hungry
Hungry	Not hungry	Hungry

a. Create a categorical frequency table

b. Create a categorical frequency histogram

HOMEWORK SET B

1. Give two examples of each type of variable.

a. Continuous variable

b. Ordinal variable

c. Categorical variable

2. Using APA format, round the following numbers:

a. 22.54218

b. 3.291621

c. 53.98523

d. 77.99852

e. 13.01368

f. 211.90610

3. You are conducting a study assessing the relationship between physical fitness and overall confidence in middle school kids. Your participants are divided into three groups—not physically fit, somewhat physically fit, and very physically fit. Their overall confidence levels are measured on a 10 point scale, with 1 being not confident and 10 being very confident. Your data is displayed in Table 2.16.

Table 2.16: Homework Set B #3 Data

Not Physically Fit	Somewhat Physically Fit	Very Physically Fit
2	5	10
3	6	9
10	1	8
4	5	8
3	6	7
10	5	9
3	7	6
3	1	6
2	6	7
3	6	9

a. Calculate the mean
b. Calculate the median
c. Calculate the mode
d. Indicate which index of central tendency is the most representative for each particular data set, or indicate if the mean, median, and mode are equally representative for the particular data set.

4. In your area, the buses are notorious for not stopping for anyone who is late in getting to the bus stop. You've noticed that when people are late for the bus, they will typically run for a short period of time, then stop once they realize the bus is not going to stop for them. You are curious whether there is a common amount of time that people typically run before they give up. Further, you think that people in business attire typically run for shorter periods of time than people in casual clothing. You sit at a bus stop and collect data, using seconds to measure how long the people ran. Your data is displayed in Table 2.17.

Table 2.17: Homework Set B #4 Data

Casual Clothing	Business Attire
20	6
12	5
6	8
3	8
8	9
22	6

For each group, calculate:
a. Deviation scores
b. Squared deviation scores
c. Sum of the squared deviation
d. Variance
e. Standard deviation
f. What do the results of your statistical analyses tell you about the variation in scores within each group?

5. You wonder if people who take higher-level computer classes tend to use more electronic gadgets overall. You ask a sample of people from a high-level computer class how many electronic gadgets they use regularly, and obtain these numbers:

8	6	7
9	5	4
10	4	6

   a. Create a frequency table
   b. Create a frequency histogram
   c. Create a frequency polygon
   d. Indicate whether the polygon is unimodal or bimodal
   e. Indicate the direction of skew, if any

6. You remember that when you were a child, adults always had change in their pockets. Since everyone has debit cards now, you theorize that fewer people have change in their pockets, and those who do have change in their pockets don't have much change. You collect data, recording the amount of change in cents.

12	0	4	13
9	26	3	0
0	0	25	11
0	52	0	0
5	0	0	0

   a. Create a grouped frequency table (using 10-cent intervals)
   b. Create a grouped frequency histogram
   c. Create a grouped frequency polygon
   d. Indicate whether the polygon is unimodal or bimodal
   e. Indicate the direction of skew, if any

7. You think that when given the option between different novels to read in literature class, the majority of the class will choose the novels that have the fewest number of pages. When your class is given the option of reading Alice Walker's *The Color Purple* or the much longer *Uncle Tom's Cabin* by Harriet Beecher Stowe, you survey your classmates on their choices.

Data:

The Color Purple	*The Color Purple*	*The Color Purple*
The Color Purple	*The Color Purple*	*The Color Purple*
The Color Purple	*The Color Purple*	*The Color Purple*
The Color Purple	*Uncle Tom's Cabin*	*The Color Purple*
The Color Purple	*The Color Purple*	*Uncle Tom's Cabin*
The Color Purple	*The Color Purple*	*The Color Purple*
The Color Purple	*The Color Purple*	

   a. Create a categorical frequency table
   b. Create a categorical frequency histogram

HOMEWORK SET A ANSWERS

1. a. height, weight—any variable that has values that vary by degree
    b. place in line, rank of finish in a race—any variable that corresponds to rank
    c. dog vs. cat, employed vs. unemployed—any variable that is scored by placement in a category
2. a. 6.17
    b. 24.35
    c. 101.96
    d. 91.47
    e. 67.01
    f. 42.00
3.

Table 2.18: Homework Set A #3 Calculations a–d

Ages of Clients: Roller Skating Rink	Ages of Clients: Paintball Arena	Ages of Clients: Racquetball Court
11	16	30
13	16	31
12	15	32
92	18	30
11	17	30
11	17	30
12	17	29
12	16	12
13	15	32
12	16	30
Mean $= M = \dfrac{\Sigma X}{N} = \dfrac{199}{10} = 19.9$	Mean $= M = \dfrac{\Sigma X}{N} = \dfrac{163}{10} = 16.3$	Mean $= M = \dfrac{\Sigma X}{N} = \dfrac{286}{10} = 28.6$
Median = 12	Median = 16	Median = 30
Mode = 12	Mode = 16	Mode = 30
The mean is not the best index of central tendency because the spry 92-year-old who came to the early-morning skate session provided an outlier in the data set. The median and mode, both 12, are better indicators of central tendency in this data set, showing that the average early-morning roller skater is 12 years old.	The mean, median, and mode are all equally good measures of central tendency in this particular data set. All three indexes demonstrate that the average early morning paintballer is 16 years old.	The mean in this data set is skewed by the 12-year-old racquetball player amongst all the 30-year-olds. The 12 is an outlier. The median and mode, both 30, are better indicators of central tendency in this data set, showing that the average early-morning racquetball player is 30 years old.

4.

Research Group A:

Table 2.19: Homework Set A #4 Research Group A Calculations a–b

X	M	Deviation Score (X–M)	Squared Deviation Score (X–M)²
2	2.6	–.6	.36
3	2.6	.4	.16
4	2.6	1.4	1.96
3	2.6	.4	.16
1	2.6	–1.6	2.56
$\sum$ = 13			$\sum$(X–M)² = 5.2
N = 5			
M = 2.6			$SD^2 = \dfrac{(X-M)^2}{N}$ = 1.04
			$SD = \sqrt{(SD)^2}$ = 1.02

a. Deviation scores—see chart
b. Squared deviation scores—see chart
c. Sum of squared deviation scores $\sum$(X–M)² = 5.2
d. Variance = $SD^2 = \dfrac{(X-M)^2}{N}$ = 1.04
e. Standard deviation = SD = $\sqrt{(SD)^2}$ = 1.02
f. The statistical analyses of Group A indicate that Group A has a mean gregarious-
    ness score of 2.6 on a 10-point scale. The standard deviation is 1.02. Therefore, the
    average gregariousness scores are very low, and there is not much variability in the
    scores. Group A is not a very gregarious group of people.

Research Group B:

Table 2.20: Homework Set A #4 Research Group B
Calculations a–b

X	M	Deviation Score (X–M)	Squared Deviation Score (X–M)²
9	8	1	1
8	8	0	0
8	8	0	0
7	8	–1	1
8	8	0	0
$\sum$ = 40			$\sum$(X–M)² = 2
N = 5			
M = 8			$SD^2 = \dfrac{(X-M)^2}{N}$ = .4
			$SD = \sqrt{(SD)^2}$ = .63

a. Deviation scores—see chart
b. Squared deviation scores—see chart
c. Sum of squared deviation scores $\sum(X–M)^2 = 2$
d. Variance = SD^2 = $\dfrac{(X-M)^2}{N}$ = .4
e. Standard deviation = SD = $\sqrt{(SD)^2}$ = .63
f. The statistical analyses of Group B indicate that Group B has a mean gregariousness score of 8 on a 10-point scale. The standard deviation is. 63. Therefore, the average gregariousness scores are very high and there is not much variability in the scores. Group A is a very gregarious group of people.

Research Group C:

Table 2.21: Homework Set A #4 Research Group C Calculations a–b

X	M	Deviation Score (X–M)	Squared Deviation Score (X–M)^2
10	5.8	4.2	17.64
2	5.8	–3.8	14.44
3	5.8	–2.8	7.84
9	5.8	3.2	10.24
5	5.8	–.8	.64
$\sum$ = 29			$\sum(X–M)^2 = 50.8$
N = 5			
M = 5.8			SD^2 = $\dfrac{(X-M)^2}{N}$ = 10.16
			SD = $\sqrt{(SD)^2}$ = 3.19

a. Deviation scores—see chart
b. Squared deviation scores—see chart
c. Sum of squared deviation scores $\sum(X–M)^2 = 50.8$
d. Variance = SD^2 = $\dfrac{(X-M)^2}{N}$ = 10.16
e. Standard deviation = SD = $\sqrt{(SD)^2}$ = 3.19
f. The statistical analyses of Group C indicate that Group C has a mean gregariousness score of 5.8 on a 10-point scale. The standard deviation is 3.19. Therefore, the average gregariousness scores are in the middle of the scale, and there is a great deal of variability in the scores. Group C contains individuals who are very gregarious and individuals who are not at all gregarious.

5.   a. See Table 2.22.

Table 2.22: Homework Set A #5a

Value	Tick Marks	Frequency
0		0
1		0
2				2
3						4
4						4
5				2

b. See Figure 2.7.

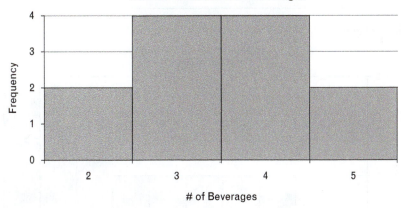

Frequency Histogram
Number of Caffeinated Beverages

FIGURE 2.7: Homework Set A #5b.

c. See Figure 2.8.

Frequency Polygon
# of Caffeinated Beverages

FIGURE 2.8: Homework Set A #5c.

   d.   The distribution is unimodal.
   e.   The distribution is not skewed.

6.   a. See Table 2.23.

Table 2.23: Homework Set A #6a

Time Studied, in Minutes	Tick Marks	Frequency
0–29		0
30–59		0
60–89	|	1
90–119	|	1
120–149	|	1
150–179	|	1
180–209	|	1
210–239	||	2
240–269	||	2
270–299	|||	3

b. See Figure 2.9.

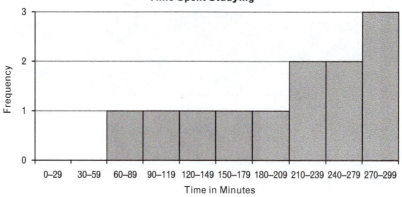

FIGURE 2.9: Homework Set A #6b.

c. See Figure 2.10.

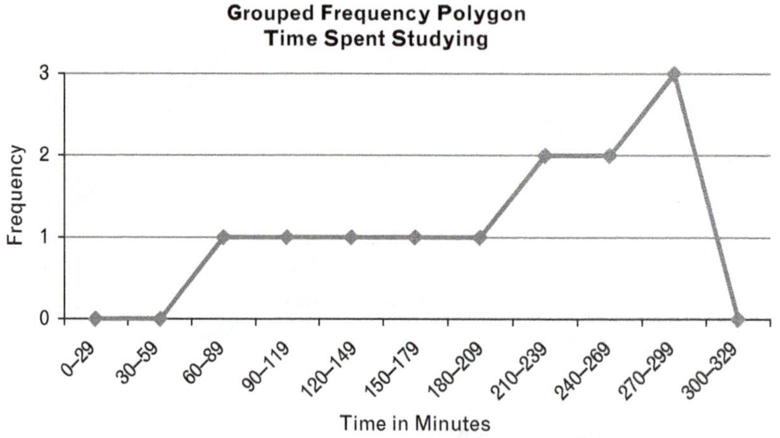

FIGURE 2.10: Homework Set A #6c.

d. This data set is unimodal. There is one most common value, which is the interval of 270–299 minutes.

e. This distribution of time spent studying is negatively skewed, with the high values clustered to the right side.

7.

a. Categorical frequency table for Hunger of Club Members

Table 2.24: Homework Set A #7a

Value (Category)	Tick Marks	Frequency	Percentage
Hungry	JHT JHT II	12	80%
Not hungry	III	3	20%

b. See Figure 2.11.

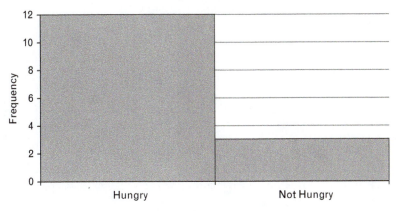

FIGURE 2.11: Homework Set A #7b.

REFERENCE

Gallant, S., Williams, L., Fisher, M., & Cox, A. (2011). Mating strategies and self-presentation in online personal advertisement photographs. *Journal of Social, Evolutionary and Cultural Psychology, 5(1),* 106–121.

C H A P T E R   3

STANDARDIZED SCORES

Standardized Scores (also called *z-scores*) comprise one of the core concepts in statistics. As we'll soon see, z-scores allow you to compare raw scores that come from different scales with one another. For instance, using z-scores, you'll have the tools to assess which is more impressive, a GPA of 3.8 or a combined GRE score of 1490. Further, z-scores will allow you to think about any score in a very clearly structured and meaningful manner—you will be able to think of any score in terms of how many standard deviations from the mean it is in a given sample or distribution. As you read more in this chapter and work out the problems, you'll see how intuitive and useful this way of thinking is. But that's not all! The reasoning underlying z-scores sets the groundwork for many of the ideas that are to follow across the remainder of this book.

Let's start with this scenario: Suppose you live in the dictatorship of Madupistan (a totally made-up nation!). In this country, very few students are allowed entry into the state-run university system. Further, once you get in, your major and your classes are determined completely based on your scores on the all-too-difficult Madupistan Aptitude Measure—a rigorous, challenging test that makes or breaks the careers and lives of the poor citizens of Madupistan.

Because of the disagreement and chaos that permeate Madupistan's culture, all the different subsections of the Madupistan Aptitude Measure are on their own scales. For instance, scores on the verbal test range from 1–10, while scores on the quantitative test range from 20–40. Test day arrives and you feel pretty good. Soon thereafter, your scores arrive in the mail. You got a 9 on the verbal test and a 35 on the quantitative measure.

What does this all mean? One thing you may do is consider your scores in terms of the possible ranges for each test. You may reason to yourself that your score on verbal was closer to the top of the possible range (1 point away) than was your score on the quantitative section (which was 5 points from the top). Based on this analysis, you may be in for four years of courses on poetry and literary analysis.

But wait. Interpreting a score involves much more than a consideration of where that score lies in terms of some arbitrary range of numbers. What if it turns out that 80 percent of students get 9 out of 10 correct on the verbal test, but you're the first student in the history of Madupistan to score as high as 35 on the quantitative test? This would complicate things a bit, wouldn't it?

Not to worry! Madupistan's government is, in fact, well aware of this issue—and they have hired professional statisticians to help with the interpretation of scores. These statisticians reason that the best way to understand where a particular score is relative to the population of interest is to compute *standardized scores*. A standardized score is a reframing of a score in units that are universal (or standard). Initially, we can't compare the verbal score of 9 with the quantitative score of 35, because they are on totally different scales. It'd be like comparing your height in inches (which may be something like 66) with the number of books you've read this year (which may be something like 9) and trying to decide if you're more tall than you are well-read—it just doesn't make sense. That's right: apples and oranges.

The beauty of standardized scores is this: These scores allow you to, metaphorically speaking, compare apples and oranges. By putting scores from different scales onto the same universal (standard) scale, you suddenly can make such comparisons.

In terms of formal statistical concepts, a z-score corresponds to the **number of standard deviations above or below the mean that a particular score is**. Recall from chapter 2 that the standard deviation of a sample is a statistical index that roughly corresponds to the average or typical amount that scores in a sample vary from one another. The standard deviation is in units that match the original scale that the data come from.

The simple formula for a z-score is this: $Z = \dfrac{X - M}{SD}$. In this formula, the different elements are defined as follows:

Z = the number of standard deviations above or below the mean that a particular raw score is (relative to the sample it was drawn from)
X = the raw score of interest that we are converting to a standardized (z) score
M = the mean of the sample that x was drawn from
SD = the standard deviation of the sample that x was drawn from.

At this point in the course, you have all the tools in your statistical toolbox to compute and understand z-scores. So here's how it works: By subtracting M from X, we get a difference score that tells us two things. First, the sign of this difference (which will correspond to the sign of the z-score) tells us if X is *greater than* the mean of the sample or if X is *less than* the mean of the sample. If X is greater than the mean, X–M (and, ultimately, Z) will be positive. If X is less than the mean, X–M (and, ultimately, Z) will be negative.

By dividing this difference (X–M) by SD, we get a sense of how different X is from M in light of the standard deviation. Is X a standard deviation different from M? Is it more than a standard deviation different from M? Further, given how z-scores are computed, the mean of z distribution is *always* 0 and the standard deviation of a z distribution is *always* 1. The nature of the z-score formula forces this to be the case. To understand why, consider the following: If X = M, then you have a score that is *not at all different* (read as **zero different**) from the mean. Such a score would be zero standard deviations from the mean—it would, in fact, **be the mean**. Mathematically, such a situation would lead to a z-score of 0 (because X–M would be 0, making Z 0 as well).

Now let's think about why the standard deviation of a z distribution must be 1. If you have a score (X) that is exactly one standard deviation above the mean, what's going to happen? Well, since $Z = \dfrac{X - M}{SD}$, the numerator (top part) of this fraction will equal the standard deviation (in raw score units). And that standard deviation divided by itself must = 1.

Consider the following three scenarios to see how intuitive this is. For each of these scenarios, assume that combined SAT scores have a mean of 1000 and a standard deviation of 200.

A. Joey got a 1200 on the SAT. What is Joey's SAT score in standardized units? In other words: What is the z-score for Joey's raw score of 1200? OR: How many standard deviations above or below the mean is Joey's particular SAT score of 1200? (Note that these questions are identical to one another).

Answer: Joey's z-score is 1 (thus, Joey's score of 1200 is 1 standard deviation above the mean of 1000).

$$\text{Here's the math: } Z = \frac{1200 - 1000}{200}. \text{ That equals } \frac{200}{200} = 1.$$

Thus, if a raw score (X) corresponds to a z-score of 1, that's the same as saying that this particular score is exactly 1 standard deviation above the mean.

B. Now consider Tommy. Tommy's combined SAT score is 800. What is Tommy's z-score? In other words, how many standard deviations above or below the mean is Tommy's raw score of 800?

$$\text{Answer: Tommy's z-score} = -1. \; (z = \frac{800 - 1000}{200} = -1).$$

Thus, Tommy's raw score (800) is exactly 1 standard deviation below the mean.

C. Julia's SAT score is 1000. What is this score converted to a standardized (Z) score? Given the definition of a z-score, the answer may be fully intuitive at this point. Z literally corresponds to how many standard deviations above or below the mean a particular raw score is. The mean given in this problem is 1000. Julia's raw score is 1000. It is not above the mean. It is not below the mean. It is equal to the mean. It deviates ZERO from the mean. Here's how the Z formula tells us this same story:

$$Z(\textbf{for Julia}) = \frac{1000 - 1000}{200} = \frac{0}{200} = 0.$$

WHEN A Z-SCORE EQUALS 0, THE RAW SCORE IT CORRESPONDS TO MUST EQUAL THE MEAN

So a z-score provides us with information about how many standard deviations a particular score is from the mean of the sample that corresponds to that particular score.

Let's get back to the Madupistan example. We're now looking at the question of which test you did better on—the verbal test (you got a 9) or the quantitative test (you got a 35). Remember, these scores are on different scales.

Here's what we're going to do: We'll compute your z-score for the verbal test and the z-score for the quantitative test. We'll then have scores that are *on the same scale*, making it reasonable to compare them with one another. Once we reconceptualize the verbal scale as a z distribution, the mean becomes 0 and the SD becomes 1. Same for the quantitative scale. Given how z-scores are computed, all z distributions are standardized—they are, by definition, on a scale with a mean of 0 and a standard deviation of 1. In this light, it is now fair to compare scores that originated from radically different scales.

To address this question using the beautiful logic of z-scores, you'll need to understand all the elements embedded in the Z formula. Recall that $Z = \dfrac{X - M}{SD}$. For both the verbal and quantitative tests, you have X (the raw scores you want converted to z-scores). X for the verbal is 9, X for the quantitative is 35. Remember, X simply means *the actual raw score of interest*. This information was given to you in the problem. You now have to figure out what M and SD are for your current purposes. Importantly, there are two different Ms and SDs—there will be the mean and standard deviation for the verbal scores and, separately, the mean and standard deviation for the quantitative scores. Given that you've completed chapter 2, you're an ace at computing these different statistics. Get those computational skills out of the toolbox—you'll need them.

Suppose that you were one of a class of seven students who took the Madupistan Aptitude Measure in one particular year. Here (see Table 3.1) are the scores for each student (you are Student #4):

Table 3.1: Verbal and Quantative Raw Scores

Student #	Verbal Score	Quantitative Score
1	4	21
2	7	30
3	9	29
4	**9**	**35**
5	5	26
6	3	20
7	8	30

So, what is the task at hand? Here's the big picture: You're looking to see (based on these test scores) which is your stronger aptitude, verbal or quantitative. As these raw scores are on different scales from one another, you can only make this comparison by converting your verbal score and your quantitative score to z-scores.

So we'll have to compute these two z-scores.

Recall that $Z = \dfrac{X - M}{SD}$. We have the two Xs (raw scores) of interest (9 for verbal, 35 for quantitative). We now need to figure out the two different means and standard deviations. Well, that's easy. Let's start with the verbal test.

Here are the steps:

1. Compute the mean for the sample $\left(M = \dfrac{\Sigma X}{N} \right)$.

$$M = \frac{45}{7} = 6.43$$

We now have $Z = \dfrac{9 - 6.43}{SD}$. Next we need to figure out the standard deviation (exactly as we did for chapter 2).

2. Computing the standard deviation. As a quick review of information from chapter 2, steps for getting the standard deviation include:

   A. Subtract the mean from each score to get difference scores (X–M)
   B. Square each difference score (X–M)^2
   C. Compute the sum of the squared difference scores Σ(X–M)^2
   D. Divide the sum of the squared difference scores by N to get the variance $(SD^2 = \dfrac{\Sigma(X-M)^2}{N})$
   E. Take the square root of the variance (SD = $\sqrt{SD^2}$)

VERBAL SCORES FOR THE MADUPISTAN APTITUDE MEASURE

3. Now compute the z-score of interest: $Z = \dfrac{X-M}{SD} = Z = \dfrac{9-6.43}{2.26} = 1.14.$

Here's how to interpret this information: Your verbal score of 9 is 1.14 standard deviations above the mean. Stated a bit more roughly, you're better than average in the verbal domain—a good bit better than average, in fact.

BACK ON TASK: Recall that we did all of this math for a particular reason. Our goal here is to figure out which is your stronger intellectual capacity: Verbal or Quantitative. Since the verbal and quantitative tests are on different scales, we're converting your raw scores on both tests to z-scores—a process that will put them both on the same scale with a straightforward and coherent interpretation (number of standard deviations from the mean that each score is). We already figured out your z-score for the verbal test—now let's follow the same process to figure out your z-score for the quantitative test. The good news: The steps are the same.

1. Compute the mean for the sample of quantitative scores $\left(M = \dfrac{\Sigma X}{N} \right)$.

$$M = \dfrac{191}{7} = 27.29$$

Table 3.2: Computing Standard Deviation for Verbal Scores

X	M	(X–M)	(X–M)^2
4	6.43	−2.43	5.90
7	6.43	.57	.32
9	6.43	2.57	6.60
9	**6.43**	**2.57**	**6.60**
5	6.43	−1.43	2.04
3	6.43	−3.43	11.76
8	6.43	1.57	2.46

$$\Sigma(X-M)^2 = 35.68$$

$$SD^2 = \dfrac{\Sigma(X-M)^2}{N} = 5.10$$

$$SD = \sqrt{SD^2} = 2.26$$

Now we have $Z = \dfrac{35 - 27.29}{SD}$. We still have to figure out the standard deviation.

2. Compute the standard deviation.

Table 3.3: Computing Standard Deviation for Quantitative Scores

X	M	(X–M)	(X–M)²
21	27.29	–6.29	39.56
30	27.29	2.71	7.34
29	27.29	1.71	2.92
35	**27.29**	**7.71**	**59.44**
26	27.29	–1.29	1.66
20	27.29	–7.29	53.14
30	27.29	2.71	7.34

$$\Sigma(X–M)^2 = 171.49$$

$$SD^2 = \frac{\Sigma(X - M)^2}{N} = 24.50$$

$$SD = \sqrt{SD^2} = 4.95$$

QUANTITATIVE SCORES FOR THE MADUPISTAN APTITUDE MEASURE

3. Now compute the z-score of interest: $Z = \dfrac{X - M}{SD} = Z = \dfrac{35 - 27.29}{4.95} = 1.56$. Your raw score on the quantitative test is 1.56 standard deviations above the mean for that test.

THE MOMENT OF TRUTH HAS ARRIVED: Well, now you have all the information you need to answer the question of interest: Which is your stronger ability (based on scores on the Madupistan Aptitude Measure)? To address this question at this point, we simply can compare your two z-scores. Z for verbal was 1.14, Z for quantitative was 1.56. On both tests, you did better than average (by more than a full standard deviation). However, given that 1.56 > 1.14, it seems that your quantitative score is particularly high. You have high aptitude in both the verbal and quantitative domains—but you seem to have slightly more aptitude when it comes to numbers. See how useful z-scores are for answering this kind of question?

EVERY RAW SCORE FOR ANY VARIABLE CORRESPONDS TO A PARTICULAR Z-SCORE

Conceptually, for every raw score that exists on any variable, there is a unique corresponding z-score. For every grade on every test you take in college, a z-score can be computed. The temperature on any given day (e.g., 72 degrees) corresponds to a z-score (e.g., 1.22 (meaning that this temperature is 1.22 standard deviations above the mean temperature for a given location)).

For the Madupistan Aptitude Measure, we've calculated your z-score for the verbal and quantitative tests. Using the same process, we can calculate z-scores for all the other students who took the test. Let's do it. Not only is this a useful exercise in developing your computational skills, but it will set you up for computing and organizing z-scores as a tool for computing correlations (which we turn to in chapter 4).

COMPUTING Z-SCORES FOR ALL STUDENTS FOR THE MADUPISTAN VERBAL TEST

To compute the z-scores for all the students, we'll use exactly the same process that we employed to calculate your particular z-score. When we're computing all the z-scores for an entire sample on some variable, we'll find it useful to organize them into a table. In fact, the table that statisticians typically use for this work is identical to the table used to compute standard deviation—with one extra column. That extra column corresponds to the z-score for each particular raw score. To compute each of these seven z-scores, we'll simply do the following:

1. Use the z-score formula $(Z = \dfrac{X - M}{SD})$ one time for each raw score (as we have seven raw scores, we'll use it seven times).
2. Note that in each case, the MEAN and the STANDARD DEVIATION will be identical. That will make things easy. In this case, for the verbal scores, M = 6.43 and SD = 2.25.
3. For instance, for the first person in the table who scored a 4 on the verbal test, we'd compute that person's z-score as follows: $Z = \dfrac{4 - 6.43}{2.25} = -1.08$.

Here are the answers in table format:

Note that this table is identical to the standard deviation table—except it now has a column for each z-score.

Table 3.4: Z-Scores for Verbal Scores

X	M	(X–M)	(X–M)²	Z
4	6.43	−2.43	5.90	−1.06
7	6.43	.57	.32	.25
9	6.43	2.57	6.60	1.14
9	**6.43**	**2.57**	**6.60**	**1.14**
5	6.43	−1.43	2.04	−.63
3	6.43	−3.43	11.76	−1.52
8	6.43	1.57	2.46	.69
			Σ(X–M)² = 35.59	

$$SD^2 = \frac{\Sigma(X - M)^2}{N} = 5.10$$

$$SD = \sqrt{SD^2} = 2.26$$

Each z-score corresponds to the particular raw score (X) in the same row—and can be interpreted in the same way that all z-scores are interpreted. For instance, the sixth student in this table had a raw score of 3 on the verbal test. The corresponding z-score is –1.48. Thus, this person's score of 3 is 1.48 standard deviations below the mean for the verbal test.

Here's the corresponding table for the **quantitative scores** (in which M = 27.29 and SD = 4.95):

Table 3.5: Z-Scores for Quantitative Scores

X	M	(X–M)	(X–M)²	Z
21	27.29	–6.29	39.56	–1.27
30	27.29	2.71	7.34	.55
29	27.29	1.71	2.92	.35
35	**27.29**	**7.71**	**59.44**	**1.56**
26	27.29	–1.29	1.66	–.26
20	27.29	–7.29	53.14	–1.47
30	27.29	2.71	7.34	.55

$$\Sigma(X-M)^2 = 171.49$$

$$SD^2 = \frac{\Sigma(X-M)^2}{N} = 24.50$$

$$SD = \sqrt{SD^2} = 4.95$$

As is the case with the table for the verbal scores, each z-score in this table corresponds to one specific raw score—and it can be interpreted in the same way that z-scores are always interpreted. For instance, take the person whose score of 21 is represented in the first row. This person's raw score (X = 21) corresponds to a z-score of –1.43. Thus, this person's quantitative score is 1.43 standard deviations below the mean (not so great) on this test.

COMPUTING RAW SCORES FROM Z-SCORES

So far, we've gone over what z-scores are, how they are computed, how they are interpreted, and what they're good for. From a computational perspective, there is one final point to be considered regarding z-scores. Just as we can compute a z-score from a raw score (as long as we have the appropriate mean and standard deviation), we can compute a raw score (X) from a z-score (again, as long as we have the mean and the standard deviation). In other words, instead of concluding that your raw score of 35 on the quantitative test corresponds to a z-score of 1.56, we can start with the z-score (of 1.56) and figure out that your raw score was 35.

This skill is partly important simply because it's needed in some advanced statistics that you'll learn later in this course. There are practical conditions in which this skill would be useful. For instance, suppose that you and your best friend Pat are at two different schools. Your school has a reputation as a solid state school (Solid State University)—and it's traditional in many respects. Pat decided to really challenge herself, and went to Advanced Technical University—a school renowned worldwide for its exceptional academic rigor. In fact, Pat informed you recently that the average GPA at Advanced Technical University is 1.6 and the standard deviation is .2. These numbers differ markedly from your nice school, which has a mean GPA of 2.5 and a standard deviation of .5.

In the midst of your conversation, you learn that Pat is, apparently, on the dean's list at Advanced Technical University this semester, with a GPA of 1.95. Ridiculous! You didn't make the dean's list yourself at Solid State, even though your GPA was 3.10—*way higher* than Pat's GPA! You demand an explanation! Then you come to your senses and realize that with your understanding of z-scores, you can shed some light on this situation. Essentially, you decided that you would like to see what Pat's GPA of 1.95 would translate into if she were at Solid State U.

COMPARING YOUR GPA OF 3.10 FROM SOLID STATE UNIVERSITY WITH PAT'S GPA OF 1.95 FROM ADVANCED TECHNICAL UNIVERSITY

The specific question you decide to ask is this: What would Pat's GPA be if she were doing just as well at her studies—but she was a student at good old Solid State U? Here are the steps you'd need to follow:

1. First, convert Pat's score to a z-score to figure out how many standard deviations different from the mean (at Advanced Technical University) her GPA is. Easy:

$Z = \dfrac{X - M}{SD}$. All this information is given (we just have to remember to use the M and SD that correspond to Advanced Technical University, as this information will allow us to first address how Pat's score fares compared with other scores at that school). Here it is again: X = 1.95, M = 1.6, SD = .2.

$$Z = \frac{.35}{.20} = 1.75$$

Thus, Pat's GPA of 1.95 is 1.75 standard deviations above the mean of the students at Advanced Technical University.

2. We now have a z-score for Pat (1.75). We can therefore ask what raw score at Solid State University corresponds to this particular z-score. In other words, we can see what specific GPA at your school corresponds to being 1.75 standard deviations above the mean (at your school). In doing so, we're converting a z-score to a raw score (X).

The formula for carrying out this conversion is simply an algebraic reshuffling of our loyal z-score formula. Essentially, we rearrange this formula so that it's designed to solve for X (instead of Z).

$$\text{If } Z = \frac{X - M}{SD}, \text{then X = M} + \left(SD * Z\right)$$

Back to the task at hand: To figure out what GPA at Solid State U. corresponds to a z-score of 1.75, we simply use this formula (with X representing the score as a GPA). Given that we're figuring out that the GPA would be at Solid State, the M and SD we use here will be the ones for Solid State.

$$X = 2.5 + (.5 * 1.75) = 3.38.$$

It now becomes clear why Pat made the dean's list and you didn't—her GPA of 1.95 at Advanced Technical University would correspond to a 3.38 at Solid State—enough higher than your 3.10 to warrant dean's list status. Problem? No problem—just work harder next semester!

EACH Z-SCORE FOR ANY VARIABLE CORRESPONDS TO A PARTICULAR RAW SCORE

Just as each raw score on a variable corresponds to a particular z-score, each z-score corresponds to a particular raw score for a given variable. As such, z-scores and raw scores may be said to have an *isomorphic relationship* (meaning they have a one-to-one correspondence to one another).

Thus, for instance, if you found a list of the GPAs for everyone in your dorm, but these GPAs were in z-score format, you should realize that it's possible to compute the specific GPA (i.e., raw score) for each of these (presented in standardized, z-score format). Not that you're the kind of person who would be interested in this information ... but if you were, consider the following:

CONVERTING Z-SCORES TO RAW SCORES (THE DORM RESIDENT EXAMPLE)

You just happened upon a list of GPAs for all students in your dorm. This list is from the Registrar's office, so you know it's legitimate. However, the GPAs are in z-score format. Being the curious creature that you are, you decide to go into your statistics toolbox and figure out what these cryptically encoded scores convert to as real GPAs.

Here's a subset of the list:

Table 3.6:

Name	GPA (in z-score format)
Ben	1.82
Kathy	.56
Joel	−1.23
Merle	−.34
Eric	1.45
Tamina	.68

Recall that to convert a particular z-score to a raw score, you need to use the following formula: $X = M + (SD*Z)$. In this case, X means the score in raw (GPA) units, M is the mean of the sample or population of interest, SD is the standard deviation of the sample or population of interest, and Z is the particular z-score that you're given. Thus, to implement these calculations, you'll need the mean and standard deviation. Let's assume that you're still at Solid State University, and the mean GPA is 2.5, while the standard deviation is .5.

Here are the answers worked out:

Table 3.7:

Name	GPA (in z-score format)	Calculations $X = M + (SD * Z)$	GPA (in raw-score format)
Ben	1.82	$X = 2.5 + (.5 * 1.82) =$	3.41
Kathy	.56	$X = 2.5 + (.5 * .56) =$	2.78
Joel	−1.23	$X = 2.5 + (.5 * −1.23) =$	1.89
Merle	−.34	$X = 2.5 + (.5 * −.34) =$	2.33
Eric	1.45	$X = 2.5 + (.5 * 1.45) =$	3.23
Tamina	.68	$X = 2.5 + (.5 * .68) =$	2.84

A REAL RESEARCH EXAMPLE

In a large cross-cultural study addressing sex differences in basic personality traits, McCrae and Terracciano (2005) sought to find out if there are basic and consistent sex differences in several personality traits worldwide. To address this question, they administered a respected personality test (the Revised NEO Personality Inventory) to more than 11,000 adults across 50 different cultures. While this personality test includes 240 items (each on a five-point scale), these researchers wanted to present information on sex differences in standardized units, so the reader can quickly understand the nature of any sex differences in terms of differences in standard deviations. Here is a summary of representative finding:

Across all participants, women scored higher than men on anxiety (the mean z-score for women was .32 standard deviation units higher than the mean z-score for men). By presenting this information in z-score units, the reader can draw inferences such as "women are, on average, about a third of a standard deviation higher on anxiety than are men." For a reader who is educated in z-scores, this presentation is highly accessible and informative.

SUMMARY

Among the different statistics that you run into, few are as basic, interpretable, and integral as the z-score. Z-scores allow you to compare scores from variables that are on different scales. Given the simple mathematical nature of z-scores, converting raw scores to z-scores and vice versa is straightforward. The simple and clean nature of z-scores—always on a scale with a mean of 0 and a standard deviation of 1—allows for a universal and clear interpretation of scores obtained from all kinds of variables. Further, as we'll see in chapter 5 (and subsequent chapters), z-scores play a major role in our understanding and implementation of nearly all the statistical concepts that follow.

KEY TERMS

Isomorphic Relationship: A situation in which the items in one set correspond perfectly to specific items in another set. In terms of raw scores and z-scores, each raw score for a variable corresponds to a specific z-score for that same variable. The relationship between raw and z-scores is, thus, isomorphic.

Raw score: An unaltered number in the original units of measurement, a number which has not been transformed in any way

Standardized score: Z-score

Z-score: A number that corresponds to the number of standard deviations a score is above or below the mean

HOMEWORK SET A

1. For each of the following raw scores (X), compute Z if the mean (M) is 36 and the standard deviation (SD) is 2. Remember, $Z = \dfrac{X - M}{SD}$. Explain in terms of standard deviation what the z-score means.
    a. 31
    b. 42
    c. 28

2. For each of the following sets of raw scores, compute the mean, standard deviation, and z-score.
    a. 18, 16, 15, 20
    b. 32, 36, 29, 30

3. You learned in this chapter how to find a raw score given a z-score, mean, and standard deviation, using the formula X = M + (SD*Z). Find the raw scores for the following z-scores, given that the mean of the distribution is 61 and the standard deviation is 3.
    a. z = 1.2
    b. z = 2.6
    c. z = −2.3

4. You participate in a study designed to determine how cool you are, according to college student standards. You are told that your z-score on the coolness scale is 1.35, and that the mean of the scale was 58, with a standard deviation of 4.02. What was your raw score on the coolness scale?

5. You feel so cool after participating in the coolness study that you decide to sign up for participation in a study designed to rate how much fun you are. You score 86 on the fun scale, which has a mean of 60 and a standard deviation of 6. What is your z-score on the fun scale?

6. You now know your raw scores and z-scores for both the coolness scale and the fun scale. Which of these scores (the raw scores or the z-scores) are you going to use to compare how cool you are to how fun you are? What are the results of the comparison?

HOMEWORK SET B

1. For each of the following raw scores (X), compute Z if the mean (M) is 6 and the standard deviation (SD) is .5. Remember, $Z = \dfrac{X - M}{SD}$. Explain in terms of standard deviation what the z-score means.
    a. 7.3
    b. 6.2
    c. 5.4

2. For the following sets of raw scores, compute the mean, standard deviation, and z-score.
    a. 6, 4, 7, 9
    b. 41, 39, 46, 43

3. Find the raw scores for the following z-scores, given that the mean of the distribution is 17 and the standard deviation is 2.5.
    a. z = −.65
    b. z = 1.8
    c. z = −2

4. You need to purchase both a computer and a television. You find both items on super one-time-only sale, but only have enough money to purchase one. You need to figure out which is the better deal. The computer costs $300 (yes, a screamin' deal!). The average (mean) cost for this computer at all stores in your region is $699, with a standard deviation of $35. The television costs $275, with an average (mean) cost in your region of $589 and a standard deviation of $25. Use these numbers to find the z-scores, and determine which item is the best deal.

5. You and a friend participate in a fitness evaluation. When the results come in, your results indicate that the mean number of sit-ups completed within the allowed time frame for all participants was 52, with a standard deviation of 3. Your z-score on the sit-ups portion of the test was 1.11 and your friend's z-score was 1.8. How many sit-ups did each of you do?

6. In the same fitness evaluation as the previous problem, you are informed that your overall fitness score was 215. The mean for the distribution was 196, with a standard deviation of 5. How many standard deviations is your score above the mean?

7. If your performance on a standardized examination on knowledge of American history shows that your raw score was 520 (compared with a distribution with a mean of 410 and a standard deviation of 13), can you compare your performance on the history evaluation with your performance on the fitness evaluation described in the prior problem? If so, describe why in terms of ideas related to z-scores. If not, describe why (also in terms of ideas related to z-scores).

ANSWERS TO SET A

1. a. $Z = \dfrac{X - M}{SD} = \dfrac{31 - 36}{2} = \dfrac{-5}{2} = -2.5$. The raw score of 31 is 2.5 standard deviations below the mean.

   b. $Z = \dfrac{X - M}{SD} = \dfrac{42 - 36}{2} = \dfrac{6}{2} = 3$. The raw score of 42 is 3 standard deviations above the mean.

   c. $Z = \dfrac{X - M}{SD} = \dfrac{28 - 36}{2} = \dfrac{-8}{2} = -4$. The raw score of 28 is 4 standard deviations below the mean.

2. a. mean (M) $= \dfrac{18 + 16 + 15 + 20}{4} = \dfrac{69}{4} = 17.25$

Standard deviation (SD) = 1.92

Table 3.8: Homework Set A #2a

X	M	X–M	(X–M)²	Z
18	17.25	.75	.56	.39
16	17.25	−1.25	1.56	−.65
15	17.25	−2.25	5.06	−1.17
20	17.25	2.75	7.56	1.43

$$\Sigma(X - M)^2 = 14.74$$

$$SD^2 = \left(\frac{\Sigma(X-M)^2}{N}\right) = \frac{14.74}{4} = 3.69$$

$$SD = \sqrt{SD^2} = \sqrt{3.68} = 1.92$$

z-score of raw score 18 $= \dfrac{X-M}{SD} = \dfrac{18-17.25}{1.92} = \dfrac{.75}{1.92} = .39.$

z-score of raw score 16 $= \dfrac{X-M}{SD} = \dfrac{16-17.25}{1.92} = \dfrac{-1.25}{1.92} = -.65.$

z-score of raw score 15 $= \dfrac{X-M}{SD} = \dfrac{15-17.25}{1.92} = \dfrac{-2.25}{1.92} = -1.17.$

z-score of raw score 20 $= \dfrac{X-M}{SD} = \dfrac{20-17.25}{1.92} = \dfrac{2.75}{1.92} = 1.43.$

b. mean (M) $= \dfrac{32+36+29+30}{4} = \dfrac{127}{4} = 31.75$

Standard deviation (SD) = 2.68

Table 3.9: Homework Set A #2b

X	M	X–M	(X–M)²	Z
32	31.75	.25	.06	.09
36	31.75	4.25	18.06	1.59
29	31.75	-2.75	7.56	-1.03
30	31.75	-1.75	3.06	-.65

$$\Sigma(X - M)^2 = 28.74$$

$$SD^2 = \left(\frac{\Sigma(X-M)^2}{N}\right) = \frac{28.74}{4} = 7.19$$

$$SD = \sqrt{SD^2} = \sqrt{7.19} = 2.68$$

z-score of raw score 32 $= \dfrac{X-M}{SD} = \dfrac{32-31.75}{2.68} = \dfrac{.25}{2.68} = .09.$

z-score of raw score 36 $= \dfrac{X-M}{SD} = \dfrac{36-31.75}{2.68} = \dfrac{4.25}{2.68} = 1.59.$

z-score of raw score 29 $= \dfrac{X-M}{SD} = \dfrac{29-31.75}{2.68} = \dfrac{-2.75}{2.68} = -1.03.$

z-score of raw score 30 $= \dfrac{X-M}{SD} = \dfrac{30-31.75}{2.68} = \dfrac{-1.75}{2.68} = -.65.$

3. a. $X = M + (SD * Z) = 61 + (3 * 1.2) = 61 + 3.6 = 64.6$
    b. $X = M + (SD * Z) = 61 + (3 * 2.6) = 61 + 7.8 = 68.8$
    c. $X = M + (SD * Z) = 61 + (3 * -2.3) = 61 - 6.9 = 54.1$
4. $X = M + (SD * Z) = 58 + (4.02 * 1.35) = 58 + 5.43 = 63.43$
5. $Z = \dfrac{X - M}{SD} = \dfrac{86 - 60}{6} = \dfrac{26}{6} = 4.33$
6. You will use the z-scores to compare how cool you are to how fun you are. Your z-score on the coolness scale was 1.35, which indicates that your score is 1.35 standard deviations above the mean, while your z-score on the fun scale was 4.33, which indicates that your score is 4.33 standard deviations above the mean. You are definitely both cool and fun, but you are even more fun than you are cool.

REFERENCE

McCrae, R. R., Terracciano, A., and 78 members of the Personality Profiles of Cultures Project. (2005). Universal Features of Personality Traits from the Observer's Perspective: Data from 50 Cultures. *Journal of Personality and Social Psychology, 88,* 547–561.

CHAPTER 4

CORRELATION

Chances are, questions of correlation permeate your thoughts on a daily basis. Consider the following:

- Did you ever notice that the hungrier you are at the grocery store, the more it costs you come checkout time?
- Ever wonder whether extremely wealthy people are happier than everyone else? Do money and happiness go hand in hand?
- Do people who exercise a lot have more energy than others—or does the exercise wipe them out?
- Ever notice that the further you get from big cities, the nicer people seem?
- Finally, as a college student, you *hopefully* have noticed that the more you study for exams, the higher you score on them.

Each of these everyday questions relates to the issue of correlation. A *correlation* is essentially a relationship between two variables. Recall from chapter 2 that we discussed different kinds of variables. These include continuous variables, ordinal variables, and categorical variables. While correlations can be computed between each of these kinds of variables with one another, the most common kind of correlation in psychological statistics is based on a relationship between two continuous variables.

Recall that continuous variables are variables for which values differ by degree. Each of the examples delineated so far can be translated into correlations between two continuous variables. For instance, consider the question of whether hungry people are spending more at the check-out than their less-hungry counterparts. Here we have two continuous variables: *Hunger* and *Amount of Money Spent*. Each of these varies by degree. You can be fully satiated, a little hungry, moderately hungry, crazy-hungry, and so on. Similarly, amount of money spent is clearly continuous. You can spend anywhere between, say, $1 and $250 at the grocery store.

When we're thinking of the most basic and common kinds of correlations used in psychological statistics, it's often useful to first think about the two variables of interest, and then to make sure to clearly conceptualize these variables as continuous variables.

CORRELATIONS ARE SUMMARIES

Importantly, when we compute a correlation between two variables, we're not making a statement about whether two variables go together for a particular person. Rather, we're making a general comment, or summary, regarding the relationship between two variables. Suppose that we find a strong correlation between level of hunger at the grocery store and amount of money spent such that hungrier people tend to spend more than others. This finding would not mean that *every* hungry person is emptying his or her bank account, nor that every non-hungry person is spending next-to-nothing. Rather, it would mean that, *overall*, we expect hungrier people to be spending more than their non-hungry counterparts. If we had to bet on how much someone spends at checkout, and we know that there is a strong correlation between these two variables, we would be smart to bet that a very hungry customer is likely to spend more than average at the checkout. However, as often happens in life, we can be wrong…

Consider another example: height and success in basketball. Sure, without question, there's a correlation between height and indices of success in basketball—such as points scored. Taller players tend to outcompete shorter ones. This makes sense, as taller players are that much closer to the basket. However, is it the case that short players *necessarily* stink at basketball? No— throughout NBA history, there have been important exceptions to this general pattern (such as Spud Webb and Muggsey Bogues—both NBA stars at less than 5'6"). Correlations summarize general patterns of relationships between variables—they never speak conclusively to individual cases.

REPRESENTING A CORRELATION GRAPHICALLY

Correlations are typically represented in one of two ways: either graphically (using something called a *scatterplot*) or mathematically (with the *r* statistic [officially referred to as the Pearson product-moment correlation coefficient]). In this section, we consider scatterplots. A scatterplot has an X- and Y-axis, and dots in two-dimensional space that each represent a particular case. As a very simple introduction to this idea, consider the following: You are interested in the relationship between hours of video games played the night before a quiz in your stats class and scores on the quiz. You have data from three students in your class. Of course, in reality, to have confidence in our analyses, it's best to have data from a good number of subjects. However, to start easy and get the concepts down, let's just consider a nice little sample of three—as follows (see Table 4.1):

Table 4.1: Raw Data for Correlation between Video Game Playing an Quiz Score

Student	Hours of Video Games Played	Quiz Score
Joe	0	8
Sally	3	5
Jill	9	2

If you knew nothing about statistics but were presented with this table, you would probably be able to make some inferences simply by looking at the numbers. This process is called *eyeballing* the data—and we all do it! Eyeballing the data essentially corresponds to looking at raw data and, without doing any systematic analyses, drawing some conclusions. If you were to eyeball these data, chances are you would conclude that playing too many video games the night before a quiz is a recipe for failure. Further, perhaps you would make the inference that studying, as opposed to playing games, would be a better way to go.

Let's create a scatterplot for these data. In making a scatterplot, the variable that goes along your x-axis is typically the one we call the *predictor variable*. Essentially, this variable is the one that you believe precedes, and perhaps causes, scores on the other variable. Often, it makes no difference which variable you conceive of as the predictor variable. If you computed a correlation between the number of belts and the number of shoes people own, you would be hard-pressed to make a case that one of these variables should be conceptualized as the predictor variable. In fact, for purposes of this chapter, it really makes no difference. However, it makes a difference for the following chapter on the concept of regression (as you'll see). As such, while it doesn't really matter which variable is assigned as the predictor variable for now, it's good to get used to thinking about which variable is the predictor variable.

The Y-axis corresponds to the *dependent* variable. This variable (also referred to as the *criterion* or *outcome* variable) is thought to be *predicted by* or is thought to *depend on* the predictor variable. In short, this variable is the one that you believe is the result of scores on the predictor variable. Again, this all will matter more for the chapter on regression—but we need to assign variables to the X and Y axes for the purposes of creating the scatterplot.

For the current example, it makes most sense to think of hours of video games played as the predictor variable (X) and scores on the quiz as the dependent variable (Y).

HERE ARE THE STEPS IN CREATING A SCATTERPLOT:

1. Decide which variable is your predictor variable (X) and which is your dependent variable (Y).
2. Draw your X and Y axes.
3. Label your X and Y axes.
4. Write the range of possible X and Y values adjacent to the axes. Here, you need to make sure that all scores in the data will fit within the range.
5. Create a dot on the space between the X- and Y-axis to represent the (X,Y) coordinate for each case in your data.

Your finished product should look like so (refer to Figure 4.1).

CORRELATION DIRECTION

Once you have created your scatterplot, you can summarize your correlation. Typically, we summarize a correlation in terms of two important criteria: *correlation direction* and *correlation strength*. The direction of the correlation pertains to whether relatively high Xs go with

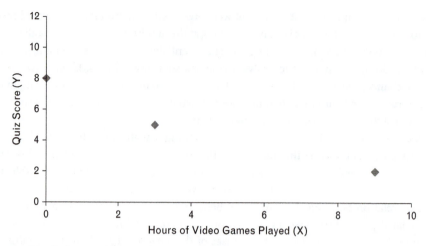

FIGURE 4.1: Simple Scatterplot.

relatively high Ys (and relatively low Xs go with relatively low Ys) [a pattern referred to as a *positive correlation*] or whether relatively high Xs go with relatively low Ys (and relatively low Xs go with relatively high Ys) [a pattern referred to as a *negative correlation*]. With the quiz score and videogame example we have at hand, we're looking at a negative correlation. Clearly, high Xs (such as 9) go with low Ys (such as 2), whereas low Xs (such as 0) go with high Ys (such as 8).

Importantly, just because a correlation is *negative*, it need not necessarily be *weak*. When it comes to interpreting correlations, *negative* and *positive* refer **exclusively** to whether the direction of the correlation corresponds to a line with negative slope (as is the case here—notice that from the Y-axis, the dots go down and to the right) or a positive slope (which would go up and to the right from the Y-axis). All too often, students will confuse a "negative" correlation for a "weak" correlation. Don't let that be you!

CORRELATION STRENGTH

Correlation strength, in fact, is fully independent of correlation direction. In the context of a scatterplot, the strength of a correlation refers to the degree of scatter among the dots. As we'll learn in the next chapter, each scatterplot has a mathematically defined line that best fits the pattern of scatter. Thus, while we don't yet have a line on our nice little scatterplot, we can imagine one that best approximates the pattern—such as the following (Figure 4.2):

The "degree of scatter" refers to the extent to which the dots on the scatterplot tend to deviate from this "best-fit" line. If the dots are relatively far from this line in general, we say that there is "a lot of scatter," which corresponds to a weak correlation. If the dots are relatively close to this line, then we say that there is "not much scatter," which corresponds to a strong correlation.

In our working example here, we have a very strong correlation (as we'll soon demonstrate mathematically). The dots approximate the best-fit line well. To understand this point, compare this scatterplot (in Figure 4.2) with a hypothetical scatterplot that has much scatter, as found in Figure 4.3.

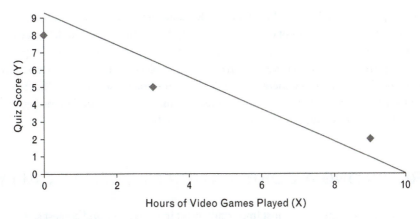

FIGURE 4.2: Simple Scatterplot with Estimated "Best Fit" Line.

Here, the direction of the correlation is similar to that in our working example (as in Figure 4.2), but the dots are, *in general*, more scattered and further from the best-fit line compared with the pattern of scatter in our working example. Because there is more scatter in this hypothetical correlation (in Figure 4.3), the correlation is relatively weak. As there is not much scatter in our working example (Figure 4.2), that correlation is strong.

If you were to summarize the findings from your scatterplot to someone who didn't know much about statistics, you would say that, generally, people who played many hours of video games did poorly on the quiz—and that those who played few hours of video games did relatively well. Further, you would be able to say that there is a negative correlation between these two variables (high Xs go with low Ys and low Xs go with high Ys) and that the correlation seems to be relatively strong (as the pattern of scatter does not deviate considerably from this imaginary best-fit line [in Figure 4.2]).

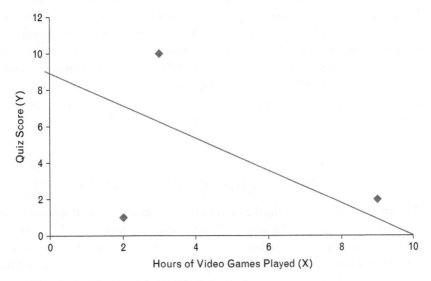

FIGURE 4.3: Hypothetical Scatterplot with "Much Scatter".

So scatterplots are cool—and allow us to understand the general nature of correlations, in addition to the integral concepts of correlational strength and directions. But let's face it—creating a scatterplot is really a fancy form of eyeballing. To say that the dots "seem to approximate a line with a negative slope" or that the pattern of scatter "looks to not deviate too much from the imaginary line that I sort of see there...I think..." is not exactly super-scientific. Scatterplots are a great start—and are extremely useful in grasping the nature of correlations between variables—but they're not as mathematical as things get in statistics.

REPRESENTING A CORRELATION MATHEMATICALLY

Meet the *r coefficient*—one of the most important, most interpretable, and coolest statistics there is! r does everything that a scatterplot does—and more. Because of how it's calculated, r will always be a number between –1 and +1. Once you understand r, you can quickly make inferences about a correlation's strength and direction.

USING r TO UNDERSTAND CORRELATION STRENGTH

Simply, as r approaches *either* –1 or +1, the correlation increases in strength. In fact, correlations of exactly 1.0 or –1.0 represent what we call *perfect correlations*. In nature, such correlations are extremely rare. In terms of a scatterplot, a perfect correlation would be one in which each and every dot was precisely on the best-fit line. The dots would not scatter at all from that pattern. In short, they would combine to make a perfect line. A correlation of +1.0 would correspond to a scatterplot for a perfect positive correlation (the dots would make a perfect line with a positive slope), whereas a correlation of –1.0 would correspond to a scatterplot for a perfect negative correlation (the dots would make a perfect line with a negative slope).

As r approaches 0, the correlation is said to be weaker. In fact, a correlation of 0 is "perfectly weak" and literally corresponds to "no mathematical relationship between two variables whatsoever." Importantly, interpreting the strength of a correlation is independent of the sign of r. In other words, for instance, a correlation of .10 is weak and a correlation of –.10 is weak. Further, they are **equally weak**. The strength of the correlation has nothing to do with the sign of r. As a very general rule of thumb (which scientists break all the time!), we can think of correlations between 0 and .3 (or between 0 and –.3) as weak, correlations between .3 and .7 (or –.3 and –.7) as moderate, and correlations between .7 and 1.0 (or –.7 and –1.0) as strong. In terms of r, correlation strength corresponds to how close r is to either 1.0 or –1.0.

USING r TO UNDERSTAND CORRELATION DIRECTION

Simply, the sign of r tells you about the direction of the correlation. If r is a positive number, the correlation is positive in direction (and the scatterplot should approximate a line with positive slope). If r is negative in sign, the correlation is negative in direction (and the scatterplot should approximate a line with a negative slope). It's that simple. Consider how the sign of r is interpreted in the subsequent section.

INTERPRETING r

Once you understand r, you will realize that you can extract a great deal of information from this single statistic. Consider the following hypothetical examples:

A.   The correlation between household income and number of children in the U.S. is –.12.
B.   The correlation between number of books read and vocabulary size among American teens is .38.
C.   The correlation between shoe size and vocabulary size is –.02.

In each case, given that you have r (referred to in these examples as *the correlation*), you have information regarding the strength and direction of each correlation.

For example A, you could infer that household income is actually negatively related to number of children (richer people have fewer children). Further, as this correlation is weak in size (–.12 is quite close to 0), you could infer that it is not a very strong relationship.

For example B, you could infer that teens who read a lot have relatively large vocabularies, while teens who do not read a lot have smaller vocabularies. Further, given the magnitude of this correlation (.38), you could infer that the correlation is moderate in size.

Finally, with example C, you could say that shoe size and vocabulary size are negatively correlated (after all, this correlation does have a negative sign). However, the fact that the correlation is –.02 (terribly close to 0) implies that this correlation is extremely weak.

CORRELATION AND STATISTICAL SIGNIFICANCE

How do we determine if a correlation is weak, *strong, negligible, worth talking* about, and so on? While we have some rules of thumb to help guide us to label correlations as weak, moderate, and strong (as delineated prior), statisticians are also very interested in whether correlations are *statistically significant*. The issue of statistical significance is complex and profound—and is addressed in (much-needed) detail in the second half of this book. Thus, we don't want to get bogged down with this issue here. However, scientists often talk about whether a correlation is statistically significant—so it seems appropriate to provide a brief discussion of what that means in this chapter.

If a correlation is described as statistically significant, that correlation, obtained from a sample, can be said to *most likely* represent a reliable pattern at the population level. Thus, for instance, suppose a researcher reported that there is a statistically significant correlation between the amount of pesticides used in an agricultural community and the number of children with attentional disorders (with communities high in pesticide use having more kids with attentional disorders). Suppose the scientific research report said, for instance, "across the 300 communities studied, we found a statistically significant correlation between the prevalence of pesticide use and the percentage of school-aged children diagnosed with attentional disorders (r = .21)."

Given what you already know, you would be able to look at a correlation of .21 and say that it is positive because .21 is positive in sign (consistent with the statement that more pesticide use goes with more kids with attentional disorders), but that it is also relatively weak (less than .3 . . . relatively close to 0). In this case, the researchers draw your attention to an additional point by saying that this r is *statistically significant*. This fact essentially means that it is *most likely* (but never certainly) the case that the pattern found in this sample (of selected children from 300 rural communities) accurately characterizes the pattern that would be found in the entire population of children who live in rural communities in which pesticides are at issue. The details of how to compute and understand this idea of statistical significance are complex—and will be covered in future chapters. For now, realize that correlations are often presented in terms of whether they are statistically significant or not—and this discussion should help you understand the implications of that concept when you come across it in reading summaries of scientific research.

COMPUTING r

In drawing on your understanding of z-scores (from chapter 3), you will see that computing r is actually quite straightforward. It is, in fact, a clear and direct extension of the reasoning used in computing z-scores.

Let's start with the formula $r = \dfrac{\Sigma ZxZy}{N}$. In computing r this way, we will obtain an index of the relationship between each x and each y, called the "cross-product of the z-scores" for each case of raw data. If a positive Zx tends to go with a positive Zy, the cross-product of these numbers will be positive in sign (e.g., if Zx = .2 and Zy = .1, ZxZy = .02, which is positive). Similarly, if negative Zxs tend to go with negative Zys, the cross-product (Zx * Zy) will be positive in sign (e.g., if Zx = −.3 and Zy = −1.0, ZxZy will be .3, again, positive in sign).

Recall that a positive correlation exists if high Xs go with high Ys and low Xs go with low Ys. This fact is fully consistent with our use of cross-products to understand an overall relationship between an X and Y variable. If there is a positive correlation between X and Y, high Xs will go with high Ys. Put another way, Xs with positive z-scores (i.e., Xs above the mean for the X variable) will tend to go with Ys with positive z-scores (i.e., Ys above the mean of the Y variable). Similarly, if X and Y are positively correlated with one another, Xs with negative z-scores should go with Ys with negative z-scores.

Computing cross-products of z-scores also makes perfect sense for understanding the nature of a negative correlation between X and Y. If X and Y are negatively correlated, high Xs tend to go with low Ys and low Xs tend to go with high Ys. Put in terms of z-scores, an X with a positive z-score should go with a Y with a negative z-score (leading to a negative cross-product; a negative times a positive equals a negative) and, similarly, an X with a negative z-score should go with a Y with a positive z-score.

As r is a summary of the overall relationship between X and Y (as opposed to a comment about whether any particular X and Y go together in a certain way), the formula for r essentially takes an average of the cross-products of the Zxs and Zys. Think again about the formula: $r = \dfrac{\Sigma ZxZy}{N}$. You're adding up all the cross-products and then dividing by N—the number of cross-products. In this way, the formula is basically saying, "Let's look at the average cross-product between the Zxs and Zys to see if the general trend is consistent with a positive correlation (high Xs tending to go with high Ys and low Xs tending to go with low Ys), a negative correlation (high Xs tending to go with low Ys and vice versa), or no correlation (Zxs and Zys tending to yield cross-products that are, on average, near 0)."

Let's look at all of this at work with our *videogame/quiz-grade* example. In other words, let's compute r to see if, in our small sample of three subjects, there is a correlation between hours of video games played and score on the quiz.

Here, again, are the raw data:

Table 4.2:

Student	Hours of Video Games Played	Quiz Score
Joe	0	8
Sally	3	5
Jill	9	2

Here are the steps to computing r:

1. **Compute a z-score for each X.** Note that you'll have to implement all the steps needed to compute z-scores learned in the prior chapters.
2. **Compute a z-score for each Y.**
3. **Compute ZxZy for each case.** In other words, compute a cross-product of each Zx with its corresponding Zy.
4. **Sum the cross-products (Σ ZxZy).**
5. **Take the average of the sum of the cross-products by dividing by N** (with N being the number of cross-products, which will correspond to the number of subjects).

Here's how it works with our example:

1. **Compute a z-score for each X.**

Table 4.3:

X (hours of video games)	M	X–M	(X–M)²	Zx
0	4	–4	16	–1.07
3	4	–1	1	–.27
9	4	5	25	1.34
	$M = \dfrac{12}{3} = 4$		SS = 42	
			$SD^2 = \dfrac{42}{3} = 14$	
			SD = 3.74	

2.   **Compute a z-score for each Y.**

Table 4.4:

Y (quiz grade)	M	X–M	$(X–M)^2$	Zx
8	5	3	9	1.22
5	5	0	0	0
2	5	–3	9	–1.22
	$M = \dfrac{15}{3} = 5$		SS = 18	
			$SD^2 = \dfrac{18}{3} = 6$	
			SD = 2.45	

3.   **Compute ZxZy for each case.**

Table 4.5:

Zx	Zy	ZxZy
–1.07	1.22	–1.31
–.27	0	0
1.34	–1.22	–1.63

4.   **Sum the cross-products (Σ ZxZy).**

$$\Sigma ZxZy = -1.31 + 0 + (-1.63) = -2.94$$

5.   **Take the average of the sum of the cross-products by dividing by N.**

$$\dfrac{-2.94}{3} = -.98. \; \mathbf{r = -.98.}$$

OK, we did it. Now we have an r to talk about, –.98. In light of our discussion of how to interpret r, you should focus your attention on two important features of this number. First, the sign is negative, indicating that the relationship between number of hours of video games played is negatively related to quiz grade. People who play a lot of video games seem to do relatively poorly on the quiz, while those who play fewer hours of video games seem to score higher.

Second, we can comment on correlation strength. Recall that as a correlation approaches either 1.0 or –1.0, it gets stronger. –.98 is quite close to –1.0. Thus, this correlation is **very strong!** In the real world, you will rarely, if ever, get correlations this strong—but sometimes it is useful to use extreme cases to learn the concept. If you look back at our raw data, you can see, clearly, that high X scores go with low Y scores and vice versa. Our scatterplot tells the same story. If the correlation between these variables in the real world were this strong, you'd likely think twice about playing video games the night before your next quiz in your stats course!

RETURN TO MADUPISTAN

Recall from our previous chapter on z-scores our example of the Madupistan Aptitude Measure, used to place students into universities in the struggling-yet-vibrant nation of Madupistan. In that example, scores on the verbal section of the test and scores on the quantitative section of the test were on very different scales. As you recall, z-scores address that issue by putting all scores on the same scale (with a mean of 0 and a standard deviation of 1). Given that z-scores are the backbone of our method for computing r, it follows that we can compute correlations between variables that are on very different scales. Thus, for instance, we can compute a correlation between someone's weight (ranging from about 100–300 pounds) and his or her annual salary (ranging from something like $20,000–$20,000,000). Or we can compute the correlation between an adult's age (ranging from 18–100 years) and the number of daily calories he or she consumes (ranging from 800–5,000 or so).

Let's see how this works by computing the correlation between verbal and quantitative scores on the Madupistan Aptitude Measure. Here are the raw data:

First, let's consider the relationship between verbal and quantitative scores represented graphically using a scatterplot as follows in Figure 4.4:

Based on the pattern of scatter, it looks like we have a strong and positive correlation between these variables. That is, the low Xs tend to go with the low Ys, the high Xs tend to go with the high Ys, and the pattern of (X,Y) coordinates seems to approximate a straight line (with a positive slope) reasonably well. The dots do not tend to scatter much from this linear (line-like) pattern.

Now let's compute r—knowing that we should obtain a strong, positive number.

Table 4.6:

Student #	Verbal Score	Quantitative Score
1	4	21
2	7	30
3	9	29
4	9	35
5	5	26
6	3	20
7	8	30

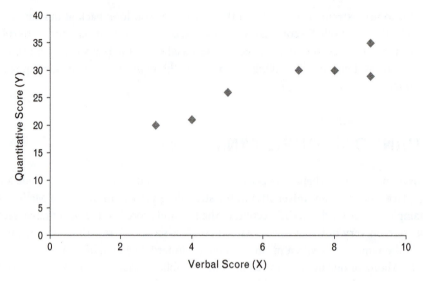

FIGURE 4.4: Madupistan Scatterplot.

Steps:

1. **Compute a z-score for each X.**

Table 4.7:

X (verbal scores)	M	X–M	(X–M)²	Zx
4	6.43	–2.43	5.90	–1.06
7	6.43	.57	.32	.25
9	6.43	2.57	6.60	1.14
9	6.43	2.57	6.60	1.14
5	6.43	–1.43	2.04	–.63
3	6.43	–3.43	11.76	–1.52
8	6.43	1.57	2.46	.69

$$M = \frac{45}{7} = 6.43 \qquad\qquad SS = 35.68$$

$$SD^2 = \frac{35.68}{7} = 5.10$$

$$SD = 2.26$$

2. **Compute a z-score for each Y.**

Table 4.8:

Y (quantitative scores)	M	Y–M	(Y–M)²	Zy
21	27.29	–6.29	39.56	–1.27
30	27.29	2.71	7.43	.55
29	27.29	1.71	2.92	.35
35	27.29	7.71	59.44	1.56
26	27.29	–1.29	1.66	–.26
20	27.29	–7.29	53.14	–1.47
30	27.29	2.71	7.43	.55

$$M = \frac{191}{7} = 27.29 \qquad\qquad SS = 171.40$$

$$SD^2 = \frac{171.40}{7} = 24.49$$

$$SD = 4.95$$

3. **Compute ZxZy for each case.**

Table 4.9:

Zx	Zy	ZxZy
–1.08	–1.27	1.36
.25	.55	.14
1.14	.35	.40
1.14	1.56	1.78
–.63	–.26	.13
–1.52	–1.47	2.23
.69	.55	.38

4. **Sum the cross-products (ΣZxZy).**

$$\Sigma ZxZy = 1.36 + .14 + .40 + 1.78 + .13 + 2.23 + .38 = 6.42$$

5. **Take the average of the sum of the cross-products by dividing by N.**

$$\frac{6.42}{7} = .92. \quad \mathbf{r = .92.}$$

A correlation of .92 is very strong and positive. It is very strong because it is close to 1.0. It is positive simply because it is positive in sign. If you were summarizing this correlation for your report to the Madupistan government, you would say that verbal and quantitative scores of the Madupistan Aptitude Measure are highly positively correlated with one another. Thus, people who scored low on the verbal tended to score low on the quantitative section and those who scored high on the verbal tended to score high on the quantitative section. Note that this interpretation is highly consistent with the scatterplot you produced (see Figure 4.4).

CORRELATION DOES NOT IMPLY CAUSATION

This course is about statistics—not about research methods. Thus, here, the focus is on understanding, computing, and interpreting the statistics used by social scientists. However, when it comes to understanding the implications of correlations that scientists compute, an extremely important methodological point needs to be raised. Simply put: Correlation does not imply causation. In other words, if you find a correlation between two variables, you simply know that the two variables are related to one another. You don't, however, know *why* the variables are related to one another. In computing a correlation, you can, in fact, never ascertain *the reason* for a relationship between variables. You only can appropriately comment on whether the variables are related to one another (and on the nature of the relationship).

Your ability to comment on the reasons underlying a correlation are under the purview of the logic of scientific research methods (typically presented in a different class altogether). In fact, the design of your research and the nature of your data collection are most relevant when it comes to the question of *why* a correlation between two variables exists.

To see why this is the case, consider our videogame/grade example. Recall that we found a strong negative correlation between the number of hours of video games played the night before a quiz and grades on the quiz. Suppose Correlational Carl simply asked people how many hours of video games they happened to play and what their quiz grades were the day after the exam. Correlational Carl finds a correlation of –.98 between these variables. He knows the variables are related, but because he has collected the data naturally—without manipulating either of the variables—he simply cannot be sure why there is a relationship. In methodological terms, this correlation may come about for the following three reasons:

A. **X *may* cause Y**. Thus, it may be the case that number of hours playing video games has a causal effect on one's quiz grade. That seems likely, for sure, but given that Carl didn't manipulate any variables, he can't be certain.

B. **Y *may* cause X!** This issue is called the *directionality* issue—and it pertains to the fact that if you have a correlation between X and Y, unless you have carefully manipulated one of the variables beforehand, you simply don't know if X and Y are related because X causes Y or because Y causes X. Perhaps scoring low on grades (Y) deflates self-esteem and leads to a college career of videogame playing as a form of emotional coping. Seems somewhat implausible, I agree. But if you have not manipulated a variable carefully, your correlation can always be interpreted in either direction.

C. **Z may cause both X and Y**. This is the notorious *third variable* issue—and it pertains to the fact that if some variable leads to multiple outcomes, these outcomes will show up as correlated with one another—but not because one causes the other. Rather, they would show up as correlated simply because they are both caused by the same third variable (Z). A classic example pertains to the reliable correlation found between ice cream sales and number of homicides. It hardly is the case that a triple-scoop sundae activates the killer in all of us. Rather, as hours of sunlight and temperature increase in summer months, we are more likely to want ice cream. Further, people spend more time outside in groups—and heat activates aggression. Both ice cream sales and homicides increase in the summer. In terms of our current example, it may be the case that being raised in an intellectual environment encourages both studying and a disdain for video games. Such a scenario would lead people from relatively intellectual upbringings to play relatively few video games and to study hard, thereby scoring well on quizzes.

Thus, while the correlation statistic is very powerful and allows us to really understand an awful lot about the relationship between variables in the world, it generally does not allow us to know which variables cause changes in other variables. Correlation does not imply causation.

A REAL RESEARCH EXAMPLE

In a major cross-cultural study of *sociosexuality* (roughly corresponding to sexual promiscuity) David Schmitt and his colleagues (2005) were interested in whether the Sociosexuality Orientation Inventory (Simpson & Gangestad, 1991), a personality scale designed to measure individual differences in sociosexuality, was correlated with several behavioral indices of promiscuity, such as the tendency to consent to sex early in a relationship and the tendency to try to "mate poach"—or have sex with someone else's long-term partner. Schmitt and his colleagues collected data from hundreds of college-aged students from 48 different nations to address these questions using a broad and diverse sample.

In their research report on this study, they presented the correlations between sociosexuality and these two outcome variables (consenting to sex and mate poaching) for each country in a table. Here are the findings from Argentina, Australia, and Austria:

Table 4.10:

Nation	Correlation between sociosexuality and consenting to sex	Correlation between sociosexuality and "mate poaching"
Argentina	.39*	.40*
Australia	.48*	.38*
Austria	.37*	.40*

* $p < .01$ (meaning that this correlation is "statistically significant" and likely reflects the pattern that would be found in the entire population of adults from this country).

In interpreting these six correlations, we use the system for interpreting r described in this chapter. Consider, for instance, the fact that sociosexuality is correlated. 39 with consenting to sex in Argentina. This correlation suggests that these variables are positively correlated with one another—and that the relationship is moderate in strength. Thus, individuals from Argentina who score as relatively promiscuous on the Sociosexuality Orientation Inventory report that they consent to sex more easily than those who score as low on sociosexuality. Note also that this correlation is asterisked as "statistically significant." This fact suggests that this particular correlation is likely representative of adults from Argentina in general—in other words, it's most likely the case that the correlation between sociosexuality and the tendency to easily consent to sex is positive at the level of this population. Importantly, each correlation in this table can be interpreted in this same manner.

SUMMARY

A correlation corresponds to a relationship between two variables. Traditionally, social scientists tend to focus on correlations between continuous variables (referred to as Pearson product-moment correlations, or r). Correlations can be represented either graphically (using a scatterplot) or mathematically (by computing r). Two important features of a correlation are the direction and the strength of the relationship. With regard to the direction of a correlation, a positive correlation exists if high X scores go with high Y scores and low X scores go with low Y scores, while a negative correlation exists if high X scores go with low Y scores, and vice versa. In terms of the strength of a correlation, correlations with rs near 1.0 or –1.0 are considered strong, while correlations near 0 are considered weak. However, whereas correlations are extremely useful for describing the nature of relationships between variables, they do not, in and of themselves, allow you to make inferences about whether one variable causes changes in another variable.

KEY TERMS

Continuous variable: Variable for which values differ by degree

Correlation: A relationship between two variables

Correlation direction: Whether the correlation is positive (high X scores go with high Y scores and low X scores go with low Y scores) or negative (high X scores go with low Y scores, and vice versa)

Correlation strength: Degree of scatter in a scatterplot; value of the r-coefficient on a scale of –1 to 1. Strong correlations are close to –1 or 1, whereas weak correlations are close to 0

Correlational statistics: Statistics which address whether multiple variables are related

Dependent variable (criterion or outcome variable): Variable that is thought to be predicted by the predictor variable; scores on the dependent variable follow from scores on the predictor variable

Negative correlation: Correlation in which high X scores go with low Y scores, and vice versa.

Positive correlation: Correlation in which high X scores go with high Y scores and low X scores go with low Y scores

Predictor variable: The variable thought to precede, and perhaps cause, scores on the other variables

r-coefficient: Also known as Pearson product-moment correlation coefficient. A number between –1 and 1 which indicates the direction and strength of a correlation.

Scatterplot: A graph with the predictor variable along the horizontal (X) axis and the dependent variable along the vertical (Y) axis, with dots in two-dimensional space that each represent a particular case

HOMEWORK SET A

1. Considering the following scatterplots, give the strength and direction of the correlation, if any.

    a.

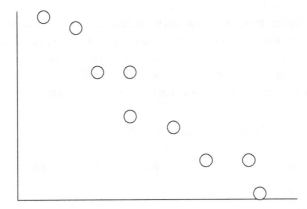

FIGURE 4.5: Homework Set A #1a.

    b.

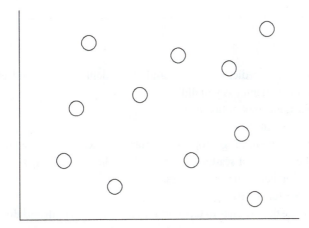

FIGURE 4.6: Homework Set A #1c.

    c.

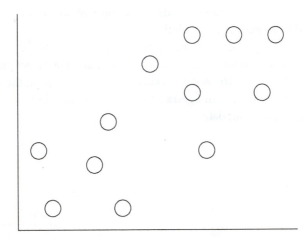

FIGURE 4.7: Homework Set A #1c.

2. Considering the following r values, give the strength and direction of the correlation.
   a.   −.22
   b.   .87
   c.   .59
   d.   −.79

3. You notice that as the time approaches for finals, more of your friends are eating choco-late. You think there may be a correlation between how stressed a person is and how many pieces of chocolate he/she consumes in a day. So you administer a measure of stress, with a score range of 1–50, to four people. Additionally, you record how many pieces of chocolate each person ate that day. Here are the data:

Table 4.11: Homework Set A #3 Data

Name	Stress Score	Pieces of chocolate eaten
Anna	30	7
Bill	48	12
Susan	12	3
Joseph	23	5

Complete a–h.
   a. Identify your predictor variable and dependent variable, and explain why you labeled the variables as you did.
   b. Create a scatterplot of the data.
   c. Draw a "best-fit" line.
   d. Summarize the findings from the scatterplot. Include the direction of the correla-tion, the amount of scatter and strength of the correlation, and the nature of the relationship between the variables.
   e. Compute r for the data given.
   f. Summarize the findings in terms of r. Include the strength and direction of the cor-relation and the nature of the relationship between the variables. Are these findings consistent with the scatterplot?
   g. Can you determine causation from all the information you now have regarding the correlation between the variables?
   h. What are three possible explanations for the correlation found?

4. You have a few friends who collect action figures, and you've noticed that they tend to go on very few dates. You decide to collect some data to see if there is a correlation between the number of action figures a guy owns and the number of dates he goes on in a month. Here are your data:

Table 4.12: Homework Set A #4 Data

Participant	# of action figures owned	Average # of dates in a month
Eli	1	8
Herbert	16	4
Steven	24	0
Garreth	6	6

Complete a–h.

a. Identify your predictor variable and dependent variable, and explain why you labeled the variables as you did.

b. Create a scatterplot of the data.

c. Draw a "best-fit" line.

d. Summarize the findings from the scatterplot. Include the direction of the correlation, the amount of scatter and strength of the correlation, and the nature of the relationship between the variables.

e. Compute r for the data given.

f. Summarize the findings in terms of r. Include the strength and direction of the correlation and the nature of the relationship between the variables. Are these findings consistent with the scatterplot?

g. Can you determine causation from all the information you now have regarding the correlation between the variables?

h. What are three possible explanations for the correlation found?

HOMEWORK SET B

1. Considering the following scatterplots, give the strength and direction of the correlation, if any.

a.

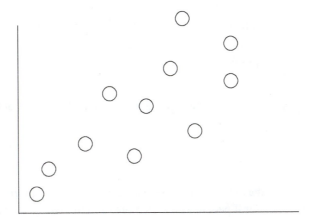

FIGURE 4.8: Homework Set B #1a.

b.

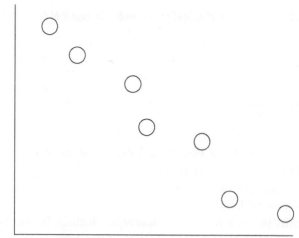

FIGURE 4.9: Homework Set B #1b.

c.

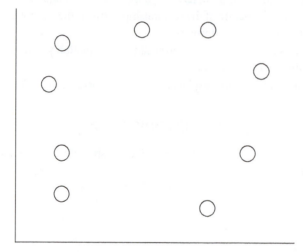

FIGURE 4.10: Homework Set B #1c.

2. Considering the following r values, give the strength and direction of the correlation.
    a.   .61
    b.   −.94
    c.   −.17
    d.   .77

3. Since you became the owner of a dog, you have been spending more time outside with your dog. You wonder if people who own more dogs tend to spend more time outside than people who own fewer dogs. You collect the following data:

Table 4.13: Homework Set B #3 Data

Participant	Number of dogs owned	Average # of minutes spent outside per day
George	3	60
Jim	0	25
Sheila	2	46

Complete a–h.

a. Identify your predictor variable and dependent variable, and explain why you labeled the variables as you did.
b. Create a scatterplot of the data.
c. Draw a "best-fit" line.
d. Summarize the findings from the scatterplot. Include the direction of the correlation, the amount of scatter and strength of the correlation, and the nature of the relationship between the variables.
e. Compute r for the data given.
f. Summarize the findings in terms of r. Include the strength and direction of the correlation and the nature of the relationship between the variables. Are these findings consistent with the scatterplot?
g. Can you determine causation from all the information you now have regarding the correlation between the variables?
h. What are three possible explanations for the correlation found?

4. At times during the academic career, you take more classes than at other times. When you have fewer classes, you attend more parties. You want to know if this pattern is true for other people as well. Here are your data:

Complete a-h.

Table 4.14: Homework Set B #4 Data

Participant	# of classes	Average # of parties attended in a month
Keisha	4	2
Kimberly	1	6
Michael	2	3
Devin	3	3

a. Identify your predictor variable and dependent variable, and explain why you labeled the variables as you did.
b. Create a scatterplot of the data.
c. Draw a "best-fit" line.
d. Summarize the findings from the scatterplot. Include the direction of the correlation, the amount of scatter and strength of the correlation, and the nature of the relationship between the variables.
e. Compute r for the data given.

f. Summarize the findings in terms of r. Include the strength and direction of the cor-
    relation and the nature of the relationship between the variables. Are these findings
    consistent with the scatterplot?

g. Can you determine causation from all the information you now have regarding the
    correlation between the variables?

h. What are three possible explanations for the correlation found?

ANSWERS TO SET A

1. a. strong, negative correlation
   b. no correlation
   c. moderate/weak, positive correlation
2. a. weak, negative correlation
   b. strong, positive correlation
   c. moderate, positive correlation
   d. strong, negative correlation
3. a. The predictor variable is the stress score, because it is thought to predict the amount
       of chocolate each person consumed. The amount of chocolate eaten is the depen-
       dent variable, because it is thought to be predicted by the level of stress each person
       is experiencing.

   b & c. See Figure 4.11.

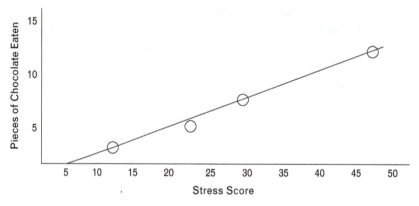

FIGURE 4.11: Homework Set A #3b & 3c.

   d. The correlation is positive and appears to be strong because there is not much scat-
       ter. It appears that people who are experiencing more stress eat more chocolate
       than people who are experiencing less stress, and vice versa.

   e.

Table 4.15: Homework Set A #3e

X (stress score)	M	X–M	(X–M)^2	Zx
30	28.25	1.75	3.06	.13
48	28.25	19.75	390.06	1.51
12	28.25	−16.25	264.06	−1.24
23	28.25	−5.25	27.56	−.40

$$M = \frac{113}{4} = 28.25 \qquad\qquad \Sigma(X–M)^2 = 684.74$$

$$SD^2 = \frac{684.71}{4} = 171.19$$

$$SD = 13.08$$

Table 4.16: Homework Set A #3e

Y (pieces of chocolate eaten)	M	Y–M	(Y–M)^2	Zy
7	6.75	.25	.06	.07
12	6.75	5.25	27.56	1.57
3	6.75	−3.75	14.06	−1.12
5	6.75	−1.75	3.06	−.52

$$M = \frac{27}{4} = 6.75 \qquad\qquad \Sigma(Y–M)^2 = 44.74$$

$$SD^2 = \frac{44.74}{4} = 11.19$$

$$SD = 3.35$$

Table 4.17: Homework Set A #3e

Zx	Zy	ZxZy
.13	.07	.01
1.51	1.57	2.37
−1.21	−1.12	1.39
−.40	−.52	.21

$$\Sigma ZxZy = .01 + 2.37 + 1.39 + .21 = 3.98$$

$$\frac{\Sigma ZxZy}{N} = \frac{3.98}{4} = .995 \text{ (or 1.00)}$$

$$r = .995 \text{ (or 1.00)}$$

f. The correlation of .995 (or 1.00) is very strong and positive. Stress scores and chocolate consumption are very highly positively correlated—in this made-up example, in fact, they are almost perfectly correlated! The more stress people experience, the more chocolate they seem to eat. These findings are consistent with the scatterplot.

g. Causation cannot be determined. Stress levels and chocolate consumption are correlated, but it cannot be determined from the findings what causes the correlation.

h. Three possible explanations for the correlation are that (1) high stress levels could cause people to eat more chocolate, (2) eating chocolate could cause people to be more stressed, or (3) something else entirely is causing both high stress levels and increased chocolate consumption.

4. a. The number of action figures owned is the predictor variable because it is thought to predict the number of dates in a month. The number of dates in a month is the dependent variable because it is thought to be predicted by the number of action figures owned.

b & c. See Figure 4.12.

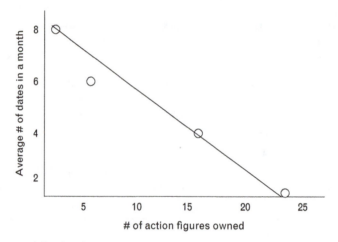

FIGURE 4.12: Homework Set A #4b & 4c.

d. The correlation is negative, and appears to be strong because there is not much scatter. It appears that guys who own many action figures tend to go on fewer dates than guys who own fewer action figures.

e.

Table 4.18: Homework Set A #4e

X (# of action figures owned)	M	X–M	(X–M)²	Zx
1	11.75	–10.75	115.56	–1.21
16	11.75	4.25	18.06	.48
24	11.75	12.25	150.06	1.38
6	11.75	–5.75	33.06	–.65

$$M = \frac{47}{4} = 11.75 \qquad \Sigma(X–M)^2 = 316.74$$

$$SD^2 = \frac{316.74}{4} = 79.19$$

$$SD = 8.90$$

Table 4.19: Homework Set A #4e

Y (# of dates in a month)	M	Y–M	(Y–M)²	Zy
8	4.5	3.5	12.25	1.18
4	4.5	–.5	.25	–.17
0	4.5	–4.5	20.25	–1.52
6	4.5	1.5	2.25	.51

$$M = \frac{18}{4} = 4.5 \qquad \Sigma(Y–M)^2 = 35$$

$$SD^2 = \frac{35}{4} = 8.75$$

$$SD = 2.96$$

Table 4.20: Homework Set A #4e

Zx	Zy	ZxZy
–1.21	1.18	–1.43
.48	–.17	–.08
1.38	–1.52	–2.10
–.65	.51	–.33

$$\Sigma ZxZy = –1.43 + –.08 + –2.10 + –.33 = –3.94$$

$$\frac{\Sigma ZxZy}{N} = \frac{–3.94}{4} = –.99$$

$$r = –.99$$

f. The co rrelation is –.99, which is a very strong negative correlation (nearly perfect). The number of action figures owned is highly negatively correlated with the number of dates a guy goes on. It appears that the more action figures a guy owns, the fewer dates he goes on in a month. The findings are consistent with the scatterplot.

g. Causation cannot be determined. Although the number of action figures owned is negatively correlated with the number of dates a guy goes on, the findings cannot indicate what causes the correlation.

h. Three possible explanations for the correlation are that (1) owning many action figures causes guys to go on fewer dates, (2) going on fewer dates causes guys to own more action figures, or (3) something else entirely causes guys to own more action figures and to go on fewer dates.

REFERENCE

Schmitt, D. P. (2005). Sociosexuality from Argentina to Zimbabwe: A 48-nation study of sex, culture, and strategies of human mating. Behavioral and Brain Sciences, 28, 247–311.

C H A P T E R   5

STATISTICAL PREDICTION
AND REGRESSION

With correlation, we discussed ways to describe how related two variables are to one another. Variables can be unrelated to one another (such as the correlation between shoe size and GPA among college students, which is likely close to zero), negatively correlated with one another (such as with the "number of hours of video games played" and "quiz score" example from Chapter 4, which yielded a correlation of –.98), or positively correlated with one another (such as with the quantitative and verbal scores on the Madupistan Aptitude Test from chapter 4 (r = .92)).

The next conceptual step has to do with prediction. If I know that two variables are related to one another, I can then use that information to make predictions about one variable from the other variable. Consider meteorology, for example. Suppose that a meteorologist is trying to predict if it is going to rain tomorrow, and she knows that the humidity (percentage of moisture in the air) is positively correlated with likelihood of rainfall. She can then use this correlation to her predictive advantage—if the humidity is high, she can increase her expectation that it will rain. **This is because these variables are correlated with one another**! If humidity were found to be uncorrelated with likelihood of precipitation, then this meteorologist would not be wise to use information about humidity in helping predict precipitation. It is only because these variables are correlated with one another that humidity is useful in making predictions about precipitation.

This point is important, because it helps us understand the interface of correlation and statistics that help us make predictions. Generally, statistics that help us predict outcomes fall under the category of *regression*. Specifically, regression analyses are analyses that allow us to predict scores on one variable from one or more other variables, *given information about the correlations between the variables.*

The simplest case of regression is referred to as *bivariate regression*. This simply denotes a situation in which you know the correlation between two variables—and you are trying to predict scores on one variable (the *dependent variable*) from scores on the other variable (the *predictor variable*). So a meteorologist, for instance, could use a bivariate regression analysis to see how well humidity predicts likelihood of rainfall. Note that the question here is slightly (but importantly) different than the question of correlation. With a correlation, one would simply want to see how interrelated two variables are. With a regression, the question pertains to how well scores on one variable predict scores on the other variable given the size and direction of the correlation between the variables.

STANDARDIZED REGRESSION

Throughout this chapter, we'll discuss two kinds of regression analyses—*standardized regression* and *unstandardized* (or *raw*) *regression*. We'll start with standardized regression, which is more useful in helping explain the nature of the process.

By definition, a *standardized regression analysis* is an analysis used to predict z-scores on the dependent (Y) variable from z-scores on the predictor (X) variable, given r_{xy} (i.e., the correlation between X and Y). Let's take a look at our "hours of video games played" and "quiz score" example from chapter 4 to explicate this process.

You'll recall that the raw data (found in Table 5.1) led to a strong negative correlation (r = –.98), meaning that as the number of hours of video games increased, the quiz score decreased (and vice versa).

So, for instance, Joe played zero hours of video games before the quiz and he got the best score in the sample (at 8). High Xs go with low Ys, and vice versa.

Based on the fact that the correlation in this example is –.98, what do we know about how well X predicts Y? Recall that a correlation gives you two basic pieces of information—how strong the relationship between the variables is as well as the direction of the relationship. A correlation of –.98 is extremely strong! (Recall that as the r approaches either –1 or +1, it increases in strength). In short, the stronger the correlation between two variables, the more predictive the one variable is of the other variable.

With regression, we set the problem up such that the variable we are *trying to predict* is the Y variable, and the *predictor variable* is the X variable. With the current example, we're trying to predict quiz scores (Y) from hours of video games played (X). Is our predictor variable useful in helping us predict quiz scores? In other words, if I want to predict someone's score on a quiz, would it be useful for me to know how many hours of video games that person played beforehand?

Table 5.1: Raw Data with Hours of Video Games Played (X) and Quiz Score (Y)

Student	Hours of Video Games Played (X)	Quiz Score (Y)
Joe	0	8
Sally	3	5
Jill	9	2

PREDICTING SCORES ON Y WITH DIFFERENT AMOUNTS OF INFORMATION

With regression, we're looking at how well we can predict our scores on some outcome (i.e., dependent, or Y) variable. A simple case, which we'll stick with for now, pertains to trying to predict scores on a quiz based on the quiz's correlation with some other variable. In the current scenario, we've stacked the deck so that quiz scores are strongly related to hours of video game playing (r = −.98). As the correlation is very close to −1, it is a very strong correlation. This will ultimately mean that this variable is strongly predictive of scores on the outcome variable (quiz scores).

But it's not always the case that you have strongly inter-correlated variables. You might have a variable that has zero correlation (or just a mild one) with your dependent variable.

Consider Scenario A: The correlation between number of hot dogs eaten in the past year and scores on the quiz equals exactly zero. That is, r = 0.

In this scenario, the number of hot dogs a student has eaten is completely unrelated to that person's quiz score. Suppose, now, that your task is to best predict a student's score on the quiz. You are asked if, in making this determination, you would like to know how many hot dogs this student has eaten in the past year. Would you want that information?

It depends on the size of the correlation. If number of hot dogs is correlated with quiz scores, then by all means, *yes*, you'd probably want to have some idea of how many hot dogs the person has had—as this variable would, due to its correlation with quiz scores, have some amount of predictive utility in guessing one's quiz score. But here, in this scenario, we have zero correlation. That means that there is exactly zero relationship between number of hot dogs eaten and quiz score. Given this fact, why in the world would you care how many hot dogs this person has eaten? You would not. The fact that there is zero correlation between these variables means that variable X (number of hot dogs) is totally unrelated to scores on variable Y (quiz scores). And if they are not related, then X does not *at all* predict Y.

Now consider Scenario B: Number of sardines eaten in the last year is positively correlated with quiz scores; r = .25.

Well, they do say that fish is brain food, so let's go with it! OK, now we have a mild-to-moderate correlation between our two variables. There is statistical correlation between number of sardines consumed and quiz score. We also know that the relationship is positive (more sardines, better score!).

Given this scenario, let's rethink about the information we'd want in making our prediction. Suppose that your task is to make your best prediction regarding someone's score on the quiz—and you are asked if you would like to know how many sardines that person has had. Guess what? Your answer is *yes*! At least "yes, given the fact that number of sardines consumed is related to the score on the quiz." From the perspective of regression, we really only care if a variable is related to another variable. And if it is, then we will find it useful in helping us predict that other variable.

That said, you can see that the strength of the correlation affects how much weight we want to give to a particular variable in helping us predict scores on the dependent variable (in this case, quiz scores). Simply: The variables that have the strongest correlations with the dependent variable are the ones that we should give more weight in the process of predicting scores on the dependent variable. A variable that is correlated −.98 with Y should be given more weight than a variable that is correlated .25 with Y...and they should both be given more weight than a variable that is correlated 0 with Y.

In fact, a variable that is correlated 0 with our dependent variable is, by definition, fully useless in helping us predict scores on Y. In this case, the number of hot dogs someone eats tells us zero about his or her quiz score.

Suppose that we knew the mean and standard deviation for the quiz (based on a large population of students who took it). Let's say the mean is 4.2 and the standard deviation is .7. Further, suppose that we know that this variable is, roughly, normally distributed, meaning that most scores are near the mean.

Now suppose that we were asked to guess the score of a random student: Pierre. We know absolutely nothing about Pierre—other than the fact that he took this quiz (and perhaps that he comes from France). All things equal, what should we guess for Pierre's score? Well, in the distribution of scores, since the mean is 4.2, and the distribution is normally distributed, the single most likely score is 4.2. Now, this does not mean that every score is 4.2. If you guess 4.2, you're still probably going to be wrong. But it is mathematically your very best possible guess as to Pierre's score *with no additional information.*

As such, if you are asked to guess someone's score on some normally distributed variable and you have zero other information, guessing the mean is always the mathematically smartest thing to do.

Now suppose that you know that Pierre had 30 hot dogs last year. Would this change your prediction of Pierre's test score? Simply: No—because you know that hot dog eating is uncorrelated with quiz scores. Since the correlation is zero, knowing something about his hot dog eating behavior tells you nothing about his quiz outcome.

In this sense, then, the weight of the predictor variable that should be used to predict scores on the Y variable is derived from the correlation between scores on that particular predictor variable and Y.

BETA WEIGHT

A *beta weight* is the specific coefficient used in a regression equation to represent how much weight a particular variable should have in predicting an outcome variable. A beta weight is a decimal between −1.0 and +1.0. The great thing is that with bivariate regression (with only one predictor variable and one dependent variable), the beta weight in your unstandardized regression equation equals r (or your correlation). This fact makes sense in light of the prior reasoning regarding how correlation relates to prediction—devoid of any other information, the correlation between X and Y is the most useful tool you have in determining how useful X is in predicting Y.

Let's revisit the example in which r = 0. If r = 0, then, β = 0 (as, simply, in bivariate regression, r = β). Recall that if X and Y have a zero correlation with one another, then X is totally useless in helping you predict Y. Thus, if number of hot dogs eaten is totally uncorrelated with quiz score, then knowing how many hot dogs someone has eaten helps you **zero** in trying to determine that person's quiz score. The number of hot dogs should therefore have **zero weight** in your efforts to predict the person's quiz score.

Recall also that if a variable is at least somewhat normally distributed and you are trying to predict a score for that variable with no other information, your mathematically best guess is the mean of the variable (which will be the most likely score). We had this example with our efforts to predict Pierre's score (knowing nothing except the number of hot dogs he has eaten (which is totally useless in predicting quiz scores due to its zero beta weight) and the mean for the quiz scores (which is 4.2). So our best guess for Pierre, recall, is 4.2.

The *unstandardized regression formula* reflects this process well. Simply, in its generic form, the formula is:

$$\hat{Z}y = (\beta)(Zx)$$

Here, $\hat{Z}y$ corresponds to "the predicted z score for the y variable." Note that the little "cap" or "hat" over this symbol means "predicted" as opposed to "actual" score. And Zx simply means "the z score for a particular raw score on the x variable."

The β refers to beta weight. When asked for the "unstandardized regression formula" for a particular data set, you'd typically fill in for β and leave the rest. Thus, if you were asked for the unstandardized regression formula for predicting quiz scores from the number of hot dogs eaten, you'd put it as follows:

$$\hat{Z}y = (0)(Zx)$$

...with 0 representing the beta weight. In this case, zero has a pretty literal interpretation. If you're trying to predict someone's z-score on the y variable and you have that person's z-score on the x variable, then you will come up with the same product for any value of Zx—as any number times zero equals zero.

Consider the values in Table 5.2 to see how this would pan out.

This all ultimately means that if X and Y are totally uncorrelated, X tells you nothing about Y. Thus, if you have to guess someone's z-score on the Y variable, you should, in this kind of instance, always just pick the mean for the Y variable (in this case, since we are dealing with standardized scores, it's the mean for the z-score of the Y variable—and the mean of any z distribution is always, by definition, zero—meaning zero standard deviations from the mean).

Table 5.2: Predicting Quiz Scores from Number of Hot Dogs Eaten if $r_{xy} = 0$

Subject	Zx	Zy	Interpretation
Harry	1.0	0.0	If Harry's z-score on the X variable is 1.0 (or Harry's hot dog eating has been 1 standard deviation above average), our best prediction of his z-score on the quiz is 0, or the mean of the Y variable (which is, by definition, zero standard deviations from the mean)
Ralph	−1.5	0.0	If Ralph's z-score on the X variable is −1.5 (or Ralph's hot dog eating has been 1.5 standard deviations below average), our best prediction of his z-score on the quiz is 0, or the mean of the Y variable (which is, by definition, zero standard deviations from the mean)

In short, if X and Y are uncorrelated, then your best guess as to the z-score for y, given the z-score for x, is the mean of Y (M_y).

To see how regression works, let's now take an example at the other extreme. Suppose that you have two variables that are perfectly correlated—imagine that the amount of chocolate someone eats (X) is perfectly and positively correlated with his or her score on a life happiness scale (Y). In this case, $r_{xy} = 1.0$. The z-score regression formula, then, would be as follows:

$$\widehat{Zy} = (1)(Zx)$$

…meaning that your best statistical guess as to the z-score for any value of Y is the z-score for the corresponding Zx times 1. For instance, suppose that Mary eats half a standard deviation more chocolate than average. Her z-score for the X variable is, thus, .5 (meaning .5 (or half of one) standard deviations above the mean).

At this point, it's important to ask if chocolate is useful in predicting happiness. In this example, it's not only useful, but given the correlation of 1.0, it's perfectly predictive. That means that if we know someone's Zx, then we know, perfectly, that person's Zy! (In reality, things are never this clean, but this works for helping teach the concept.) OK—so, if Mary's Zx is .5, then we can plug this number into the standardized regression equation—and we get a Zŷ of .5.

$$\widehat{Zy} = (\beta)(Zx)$$
$$\widehat{Zy} = (.5)(1) = .5$$

In short, this means that our best mathematical guess for Mary's happiness is half a standard deviation above the mean—exactly as extreme as her chocolate score.

There's an important lesson in this: With regression, the most extreme score that can be predicted for the Y variable is based on how extreme the X score is. With a perfect correlation between X and Y, our predicted Zy is as extremely different from the mean as Zx. It's not more extreme.

And recall that with a zero correlation between X and Y, our predicted Zy will always be exactly the mean of Zy, or 0.

Our predicted Zy scores, then, vary between 0 (meaning the mean of the Zy distribution) and Zx.

If our correlation between Zx and Zy is imperfect (which is usually the case in the real world), the predicted Zy *regresses* toward the mean. That is, the equation first assumes that the predicted Zy will be as extreme as Zx, but then as β approaches zero, the predicted Zy moves toward the mean for the Y variable—it regresses toward the mean.

So suppose that there is a correlation between exercise (X) and GPA (Y) that's found to be .4. The standardized regression equation to predict z-scores for GPA from z-scores for exercise would be as follows:

$$\widehat{Zy} = (.4)(Zx)$$

Now suppose that Joe's exercise score (in z-score units) is 1.2. That is, Joe exercises 1.2 standard deviations more than average. What's our best guess as to Joe's z-score for the GPA (Y) variable? In using the equation, we see that 1.2 * .4 = .48. Note that .48 is not as extremely different from the mean as is 1.2, but it's more extreme than 0. So the z-score of .48 is essentially reflective of the fact that X and Y are *somewhat correlated*. The fact that X and Y are somewhat correlated essentially says that our prediction for Zy need not be the mean of Zy (or 0). We can predict better than that. But let's not predict a score as extreme (in z-score units) as Zx, as X and Y are only somewhat inter-correlated. Thus, our prediction of Zy should not be as extreme as Zx, but, rather, it should regress toward the mean (.48 is between 1.2 (Zx) and 0 (the mean of Zy)).

The reason that it is logical to assume that a predicted score regresses toward the mean is based on the general idea that in normally distributed variables, scores tend to regress toward the mean. So, for instance, if a student scores 2 standard deviations above the mean on his or her first exam, that person will likely do well on the second exam, but the second exam score will probably not be as extreme as the first exam score; it will likely (albeit not necessarily) regress toward the mean. Extreme scores are rare, and often reflect statistical aberrations. All things equal, scores tend to regress toward the mean.

UNSTANDARDIZED REGRESSION EQUATION

Given that we used z-scores to help us understand how correlation works, it's always easiest to first grasp regression with the standardized regression formula (trying to predict z-scores rather than raw scores). Simply: z-scores are key for teaching the basics of so many statistical concepts.

However, in the real world, go ahead and try explaining to the Average Joe or the Average Mary that your model predicts that someone's score on the test will be .4 standard deviations above the mean. Both Joe and Mary will probably look at you quizzically, pack their bags, and head to the other side of the room!

Standardized scores are not complicated, but they *are* technical—they have specific meaning within the confines of the beautiful but unique world of Statistics. In the real world, people deal in raw scores. If you tell Joe and Mary that your model predicts that Fred will score a 78 on the exam, they get it—they know what you're talking about, and they'll perhaps agree to sit with you at lunch again in the near future!

For various reasons, it's useful to understand the details of raw-score regression modeling. In its generic form, the formula for a raw-score regression model is as follows:

$$\hat{Y} = a + b(X)$$

where

$b = B\left(\dfrac{SDy}{SDx}\right)$ (known as the *raw score regression coefficient*), and

$a = My - (b)Mx$ (this is the *regression constant*, also known as the *Y-intercept*, or *the point at which the regression line hits the y-axis*).

Yes, if you recall your 8th-grade algebra (and humor us, pretend you do!), you'll recognize this equation as the equation for a straight (linear) line. The raw-score regression equation, thus, is, as it turns out, the equation for the line that best approximates the scatterplot of some X and Y variables.

We can therefore think of the raw-score regression equation as two things. First, it's the equation that produces a straight line that best approximates the dots in a scatterplot of X and Y.

Second, it's a formula that we can use in the context of *prediction* (remember, that's the whole point of this stuff!). The raw-score regression formula allows us to best predict raw scores on Y from raw scores on X, knowing the relationship between X and Y. However, it differs from the standardized regression formula in a critical way—here, instead of predicting z-scores for the Y variable, you are predicting actual raw-scores for the Y variable. In other words, you are actually predicting scores on the Y variable in a way that would make sense to Joe and Mary!

Let's go back to our example regarding whether the number of hours of video games played predicts quiz scores (see Table 5.3). With our z-score prediction model, we concluded that these two variables have a strong negative correlation (−.98) and that video game playing is very predictive of quiz score (in a negative direction: More video game playing leads to lower quiz score (yes, there's a small lesson here!)).

However, that z-score model ($Z\hat{y} = -.98 * Zx$) only allows us to predict quiz scores in standardized (Z) units. But what, again, of Joe and Mary? They never took this class and they just want to know what the predicted scores are in a straightforward manner!

Well, help is on the way—the raw-score regression model will allow us to come up with such predicted raw scores. In this particular case, the raw-score regression model is determined as follows:

$$^*b = B\left(\frac{SDy}{SDx}\right) = -.98\left(\frac{2.45}{3.74}\right) = -.64$$

And

$$^*a = My - b(Mx) = 5 - [(-.64)(4)] = 7.56$$

Thus,

$$\hat{Y} = 7.56 + (-.64)(X)$$

If I know that Joe played one hour of video games, then $\hat{Y}$ would equal $7.56 + (-.64) * (1) = 6.92$. Knowing Joe's video game playing behavior, coupled with our understanding of the relationship between video game playing and quiz score, our best mathematical guess as to Joe's score on the test would be 6.92. Let's hope that both Joe and Mary are happy with that!

So, a great benefit of the raw-score regression model is its ability to allow you to predict scores on Y that are on the raw Y scale.

Table 5.3: Raw Data with Hours of Video Games Played (X) and Quiz Score (Y)

Student	Hours of Video Games Played (X)	Quiz Score (Y)
Joe	0	8
Sally	3	5
Jill	9	2

THE REGRESSION LINE

For any of your friends who make you feel self-conscious about your love of statistics—who make you feel that statistics is just *not cool*, might we suggest you introduce them to the regression line! Honestly, this is about as cool as things get in statistics.

The regression line is formed based on the raw-score regression equation, and it can be superimposed on the appropriate scatterplot to give a sense of how well the model conforms to the actual data. If the model strongly maps onto (or predicts) the data in the scatterplot, then the line will be in close proximity to the dots in the scatterplot (on average; See Figure 5.1). On the other hand, if the regression model does not strongly predict the pattern of data in the X and Y scores, then the line will generally misrepresent the dots in the scatterplot (see Figure 5.2).

Here are the simple steps to create a regression line from a raw-score regression model:

1. Draw your scatterplot for X and Y.
2. Write out the raw-score regression model:

    $$\hat{Y} = 7.56 + (-.64)(X)$$

3. Think of *any* two possible values of X. It's good to have these be on a scale that is readily interpretable, but it's not necessary, as any two points, when connected, will give you the same line to overlay on your scatterplot.
4. With these two Xs, compute two $(X,\hat{Y})$ coordinates by plugging X into the raw-score regression equation.
5. Put a mark for each $(X,\hat{Y})$ coordinate right on the scatterplot (go on, you can do it!).
6. Connect these two points. Voila—you've created your regression line!

This regression line includes an infinite number of $(X, \hat{Y})$ points—it gives you the predicted Y for any possible value of X.

Let's go through these three steps for creating the regression line for the video game data.

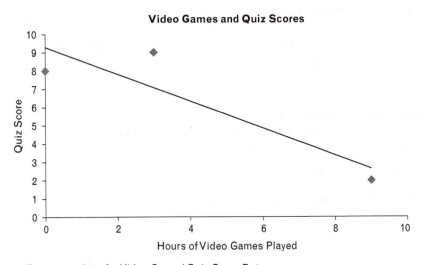

FIGURE 5.1: Regression Line for Video Game / Quiz Score Data.

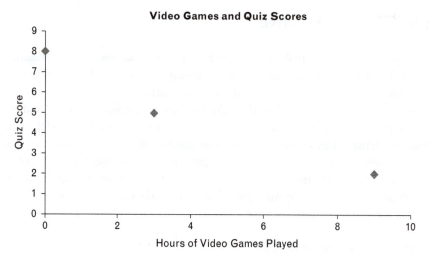

FIGURE 5.2: Scatterplot Without Regression Line.

1. Draw your scatterplot for X and Y.
2. Write out the raw-score regression model:

$$\hat{Y} = 7.56 + (-.64)(X)$$

3. Think of *any* two possible values of X. It's good to have these be on a scale that is readily interpretable, but it's not necessary, as any two points, when connected, will give you the same line to overlay on your scatterplot.

So let's, arbitrarily, use 0 and 9 for our values of X in coming up with X, $\hat{Y}$ coordinates (you'll actually see that using these two particular points, as they correspond to real Xs in the data set, will have some solid benefits for us as we progress—but, again, remember that *any* two Xs will do for creating the regression line).

4. With these two Xs, compute two (X, $\hat{Y}$) coordinates by plugging X into the raw-score regression equation.

If we put 0 into the equation, $\hat{Y} = 7.56$
If we put 9 into the equation, $\hat{Y} = 1.80$
Remember, we're just putting these arbitrary Xs (0 and 9) into the regression equation to compute values for $\hat{Y}$—with the regression equation being:

$$\hat{Y} = 7.56 + (-.64)(X)$$

So here are two X, $\hat{Y}$ coordinates:
(0, 7.56) and (9, 1.80)

5. Put a mark for each (X, $\hat{Y}$) coordinate right on the scatterplot (go on, you can do it!).
6. Connect these two points. Voila—you've created your regression line!

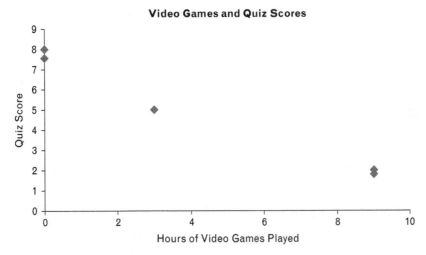

FIGURE 5.3: Scatterplot with two X, Ŷ Coordinates.

This regression line includes an infinite number of (X, Ŷ) points—it gives you the predicted Y for any possible value of X.

Given the current example, with hours of video games played and quiz scores, the correlation is very strong (–.98); thus, Beta is very strong (also –.98). In this example, hours of video games played very strongly maps onto how well students do on the quiz. In terms of regression, you can see from the regression line in Figure 5.3 that the actual points in the scatterplot correspond very closely to the regression line. That makes sense, as the regression model strongly predicts scores. In fact, if we compare how close scores are to the regression line relative to a flat line representing just the mean of Y (of 5), you'll see that in nearly each case, the actual (X, Y) score, representing an actual data point, is closer to the regression line than to the line representing the mean (see Figure 5.5). Based on this visual inspection, we can see that the regression model predicts the actual (X, Y) scores better than the mean does (on average).

However, as we've seen before with statistics, statisticians like numbers…

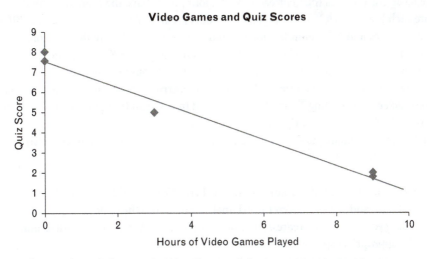

FIGURE 5.4: Scatterplot with Regresssion Line Demarcated.

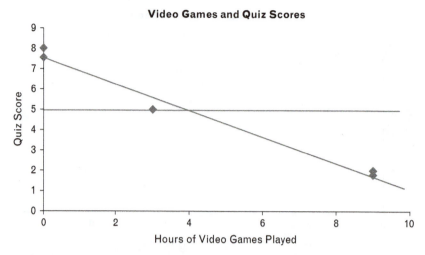

FIGURE 5.5: Scatterplot with Regression Line and Line Representing Mean of Y.

QUANTITATIVELY ESTIMATING THE PREDICTIVE POWER OF YOUR REGRESSION MODEL

If you simply told people "look, the dots on the actual scatterplot representing the real (X, Y) data points are closer to the regression line than to the mean of Y," people might be skeptical. They would likely want to see some numeric evidence of this point. Enter "r squared." (i.e., r^2). r squared is one of the coolest statistics going—because it answers precisely the question of just how much better your regression model predicts actual scores relative to simply guessing the mean.

Formally, r squared represents the *proportionate reduction of error in predicting Y relative to simply guessing the mean of Y*. That sounds like a lot. And it sort of is. But you can handle it. In fact, the way we'll compute and conceptualize r squared is quite similar to how we have dealt with the old standby, standard deviation.

The basic reasoning is this: For each (X, Y) point, if we have the regression model, we can compare each Y with each $\hat{Y}$. If our regression model predicts Y scores well, then the differences between Y scores and $\hat{Y}$s should be small. If our regression model predicts Y scores perfectly, then each $\hat{Y}$ (representing a predicted Y score) should equal each Y. If our regression model is bad, then our $\hat{Y}$s and Y scores should deviate considerably from one another.

We now have the basis of a term called *error*. Here, error simply refers to how different each Y is from each corresponding $\hat{Y}$ (see Table 5.4). And in case you thought it was complicated, it's not: Error = $Y-\hat{Y}$. Makes sense, right?

You'll see that r squared is simply a statistic that is rooted in this idea of error. To compute r squared, we do the following:

1. Create a table with five columns: X, Y, $\hat{Y}$, Error ($Y-\hat{Y}$), and Error² $(Y-\hat{Y})^2$
2. Put all X and Y scores from the original raw data into the table.
3. Using your raw-score regression model, compute each $\hat{Y}$, and enter these numbers into the appropriate spots in the table.
4. Compute an error term for each (X, Y) coordinate.

Table 5.4: Computing r square (proportionate reduction of error) for the video game / quiz score example

X	Y	Ycap	(Y–Ycap) (ERROR)	(Y–Ycap)² (ERROR)²
0	8	7.56	.44	.19
3	5	5.64	−.64	.41
9	2	1.80	.20	.04
				SSe = .64
				SSt = 18*
				$r^2 = \dfrac{SSt - SSe}{SSt}$
				.96

*SSt = SSy; this was computed during the process of calculating standard deviation for the Y variable; the sum of the squared deviation scores was 18.

5. As the sum of these error terms will come to zero (due to the same reasons we ran into in computing standard deviation), we now square our error terms (and put each in the appropriate spot in the table).

6. For an index of the overall amount of squared error, sum the squared error column for SSe (Sum of the squared error terms). In this case, SSe = .64.

7. R squared = $\dfrac{SSt - SSe}{SSt}$, with SSt = SSy (meaning the sum of the squared deviation scores for the Y variable). Here, it's referred to as "SSt," with "t" standing for "total"—meaning, literally, the total amount of variability in Y in terms of sum of squared deviation scores. Thus, the equation we have here partials out how much variability there is between the Y and Ŷs relative to the total variability there is in Y scores (they're both in "sum of squared deviation score" units, so they're on the same scale). Here, r^2 = (18–.64) / 18 = .96.

You may have at this point figured out that r^2 has a very literal computational meaning: r^2 = r * r = (−.98) * (−.98) = .96. But hopefully you agree that going through the computational process presented here provides a useful conceptual way of understanding *why* r^2 is a good index of how well your regression model predicts Y scores.

INTERPRETING r^2

The most literal meaning of r^2 corresponds to this idea of *proportionate reduction of error in predicting Y relative to simply guessing the mean of Y*. It is literally a ratio of variability—how much variability there is in terms of the degree that actual Y scores deviate from predicted Y scores (error)—**relative to** the amount of overall variability from the mean of the Y variable. If the error is small relative to the amount of overall variability that scores vary from the mean, r^2 will be relatively large. If r^2 is large, as it is in our working example, then our ability to predict Y scores (in this case, quiz scores) has improved **a lot** based on just predicting the mean of Y. How much is **a lot**? Happily, we can answer that question with precision: 96%. Our ability to predict scores on Y has improved 96% as a function of our regression model relative to just predicting the mean for each value of X. That's a lot! If you were trying to use your research to make the case that students shouldn't play too much in the way of video games before their quizzes, you may well be able to use this kind of data to help you make that point (if, of course, your participants have the ability to look up from their iPhones while you're explaining your findings…).

r squared is often also referred to as "the amount of variability in your Y variable accounted for by the relationship between X and Y." Again, this is often presented as a percentage—and it's the same percentage we've seen in terms of the *proportionate reduction of error* conceptualization—just framed slightly differently. Here, we'd say something like "the relationship between video games and quiz scores accounts for 96% of the variability in quiz scores." This way of summarizing / interpreting r² is slightly more common than the *proportionate reduction of error* conception, but it's actually slightly less accurate and intuitive. Still, there you have it!

Bottom line: r² is our ultimate regression statistic—it provides a finely tuned and coherent summary of how well our regression model predicts scores on our outcome (Y) variable compared with having no information whatsoever.

A REAL RESEARCH EXAMPLE

In a recent study examining factors that predict preferences for different kinds of sexual acts, Peterson, Geher, and Kaufman (2011) conducted a multiple regression analysis. This kind of analysis is just like the bivariate regression analysis that you've been exposed to in this chapter— with one exception: With multiple regression, instead of trying to predict scores on an outcome variable from a single predictor variable, you are trying to predict scores on one outcome variable from multiple predictor variables. In this case, we were attempting to predict preference for vaginal (as opposed to other forms of) intercourse. Here's how we presented to the regression analysis:

For preference for vaginal sex, the predictor variables accounted for a significant portion of the variability ($R^2 = .11$, $F(9, 361) = 4.91$, $p < .01$). Therefore, sex, personality, life history strategy, sociosexuality, and mating intelligence accounted for 11% of the variance in the preference for vaginal sex. For individual unstandardized regression coefficients (β), intercept, and standardized regression coefficients (β) for each variable, see Table 5.5. In terms of individual relationships between the predictor variables and the preference for vaginal sex, openness ($t = -2.63$, $p < .01$), sociosexuality ($t = 4.17$, $p < .01$), and mating intelligence ($t = 3.50$, $p < .01$) each significantly predicted preference for vaginal sex. Therefore, individuals who are sociosexually unrestricted and high in openness and mating intelligence are likely to have strong preferences for vaginal sex.

OK—so this is a bit more complex than the examples that we've run into in this chapter—but it's a very typical kind of analysis that you'll encounter in the literature. Also, importantly, note that in Appendix E, when we examine advanced statistics, a relatively full summary of multiple regression will be presented. That said, let's see how our current understanding of regression can help us make sense of the findings presented here.

First, note the starting sentence here: "For preference for vaginal sex, the predictor variables accounted for a significant portion of the variability ($R^2 = .11$, $F(9, 361) = 4.91$, $p < .01$)." Let's dissect! Observe that here, we are presented with capital R^2 as opposed to lowercase r². This is

Table 5.5: Multiple Regression Predicting Preference for Vaginal
Sex from Predictor Variables

Predictor Variable	b	SE(b)	β	t
Mating Intelligence[1]	.07	.02	.20	3.50**
Life History[2]	.03	.12	.02	.25
Openness[3]	−.32	.11	−.14	−2.63**
Neuroticism[3]	−.01	.09	−.01	−.10
Conscientiousness[3]	.22	.12	.10	1.90
Agreeableness[3]	.08	.12	.04	.64
Extraversion[3]	−.02	.09	−.01	−.16
Sociosexuality[4]	.03	.01	.23	4.17**
Sex[5]	−.11	.18	−.03	−.61

Note.

$R^2 = .11**$

$*p < .05; **p > .01$
Key
[1] For mating intelligence, high scores correspond to individuals with high mating intelligence and low scores correspond to individuals with low mating intelligence. *Range* = 0–24.
[2] For life history, high scores correspond to individuals endorsing a slow life history strategy (i.e., *high K*) and low scores correspond to individuals endorsing a fast life history strategy (i.e., *low K*). *Range* = −3–3.
[3] For the traits of the Big Five, high scores correspond to individuals being high in the trait and low scores correspond to individuals being low in the trait. *Range* = 1–5.
[4] For sociosexuality, high scores correspond to individuals endorsing an unrestricted sociosexuality and low scores correspond to individuals endorsing a restricted sociosexuality. *Range* = 0–81.
[5] For sex, Female = 0; Male = 1. (from Peterson, A., Geher, G., & Kaufman, S. B. (2011). Predicting preferences for sex acts: Which traits matter and why? *Evolutionary Psychology, 9*, 371–389).

simply because we have multiple regression (with multiple predictor variables) as opposed to bivariate regression (with just one predictor variable). Here, $R^2 = .11$. That means, simply, that the regression model has improved our ability to predict variability in preference for vaginal intercourse by 11% over knowing just the mean for this preference. And the subsequent stuff—$(F(9, 361) = 4.91, p < .01)$—means that this 11% is significantly more than we would expect by chance. So, it's not 96%, but it's still significant and substantial.

The table, then, (5.5) provides information on which particular variables are significantly predictive of preference for vaginal intercourse. There's a lot of information there, but in this case we will ultimately look to the asterisks—asterisked variables are variables that have "significant Beta weights" in predicting the outcome variable. Here, we see that there are three significant beta weights—for mating intelligence (Beta = .20), open-mindedness (−.14), and sociosexuality/promiscuity (.23). These are all interpreted in a manner very similar to correlations. People high in mating intelligence, then, generally prefer vaginal intercourse over those who don't— and this relationship accounts for a significant amount of variability in preference for vaginal intercourse. On the other hand, with a negative beta, open-minded individuals seem to actually not prefer vaginal intercourse relative to closed-minded individuals. Finally, promiscuous individuals (those high in sociosexuality) seem to prefer vaginal intercourse compared with their non-promiscuous counterparts.

CONCLUSION

Statistics are ultimately tools designed to help us predict what will happen in the world. Regression is the particular statistic that most directly bears on this idea of predicting outcomes. Regression allows us to make our best mathematical predictions of outcomes given that we have some understanding of the relationships between variables (i.e., given that we know how inter-correlated variables are with one another). If two variables are strongly correlated with one another, the regression model will do a good job of predicting scores on the outcome variable. If two variables are negligibly correlated with one another, the regression model will not improve your predictive ability much at all.

KEY TERMS

Beta weight: Specific coefficient between –1.0 and +1.0 used in a regression equation to represent how much weight a particular variable should have in predicting an outcome variable.

Bivariate regression: Statistical analyses that allows for the prediction of scores on a dependent variable based on scores from a predictor variable.

Error: How different each Y is from each corresponding ŷ. $Y - \hat{Y}$ = Error.

r squared (r^2): The proportionate reduction of error in predicting Y relative to simply guessing the mean of Y, or the amount of variability in the Y variable that is accounted for by the relationship between X and Y.

Regression: Statistics that predict outcomes.

Regression analyses: Analyses that allow the prediction of scores on one variable from other variables, given information about the correlations between the variables.

Standardized regression analysis: An analysis used to predict z-scores on the dependent (Y) variable from z-scores on the predictor (X) variable, given r_{xy} (the correlation between X and Y).

HOMEWORK SET A

1. Your grade in one of your classes is based entirely on the work product of your group rather than your own individual work product. Therefore, you need to choose the members of your group wisely. You are gathering information from class members to determine who to choose. You know the correlations between grades and certain other variables are as follows: See Table 5.6 for data.

Table 5.6: Homework Set A #1

Variable	Correlation with Grades
Amount of time spent planning last year's Halloween costume	0
Amount of time spent preparing for the last midterm	.56
Number of alcoholic beverages consumed in the last week	−.43
Knife-throwing skills	.12
Recognition of quotes from the movie Tommy Boy	.08
Hours spent on Facebook in the last week	−.39

Rank these variables from 1–6, with #1 being the most valuable in determining who to choose for your group, and #6 being the least valuable in determining who to choose for your group. Keep in mind, your goal is to get the highest grade possible!

2. You have signed up to participate in a research project. You know that the average amount of time required to complete the task is 8.24 minutes, and the distribution is normally distributed.
   a. With no additional information, what is your best guess as to the amount of time it will take you to finish the task?
   b. It took you 12 minutes to get from your home to the research site, which corresponds to a z-score of .23, and you know that there is a correlation of 0 between the amount of time it takes to arrive at the research site and the amount of time it takes to complete the task. Give $Z\hat{y}$ and $\hat{Y}$, based on the amount of time it took you to arrive at the research site.
   c. You have been told that people who get adequate sleep the week before attempting the task tend to complete the task faster, with a correlation of .36. Calculate $Z\hat{y}$, knowing that your z-score for amount of sleep is −.61.

3. In chapter 4, we investigated the relationship between stress levels and number of pieces of chocolate consumed in a day and found the correlation between these two variables was 1.00. Recall that the sum of the squared deviation scores for the y-variable (SSy, or SSt) was 44.74. See Table 5.7 for data.

Table 5.7: Homework Set A #3

Name	Stress Score	Pieces of chocolate eaten
Anna	30	7
Bill	48	12
Susan	12	3
Joseph	23	5
	M = 28.25	M = 6.75
	SD = 13.08	SD = 3.35

    a.   Compute the raw-score regression model for this data set.
    b.   Calculate the predicted number of pieces of chocolate eaten if the stress score is 16.
    c.   Create a regression line.
    d.   Compute r^2.
    e.   How much of the variability in the y-variable is accounted for by the relationship between x and y?

4.   Previously, we found a correlation of –.99 for a data set involving the number of action figures a guy owns and the average number of dates he goes on in a month. Recall that the sum of the squared deviation scores for the y-variable (SSy, or SSt) was 35. See Table 5.8 for data.

Table 5.8: Homework Set A #4

Participant	# of action figures owned	Average # of dates in a month
Eli	1	8
Herbert	16	4
Steven	24	0
Garreth	6	6
	Mean = 11.75	Mean = 4.5
	SD = 8.90	SD = 2.96

    a.   Compute the raw score regression model for this data set.
    b.   Calculate the predicted number of dates in a month if the number of action figures owned is 10.
    c.   Create a regression line.
    d.   Compute r^2.
    e.   How much of the variability in the y-variable is accounted for by the relationship between x and y?

HOMEWORK SET B

1.   You are required to complete a community service project. You have procrastinated until cleaning up messy local dog parks is the only project left with openings. However, you have your choice between two groups to join. With finals to study for, and considering the job you will be doing, you want to complete the task as quickly as possible.

Given the following variables and their correlations to how quickly the group is likely to work, rank the variables from 1–6, with #1 being the most valuable in determining how fast the group will finish the clean-up and #6 being the least valuable in determining how fast the group will finish. See Table 5.9 for data.

Table 5.9: Homework Set B #1

Variable	Correlation to how fast the group will finish the clean-up
Number of people in the group	.95
Roosters running loose in the dog park	−.86
Number of people in the group who firmly believe in the paranormal	0
Number of people in the group with ankle injuries requiring crutches	−.41
Overall skill in canoeing within the group	.02
Number of boy scouts and girl scouts in the group	.26

2. You are predicting stress levels amongst first-year college students, which is a normal distribution with a mean of 20.
    a. What is your best guess for the stress level of any first-year college student, with no other information available?
    b. If self-confidence is correlated with stress levels, with r = −.44, and Sabrina's z-score in confidence is 2.2, what is Sabrina's $Z\hat{y}$ for stress level?
    c. If loneliness has a .35 correlation with stress levels, and Patrick has a z-score of 1.3 on loneliness, what is his $Z\hat{y}$ for stress level?
    d. Knowing that the ability to blow really big bubble gum bubbles has no correlation with stress levels, and knowing that Teagan excels at bubble gum bubble blowing, with a z-score of 3, what is Teagan's $Z\hat{y}$ for stress level? Can you give an actual score for Teagan's stress level, knowing his $Z\hat{y}$?
3. Recall from chapter 4 when we found a correlation of 1.00 between the number of dogs owned and the average number of minutes spent outside per day. Remember that the sum of the squared deviation scores for the y-variable (SSy, or SSt) was 620.67. See Table 5.10 for data.

Table 5.10: Homework Set B #3

Participant	Number of dogs owned	Average # of minutes spent outside per day
George	3	60
Jim	0	25
Sheila	2	46
	Mean = 1.67	Mean = 43.67
	SD = 1.25	SD = 14.38

    a.   Compute the raw score regression model for this data set.

    b.   Calculate the predicted number of minutes spent outside if the number of dogs owned is 4.

    c.   Create a regression line.

    d.   Compute r^2.

    e.   How much of the variability in the y-variable is accounted for by the relationship between x and y?

4.   Previously, we found that the more classes students take, the fewer parties they tend to attend, with a correlation of –.90. Recall that the sum of the squared deviation scores for the y-variable (SSy, or SSt) was 9. See Table 5.11 for data

Table 5.11: Homework Set B #4

Participant	# of classes	Average # of parties attended in a month
Keisha	4	2
Kimberly	1	6
Michael	2	3
Devin	3	3
	Mean = 2.5	Mean = 3.5
	SD = 1.12	SD = 1.5

    a.   Compute the raw score regression model for this data set.

    b.   Calculate the predicted number of parties attended if the number of classes is 5.

    c.   Create a regression line.

    d.   Compute r^2.

    e.   How much of the variability in the y-variable is accounted for by the relationship between x and y?

HOMEWORK SET A ANSWERS

1.   #1–Amount of time spent preparing for the last midterm

    #2–Number of alcoholic beverages consumed in the last week

    #3–Hours spent on Facebook in the last week

    #4–Knife-throwing skills

    #5–Recognition of quotes from the movie Tommy Boy

    #6–Amount of time spent planning last year's Halloween costume

2.   a.   8.24 minutes, which is equal to the mean

    b. $\hat{Z}y = (\beta)(Zx)$

        $\hat{Z}y = (0)(.23) = 0$

$\hat{Z}y = 0$, which means 0 standard deviations from the mean, which is equal to the mean, which is 8.24 minutes. So $\hat{Y} = 8.24$ minutes.

c. $\widehat{Zy} = (\beta)(Zx)$

$\widehat{Zy} = (.36)(-.61)$

$\widehat{Zy} = -.22$

3. a. $b = 1\left(\dfrac{3.35}{13.08}\right) 1(.26) = .26$

$a = 6.75 - .26(28.25) = 6.75 - 7.35 = -.6$

$\hat{Y} = -.6 + .26(x)$

b. $\hat{Y} = -.6 + .26(16) = -.6 + 4.16 = 3.56$

$\hat{Y} = 3.56$ pieces of chocolate

c.

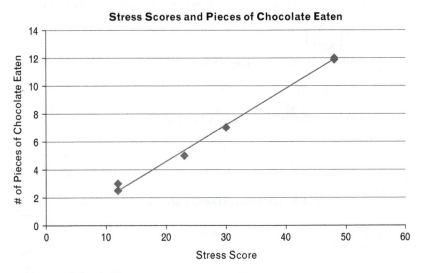

FIGURE 5.6: Homework Set A #3c.

pt. 1 = $\hat{Y}$ = -.6 + .26(12) = -.6 + 3.12 = 2.52
pt. 1 = (12, 2.52)
pt. 2 = $\hat{Y}$ = -.6 + .26(48) = -.6 + 12.48 = 11.88
pt 2 = (48, 11.88)
d.

Table 5.12: Homework Set A # 3d Answers

X	Y	$\hat{Y}$	(Y–$\hat{Y}$) (Error)	(Y–$\hat{Y}$)² (Error)²
30	7	7.2	–.2	.04
48	12	11.88	.12	.01
12	3	2.52	.48	.23
23	5	5.38	–.38	.14

SSe = .42

SSt = 44.74

$$r^2 = \frac{SSt - SSe}{SSt} = \frac{44.74 - .42}{44.74} = \frac{44.32}{44.74} = .99$$

$$r^2 = .99$$

e. 99% of the variability in the number of pieces of chocolate consumed can be accounted for by the relationship between stress and chocolate consumption.

4. a. $b = -.99\left(\dfrac{2.96}{8.90}\right) - .99(.33) = -.33$

   $a = 4.5 - (-.33)(11.75) = 4.5 - (-3.88) = 8.38$

   $\hat{Y} = 8.38 + -.33(x)$ or $\hat{Y} = 8.38 - .33(x)$

   b. $\hat{Y} = 8.38 + (-.33)(10) = 8.38 + (-.3.3) = 5.08$

   $\hat{Y} = 5.08$ dates

   c.

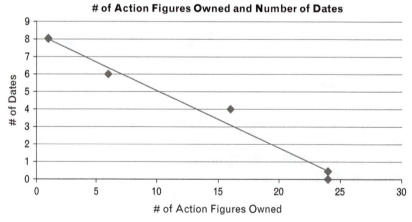

FIGURE 5.7: Homework Set A #4c.

pt. 1 = Ŷ = 8.38 + (−.33)(1) = 8.38 + (−.33) = 8.05
pt. 1 = (1, 8.05)
pt. 2 = Ŷ = 8.38 + (−.33)(24) = 8.38 + (−7.92) = .46
pt. 2 = (24, .46)
d.

Table 5.13: Homework Set A # 4d Answers

X	Y	Ŷ	$(Y-\hat{Y})$ (Error)	$(Y-\hat{Y})^2$ (Error)^2
1	8	8.05	−.05	0
16	4	3.1	.9	.81
24	0	.46	−.46	.21
6	6	6.4	−.4	.16
				SSe = 1.18
				SSt = 35

$$r^2 = \frac{SSt - SSe}{SSt} = \frac{35 - 1.18}{35} = \frac{33.82}{35} = .97$$

$$r^2 = .97$$

e.   97% of the variability in the number of dates in this data set is accounted for by the relationship between the number of action figures owned and the number of dates in a month.

REFERENCE

Peterson, A., Geher, G., & Kaufman, S. B. (2011). Predicting preferences for sex acts: Which traits matter and why? *Evolutionary Psychology, 9,* 371–389.

C H A P T E R   6

THE BASIC ELEMENTS
OF HYPOTHESIS TESTING

To this point, we've addressed *descriptive statistics*—statistics that describe variables, either single variables (e.g., the mean of a continuous variable) or relationships among multiple variables (e.g., the correlation between two continuous variables). Enter *inferential statistics*—an approach to statistics that addresses whether statistical effects are *beyond what would be expected by chance*. As you'll see, there's quite a bit to the reasoning underlying inferential statistics. This chapter focuses on some of the basic elements that underlie inferential statistics.

When statisticians talk about *hypothesis testing*, we are referring to *inferential statistics*—these concepts are essentially one and the same. Specifically, *hypothesis testing* corresponds to determining if some effect found in a sample is likely reflective of patterns in the population. Whereas the complementary concept of *inferential statistics* corresponds to statistics that are designed to allow us to infer whether some pattern found in a sample likely reflects a pattern found in the population (as you can see, it's basically the same idea).

Inferential statistics are useful because they allow you to see whether effects you observe in your world are likely reflective of anything *real* or anything that matters—or, in other words, how the world really is. For example, suppose that you are a professor teaching two sections of statistics—one at 8:00 a.m. and one at 2:00 p.m. You find that the early birds seem a little better in terms of understanding the material. But, at this point, it's pretty much just a hunch. Then you give the first exam and your data seem to support your hunch. The grades in the two sections are as follows (see Table 6.1):

Table 6.1: Exam Scores for Students in Two Sections
of Class (8:00 a.m. and 2:00 p.m.)

8:00 a.m. class	2:00 p.m. class
80	98
95	88
90	74
95	85
85	89

Table 6.2: Mean Exam Scores for Students in Two Sections of Class

Mean for 8:00 a.m. class = 89	Mean for 2:00 p.m. class = 86.8

So here you have two variables—scores from Class 1 and scores from Class 2. Given what you know so far about statistics, you realize that you need to use some statistic to capture the central tendency of each variable. And given how much the mean has been stressed to this point as the best overall index of central tendency, you conclude that you'll start testing your hunch by calculating the mean for each sample. Your findings are as follows (see Table 6.2):

Thus, we're pretty much looking at a difference of 89 versus 87. In most grading scales, these are both B+ grades. Well, what of your hunch? Have you convinced yourself that students who choose to take the class early in the morning are better statistics students than those who take it in the afternoon? Based on this difference, would you be confident enough to go on record saying that early-morning statistics students are academically superior to afternoon statistics students in general?

The answer here is "probably not"—with the reason being as follows: The difference between these means is just not that big. Concurrently, the sizes of the samples are not that big. These data don't scream out "Look! These two groups obviously differ in terms of their academic performance!" In fact, the data barely eke out this point.

But to play devil's advocate, on the other hand, we simply don't know. Based on the information presented thus far, we have no way of knowing if the pattern found in the samples reflects a real difference between the means at the population level. Here, the *population level* would refer to all the students who take statistics at 8:00 a.m. versus all the students who take statistics at 2:00 p.m. (you can see that sometimes the *population level* is really a hypothetical concept...).

As we'll see in the next several chapters, inferential statistics allow us to make these kinds of inferences—whether some pattern found in some samples reflects how things likely are at the population level.

The reasoning involved in inferential statistics is actually highly counterintuitive—and is premised on several abstract concepts. This chapter is dedicated to introducing these abstract concepts that comprise the reasoning included in inferential statistics.

THE BASIC ELEMENTS OF INFERENTIAL STATISTICS

Inferential statistics are mostly premised on the concept of probability. This is because if you do make an inference that some pattern in a sample likely reflects a pattern in the population, you've got that word *likely* in there—you are, in fact, never making a hard-and-fast claim. Rather, with inferential statistics, the best you can ever do is to show that some effect *likely* reflects how things are at the population level. For this reason (as you'll see in more detail in the upcoming chapters), statisticians never *prove* anything—thereby making *prove* something of a dirty word in the world of statistics! This, by the way, is not a bad point to keep in mind when examining how people in all kinds of areas present information. Being wary of any findings that claim to *prove* any point is usually a healthy form of skepticism.

PROBABILITY IN INFERENTIAL STATISTICS

We need to have some basic understanding of probability to understand inferential statistics—but don't worry. The level of understanding of probability needed to comprehend inferential statistics is actually pretty basic. For our purposes, probability can be defined as the *expected relative frequency of some outcome*. In other words, how likely would you expect some outcome to be? How probable is some particular outcome?

The simplest example to think about may well be a coin flip. If you have a fair (unbiased) coin, what are the odds of getting a head? Simple: Half the time you'll get a head—expressed as *p* (i.e., probability), that's .5. (Probabilities are expressed simply as decimals—with .0 meaning "no probability," 1.0 being "a definite probability—100%"—and numbers in between corresponding to intermediary levels of probability (e.g., p = .43 means that some outcome has a .43 or 43% chance of happening).

Thus, the odds (or probability) of getting a head on one flip is .5; the probability of getting a tail is also .5.

Probability is often expressed as follows: p(.5); meaning that the probability (of whatever the event is) is .5 (or is likely to happen, in this case, 50% of the time).

PROBABILITY AS THE EXPECTED RELATIVE FREQUENCY OF SOME OUTCOME

One way to define probability is to think of it as the *expected relative frequency of some outcome*. How often would we expect a certain outcome to occur?

With this conception of probability, we can think about how often an event is likely to happen out of a number of trials or times. Thus, while the probability of getting a head on a single coin flip is .5, we can also think about the probability of, for instance, getting one head if we flip a coin twice.

To address this mildly more complex form of probability, we'll need to think about a *probability distribution*—which will give us a sense of how likely (or expected) several possible outcomes are. And, as you'll see, analyzing probability distributions ends up being one of the primary activities of people who use statistics in the behavioral sciences.

CREATING A PROBABILITY DISTRIBUTION

Most probability distributions that behavioral scientists use are existing mathematical functions that have already been determined and laid out by mathematicians who study probability. As you'll see in subsequent chapters, these include the *normal* distribution, the *t* distribution, the *F* distribution, and more! For purposes of utilizing statistics in the behavioral sciences, you don't need to know how to create these distributions—they're laid out already and are included in the appendices in this book. However, to get a sense of where such distributions come from, it's useful to go through the steps of creating a simple probability distribution from scratch.

As an example, let's consider the situation in which we want to understand the probability distribution corresponding to getting one head on two coin flips. To understand how to create this distribution, we'll need to unleash a few basic concepts in probability.

To start, consider the following (see Table 6.3):

Table 6.3: Probabilities Associated with Numbers of Heads Likely on Two Coin Flips

Flip #1	Flip #2	Probability of Flips 1 and 2 happening jointly
Head (p = .5)	Head (p = .5)	.25
Head (p = .5)	Tail (p = .5)	.25
Tail (p = .5)	Head (p = .5)	.25
Tail (p = .5)	Tail (p = .5)	.25
		$\Sigma = 1.00$

Sorry if this table seems a bit dull. That's right, on the surface, not much is happening here!

One thing you'll notice is that the probability of either a tail or a head on each flip is .5. That's always true! And each flip is *independent*. In other words, no matter what happened the last thousand-or-so times I flipped a coin, the odds of a head on any particular flip is exactly .5. What happens now is *not* contingent on what happened in the past.

As something of an important side note, consider the *gambler's fallacy*—which is the tendency to think that the probability of some independent outcome depends on what happened in the past. For instance, imagine Kelly—she's very nice, but not a very bright gambler. So here she is in Vegas playing roulette and she just lost betting red (over black) three times in row. "Aha!" thinks Kelly. Since the last three times turned out red, I'm going to bet $1,000 on black (reasoning, erroneously, that black is now more likely than it was in the past because it follows three red outcomes). You know the rest—Kelly loses it all and ends up not being able to pay her hotel bill—things go down dramatically from there!

The short version: The probability of each individual event is (generally) not contingent on what has happened in the past. The probability distribution we are creating here follows this algorithm. Thus, the probability of either a head or a tail on Flip #2 is always exactly .5; it is *not* contingent on the outcome of Flip 1 (and yes, if you think about it, there are some important life lessons that follow from this idea!).

Additionally, you'll note that the probability of each joint outcome (i.e., the probability of X for Flip #1 and Y for Flip #2) is always .25. That's because the probability of one event *and* another event is calculated simply as follows:

$P(X \text{ and } Y) = P(X) * P(Y)$. So, with each of our examples in Table 6.3, we're looking at .5 *. 5, or .25.

With probability, then, the term *and* leads us to multiplication—and leads to a product that is smaller than either of the individual elements! This is because the probability of having to get one outcome *and* having to get another outcome must be smaller than the probability of getting either of the individual outcomes alone. The probability of getting two heads on two flips is, put another way, half the probability of getting one head on one flip (.5 * .5).

On the other hand, in probability, the word *or* is a tipoff for adding. So suppose we wanted to know the probability of getting, on a single flip, a tail **or** a head. Well, that sort of has to happen, now, doesn't it? Mathematically, that'll correspond to $P(\text{Tail} = .5) + P(\text{Head} = .5)$, which equals 1.0 (or 100%).

You'll see that if the four rows in Table 6.3 comprise all possible outcomes, then the total sum of all the probabilities should be 1.0—and this is the case. So if you flip a coin twice, all the possible outcomes are demarcated in Table 6.3.

Now let's put the distribution together, and you'll see that things get a smidge more interesting. Figure 6.1 is a probability distribution for the working example. Note a few things about this figure that reflect probability distributions in general.

1. The X-axis includes all possible values of the X variable.
2. The Y-axis includes all possible probabilities (from 0 to the highest probability in the figure, which is .5 in this case).
3. The probabilities are demarcated by either bars (as in a histogram) or lines (as in a frequency polygon).

Importantly, you'll see a strong connection between a probability distribution and a frequency distribution (per chapter 2). A probability distribution is a distribution of possibilities. It's a mathematically derived function regarding *how likely* different values are expected to occur. On the other hand, a frequency distribution is a representation of reality. It is a distribution of *how frequently* each value in a distribution of real scores *actually* occurs. Other than this important distinction between possibilities and reality, frequency distributions and probability distributions have remarkable conceptual overlap. But, of course, the distinction between what's real and what's possible is no small detail…

The X-axis in Figure 6.1 represents possible X values. In this case, it refers to how many heads one might get if he or she flips a coin twice. All possible values for this variable include: 0 heads, 1 head, and 2 heads.

The Y-axis represents the probability of each value of X, ranging from 0 to .5 (but, as you can see, we can make it from .25 to .5—or perhaps from 0 to 1.0—depending on our presentational purposes).

To interpret our probability distribution, we'll simply say that the probability of getting two heads on two flips is .25 (it'll happen 25% of the time), the probability of getting one head is .5 (it'll happen 50% of the time), and the probability of getting two tails is .25 (it'll happen 25% of the time).

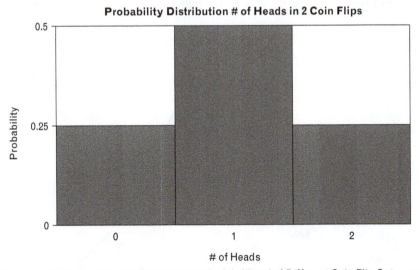

FIGURE 6.1: Probability Distribution Representing the Likelihood of Different Coin Flip Outcomes (Number of Heads Occurring in Two Flips).

How is it that P(1 head) = .5? The answer is reflected in the fact that two of the outcomes in Table 6.1 will lead to this result. These are: (a) getting one head and then one tail, and (b) getting one tail and then one head. Each of these possible outcomes has a probability of .25. But to get one head in two flips, you need to **either** get a *head and then a tail* **or** get a *tail and then a head*. Recall that in probability, the term *or* is a tipoff for addition. Here we'll add the probabilities: .25 +.25 = .5.

THE NORMAL DISTRIBUTION

The cat's meow of probability distributions is the normal distribution (see Figure 6.2). This distribution, discovered by the German mathematician Friedrich Gauss (it's also called the *Gaussian Distribution*) is a special probability distribution that encapsulates how an extraordinarily large number of variables in the natural world are distributed.

Like all probability distributions, including the one that we created regarding the coin flips earlier in this chapter, the normal distribution is a mathematically created distribution reflecting how probable different values of some variable are—or how likely different values are to occur. In the behavioral sciences (as in the physical sciences, by the way), an exceptional number of variables end up as normally distributed. As some quick examples, these include major personality variables (e.g., how open-minded versus closed-minded people are), rates of responding to stimuli in cognitively oriented research, scores on measures of health psychology (such as how Type A a person is), and on and on. Most psychological variables tend to be normally distributed—that is, they tend to, at least roughly, follow the pattern of a normal distribution.

The normal distribution is so special this way due to various qualities of this kind of distribution. First off, you'll notice that the distribution is symmetrical. That essentially means that the pattern of scores above the mean of a normally distributed variable is a mirror image of the pattern of scores that fall below the mean for this same variable. It's also important to note that the normal distribution peaks at the middle (typically reflecting the mean of the variable). This

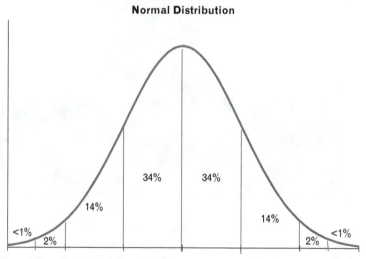

FIGURE 6.2: Normal Distribution with Standard Deviation Sections Demarcated.

Normal Distribution

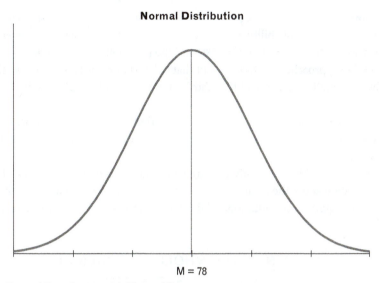

M = 78

FIGURE 6.3: Normal Distribution with Mean of 78.

essentially means that the average score is the most likely score to be randomly selected from the distribution.

Let's analyze this idea a bit. The average score is the most likely score for all normally distributed variables. That essentially means that if you were going to blindly guess someone's score on a variable, typically the mean is the best guess (as you likely remember from our earlier chapter on regression). Suppose, then, that test scores for the first statistics exam were normally distributed—and the mean was 78. A probability distribution reflecting this variable would have 78 as the mean, which would correspond to the highest peak in the distribution, and scores higher and lower than 78 would become increasingly less common as they approach the tails of the distribution (see Figure 6.3).

Just as our homemade coin flip distribution has known probabilities for all the different values (based on its having been created mathematically), the probabilities associated with different values of the normal distribution are also known. With a normal distribution, in addition to talking about how probable any particular value is, we'll also often talk about how probable entire sections of the distribution are. For instance, we can talk about how probable it is to get a score above the mean. In this case, as half the scores are above the mean—and it's a symmetrical distribution—the answer is .5, or 50%.

You'll discover that the probabilities of other sections of the normal distribution are known as well. One way to easily think about this concept pertains to seeing the normal distribution in terms of z-scores (see Figure 6.4). Given that the probabilities of the different sections of the normal distribution are known, it's actually quite useful to think of the normal distribution as a z-score distribution. And, in fact, we can always convert a normal distribution that is framed in terms of raw scores to a z-score distribution (as we'll see later in this chapter).

With a normal distribution framed as z-scores, the probabilities of getting a score in specific sections associated with whole-number z-scores are known (see Figure 6.4). Specifically, as you can see in Figure 6.4, the probability of getting a score that is between the mean and one standard deviation above the mean is .34; the probability of getting between 1 and 2 standard deviations above the mean is .14; the probability of getting between 2 and 3 standard deviations above the mean is .2; the probability of getting a score greater than 3 standard deviations above the mean is *itty bitty* (that is, it's less than 1%, and the probability of scores drops off as the tail of the distribution approaches the X-axis—but that tail never touches the X-axis, so the tail goes on infinitely. But functionally, 50% of the distribution (34% + 14% + 2% (- *itty bitty*)) is above the mean.

The probabilities (which, as you see, can be converted to percentages) associated with getting scores less than the mean, relative to whole z-scores, are a mirror image of the pattern found above the mean.

Note that at this point, we're only dealing with whole z-scores (such as 1, which means "1 standard deviation above the mean"). At some point soon, we'll deal with non-whole z-scores (e.g., 1.5), which requires some additional skills that we'll work on later in this chapter.

DEALING WITH WHOLE Z-SCORES IN A NORMAL DISTRIBUTION

Suppose the mean GPA at your university is 2.5 and the standard deviation is .5 (see Figure 6.4).

Note that in Figure 6.4, each standard deviation point corresponds to a particular raw value and a particular z value. For instance, two standard deviations below the mean corresponds to a raw value of 1.5 and z of –2. As you likely recall from our chapter on z-scores, these are one-and-the-same. 1.5 simply is the person's GPA as a raw score—and –2 is the same GPA represented as a z-score (here meaning "two standard deviations below the mean").

Let's think about this score of 1.5. If your GPA is 1.5, you're (no offense!) not doing all that great (of course, you're young yet and have plenty of time to turn things around!). Based on the percentages in Figure 6.2, you'll see that in this case, 16% of people in the population scored lower than you—and 84% scored higher. We can make this inference simply by adding the percentage of the distribution below a particular score and then, conversely, adding the percentage of the distribution above a particular score.

Standard Deviations and Z-scores

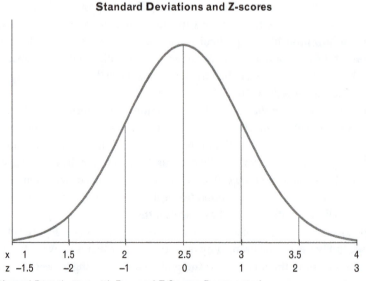

x	1	1.5	2	2.5	3	3.5	4
z	–1.5	–2	–1	0	1	2	3

FIGURE 6.4: Normal Distribution with Raw and Z Scores Demarcated.

Let's try another. Suppose you're now in a better place, and your GPA is 3.5. Using Figure 6.2, we can conclude that 98% of people in the population scored lower than you and 2% scored higher. Again, to arrive at these numbers, we simply come up with the sums of the sections of the distribution that correspond to the particular question of interest. In this case, if the question of interest is "What percentage of the scores are above your score?" we see that above a GPA with a z-score of 2 (which corresponds to a raw score of 3.5) is 2% + *itty bitty*, which equals 2%.

To address the question of "What percentage of scores are below your particular score (of 3.5)?" we sum all the percentages in the normal distribution that are below that point of a z-score of 2; you'll see based on Figure 6.2 that this comes to 98%.

You might also be asked the converse kind of question, which goes something like the following:

> *The Mean GPA in a population is 2.5, and the population standard deviation is .5. Given this infor-mation, suppose that we know that 16% of people in the population scored higher than Joe did. What is Joe's raw GPA score? (Refer to Figure 6.4 to determine your answer.)*

Here, we're given percentage-based information and we're asked to come up with Joe's score based on this information. OK. So let's look at Figure 6.2. What point on the X-axis corresponds to the value at which 16% of the scores are above it? Well, if we're at a Z of 1 (i.e., a raw score of 3.0), we have 14% of scores between that score and the next standard deviation; then there are 2% of the scores above that. So that point of the distribution, with a Z of 1, corresponds to the point at which 16% of the scores are above in a normal distribution.

To convert that z-score of 1 to a raw score, we can simply use Figure 6.2 and see that a z of 1 corresponds to a raw score of 3.0.

Alternatively (anticipating our next section), we can use our old z-score formulas from chapter 3 to help inform this process. To convert a z-score to a raw score (knowing the mean and the standard deviation), we do as follows: $X = Z(SD) + M = 1(.5) + 2.5 = 3.0$.

Similarly, in working with a z-version of a normal distribution of scores, we may need to convert a raw score to a z-score. For instance, you may be asked the following:

> *The Mean GPA in a population is 2.5, and the population standard deviation is .5. Given this infor-mation, suppose that we know that Frankie's GPA in raw-score units is 2.0. What is Frankie's GPA represented as a z-score?*

Here, we simply use our trusty old formula for z: $z = (X-M)/SD$. So in this case, $z = \dfrac{2.0 - 2.5}{.5} = -1$.

This makes sense, as Frankie's z-score is one standard deviation below the mean and that's exactly how we interpret the idea of a z-score of -1.0.

WORKING WITH A NORMAL DISTRIBUTION WITH Z-SCORES THAT ARE NOT WHOLE NUMBERS

So far, we've dealt with some relatively straightforward scenarios. Figure 6.4 allows us to inter-pret percentages of scores above or below a particular score in a distribution, assuming that the particular score corresponds to a z-score that is a round number (e.g., $z = -2$; $z = 1$; etc.). The real world is not that clean.

Suppose that Susan's GPA corresponds to a z-score of 1.5. And we're asked to compute the percentage of scores above or below Susan's score. Can we do this simply with the information in Figure 6.2? No. Figure 6.4 only has information that pertains to whole z-scores. 1.5 is not a whole number.

What should we do? Should we freak out? Start crying? No need! When Gauss discovered the details of the normal distribution, he came up with a formula to derive the specific probabilities of scores across the entire X-axis—regardless of whether or not they correspond to whole numbers. Thank you, Gauss!

These days, we have a special table called a *Z-Score Table* that allows us to derive information needed when scores are not whole numbers (See Appendix A). Simply put, the z-score table is awesome! Once you understand how to use it, given the appropriate information (e.g., the raw mean and standard deviation of a distribution and the fact that the distribution is normally distributed), you can make the kinds of inferences that we have been making (e.g,. percentage of score above a particular raw score) for scores with z-scores that are not necessarily whole numbers.

Let's go back to Susan's example with a z-score of 1.5. Suppose that for this example, we're asked for the following:

A. What is Susan's raw score?
B. What percentage of people scored below Susan?
C. What percentage of people scored above Susan?

Here's how we'd address these in turn:

A. What is Susan's raw score?

Here, we'd simply use the Z-to-X conversion formula: $X = Z(SD) + M$
$$= 1.5(.5) + 2.5 = 3.25$$

B. What percentage of people scored below Susan?

Here, we need to develop a new skill. We can't rely on Figure 6.2 (or a comparable figure) any more. We'll now refer to our z-table (See Appendix A). Note that the table has two columns: Z and *% Mean to Z*. That first column considers a particular z-score of interest (e.g., 1.5). The second column provides the percentage of z-scores that is between that Z and the mean of the distribution (that's what's meant by *% Mean to Z*). So if we look up 1.5, we'll see the following:

Z	% Mean to Z
1.5	43.32

Importantly, note that 43.32 is a percentage (43.32%). Thus, for a z-score of 1.5, 43.32% of the scores are *between that score and the mean of the distribution*. When dealing with this kind of problem, it's useful to create a brand-new normal distribution, precisely for use with this specific problem. We've done so in Figure 6.5.

So remember, we're trying to figure out the percentage of people who scored below Susan. We will find it useful to label parts of the normal distribution that we just made. In doing so, it's useful to divide the distribution into three sections, A, B, and C (see Figure 6.6). Here's a crucial tip: **The % Mean to z from the z Table *always* will correspond to section B when we divide**

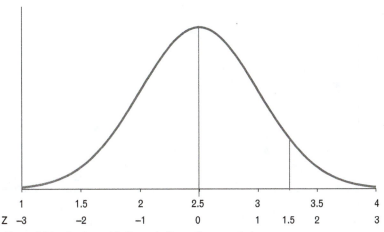

	1	1.5	2	2.5	3	3.5	4
Z	−3	−2	−1	0	1	1.5 2	3

FIGURE 6.5: Normal Distribution with Susan's Score Demarcated.

things up this way. That will be true every time, whether our z-score is negative or positive in sign. If we capitalize on this fact, this process will be easy.

The 43.32% we got from the table corresponds to Section B (in Figure 6.6)—which is, literally, the percentage of scores in the normal distribution between the particular z-score and the mean. Trick question right about…now: Is the answer to the question here (*what percentage of scores are below Susan's score*) 43.32?

No.

The answer is *no* because the question implies "the entire distribution"—as in "what percentage of scores *in the entire distribution* are below Susan's score?" And 43.32% only refers to the percentage that is between Susan's score and the mean. Sure, these scores are all below Susan's score, but there's an entire half of the distribution (Section A in Figure 6.6) that is lower still! So to compute the entire percentage of scores below Susan's, we'll add the entire percentage in Section A (50%) to 43.32% (see Figure 6.7) to get 93.32%.

C. Finally, we're asked for *the percentage of scores above Susan's score*. Here, we can use very simple math. If we know that 93.32% scored below Susan, this means that only the folks in Section C (which corresponds to scores above Susan's score) should be counted. If the entire distribution is 100% (and it is), then Section C = 100%–93.32% = 6.68%.

You'll note that the Z-Score Table only includes positive numbers. This is because the normal distribution is symmetrical. Thus, the percentages of scores for negative z-scores will be identical to the percentages of scores for positive z-scores. If 43.32% of scores are between a z of 1.5 and the mean, then that same percentage (43.32%) is between a z of −.1.5 and the mean (see Figure 6.8).

Let's try one more example with a score that is below the mean. Suppose that Gustav has a GPA of 1.44. Using the X-to-Z formula, $Z = \dfrac{X - M}{SD} = \dfrac{1.44 - 2.5}{.5} = -2.12$.

    A.   What percentage of scores is above Gustav's score?
    B.   What percentage of scores is below Gustav's score?

First, it's helpful to draw a brand-new normal distribution for this problem. We can label two points, the mean and Gustav's score (see Figure 6.9). In doing so, we should label sections A, B,

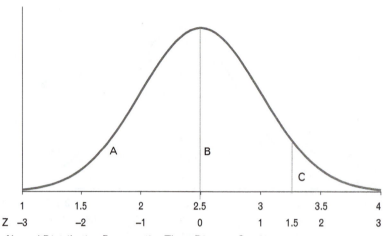

FIGURE 6.6: Normal Distribution Demarcating Three Discrete Sections.

and C. Here, you'll see that Section B is still the section between the particular score of interest and the mean—it just now so happens that the particular score of interest is to the left of the mean (it's a relatively *low* score).

First, we're asked the percentage of scores that are above Gustav's score (see Figure 6.10). In terms of Figure 6.10, that's Sections B and C (now shaded to be clear). Next, we now need to know what percentage of the entire distribution is encompassed in Sections B and C. Section C is easy; it's the section above the mean—it's half of this symmetrical, normal distribution: 50%. But how do we figure out Section B? Simple—just as we did in the prior example. We'll use the table—by looking up the relevant z-score. Importantly, note that Gustav's z-score is negative—and there are no negatives in the table—but if we look up the same score as a positive number,

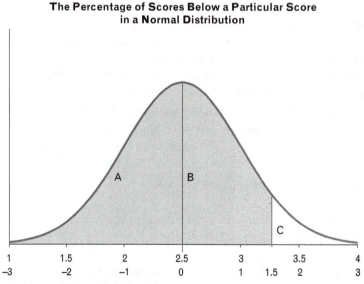

FIGURE 6.7: Shaded Area of Normal Distribution.

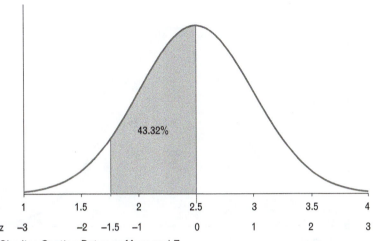

FIGURE 6.8: Shading Section Between Mean and Z.

the percentage between that score and the mean will be identical to what it would be for the positive number. Gustav's z-score is -2.12. So let's look up the % Mean to z for a z-score of 2.12:

Z   %Mean to Z
2.12   48.30

Remember, the "% Mean to z" always corresponds to Section B. So 48.30% of the distribution is between Gustav's score and the mean. Is the answer to the big question here 48.30%? No!

Remember, we're being asked for the % of scores above Gustav's score. That's all of Section C *and* all of Section B. Or 50% + 48.30% = 98.30%. Gustav has some room for improvement!

Finally, we're asked the percentage of scores that are below Gustav's score. Referring to Figure 6.10, we'll see that this corresponds to Section A. If we know that the sum of Sections B and C is 98.30%, then to compute Section A, we'll simply do 100%–98.30% = 1.7%.

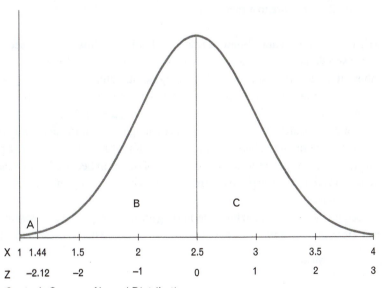

FIGURE 6.9: Gustav's Score on Normal Distribution.

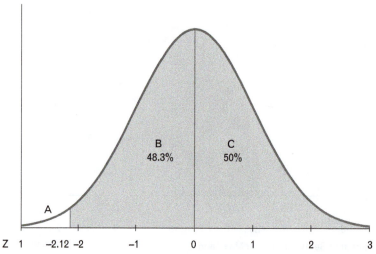

FIGURE 6.10: Percentage of Scores that are Above Gustav's Score.

Importantly, for these kinds of problems, you'll see that there is not really a single equation that will allow you to answer questions. Each problem will be unique—and will require you to really understand the concepts and to really use the z-table accurately. For this reason, several practice problems are given so that you get the hang of it. As a tip, make sure to **always** draw a new normal distribution for each such problem and **always** label Sections, A, B, and C, as we have here.

A final kind of problem we may need to work on pertains to the situation in which we are given percentage-based information and asked to derive a particular score (z and/or raw). To consider this kind of problem, let's use the example of Nick. 75% of students in the population have a GPA higher than Nick's GPA.

To figure out this kind of problem, we'll need to:

A. Figure out Nick's z-score; and
B. Convert Nick's z-score to a raw score

First, we'll need to draw a brand-new normal distribution for this problem (see Figure 6.11). In doing so, we should label the mean and Nick's score. Where is Nick's score? Well, if 75% of scores are above it, it's less than the mean. In placing it, estimate, but don't worry about getting it in exactly the right spot. All that matters is that it's on the correct (left) side of the mean given the problem. After we label Nick's score, we'll label Sections A, B, and C.

Now things are a bit different than before. Instead of figuring out the percentages based on a score, we're figuring out the score based on percentages. It's actually a less intensive process. The first thing we need to know pertains to the percentage of scores in Section B. The reason Section B matters so much is that it corresponds to the way the table is organized—remember–% Mean to Z—and that's always Section B.

Now let's look up the percentage in the table, finding the percentage that is closest to the percentage of interest. Here, our percentage of interest is 25%. So let's see what's closest to that in the table:

Z	% Mean to Z
.67	24.86%
.68	25.17%

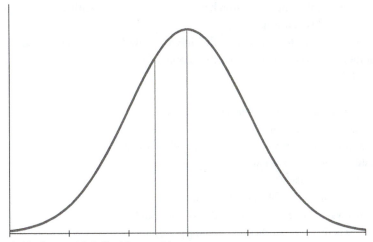

FIGURE 6.11: Nick's Score with 75% of Scores Above.

As we suspected, our exact percentage of interest (25%) is not in the table. But one just above it (25.17%) and one just below it (24.86%) are included. Here, we'll simply choose the z corresponding to the one that is closest to the percentage of interest. (In rare cases in which the two percentages are equal, you typically can choose either z-score). In this case, the percentage corresponding to a z of .67 is closest (24.86 is closer to 25 than is 25.17). So we'll go with that.

One final thing to consider: Is Nick's score above the mean or below the mean? If it's above the mean, it will be positive, and if it's below the mean, it will be negative. Recall that the z table will not provide negative numbers—it's an optimist, always positive! Thus, if there's a negative sign to be given out, you'll have to make that determination—and you should do it based on the information at hand (easily identifiable in Figure 6.11). Nick's z-score, then, is negative (as his score is below the mean); his z-score therefore is −.67.

Our final step here is to compute that z-score into a raw score (X). $X = Z(SD) + M = -.67(.5) + 2.5 = 1.33$.

Again, as with the prior examples, note that there is not a single equation to get these kinds of problems right. You simply must understand the concepts and work through several problems, creating a well-labeled normal distribution each time.

A REAL RESEARCH EXAMPLE

Probability and the normal distribution emerge in research in several different ways. Personality psychologist Daniel Nettle (2006) is interested in why the basic trait dimensions of human personality—extraversion, neuroticism, openness, agreeableness, and conscientiousness (collectively known as *The Big Five*)—are normally distributed when studied in large populations.

Let's consider what that means for one such trait: Neuroticism (or emotional instability). People vary in terms of how generally neurotic they are—some of us are solid like rocks, with nothing able to shake our emotional core, while others are highly neurotic—constantly experiencing negative moods and emotional fluctuations. And most of us are somewhere in between. Research on this trait dimension has found that it consistently comes out in a way that approaches a normal distribution.

Nettle (2006) is interested in why both high and low levels of neuroticism are adaptive (or beneficial for survival). He thinks that the adaptive benefits of low neuroticism are obvious, but writes (p. 626):

> A much more challenging issue, then, is finding any
> compensatory benefit to neuroticism. However, given the
> normal distribution observed in the human population, and
> the persistence of lineages demonstrably high in the trait,
> such a benefit seems likely.
> Studies in nonhuman animals, such as guppies (see the
> Evolution of Variation section), suggest that vigilance and
> wariness are both highly beneficial in avoiding predation
> and highly costly because they are quickly lost when predation
> pressure is absent. In ancestral environments, a level
> of neuroticism may have been necessary for avoidance of
> acute dangers. Anxiety, of which neuroticism can be considered
> a trait measure, enhances detection of threatening
> stimuli by speeding up the reaction to them, interpreting
> ambiguous stimuli as negative, and locking attention onto
> them (Mathews, Mackintosh, & Fulcher, 1997).

Clearly, the idea of the normal distribution is essential to Nettle's reasoning—a fact that has led to insights into why so many people (and guppies, apparently) demonstrate high levels of anxiety and emotional vigilance. The normally distributed nature of so many variables has led behavioral scientists to simply learn so much about the nature of behavior.

SUMMARY

Hypothesis testing, which tests whether some pattern found in a sample is likely to generalize to a broader population, is founded on some basic concepts. Statistics used for the behavioral sciences focus on probability and the normal distribution as foundational for understanding hypothesis testing. Probability corresponds to how likely some outcome is (it is represented by a decimal, with 0.00 corresponding to *no probability*, 1.00 corresponding to *100% certain*, and numbers in between representing intermediate probabilities). A *probability distribution* is a theoretical, mathematically derived distribution that presents information on how likely different values are expected to be in a distribution of scores. The *normal distribution* is perhaps the best-known and most useful probability distribution—and it's often used in the behavioral sciences as many behavioral variables are normally distributed. In thinking of a normal distribution as a z distribution, we can make many inferences about how likely scores are and how many scores would be expected to be above or below any particular score. These ideas will ultimately serve as the basis for the logic that underlies statistics hypothesis testing.

KEY TERMS

Hypothesis testing: Determining if some effect found in a sample is likely reflective of patterns in the population.

Inferential statistics: Statistics designed to allow us to infer whether some pattern found in a sample likely reflects a pattern found in the population; statistics designed to address whether statistical effects are beyond what would be expected by chance.

Probability: The expected relative frequency of some outcome.

Probability distribution: A distribution of possibilities; a mathematically derived function regarding how likely different values are expected to occur.

HOMEWORK SET A

1. Given the following probabilities, how likely is the event, in percentages?
    a. p(.47)
    b. p(.94)
    c. p(.06)

2. You buy bags of red and white M&Ms, each bag having equal numbers of red and white.
    a. You reach into the first bag without looking and grab an M&M. What is the probability that the M&M you grab will be red?
    b. You reach into the second bag without looking and grab an M&M. What is the probability that the M&M you grab will be red?
    c. You reach into the third bag without looking and grab an M&M. What is the probability that the M&M you grab will be red?
    d. You reach into a bag and grab an M&M. What is the probability that the M&M you grab will be red *or* white?
    e. You reach into one bag and grab an M&M, then into another bag and grab an M&M. What is the probability that you will get a red on the first grab *and* a red on the second grab?

3. Your score on a test is 1 standard deviation above the mean.
    a. What is your z-score?
    b. What percentage of the class scored higher than you?
    c. What percentage of the class scored lower than you?

4. The professor in your favorite class tells you that the mean for the latest test was 50 and the standard deviation was 5, and that your z-score on the quiz was 1.3.
    a. What was your raw score?
    b. What percentage of the class scored lower than you?
    c. What percentage of the class scored higher than you?

5. Your friend, Gabe, is in your favorite class, but is not as enthusiastic about the class as you are. He had a z-score of –1.2 on the test that had a mean of 50 and a standard deviation of 5.
    a. What was Gabe's raw score?
    b. What percentage of the class scored lower than Gabe?
    c. What percentage of the class scored higher than Gabe?

6. The professor for your least favorite class tells you that the mean for the latest test was 75, the standard deviation was 8, and your score was 62.
    a. What was your z-score?
    b. What percentage of the class scored lower than you?
    c. What percentage of the class scored higher than you?

7. Gabe loves your least favorite class, and scored 90 on the test, with a mean of 75 and a standard deviation of 8.
    a. What was Gabe's z-score?
    b. What percentage of the class scored lower than Gabe?
    c. What percentage of the class scored higher than Gabe?

8. You initially struggled in one of your classes, and on the first test, 67% of the class scored higher than you. You focused your energies, studied hard, and scored higher than 82% of the class on the next class. Both tests had a mean of 70 and a standard deviation of 4.
   a. What was your z-score on the first test?
   b. What was your raw score on the first test?
   c. What was your z-score on the second test?
   d. What was your raw score on the second test?

HOMEWORK SET B

1. Given the following probabilities, how likely is the event, in percentages?
   a. p(.81)
   b. p(.23)
   c. p(.01)
2. Your friend has a small Chihuahua that is going to have puppies. Being so small, this Chihuahua will likely only have 3 puppies.
   a. What is the probability that the first puppy born will be a boy?
   b. What is the probability that the second puppy born will be a girl?
   c. What is the probability that the third puppy will be a boy?
   d. What is the probability that the first puppy will be a boy, the second puppy will be a girl, and the third puppy will be a boy?
   e. What is the probability that all three puppies will be girls?
3. You receive the results of an aptitude test, and learn that in the section involving engineering concepts, you got a z-score of 1.6. The mean was 110, and the standard deviation was 8.
   a. What was your raw score?
   b. What percentage of the test-takers scored lower than you?
   c. What percentage of the test-takers scored higher than you?
4. In the section regarding electronics knowledge of the aptitude test, you got a z-score of − .69. The mean was 85 and the standard deviation was 4.
   a. What was your raw score?
   b. What percentage of the test-takers scored lower than you?
   c. What percentage of the test-takers scored higher than you?
5. In the creative writing section of the aptitude test, you scored 56. The mean was 60 and the standard deviation was 3.
   a. What was your z-score?
   b. What percentage of the test-takers scored lower than you?
   c. What percentage of the test-takers scored higher than you?
6. In the mathematics section of the aptitude test, you scored 115. The mean was 100 and the standard deviation was 10.
   a. What was your z-score?
   b. What percentage of the test-takers scored lower than you?
   c. What percentage of the test-takers scored higher than you?

7. You are involved in tutoring elementary school kids in mathematics. The child you are currently tutoring scored lower than 60% of his class on the first test. After three months of tutoring, he is retested, and scores higher than 80% of his class. The tests had a mean of 60 and a standard deviation of 5.

    a. What was his z-score on the first test?
    b. What was his raw score on the first test?
    c. What was his z-score on the second test?
    d. What was his raw score on the second test?

HOMEWORK SET A ANSWERS

1. a. 47%
    b. 94%
    c. 6%
2. a. p(.5) or 50%
    b. p(.5) or 50%
    c. p(.5) or 50%
    d. p(.5) + p(.5) = 1 or 100%
    e. (.5) * (.5) = .25 or 25%
3. a. z = 1
    b. 16%
    c. 84%
4. a. X = Z(SD) + M
        X = 1.3(5) + 50
        X = 56.5 = your raw score
    b. 50 + 40.32 = 90.32% of the class scored lower than you
    c. 100–90.32 = 9.68% of the class scored higher than you

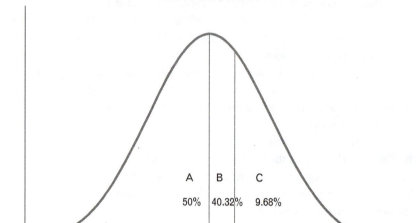

Homework Set A #4

Z = 1.3

FIGURE 6.12: Homework Set A #4.

5. a.   X = Z(SD) + M
         X = −1.2(5) + 50
         X = 44 = Gabe's raw score
    b.   50–38.49 = 11.51% of the class scored lower than Gabe
    c.   100–11.51 = 88.49% of the class scored higher than Gabe

Homework Set A #5

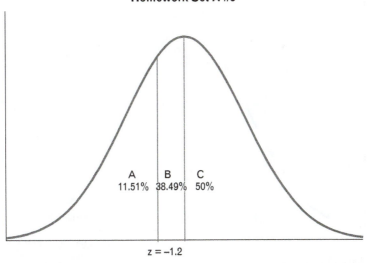

z = −1.2

FIGURE 6.13: Homework Set A #5.

6. a.   Z = (X–M)/SD
         Z = (62–75)/8
         Z = −1.63
    b.   50–44.84 = 5.16% scored lower than you
    c.   50 + 44.84 = 94.84% of the class scored higher than you

Homework Set A #6

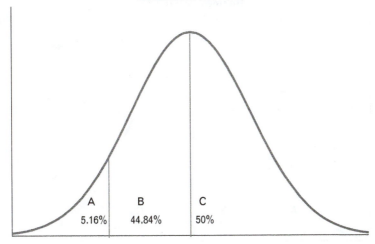

z = −1.63

FIGURE 6.14: Homework Set A #6.

7. a. $Z = (X-M)/SD$
        $Z = (90-75)/8$
        $Z = 1.88$
    b. $50 + 46.99 = 96.99\%$ of the class scored lower than Gabe
    c. $100-96.99 = 3.01\%$ of the class scored higher than Gabe

Homework Set A #7

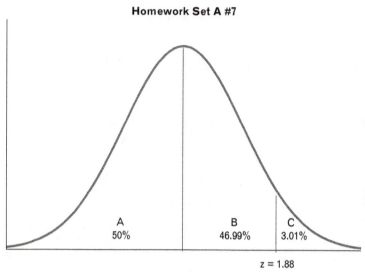

z = 1.88

FIGURE 6.15: Homework Set A #7.

8. a.   Your z-score on the first test is $-.44$ (17.00 on the % Mean to Z table)
    b. $X = Z(SD) + M$
        $X = -.44(4) + 70 = 68.24 =$ Your raw score on the first test
    c.   Your z-score on the second test was .92 (32.12 on the % Mean to Z table)
    d. $X = Z(SD) + M$
        $X = .92(4) + 70 = 73.68 =$ Your raw score on the second test

Homework Set A #8

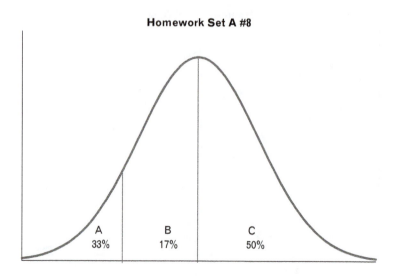

Your score on the first test

FIGURE 6.16: Homework Set A #8.

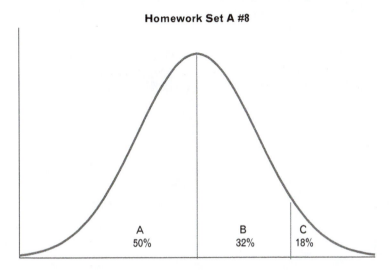

FIGURE 6.17: Homework Set A #8.

REFERENCES

Mathews, A., Mackintosh, B., & Fulcher, E. P. (1997). Cognitive biases in anxiety and attention to threat. *Trends in Cognitive Sciences, 1,* 340–345.

Nettle, D. (2006). The evolution of personality variation and humans and other animals. *The American Psychologist, 6,* 621–631.

INTRODUCTION TO HYPOTHESIS TESTING

The reasoning of hypothesis testing is both abstract and unique. For this reason, the process and the rationale underlying the process are described slowly—across several chapters (chapters 6–9, to be exact). This chapter is dedicated to the fundamentals of the process—the basic idea is delineated here.

Suppose that I wanted to test if one teaching method of statistics is superior to another method. Specifically, suppose I were interested in whether students who are assigned homework and textbook reading perform significantly better than other students on the final examination in some statistics class.

Suppose that the students in the two classes were given the same final exams, and the scores were as follows:

Two questions. First, based on the information presented in Table 7.1, who did better? Answer—simple: The group that had both textbook reading *and* homework did better (as their final exam mean of 83.00 is higher than the mean for the other group (at 79.75)).

Now for the second—and more difficult—question: Did the group that had homework assigned do so much better on the exam that you're convinced, **based solely on these data**, that all statistics students around the world should be assigned homework? Are the data findings robust enough to allow you to feel confident that the pattern found in this sample (with the homework group scoring higher than the other group, on average) would likely replicate to the entire population of statistics students across the globe?

This second question *is* harder than the first, now, isn't it? Here are some possible thoughts:

- Yes. Since the average for the homework group is higher than the average for the other group, this is evidence that homework helps the learning of statistics in general, regardless of the sample.
- Maybe not. The average for the homework group (83.00) is only a little higher than the average for the other group (79.75)—these means are not different enough for us to confidently infer that homework helps the learning of statistics in general.

Table 7.1: Hypothetical Final Exam Scores for Two
Groups of Statistics Students

Student #	Textbook Reading Only	Textbook Reading and Homework
1	80	76
2	75	90
3	76	84
4	88	82
MEAN	79.75	83.00

- It would help if we computed the standard deviation—as we could then see how different the means are from one another in light of the amount that scores tend to vary from one another more generally. Without the standard deviation, we are not in a position to make this kind of inference.
- Maybe we need to learn a new process by which to see if a pattern found in a sample is likely (based on probability) to generalize to the population of interest.

These are all reasonable thoughts when faced with a situation like this. In this chapter, we'll focus on elaborating the final point—that we need to know a specific process for making this kind of inference. And that specific process goes by the term *hypothesis testing*.

THE BASIC RATIONALE OF HYPOTHESIS TESTING

The example included in the prior section speaks to the kind of situation in which hypothesis testing is helpful. We use hypothesis testing to see if some pattern found in a sample is likely to characterize how things are at the population level. Here are some examples of situations in which the best answer could be determined via hypothesis testing:

- Joe notices that he does better on examinations in his morning classes than in his afternoon classes. He wonders if college students in general do better in morning classes.
- Gina notices that she's in a good mood for several days after visiting her cousins who live in Ohio. She wonders if spending time with close family members generally makes people happier.
- Ralph is a supervisor who tries to create a very warm environment for his department. His brother Alex, a supervisor for another company, takes the opposite approach—trying to assert his leadership and intimidate his employees. Ralph is curious whether these differing leadership styles have general effects on the productivity of workers—and, if so, he wonders which style leads to *more* productivity.
- Cindy has two hamsters and two hermit crabs. When she is feeling lonely, she finds herself playing with the hamsters more frequently than with the hermit crabs. She wonders if humans generally prefer furry pets to help improve their moods.

For each question here, you can imagine a study in which data are collected. For instance, in Cindy's case, we might have 100 people who are randomly selected to play with hermit crabs and another hundred who are randomly selected to play with hamsters. You could then give all the participants a mood scale and see the people in the hamster condition report more positive moods than people in the hermit-crab condition.

However, even if the moods of the people in the hamster condition are more positive, on average, than the hermit-crab participants, we still have the problem that we encountered with the different kinds of statistics classes in the prior example—how big does the effect have to be for us to infer that it probably generalizes to the broader population of interest?

UNDERSTANDING THE BROADER POPULATION OF INTEREST

The basic question of hypothesis testing is this: Is the effect found in some sample likely to generalize to the broader population of interest? Let's work with Cindy's soon-to-be-renowned *Hamster Hypothesis*. Her basic hypothesis is that playing with furry, cute little mammals improves mood. Let's expand this hypothesis a bit. A question that arises here pertains to **whom?** For whom does playing with hamster-like critters improve mood? Well, Cindy hasn't yet specified, but when pushed on this, she states that she thinks this should be true for **all people**. In other words, the hypothesis is that *for people in general*, playing with hamsters should improve mood.

In fact, while there are other relevant populations of interest in research, the implicit population of interest is, quite often, all people or people in general. That's an interesting feature of research—with lots of implications. In any case, one of the first steps in hypothesis testing is to specify the population of interest.

Now, of course, Cindy isn't about to study all of the 7 billion+ people in the world to examine the mood-related effects of hamsters. So she'll do what any good researcher is typically forced to do—she'll find a random sample of people for this study.

Briefly, what she'd do to test this hypothesis (in the simplest way) would be to find some mood scale with a known mean and standard deviation (based on a large population). She'd then have a sample of individuals play with a hamster for, say, 15 minutes. Following this, she'd test the mood of the people in that sample with the standardized mood scale—and she'd see if the mean for the sample is higher than the standard mean for this measure. If the mean *is*, in fact, higher for the sample who played with the hamsters, she would then engage in hypothesis testing to see if the mean for the sample is enough higher than the mean of the general population to allow her to infer that the average mood of people who play with hamsters is probably higher than the average mood of people in general.

This is basically what we're doing with hypothesis testing—seeing if a pattern found with some sample is likely reflective of a pattern found at the population level.

POPULATION VERSUS SAMPLE PARAMETERS

When we talk about *population versus sample parameters*, we are talking about symbols used to represent different basic statistics at the level of the sample versus the level of the population.

Table 7.2: Population versus Sample Parameters to Represent Mean, Variance, and Standard Deviation

	Population Parameter	Sample Parameter
Mean	μ	M
Variance	σ^2	SD^2
Standard Deviation	σ	SD

Note that μ is pronounced "MYOO" by English-speaking statisticians (the actual Greek pronunciation is apparently "MEH") and σ is pronounced "sigma"—it is the Greek lowercase version of the summation sign that we've run into time and again, with, of course, a completely different meaning!

The three basic statistics that we'll address here (that are relevant to simple hypothesis testing) correspond to the mean, the variance, and the standard deviation (see Table 7.2).

The only differences between the population parameters and their "sample parameter" counterparts is that the population parameters refer to means, variance, and standard deviation of a population, while the sample parameters refer to these statistics for a specific sample.

When we are articulating our hypotheses in the hypothesis-testing procedure, we specify our parameters in terms of population parameters—because we are ultimately interested in patterns at the level of the population of interest. For this reason, it's important to have different nomenclature (symbols) to reflect whether we are thinking about the level of a sample or the level of some broader population. As you'll see in chapter 8 and beyond, there actually end up being additional parameters for additional kinds of distributions that will be of interest with more advanced forms of hypothesis testing.

THE FIVE BASIC STEPS OF HYPOTHESIS TESTING

Whatever the form of hypothesis testing, there are five basic, universal steps of the process. And these five steps in hypothesis testing will, in the generic sense, characterize all forms of hypothesis testing in the domain of statistics. Generally, these steps are as follows:

1. **Articulate the *research* and *null* hypotheses**. Generally, the research hypothesis is the hypothesis that you, the researcher, think is right. The null hypothesis is the opposite of your research hypothesis.
2. **Describe the comparison distribution**. In hypothesis testing, you'll compare findings from some sample with a distribution representing something else—such as a population distribution for a general population. You need to accurately describe this comparison distribution and articulate its relevant parameters (i.e., mean, variance, and standard deviation).
3. **Determine the *cutoff score* and related *alpha region***. In hypothesis testing, we'll see if our score (or mean) from our sample is extreme enough on the comparison distribution to be unlikely to have come from that distribution. To make this case, we need to figure out the score on that comparison distribution that we will define as

extreme—corresponding to the *alpha region*—or the part of the distribution that is so probabilistically unlikely that we can reject the idea that our sample has a mean that's the same as the mean of the comparison distribution.

4. **Determine the score that best represents your sample and compare it with critical value.** If we're going to compare our sample with the comparison distribution, we'll need to get a specific, numerical score to use that best represents our sample.

5. **Comment on the Null Hypothesis/Determine if your sample is unlikely to come from the population represented by the comparison distribution.** As we'll see in a few pages (when we work out a real example), the comparison distribution represents the prediction of the null hypothesis—the hypothesis that assumes that your research hypothesis is dead wrong. Once you have figured out a formal "cutoff point" (in step 4), you can now see if your score that represents your sample is more extreme than that point—or not. If your score *is* more extreme than the cutoff score, you'll then *reject the null hypothesis* (thereby supporting the research hypothesis). Importantly, note that *rejecting the null hypothesis* is identical to *finding statistical significance* or *obtaining a significant finding.*

If, on the other hand, the score representing your sample is *not as extreme* as the cutoff score, you'll *fail to reject the null hypothesis*—meaning that you simply don't have any reason to believe that your research hypothesis is correct at this point. Importantly, your research hypothesis, in fact, may be correct at this point—but if you *fail to reject* the null hypothesis, you have not provided a strong case for your research hypothesis.

The Five Steps in Hypothesis Testing Spelled out with an Example. When students first run into the formal steps of hypothesis testing, there's usually something akin to mass confusion that runs through their minds! Seeing these steps applied to examples is really the key to understanding how it all works.

For our first example, we'll do the following: (a) we'll stick with Cindy's Hamster Hypothesis, as it's simple and fresh; and (b) we'll use an *N of 1* as our sample. That is, we'll have a single score represent our sample when we do our comparisons. Of course, if our goal is to best generalize to some broad population (such as the population of all people on earth!), the general rule is the larger the sample, the better. Yes, this is true! However, for pedagogical reasons (i.e., for the purpose of teaching this stuff), it's much better to start with examples in which N = 1. This is simply a matter of practicality—there are elaborate conceptual issues that emerge once we start talking about having a sample with an N > 1. For most students, the concepts here are complex enough—we don't need to add complexity to the basic hypothesis testing process! We will, in fact, devote an entire chapter to the complexities associated with hypothesis testing with a larger N. But for this chapter, just to master the concepts of basic hypothesis testing, we'll go with examples of N = 1.

In addressing the five steps of hypothesis testing, note that it's important to be able to address these in terms of appropriate statistical symbols as well as in words (to demonstrate an understanding of the concepts). As such, you'll see that when we work out this problem, we'll be using both methods of representing our ideas.

Here goes:

Cindy loves her hamster named Springtime—and she's convinced that playing with Springtime leaves her in a better mood than when she started. As a psychology major, and as a natural curious thinker, Cindy wonders if playing with hamsters (especially when they don't bite, pee, or run away!) has this same mood-improving effect on people in general. To test this hypothesis, she finds Zung's (1986) highly validated depression inventory—a scale that has been used to measure depression symptoms on thousands of adults for years. Across several studies using large samples of adults across the world, the mean of this scale has been estimated at 65.68 with a standard deviation of 15.65. This scale is a straightforward checklist of depression and anxiety-related items given to participants (they indicate if they have the symptom or not).

Cindy's younger brother Alex happens to be home from college during this time, and Cindy concludes that he'd be the perfect candidate to participate in her study. After all, Alex has been a guinea pig for Cindy's studies since he came home from the hospital after being born 21 years ago! As always, after a mild expression of skepticism, Alex agrees to participate.

Cindy takes Springtime out of the cage and asks Alex to play with her for 15 minutes. Alex does so happily. She then asks him to complete the scale. He scores a 42. (Note that with Zung's (1986) depression scale, lower scores reflect a more positive mood.) Now, Cindy is pretty smart—and she realizes some of the limitations of this study. She realizes that Alex may be biased in how he completes this scale. She also realizes that he took the scale only once—after handling Springtime—thereby not allowing her to assess any changes in his mood. She also realizes that this study has a single participant—her little brother! So the study is not perfect! As you'll see, improved research comes with larger samples—and we'll get into that in the next chapter. But for now, we'll stick with Cindy and her slightly imperfect study of the mood-affecting outcomes associated with hamster handling!

Two other things to note: First, it's important to realize that Cindy has a prediction *in a specific direction*. That is, she's not just predicting a change in mood as a function of hamster handling—she's specifically predicting an *improvement* in mood. Second, note that Cindy has to make a call regarding how conservative she wants her test to be (you'll see in step three, below, that we always have to make this call—before our study gets off the ground). Since Cindy's doing this study just for kicks, and realizes that it's already far from perfect, she decides to go with a standard (as opposed to especially stringent) level of conservatism (this point will, again, make more sense as we get to step 3).

1. **Articulate the *research* and *null* hypotheses**. Let's start in words. Cindy's research hypothesis is simple—she expects that people who have just handled hamsters will be in better moods than people in general. As is true with all hypotheses, this hypothesis is being stated at the population level.

Here's how we'll represent these ideas symbolically:

μ_1: This is the mean score of the *special* population—the one predicted to differ from the general population. In the current example, this specifically corresponds to the mean on Zung's (1986) mood scale for people who have just handled hamsters. Note that, given the meaning of population parameters, this theoretically refers to the entire population of all humans who've just handled hamsters.

μ_2: This refers to the mean score for the general population on Zung's (1986) mood scale. Note that the special population (represented by μ_1) is something of a subset of the general population (represented by μ_2); this is an artifact of simple hypothesis testing. When comparing means of different populations against one another head-to-head (as we will in later chapters), the special population is not a subset of the general population. But, for now, and for the next few chapters, to reduce superfluous complexities, we'll stick with instances in which the special population (represented by μ_1) is conceptually a subset of some general population (represented by μ_2).

H_1: This is the research hypothesis—the hypothesis that drives the research. Note that this hypothesis **always** predicts a difference between two population means. We can reflect this in terms of both words and symbols. With the current example, in words, the research hypothesis is this: People who have just handled hamsters are predicted to score lower on Zung's (1986) depression scale compared with people in general (note here that lower scores correspond to a more positive mood).

In symbols, we can represent this hypothesis accordingly:

$$H_1: \mu_1 < \mu_2$$

H_0: The null hypothesis is the opposite of the research hypothesis and it *always* includes an equal sign. In combination, the research hypothesis and the null hypothesis are *mutually exhaustive* (i.e., they include all possibilities) and *exclusive* (i.e., a possibility found in one of the hypotheses cannot be found in the other). Thus, in words, the null hypothesis here is:

People who handle hamsters have *higher* scores than the general population on Zung's (1986) depression scale, *or*

People who handle hamsters have, on average, the same score as the general population.

In symbols, the null hypothesis here will look like so:

$$H_0: \mu_1 \geq \mu_2$$

2. **Describe the comparison distribution**. Recall that ultimately, we are going to compare a score derived to represent our special population (population #1) with the general population (population #2). Thus, our comparison distribution will be the *population of individual scores that represents the general population*. Before getting too into the details, note the following assumption: We'll suppose that the scores in the population are normally distributed (thus making the comparison distribution a normal distribution). This assumption, while not always accurate, is usually accurate enough given the highly prevalent nature of normal distributions in natural variables.

Thus, here, the comparison distribution will be a normal distribution representing the general population's scores on Zung's (1986) measure of depression. Recall from the information given about this problem that the mean for this scale at the population level is 65.68 and the standard deviation is 15.65. Thus, our comparison distribution is found here, in Figure 7.1.

If the score representing our sample is extremely unlikely to come out of this distribution, then we may be able to reject the null hypothesis at the end of the day. But we can only know that by representing our comparison distribution as it is here in Figure 7.1.

3. **Determine the *cutoff score* and related *alpha region***. The *alpha region* is the part of your comparison distribution that you define, a priori (beforehand), as *so low in probability that you'll reject the idea of a score landing in that region by chance alone*. In other words, it's a part of the distribution that you define, ahead of time, as very low in probability. So if you look at Figure 7.2, you'll see a shaded region—labeled *alpha region = .05*—in the left tail of the distribution.

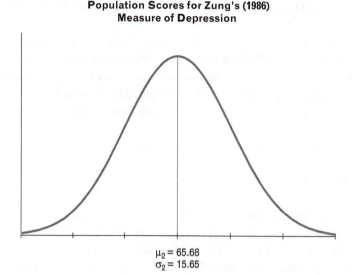

Population Scores for Zung's (1986)
Measure of Depression

$\mu_2 = 65.68$
$\sigma_2 = 15.65$

FIGURE 7.1: Comparison Distribution for Hypothesis Testing Example; Representing Population Scores for Zung's (1986) Measure of Depression.

There are a few things we need to know.

A.   Note that this region is on the left side of the distribution because the *alpha region follows the prediction of the research hypothesis*. Here, H_1 predicts that $\mu_1 < \mu_2$. So the mean of the special population is predicted to be **lower** than the mean of the general population. Thus, that mean is supposed to be to the left of the mean of the comparison distribution (as "left on the X-axis" corresponds to lower scores).

B.   When statisticians started with hypothesis testing, they agreed that predetermined a priori alpha levels need to be utilized. An alpha level is *a section of the comparison distribution that is determined to be so low in probability that scores in that section are unlikely to come about by chance*. But *what exactly* constitutes a *low probability*? Is 1% a low probability? How about 6%? How about 10%? Early statisticians realized that some lines needed to be drawn in the sand. The standard alpha level (corresponding to the standard alpha region) for statisticians in the behavioral sciences is 5%, meaning that if some result has a probability of coming about 5% of the time—or less—it's considered very unlikely to have come about by chance.

Now, to be sure, things that happen 5% of the time happen 5% of the time! That's 1 of 20. Some people think that's not so unlikely. And there's danger in having an alpha level that's not conservative enough. If our alpha level is not sufficiently conservative, then we may end up rejecting our null hypothesis when, in fact, the research hypothesis is incorrect (more on this issue in later section on *Type I and Type II Error*). Some folks therefore argue for an alpha level of .01 (or 1%). In reality, it often depends on the research situation—usually, .05 is agreed-upon as sufficient. Under some conditions, it makes sense to use the more conservative alpha level of .01. In the behavioral sciences, these are really the only two alpha levels that are used in practicality.

Population Scores for Zung's (1986)
Measure of Depression

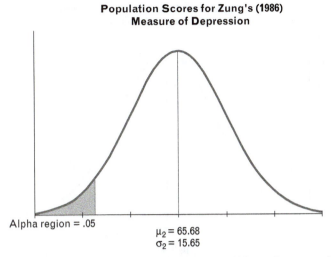

Alpha region = .05

$\mu_2 = 65.68$
$\sigma_2 = 15.65$

FIGURE 7.2: Comparison Distribution with Alpha Region and Cutoff Score Demarcated.

C. An alpha region corresponds to a particular cutoff point in the distribution. The *cutoff value* or *critical value* is the specific point that sits at the start of the alpha region. And this score marks the point that defines this "highly unlikely" section of the distribution. And the critical value is determined by using the z-score tools that we learned in chapter 6.

To put this all together, note that we'll have to refer to our z-score table. If we're going with the standard alpha level of .05 (which is what Cindy wants to do—and she's the boss here!), then we need to set a section on the left side of the comparison distribution that corresponds to 5% of the total distribution (see Figure 7.2). In doing so, we need to figure out, in z-score units (because, as you'll soon see, we'll be working with our friends the z-scores!) what particular z-score corresponds to having 5% of the full comparison distribution to the left of it.

Since you have mastered chapter 6, you may well know exactly what to do now! But if not, don't fret! Check out Figure 7.3. Here, you'll see that one particular z-score (labeled $Z_{crit} = -1.64$) is demarcated, as is the mean of the distribution. Importantly, while the mean is 65.68 in raw-score units, in z-score units, this mean is 0 (because the mean of any distribution, in z-score units, is 0). Thus, note that here, the mean is labeled both in raw and z-score units. Recall the z-score table. Remember that it gives two columns—Z and % *Mean to Z*. In the current problem, we are looking for Z and we need to derive that from the % between that z and the mean. We know that 5% of the scores are in Section A (in Figure 7.3). So what percentage of the scores is between that point and the mean of the distribution? Well, if 5% is to the left in Section A, then 50%–5%, or 45%, is in Section B (between the z and the mean). If you look up 45% on the table, you can find the corresponding z-score—and that will be Z_{crit}, or "Z-critical"—the particular z-score that corresponds to the start of the alpha region. When you look this up on the table, you'll see that 1.64 and 1.65 are equally close to % *Mean-to-Z* of 45%. Statisticians will typically go with 1.64.

But there's one more consideration. Recall that when we're dealing with z-scores that are below the mean, the scores are negative. This particular Z_{crit} happens to be below the mean. The

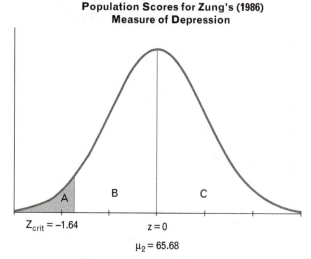

FIGURE 7.3: Determining the Critical Value (Z_{crit}).

z-table doesn't give you negative signs, so you have to write them in when appropriate—and it's now appropriate!

$$Z_{crit} = -1.64$$

So that's where the -1.64 on Figure 7.3 comes from. Done.

4. **Determine the score that best represents your sample and compare it with critical value.** In raw score units, this is easy. Alex's score on the Zung (1986) depression measure is 42. We can't compare 42 with Z_{crit} for the simple reason that Z_{crit} is in Z units and 42 is in raw units. So we have to convert this raw score to a z-score. As you may recall from earlier chapters, $Z = \dfrac{X - M}{SD}$. The only changes we'll make here correspond to the changes in the parameters. Our comparison distribution is not a sample distribution— it's a population distribution that we're treating as a probability distribution. As such, for this kind of problem, we need to slightly alter our equation for Z as follows:

$$\mathbf{Z} = \frac{X - \mu_2}{\sigma_2}.$$

That is, the z for this particular score (of X) is that score (X) minus the mean of the distribution of interest (μ_2) divided by the standard deviation of the distribution of interest (σ_2). We'll want to keep this general algorithm for computing z in mind, as we'll meet some derivative Z equations in the next few chapters. In any case, if X

$$= 42, Z = \frac{42 - 65.68}{15.65} = -1.51.$$

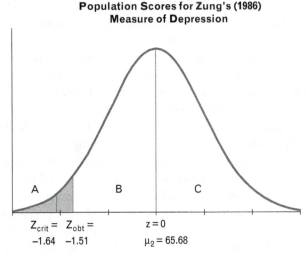

Population Scores for Zung's (1986)
Measure of Depression

$Z_{crit} =$ $Z_{obt} =$ $z = 0$
-1.64 -1.51 $\mu_2 = 65.68$

A   B   C

FIGURE 7.4: Comparing Z_{obt} with Z_{crit}.

To discriminate this particular z-score from the Z_{crit}, we'll often refer to this as Z_{obt} (meaning "Z obtained" or "the Z that was obtained in our calculations"). In short:

$$Z_{obt} = -1.51$$

Finally, we need to compare this score with Z_{crit} on our comparison distribution (see Figure 7.4). If you like simplicity, you'll enjoy this part. We now simply determine if Z_{obt} is more extreme than Z_{crit}. Or, even more simply, we ask: Is Z_{obt} in the alpha region? Here, the answer is *no*.

5. **Comment on the Null Hypothesis / Determine if your sample is unlikely to come from the population represented by the comparison distribution.**

When it comes to commenting on the null hypothesis, there are exactly two possibilities— rejecting H_0 or failing to reject H_0. In this case, *we have failed to reject H_0*—or, put another way, we have *failed to obtain statistical significance*. As such, we have not provided support for Cindy's Hamster Hypothesis. Perhaps handling hamsters makes people happier, but Cindy's findings did not conclusively document this point.

WHAT DOES IT MEAN TO *REJECT* OR *FAIL* *TO REJECT* THE NULL HYPOTHESIS?

Hypothesis testing is a dichotomous endeavor. We either reject or fail to reject H_0. Importantly, neither of these outcomes has anything to do with *proving*! And this is an important point—one that's often missed by the media and laypeople. So listen up!

The hypothesis-testing process is fallible. Always! Whatever you conclude, you may end up being wrong! The best we can do, then, is to understand the process and use our analytical skills to make our best determinations about reality.

Consider Cindy's research. Cindy found that her participant who handled the hamster had a score on Zung's (1986) scale of 42. That was considerably lower than the mean for that scale. In fact, specifically, that score was 1.51 standard deviations below the mean of the scale (that's how we interpret z-scores). But statistics are smart! And Cindy's research design was penalized for not having a large sample. With a small sample—indeed, with a sample of one person!—the statistics are essentially skeptical. And, as we'll see in upcoming chapters, the statistics become less skeptical as the sample increases. In any case, we failed to reject the null hypothesis. But that doesn't mean that the population of hamster handlers has an identical mean as the population of people in general; it simply means that our findings are inconclusive.

Similarly, if you reject the null hypothesis, you may well want to call your mom, throw a party, and celebrate. But don't open the bottle of Mountain Dew so quickly! You may be wrong. It is entirely possible to reject the null hypothesis (i.e., to have Z_{obt} be more extreme than Z_{crit}) and be wrong! All you're doing when you're rejecting the null hypothesis is showing that it's very unlikely that the research hypothesis is incorrect—but, again, you can never be sure.

As such, wording matters a lot here. When your Z_{obt} is more extreme than Z_{crit}, you can say that you've *rejected the null hypothesis* and that *you have provided support for your research hypothesis*.

Conversely, when your Z_{obt} is *not* more extreme than Z_{crit}, you can say that you have *failed to reject the null hypothesis* and that your results are *inconclusive*.

Inferential statistics help us understand reality better—these statistics assist us in ruling out possibilities that are way off. Understanding statistics helps us get a better handle on what the world is probably like. But, to be sure, statistics do not *prove* or *disprove* anything. We realize that this may be a bit of a downer, but one thing you ultimately learn in college is that reality is contextual and elusive. Statistics, on one hand, helps us better understand reality, but, on the other, it humbles. And that's not a bad thing.

ONE-TAILED VERSUS TWO-TAILED TESTS

The example we've worked with so far, regarding Cindy's famous Hamster Hypothesis, is an example of a *one-tailed test*. Simply, a one-tailed test is a *directional test*, in which your research hypothesis specifies that the special population mean differs from the general population mean in a particular direction. In the case of Cindy's hypothesis, the prediction was that the special population had a mean that was not only different from the general population mean, but that was, also, *lower* than the general population mean. An implication of this kind of hypothesis is the fact that the alpha region is specifically (and exclusively) on the left side of the distribution. Only a Z_{obt} in that part of the distribution would reject H_0.

Occasionally, we do research with no directional prediction. There are several reasons that such research may emerge. Sometimes two collaborating researchers have opposing predictions (e.g., two students working on a project regarding the effects of media on body image may disagree about whether viewing muscular and powerful women would lead to an increase or decrease in self-esteem of female participants). Sometimes you are interested in the effects of something, but you have no basis for predicting the effects (will watching too much SpongeBob make someone relatively witty (it *is* a funny show!) or relatively dull (TV *does* melt your brain!)?). And so on.

These kinds of research questions are referred to as *non-directional* and lead to what we refer to as *two-tailed tests*. A two-tailed test is as it implies—it's one in which there are two alpha regions—one in each tail of the test. The way it works is pretty simple—you take your a priori alpha level as you would in any case. If you determine your test is a two-tailed test, you divide alpha by 2 and distribute it, then, evenly between each tail. The basic hypothesis-testing procedure stays the same, but with a few minor changes to accommodate issues associated with a non-directional test.

AN EXAMPLE OF A TWO-TAILED TEST

Suppose that two undergraduate students, Joe and Josie, are conducting a project for their Research Methods class. They both use Facebook—but Joe doesn't like it very much. He claims that it makes people less social because it causes them to get addicted to artificial social outlets (typing and looking at a screen) and pulls them away from real social situations. Josie disagrees. She thinks Facebook is the best thing since the automobile, claiming that it helps her keep in close contact with all her family members and friends from different social groups. Josie is sure that Facebook has positive social benefits—and that people who use Facebook a lot are probably more sociable (on average) than people in the general population.

For their project, they put this question to the test. Since they disagree on whether Facebook leads to better or worse social outcomes, they decide this test must be a two-tailed test. And since they really cannot agree on the prediction at all, they decide that it would be best to use the relatively conservative alpha level of .01.

To test this hypothesis, they find a measure of *social efficacy* in the literature. This (fabricated!) test has a population mean of 10 and a standard deviation of 2. Now they need a sample. They decide to walk outside the psychology building and approach the first person they see in the quad to ask if he or she would participate. They find Bob—and he's happy to take part. They ask him two questions. First, they inquire if he considers himself a frequent user of Facebook. Then they give him the social efficacy scale to complete. Bob says, "I'll be in your study, but I can't *stand* Facebook!" He then completes the scale. His score is 3. Here's how we'll carry out the hypothesis test.

1. **Articulate the *research* and *null* hypotheses**. In words, the hypothesis for a two-tailed test is *always* simply that a difference between the population means is predicted. This difference might be such that the population mean for the special population (here, non-Facebook users) is *greater than* **or** is *less than* the mean for the general population.

In symbols, the research and null hypotheses for a two-tailed test are as follows:

$$H_1: \mu_1 \neq \mu_2$$
$$H_0: \mu_1 = \mu_2$$

2. **Describe the comparison distribution**. With a two-tailed test, this process is identical to the process for the one-tailed test. The comparison distribution will be a normal

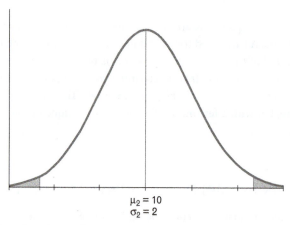

Fabricated Measure of Social Efficacy

$$\mu_2 = 10$$
$$\sigma_2 = 2$$

FIGURE 7.5: Comparison Distribution Representing Population of Scores for Social Efficacy Measure.

distribution representing the population mean for the general population. The specific variable will be social efficacy. Recall that this measure has a population mean of 10 and a population standard deviation of 2. This distribution is represented in Figure 7.5.

3. **Determine the *cutoff score* and related *alpha region*.** Here, we have to take two points into account. First, we need to figure out if this is a one- or two-tailed test. Duh! This whole example is about a two-tailed test! That was easy. Second, we need to consider the alpha level. Recall that this level is determined by the researchers (a priori) and is traditionally either .05 (most common) or .01 (if the researchers have reason to be very conservative in terms of what they call a *significant finding* that *rejects the null hypothesis*). Based on the given information for this problem, the alpha level is .01 (Joe and Josie chose this α level).

With a two-tailed test, the alpha needs to be equally divided across the extremes of the two tails of the distribution. Thus, we need to divide 1% (i.e., .01) in half—and this amount (.5%) will comprise each alpha region. These two alpha regions are represented in Figure 7.6. Note that we also need to figure out the z-scores that reflect these cutoff points. Here, with a two-tailed test, we'll have two Z_{crits}—one corresponding to the alpha region above the mean and the other corresponding to the lower alpha region. These Z-critical scores will be equal to each other in absolute value—they will only differ in sign.

As with the prior hypothesis-testing example, we'll need our z-table (see Appendix A). Recall that the table provides you with the Z that corresponds to the percentage of scores between that particular z-score and the mean of the distribution. Let's consider the Z_{crit} on the right side first. Here, .5% (i.e., half of 1%) of the distribution is above this point. Thus, 50–.5, or 49.5% of the scores are between this particular score and the mean. So let's look up 49.5% in the table. We'll see that z-scores of 2.57 and 2.58 are equally close to having 49.5% of the scores between them and the mean. Statisticians use 2.57 (which makes sense when the decimals are carried out further). So one Z_{crit}, the one that demarcates the upper alpha region, is 2.57.

Recall that in a two-tailed hypothesis test, the Z_{crits} differ from one another only in sign. Thus, the lower $Z_{crit} = -2.57$ (see Figure 7.6).

Fabricated Measure of Social Efficacy

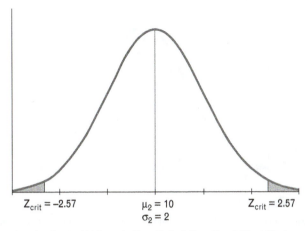

$Z_{crit} = -2.57$ $\mu_2 = 10$ $Z_{crit} = 2.57$
$\sigma_2 = 2$

FIGURE 7.6: Determining the Critical Value of a Two-Tailed Hypothesis Test (Z_{crit}).

Given that there are two alpha regions, we have two very different ways that we can reject the null hypothesis. If the sample score that represents the special population (non-Facebook users) is in the upper alpha region, we'll support the idea that not using Facebook is associated with relatively high social efficacy (backing Joe's stance). Alternatively, if our sample score representing the special population (of non-Facebook users) is in our lower alpha region, we'll support Josie's stance that not using Facebook is associated with relatively low social functioning.

4. **Determine the score that best represents your sample and compare it with critical value.** This step is identical to how things progress with a one-tailed test. We'll compute Z_{obt} for the sample score to see if the sample representing the special population is in either of the alpha regions. Recall that $Z_{obt} = (X - \mu_2) / \sigma_2$. With the current example, that means $Z_{obt} = \dfrac{3 - 10}{2} = -3.5$.

We now get to use our very simple algorithm by comparing this Z_{obt} with the two Z_{crit} scores—asking, simply, "Is this z-score in either of the alpha regions?" Intuitively, you may know that −3.5 is more extreme than −2.57—but if not, no worries; check out Figure 7.7. Clearly, our obtained z-score for Bob is lower than −2.57 and is, thus, in the alpha region.

5. **Comment on the Null Hypothesis / Determine if your sample is unlikely to come from the population represented by the comparison distribution.**

Our Z_{obt} is in one of our alpha regions. Thus, we reject H_0, supporting H_1—and even *finding statistical significance*. Importantly, since the research hypothesis for a two-tailed test is non-directional, finding a significant effect actually doesn't tell us that much! At this point, we don't yet know who's right out of Joe and Josie—all we know is that one of them is right!

To complete this kind of problem, we need to revisit Figure 7.7—seeing if the sample that represents the special population is significantly *above* or *below* the mean for the general population. And we really need to do this only if we've, first, rejected the null hypothesis. Looking at

Fabricated Measure of Social Efficacy

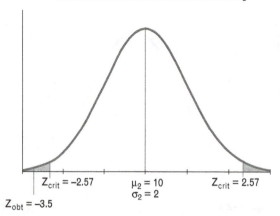

FIGURE 7.7: Comparing the Obtained Z-Score with the Critical Z-Scores in a Two-Tailed Example.

Figure 7.7, we see that not only have we rejected H_0, but, more specifically, we've found that the sample score (representing the special population of non-Facebook users) is **below** the mean for the general population. Recall that this variable represents social efficacy. So we've provided evidence that non-Facebook users may have a population mean that is lower than the general population in social efficacy. Based on the data presented here, it looks like Josie may have been right!

A DEEPER INTERPRETATION OF REJECTING
THE NULL HYPOTHESIS

To this point, we've presented enough to help guide you through the basic concepts involved in hypothesis testing. But there is one additional way of thinking about this process that is actually really useful. Let's get back to Joe and Josie's example. Recall that we found evidence supporting the idea that non-Facebook users have a population mean in social efficacy that is lower than that of the general population.

This essentially means that Bob's score of 3 was so low relative to the mean and standard deviation, that we **reject** the idea that this score came from this population (as it's very unlikely in that population) and we support the alternative idea that this score came from a population in which the score was actually more typical (as given the normal distribution, most scores in a normal distribution, simply, are near the mean of the distribution—and scores at the tails are unlikely). As such, when we reject the null hypothesis for this example, we're rejecting the idea that the means of the two populations have an identical mean—and, rather, we support the idea that the sample score came from a population with a mean that is, in this case, *lower* than the mean for the general population. Bob's score of 3 is outlandishly low relative to the general population mean (given the comparison distribution)—but it is typical for a population distribution with a lower mean score (such as 4, for instance). In a distribution with a population mean of 4 and a population standard deviation of 2, Bob's score of 3 is actually not all that surprising.

In fact, *this* is what we mean when we reject the null hypothesis. We reject the idea that Bob's score came from the general population distribution—and we, alternatively, support the idea that it came from a distribution with a lower mean—in which Bob's score would not be all that low in probability.

TYPE-I AND TYPE-II ERROR IN HYPOTHESIS TESTING

As mentioned earlier, hypothesis testing is fun and informative, but by its very nature, it's not perfect. Conceptually, there are four possible results when it comes to hypothesis testing. To contemplate this issue, it's useful to think abstractly about different possibilities. Regarding the research hypothesis—in reality, it's actually true or false. Of course, we typically cannot know the actual answer regarding whether it's true or false (as this would usually entail having full population-level data)—but let's suspend reality for a moment. In reality, H_1 is, actually, either true or false.

Another dimension to consider is the fact that in hypothesis testing, we either *reject H_0* or we *fail to reject H_0*. In a perfect world, we would only reject H_0 when the research hypothesis is true—and we'd only fail to reject H_0 when the research hypothesis is false.

But if you're old enough to read this book, then we can assert with certainty the following: You already know that this is not a perfect world...

As is the case with hypothesis testing. Given how we've set things up, we can think of hypothesis-testing outcomes in terms of a 2x2 contingency table, as follows (see Table 7.3):

Table 7.3: The Four Possible Outcomes Associated with Hypothesis Testing

	The Truth Regarding the Research Hypothesis (H1)	
Decision Regarding the Null Hypothesis (H_0)	H_1 True	H_1 False
Reject H_0	Correct Decision	Type-I Error
Fail to Reject H_0	Type-II Error	Correct Decision

Let's dissect the outcomes from Table 7.3. First, we can think of the *correct decision* resulting from rejecting the null hypothesis when the research hypothesis is true. Not only is this a correct decision, but it's the correct decision that you, the researcher, are typically shooting for. Furthermore, you have not only supported your research hypothesis (by rejecting the null hypothesis), but you've done so correctly—in a world in which the research hypothesis is true (at the population level). Dandy—this is exactly what you want.

Next, we have a less exciting but similarly accurate form of *correct decision*—this occurs when you fail to reject the null hypothesis—but the research hypothesis is actually, at the population level, incorrect. So you've done the right thing. There was nothing to be found—and this is in essence what you've discovered! Again, not as exciting as the other kind of correct decision—but it's actually an extremely common outcome in real research—and if you seek a career in research, you need to get used to this one!

Type-I Error occurs when you've rejected the null hypothesis incorrectly. In reality, the research hypothesis is false, so you should not have rejected the null hypothesis. But, again, as the entire enterprise is somewhat fallible, it's possible for this to happen. Interestingly, this kind of error is actually an error in the researcher's favor. Think about it. You've "found significance"— and supported your research hypothesis—but, in reality, your research hypothesis is false at the population level. As you may sense, there is a sort of danger here. Researchers, for so many reasons (to get tenure, to get published, to obtain grant monies, to impress their mates, etc.), actually benefit from Type-I Error. For this reason, we need to pay particular attention to this issue—and we need to come up with ways to essentially tie our hands behind our backs so that we aren't tempted to capitalize on Type-I Error. There are many ways that researchers can guard against Type-I Error—most of which are described in detail in advanced textbooks. One example you're already aware of pertains to your choice of alpha level. Using a relatively conservative alpha level (e.g., .01 instead of .05) is, from this vantage point, a way to guard against Type-I Error. In a way, using a two-tailed test instead of a one-tailed test has a similar effect. In the real world, the true watchdogs on this issue are other researchers—accusing a researcher of capitalizing on Type-I Error is actually one of the most common criticisms that researchers launch at one another—particularly when they disagree on theoretical grounds.

Finally, there's Type-II Error. While Type-I Error is an error in the researcher's favor, Type-II Error is exactly the opposite. It occurs when you fail to reject the null hypothesis (i.e., fail to support your research hypothesis), but your research hypothesis is actually true! You were correct, but simply failed to show it! This is sort of the "aw, shucks" error. As with Type-I Error, or any error, really, you want to reduce the likelihood of making Type-II Error. And that's particularly true for Type-II Error as this is an error that works *against you*. We'll see ways to reduce the likelihood of making Type-II Error in upcoming chapters. For now, it's probably useful to know that the simplest and most powerful way to reduce Type-II Error is to increase the size of the sample in your research.

A REAL RESEARCH EXAMPLE

Hypothesis testing sits at the core of so much research in the behavioral sciences. Any time a researcher talks about a *significant finding*, he or she is ultimately talking about the results of a hypothesis test.

In a study that we authors conducted together a few years back, we were interested in understanding children diagnosed with *Reactive Attachment Disorder*, a disorder of childhood caused by a lack of appropriate attachments to adult caregivers that leads to several adverse outcomes. In one study (Hall & Geher, 2003), we sought to determine if children diagnosed with reactive attachment disorder differed significantly from a group of control children in terms of several dimensions (including social problems, withdrawal, somatic complaints, anxiety/depression, thought problems, attention problems, delinquent behavior, and aggressive behavior). As you can see in Table 7.4 (adapted from our article, which was published in the *Journal of Psychology*),

Table 7.4: Differences Between Children with Reactive Attachment Disorder versus Control Children on a Number of Psychological Attributes

Scale/subscale	RAD (n = 21) M	RAD (n = 21) SD	Non-RAD (n = 21) M	Non-RAD (n = 21) SD	Univariate F (1, 40)
Anxiety/Depression	11.67	3.83	2.57	4.88	45.13**
Aggressive Behavior	26.00	7.88	7.29	10.50	42.66**
Delinquent Behavior	9.57	4.34	2.86	5.62	18.75**
Attention Problems	11.19	4.60	3.57	5.13	25.55**
Somatic Complaints	3.19	3.49	1.29	2.05	4.65*
Social Problems	8.19	3.34	1.76	2.10	53.23**
Withdrawal	6.48	4.33	2.00	3.73	12.88**
Thought Problems	4.67	2.90	1.24	3.05	13.16**

* p < .05
** p < .01

children with Reactive Attachment Disorder scored as significantly more likely to have issues with anxiety/depression, aggressive behavior, delinquent behavior, attention problems, somatic complaints, social problems, withdrawal, and thought problems. You'll note that "significant findings" are demarcated with asterisks that point toward footnotes—typically indicating either "* $p < .05$," meaning that a finding was significant based on an alpha level of .05, or "** $p < .01$," meaning that a finding was significant with an alpha level of .01. Nowadays, it's also common to report the precise probability of a particular outcome (e.g., instead of saying " $p < .05$," you may see something like "$p = .03$." Some consider it simply a matter of preference whether you report your probability relative to an alpha level or in absolute terms.

SUMMARY

Hypothesis testing resides at the core of inferential statistics. In this chapter, we learned the basic rationale underlying hypothesis testing, along with the five steps that are universal across hypothesis-testing procedures. Hypothesis testing is a probabilistic method for assessing if some population mean is likely different from some other population mean. The process is informative but not perfect, and always needs to be monitored in terms of the two common kinds of hypothesis-testing errors (Type-I Error, finding that a result is *significant* even if your data are not representative of the population-level means and Type-II Error, finding that your result is not significant, even though the population-level means truly are different).

KEY TERMS

Alpha region: The portion of the comparison distribution that is determined to be so low in probability that the idea of a score landing in that region by chance alone is rejected.

Critical value (or cutoff value): A specific value that sits at the start of the alpha region, which, if reached or exceeded, results in the rejection of the null hypothesis.

Hypothesis testing: A process for determining if some effect found in a sample is likely reflective of patterns in the population.

Null hypothesis: The hypothesis that assumes there is no difference between populations; the hypothesis that assumes that your research hypothesis is wrong.

One tailed test (directional test): Type of test used when the research hypothesis specifies that the special population mean differs from the general population mean in a particular direction; there is one alpha region at the tail of one end of the distribution.

Two tailed test (non-directional test): Type of test used when the research hypothesis does not specify the direction in which the special population mean differs from the general population mean; there are 2 alpha regions, on at each tail of the distribution.

Type I error: Rejecting the null hypothesis incorrectly; rejecting the null hypothesis when it is true.

Type II error: Incorrectly failing to reject the null hypothesis; failing to reject the null hypothesis when it is false.

HOMEWORK SET A

1. You spent the weekend landscaping your front yard. Looking at your front yard, you feel an elevation in mood. You think that other people who finish landscaping projects must experience this same elevation in mood. You notice that your neighbor, Bill, has undertaken a landscaping project in his front yard, and, upon completion of the project, you ask if Bill would be willing to complete an assessment of mood. The mean for the questionnaire is 50, and the standard deviation is 12. Bill scored 53. You decide on an alpha level of .05.

   a. Complete the 5 steps of hypothesis testing:
      1. Articulate the research and null hypotheses, in words and in equations.
      2. Describe the comparison distribution, both with words and with a normal distribution graph with the mean labeled.
      3. Determine the cutoff score and related alpha region. Label Z_{crit} and show the alpha region on the normal distribution graph by shading it.
      4. Determine the score that best represents your sample and compare it with the critical value. Label Z_{obt} on the normal distribution graph.
      5. Comment on the null hypothesis / Determine if your sample is unlikely to come from the population represented by the comparison distribution.

   b. Do the results of the research prove or disprove anything? Comment on your results.

   c. If an error were made, what type of error would it be?

2. Your recreational basketball team spends a lot of time together. You feel that the increased amount of time spent together gives your team an advantage in games. As you are preparing a study of the amount of time a team spends together and the performance of the team in games, your cousin calls and complains about how much time his recreational basketball team spends together. He states that the increased time together is likely having an adverse effect on the team's performance in games. Intrigued, you ask your cousin to assist in the research. Your cousin believes that less time spent together outside of practice would lead to a more efficient team, but you disagree. Knowing that Spencer plays on a recreational basketball team, you ask Spencer about his team, and he tells you that his team doesn't spend much time together outside of practice, but they annihilate the other teams in games. Spencer scored his team as a 44 on a team efficiency scale, which has a mean of 30 and a standard deviation of 5. You decide on an alpha level of .05.

   a. Complete the 5 steps of hypothesis testing:
      1. Articulate the research and null hypotheses, in words and in equations.
      2. Describe the comparison distribution, both with words and with a normal distribution graph with the mean labeled.
      3. Determine the cutoff score and related alpha region. Label Z_{crit} and show the alpha region on the normal distribution graph by shading it.
      4. Determine the score that best represents your sample and compare it with the critical value. Label Z_{obt} on the normal distribution graph.
      5. Comment on the null hypothesis / Determine if your sample is unlikely to come from the population represented by the comparison distribution.

   b. Do the results of the research prove or disprove anything? Comment on your results.

   c. If an error were made, what type of error would it be?

3. Your mother is constantly telling your brother that if he texts while spending time with his friends, he will wind up with weak friendships. She reasons that the texting will send the message to the person he is with that he doesn't value their friendship. Your brother always counters that by texting, he is nurturing more than one friendship at a time, which will enable him to keep all of his friendships strong. You set out to discover who is right. You ask Molly to complete a friendship strength questionnaire, considering a friend who texts often. Higher scores indicate stronger friendships. The mean for the questionnaire is 25, and the standard deviation is 2. Molly scores her friendship as 19. You decide on an alpha level of .01.

    a. Complete the 5 steps of hypothesis testing
        1. Articulate the research and null hypotheses, in words and in equations.
        2. Describe the comparison distribution, both with words and with a normal distribution graph with the mean labeled.
        3. Determine the cutoff score and related alpha region. Label Z_{crit} and show the alpha region on the normal distribution graph by shading it.
        4. Determine the score that best represents your sample and compare it with the critical value. Label Z_{obt} on the normal distribution graph.
        5. Comment on the null hypothesis / Determine if your sample is unlikely to come from the population represented by the comparison distribution.
    b. Do the results of the research prove or disprove anything? Comment on your results.
    c. If an error were made, what type of error would it be?

HOMEWORK SET B

1. You think that showering in the morning sets you up for a productive day, as you get out of the shower refreshed, motivated, and ready to tackle anything. You assume everyone feels this way, until your friend tells you that showers make him feel sleepy, and that when he showers in the morning, he feels sluggish and unmotivated all day. You decide to stand outside the door to the showers in the nearest dorm in the morning, and accost someone as s/he exits the shower facilities (fully clothed, of course!), asking him or her to complete a measure of motivation. Flynn agrees to participate, and scores 15 on the motivation questionnaire, which has a mean of 14 and a standard deviation of 3. You decide on an alpha level of .01.

    a. Complete the 5 steps of hypothesis testing
        1. Articulate the research and null hypotheses, in words and in equations.
        2. Describe the comparison distribution, both with words and with a normal distribution graph with the mean labeled.
        3. Determine the cutoff score and related alpha region. Label Z_{crit} and show the alpha region on the normal distribution graph by shading it.
        4. Determine the score that best represents your sample and compare it with the critical value. Label Z_{obt} on the normal distribution graph.
        5. Comment on the null hypothesis / Determine if your sample is unlikely to come from the population represented by the comparison distribution.
    b. Do the results of the research prove or disprove anything? Comment on your results.

   c. If an error were made, what type of error would it be?

2. Your sister has become very anxious in social situations, and you think that her social anxiety is related to her loss of employment and subsequent inability to find another job in her field. You surmise that people who have been unemployed for more than 6 months may experience an increase in social anxiety. You ask Caroline, who has been looking for work for 8 months, to complete an evaluation of social anxiety, for which high scores correspond to high social anxiety. Caroline's score is 44 on the evaluation, which has a mean of 35 and a standard deviation of 5. You decide on an alpha level of .05

   a. Complete the 5 steps of hypothesis testing:
      1. Articulate the research and null hypotheses, in words and in equations.
      2. Describe the comparison distribution, both with words and with a normal distribution graph with the mean labeled.
      3. Determine the cutoff score and related alpha region. Label Z_{crit} and show the alpha region on the normal distribution graph by shading it.
      4. Determine the score that best represents your sample and compare it with the critical value. Label Z_{obt} on the normal distribution graph.
      5. Comment on the null hypothesis / Determine if your sample is unlikely to come from the population represented by the comparison distribution.

   b. Do the results of the research prove or disprove anything? Comment on your results.

   c. If an error were made, what type of error would it be?

3. You have a friend who seems to demonstrate very low standards when it comes to choosing a mate. She doesn't care if her current romantic partner is particularly smart or good looking or employed, or any of the things that matter to you. However, your friend always seems happy in her relationships. You are looking for someone hard working, smart, ambitious, witty, confident, loyal, and kind, among other things that you believe will lead to a successful long-term relationship. You, thus far, have been somewhat dissatisfied in all of your relationships. You wonder if having fewer standards actually makes relationships happier. You find Brady, who indicates that he has few standards when it comes to romantic partners, and you ask him to complete a relationship satisfaction survey. Brady's score is 28 on the survey, which has a mean of 20 and a standard deviation of 3. You decide on an alpha level of .01.

   a. Complete the 5 steps of hypothesis testing:
      1. Articulate the research and null hypotheses, in words and in equations.
      2. Describe the comparison distribution, both with words and with a normal distribution graph with the mean labeled.
      3. Determine the cutoff score and related alpha region. Label Z_{crit} and show the alpha region on the normal distribution graph by shading it.
      4. Determine the score that best represents your sample and compare it with the critical value. Label Z_{obt} on the normal distribution graph.
      5. Comment on the null hypothesis / Determine if your sample is unlikely to come from the population represented by the comparison distribution.

   b. Do the results of the research prove or disprove anything? Comment on your results.

   c. If an error were made, what type of error would it be?

HOMEWORK SET A ANSWERS

1. a.   1.   Research hypothesis: People who have finished landscaping projects will score higher on an assessment of mood than people in general.

$$H_1 = \mu_1 > \mu_2$$

Null hypothesis: People who have finished landscaping projects will score lower than, or equal to, the general population on an assessment of mood.

$$H_0 = \mu_1 \leq \mu_2$$

2.   The comparison distribution is the population of individual scores on the mood assessment that represents the general population, with a mean of 50 and a standard deviation of 12.

Population Scores for Mood Assessment

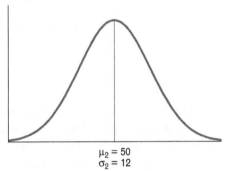

$\mu_2 = 50$
$\sigma_2 = 12$

FIGURE 7.8: Homework Set A #1a3.

3.   Alpha level is .05. Cutoff score (from % Mean-to-Z table) is 1.64.

Population Scores for Mood Assessment

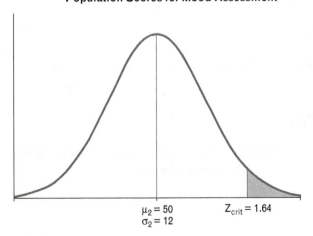

$\mu_2 = 50$ $Z_{crit} = 1.64$
$\sigma_2 = 12$

FIGURE 7.9: Homework Set A #1a3.

4. $Z = \dfrac{(X - \mu_2)}{\sigma_2}$

$Z = \dfrac{(53 - 50)}{12}$

$Z = .25 = Z_{obt}$

Population Scores for Mood Assessment

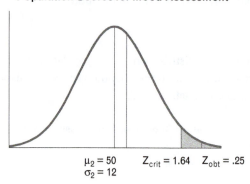

$\mu_2 = 50$ $Z_{crit} = 1.64$ $Z_{obt} = .25$
$\sigma_2 = 12$

FIGURE 7.10: Homework Set A #2a2.

5. We failed to reject the null hypothesis. It is likely that the sample comes from the comparison distribution, rather than a different distribution.

a. Our results are inconclusive, for we failed to reject the null hypothesis. Statistics do not prove or disprove anything, but we did not find support for the hypothesis that completing landscaping projects elevates mood.

b. Type II Error, failing to reject H_0 when H_1 is actually true.

2. a. 1. Research hypothesis: Teams who spend a lot of time together are more or less efficient in games than the general population of teams.

$H_1 : \mu_1 \neq \mu_2$

Null hypothesis: Teams who spend a lot of time together are not more or less efficient than the general population of teams.

$H_1 : \mu_1 = \mu_2$

2. Comparison distribution is the normal distribution of team efficiency, with a mean of 30 and a standard deviation of 5.

Team Efficiency

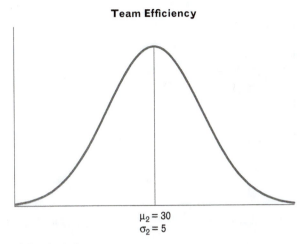

$\mu_2 = 30$
$\sigma_2 = 5$

FIGURE 7.11: Homework Set A #2a2.

3.   The alpha level is .05 and this is a 2-tailed test, so the cutoff scores are 1.96 and
   −1.96, which makes the alpha region the most extreme 2.5% of each tail.

Team Efficiency

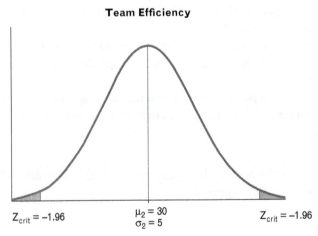

$Z_{crit} = -1.96$ $\mu_2 = 30$ $Z_{crit} = -1.96$
                               $\sigma_2 = 5$

FIGURE 7.12: Homework Set A #2a3.

4. $Z = \dfrac{(X - \mu_2)}{\sigma_2}$

$Z = \dfrac{(44 - 30)}{5}$

$Z = 2.8 = Z_{obt}$

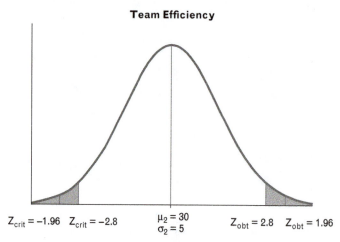

Team Efficiency

$Z_{crit} = -1.96$ $Z_{crit} = -2.8$ $\mu_2 = 30$ $Z_{obt} = 2.8$ $Z_{obt} = 1.96$
                                        $\sigma_2 = 5$

FIGURE 7.13: Homework Set A #2a4.

5. Z_{obt} is in the alpha region, so we reject H_0, supporting H_1. Based on the results, it is likely that the sample may come from a different distribution than the comparison distribution.

b. While the results do not prove or disprove anything, they do support the research hypothesis that spending little time together outside of practice may increase the efficiency of teams during games.

c. If an error were made in this research, it would be a type-I error, rejecting the null hypothesis when the research hypothesis is actually false.

3. a. 1. Research hypothesis: People who text while spending time with friends have stronger or weaker friendships than people in general.

$H_1 : \mu_1 \neq \mu_2$

Null hypothesis: People who text while spending time with friends do not have stronger or weaker friendships than people in general.

$H_0 : \mu_1 = \mu_2$

2. The comparison distribution is a normal distribution that represents the population of scores on the friendship questionnaire, with a mean of 25 and a standard deviation of 2.

Population Scores for Friendship Questionnaire

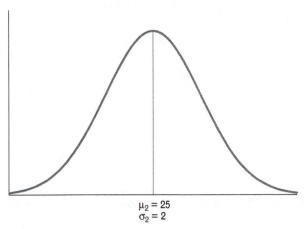

$\mu_2 = 25$
$\sigma_2 = 2$

FIGURE 7.14: Homework Set A #3a2.

3. The alpha level is .01, which is divided, making the cutoff scores −2.57 and 2.57.

Population Scores for Friendship Questionnaire

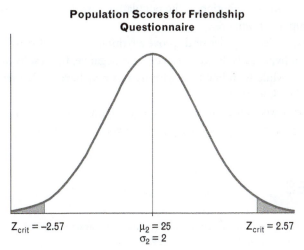

$Z_{crit} = -2.57$ $\mu_2 = 25$ $Z_{crit} = 2.57$
                  $\sigma_2 = 2$

FIGURE 7.15: Homework Set A #3a3.

4. $Z = \dfrac{(X - \mu_2)}{\sigma_2}$

$Z = \dfrac{(19 - 25)}{2}$

$Z = -3 = Z_{obt}$

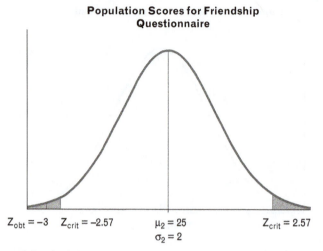

FIGURE 7.16: Homework Set A #3a4.

5. We rejected the null hypothesis, finding support for the research hypothesis. The sample is extreme enough to consider that the sample may not come from the same distribution as the population distribution for scores on the friendship questionnaire.

b. The results do not prove or disprove anything, but they do provide support for the research hypothesis. Further, since Z_{obt} is negative, the results indicate that people who text while spending time with friends may have weaker friendships. Perhaps Mom does know best!

c. If an error were made in this research, it would be a type-I error, rejecting the null hypothesis when the research hypothesis was, in fact, false.

REFERENCES

Hall, S. E. K., & Geher, G. (2003). Behavior and Personality Characteristics of Children with Reactive Attachment Disorder. *Journal of Psychology, 137,* 145–162.

Zung, W. W. K. (1986). Zung self-rating depression scale and depression status inventory. *In N. Sartorius & T. A. Ban (Eds.), Assessment of depression (pp. 221–231). Berlin: Springer Verlag.*

HYPOTHESIS TESTING IF N > 1

Chapter 7 is all about introducing the basic idea of hypothesis testing to a student of statistics. The reasoning of hypothesis testing is a bit complex and includes lots of novel ideas. Thus, we try to keep the ideas down to a manageable size at any given time.

Partly as a result, chapter 7 includes a unique form of hypothesis testing—hypothesis testing when using a single randomly selected score to represent a population. This detail allows us to introduce hypothesis testing in a pretty streamlined manner—but it also makes it so that the specifics of the process included in chapter 7 deal with an unlikely kind of scenario. Using a single score to estimate the central tendency of an entire population of scores is, well, kind of dumb. In reality, you wouldn't do that very often—simply based on the reasoning that the larger your sample is, the better your estimate of the population mean will be.

The primary reason that we introduced hypothesis testing this way pertains to reducing complexity for presentational and learning purposes. When you're hypothesis testing with an N of greater than 1, your comparison distribution is not a distribution of individual scores. Rather, it's a *distribution of means* (which is a form of a *sampling distribution*). As you'll see, the details of a distribution of means are fully within your grasp. However, you'll also see that there's a bunch of reasoning behind the nature of this kind of distribution and, simply, introducing all that complexity on top of the complexities associated with hypothesis testing itself would just be too much. So we compartmentalize our presentation. The last chapter was all about the basics of hypothesis testing. This chapter gets into the nuances associated with the distribution of means and how this all relates to the nature of hypothesis testing.

THE DISTRIBUTION OF MEANS

As we saw in chapter 7, if N = 1, that means that you have one score to represent your special population in the hypothesis-testing process. Thus, your comparison distribution is a distribution of individual scores—you are comparing a single score with a distribution of individual scores.

But if the sample of scores designed to represent your population is greater than one (e.g., you have five scores in your sample), then you can't use a population of individual scores as your comparison distribution in hypothesis testing. Suppose, for instance, you wanted to test the age-old theory (wives' tale?) that people who drive red cars drive faster than drivers in general. You randomly select five red cars that pass through a particular stretch of highway and clock their speeds (because you happen to have gotten a great radar gun for your birthday!). You find these scores (in miles per hour) as follows: 84, 71, 75, 93, and 90.

How can you best summarize this sample? What's the best way to represent the central tendency of these scores? Well, by now you know that, generally speaking, the best way to represent the central tendency of a sample of scores is with the mean. We therefore want to compute the mean of the sample (recall that $M = \dfrac{\sum X}{N} = \dfrac{84+71+75+93+90}{5} = 82.6$). Now you now have a mean to represent your special population (of red-car drivers)—and this is what you can use to compare with a comparison distribution in the hypothesis-testing process.

However, simply as a matter of apples-to-apples, you can't compare a mean with a distribution of individual scores. If you compare an individual score with a distribution of individual scores (as in chapter 7), you need to compare a mean with a distribution of means. A distribution of means is similar to a distribution of individual scores, but it has some critical differences that affect the nature of hypothesis testing.

Conceptually, once you have an $N > 1$, the parameters of hypothesis testing must accommodate this fact. As such, we'll use special symbols to represent our parameters when dealing with a situation of $N > 1$. Table 8.1 presents symbols used for parameters as a function of whether you're talking about a sample, a population distribution, or a distribution of means.

Thus, once $N > 1$, we'll be dealing with the appropriate parameters that correspond to a distribution of means.

But what exactly *is* a distribution of means? The idea is very conceptual in nature. A distribution of means is an abstract distribution based on a *population distribution* as well as information about the *population standard deviation* and the *sample size*.

You'll see, then, that the details of a distribution of means vary as a function of both N and the population parameters dealing with mean (μ) and standard deviation (σ).

Suppose that the population mean (μ) for the GPA at your school is 2.5 and the population standard deviation (σ) is .5. The population distribution (per Figure 8.1) is a distribution of individual scores with these parameters. And it's a normal distribution.

You'll note that in Figure 8.1, we have labeled the N (N = 1). The point is to show that this distribution is a distribution of individual scores.

Table 8.1: Parameters for Samples, Distributions of Individual Scores, and Distributions of Means

	Sample	Distribution of Individual Scores	Distribution of Means
Mean	M	μ	μ_M
Variance	SD^2	σ^2	σ^2_M
Standard Deviation	SD	σ	σ_M

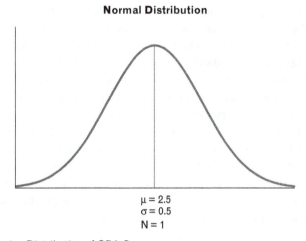

FIGURE 8.1: Population Distribution of GPA Scores.

A distribution of means is essentially a distribution based on the idea of randomly selecting scores of a specified sample size—infinitely—from a population distribution with known parameters. So suppose we were going to conduct a study to see if some special population (say psychology majors) had a mean GPA that differed from the general population. Say that our study sampled 5 individuals from the special population. In this example, we'd create a distribution of means based on an N of 5 and based on the population parameters of $\mu = 2.5$ and $\sigma = .5$. This distribution, represented in Figure 8.2, varies from the population distribution in a few ways.

First, you'll note that the mean is now represented by μ_M instead of μ and the standard deviation is represented by σ_M instead of σ. This lets us know that the distribution is a distribution of means and not a population distribution. Further, you'll see that the distribution is skinnier than the population distribution (shown on the left side of the figure). This is because the variance and standard deviation of a distribution of means is lower than the distribution of individual scores from which it is created. The reason for this pertains to how the distribution of means is created.

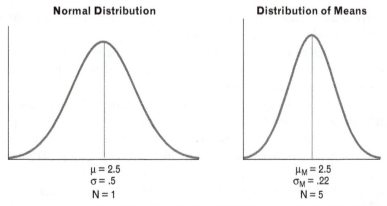

FIGURE 8.2: A comparison of a Population Distribution of GPA Scores and a Distribution of Means Based on an N of 5.

To understand how a distribution of means is created, consider the following example. Suppose that all the students in your school were put into a huge goldfish bowl. I know, not practical—but go with it! A friendly giant who is interested in statistics wants to plot three distributions—a distribution of individual scores (N = 1), a distribution of means based on a sample of 2 (N = 2), and a distribution of individual scores based on a sample of 20 (N = 20). Each giant has his own thing. Refer to Figure 8.3 to see the giant in action!

These distributions are presented in Figure 8.4. You'll notice that as N increases, the distribution decreases in variability (the normal distribution gets "skinnier"). This is the result of the Giant's work. When he creates the distribution of individual scores, he plucks one student from the bowl at a time, asks for his or her GPA, records it, and gently places the student back. He does this infinitely—or as close to it as he can! He then takes all these individual scores and graphs them in a frequency distribution. This distribution is a population distribution based on an N of 1. It's got the mean of 2.5 and the standard deviation of .5.

FIGURE 8.3: The Statistics-Friendly Giant Choosing Students for his Distributions. Credit: Michael Hubbard.

For the second distribution, based on N =2, he's now got a slightly more complex task on his hands. He randomly selects two students at a time. He gently asks for their GPAs, records the mean of the two in each case, and then places them back in the bowl. He does this millions of times—doing his best to approach infinity. He then graphs each mean. He's not graphing individual scores, but, rather, means based on an N of 2.

Now, when you are randomly selecting two scores at a time and taking the mean, you can run into all kinds of situations. You may find a situation in which you happen upon two very poorly performing students, and the mean is 1.5. You may randomly select two all-stars, and get a mean of 3.8. Or you may get a student with a high GPA and one a low GPA, resulting in a sample mean of 2.53 (close to the population mean). The scores (which are means of samples based on an N of 2) will vary less from one another than will individual scores, but they'll still vary quite a bit.

The formula for the variance of the distribution of means is as follows:

$$\sigma^2_M = \frac{\sigma^2}{N}$$

This simply means that the variance of the distribution of means goes down directly as a function of the size of the sample. As the sample size increases, the variance of the distribution of means goes down. Thus, in the current case, we can compute the variance of the distribution of means for the situation in which N = 2 as follows:

$\sigma = .5$; thus

$\sigma^2 = .25$;

$$\sigma^2_M = \frac{\sigma^2}{N} = \frac{.25}{2} = .13$$

As you may surmise, the standard deviation of the distribution of means is computed as follows:

$$\sigma_M = \sqrt{\sigma^2_M}$$

Often, this term (σ_M) is referred to as the *standard error of the mean* (which is synonymous with the *standard deviation of the distribution of means*).

So the standard deviation for the distribution of means corresponding to the situation in which N = 2 is $\sqrt{.13} = .36$ (see Figure 8.4). You'll note that this is smaller than the standard deviation of the population distribution (when N = 1), which is .5. As the N increases, the standard deviation of the distribution of means goes down.

All this said, note that the mean of all these samples of means will (as long as random selection is occurring) be equal to the mean of the population distribution from which they are drawn. Thus, $\mu_M = \mu$ (see Figure 8.4).

The Giant is curious. What happens as N increases even more? What happens if N = 20 (this distribution is also represented in Figure 8.4)?

Let's think what it would mean from the Giant's perspective if N = 20. In this case, the Giant would randomly (but politely!) select 20 students at a time from the bowl, obtain

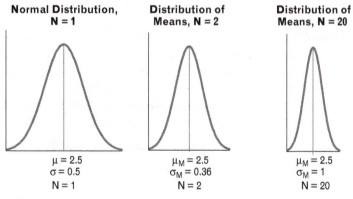

Normal Distribution, N = 1	Distribution of Means, N = 2	Distribution of Means, N = 20
$\mu = 2.5$	$\mu_M = 2.5$	$\mu_M = 2.5$
$\sigma = 0.5$	$\sigma_M = 0.36$	$\sigma_M = 1$
N = 1	N = 2	N = 20

FIGURE 8.4: Distribution of Means as N Increases.

their GPAs, record these numbers, and gently place these nice young individuals back in the bowl. He'd do this millions of times, approaching infinity as best he could. Think about how much these sample means would vary from one another. With an N of 20, the sample means are likely to all be pretty close to the mean itself. They are not likely to vary much from one another. Any very extreme score selected from the pool (e.g., a GPA of .02) will likely be counter-balanced by extreme scores the other way and scores near the mean. As N increases, extreme scores have a lower impact on the mean of a sample. So the variability indices for the distribution of means if N = 20 will all show much less variability for this distribution compared with the variability for the distributions based on smaller Ns. Specifically, if N = 20:

$\sigma = .5$;

$\sigma^2 = .25$;

$$\sigma^2_M = \frac{\sigma^2}{N} = \frac{.25}{20} = .01$$

And

$$\sigma_M = \sqrt{\sigma^2_M} = \sqrt{.01} = .1 \text{ (see Figure 8.4)}$$

Clearly, as N increases, the standard deviation of the distribution of means decreases. The Giant is pleased with this new information and lets the students all proceed to carry on with their enjoyable and productive academic lives.

STEPS IN HYPOTHESIS TESTING IF N > 1

If you're hypothesis testing with an N > 1, the steps in the process are identical to hypothesis testing if N = 1 ... with the exception that your comparison distribution is now a distribution of means. This fundamental point affects things at a number of places in the process—but, as you'll see, the process is pretty straightforward.

From the prior section, let's continue with the hypothesis that drivers of red cars speed—that they drive faster than the general population of drivers. Here, we clearly have a one-tailed (or *directional*) hypothesis. And to keep things simple, we can stick with our standard alpha level of .05.

With a problem of this variety, we'll need some other given information. Specifically, we'll need the mean and standard deviation of the general population (let's say that $\mu_2 = 70$ and $\sigma_2 = 10$). These numbers essentially say that the average speed for cars on this particular stretch of road is 70 and that standard deviation at the population level is 10.

We'll also need some raw data to represent the special population (here, that would be the population of red-car drivers). Suppose we select and record the speeds of five randomly selected red-car drivers (per our prior information; their scores are $\frac{84, 71, 75, 93, 90}{5}$, for a sample mean of 82.6). The steps in hypothesis testing would be as follows:

1. ARTICULATE THE RESEARCH AND NULL HYPOTHESES

This part of the process is identical to the process for hypothesis testing if $N = 1$. We'll continue to frame our hypotheses in terms of population-level parameters. In the current example, the research hypothesis is that the mean population speed for red-car drivers is greater than the mean speed for the general population. And the null hypothesis is the converse. In symbols, this can be represented as follows:

μ_1: Population mean for red-car drivers
μ_2: Population mean for general population of drivers

$$H_1: \mu_1 > \mu_2$$
$$H_0: \mu_1 \leq \mu_2$$

2. DETERMINE THE CHARACTERISTICS OF THE COMPARISON DISTRIBUTION

This is where things will change as a function of the fact that $N > 1$. The comparison distribution is based on the general population, but we're now looking at a distribution of means given that $N = 5$. Thus, all the characteristics of a distribution of means will come into play.

In terms of the mean, we'll now represent this with μ_{M2} instead of μ_2. That's to signify the fact that we're still basing this information on the mean for the general population, but that we're dealing with a distribution of means, not a population distribution. That said, $\mu_{M2} = \mu_2$. In this case, the mean of this distribution is 70 (see Figure 8.5). But we use different symbols to make it clear that we're talking about a different kind of conceptual distribution.

Naturally, we need to incorporate the fact that we're now dealing with a distribution of means in the indices of variability. Thus, the standard deviation of the comparison distribution will be represented by σ_M instead of σ.

To compute σ_M, we'll use the following:

$$\sigma = 10;$$
$$\sigma^2 = 100;$$

$$\sigma^2_M = \frac{\sigma^2}{N} = \frac{100}{5} = 20$$

And

$$\sigma_M = \sqrt{\sigma^2_M} \ \sqrt{20} = 4.47 \ \ (\text{see Figure 8.5})$$

3. DETERMINE CRITICAL VALUE

With an alpha of .05 and our research hypothesis (which predicts that the mean for the special population is greater than the mean for the general population), we know that our critical value (Z_{crit}) will be on the right side of the comparison distribution. We figure out Z_{crit} using the same process as we've used in the past few chapters. If 5% of the distribution is greater than Z_{crit}, then 45% is between Z_{crit} and the mean. Based on the information in the Z-to-Mean Table (Appendix A), this gives us a z-score of 1.64. So Z_{crit} = 1.64. See Figure 8.6.

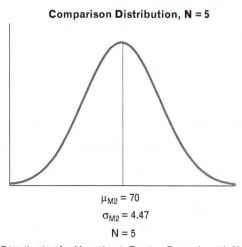

Comparison Distribution, N = 5

$\mu_{M2} = 70$
$\sigma_{M2} = 4.47$
$N = 5$

FIGURE 8.5: Comparison Distribution for Hypothesis Testing Example with N = 5.

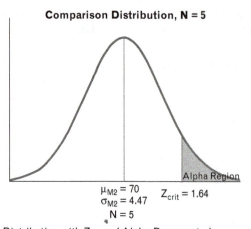

Comparison Distribution, N = 5

Alpha Region

$\mu_{M2} = 70$ $Z_{crit} = 1.64$
$\sigma_{M2} = 4.47$
$N = 5$

FIGURE 8.6: Comparison Distribution with Z_{crit} and Alpha Demarcated.

4. COMPARE Z_{OBT} BASED ON SAMPLE WITH Z_{CRIT}

This process is pretty much the same as what we've done in chapter 7. The primary difference is the fact that we're now computing a z-score based on the fact that we're dealing with a distribution of means. Thus, if we're dealing with a situation in which N > 1, we have to use the appropriate formula for Z_{obt}. In this case, if N > 1, we'll use the following:

$$Z_{obt} = \frac{M - \mu_{M2}}{\sigma_{M2}}$$

Note here that we use the parameters for the distribution of means. Also, the score that we are using to compare against the mean of the distribution of means (against μ_{M2}) is M, or the sample mean. That's because any particular "score" in a distribution of means is actually a sample mean. So we're comparing a sample mean with the mean of the distribution of means. Computationally, this is as follows:

$$Z_{obt} = \frac{82.6 - 70}{4.47} = 8.13$$

This information is visually demarcated in Figure 8.7.

5. COMMENT ON NULL HYPOTHESIS

This part of the process is identical to what we've done in chapter 7. We'll compare Z_{obt} with Z_{crit} on the comparison distribution (see Figure 8.7). Clearly, Z_{crit} is greater than Z_{obt}. As such, we reject the null hypothesis. In this case, it looks like the stereotype may be correct—these data suggest that red-car drivers drive faster than drivers in general.

If Z_{obt} were not as extreme as Z_{crit} and was, thus, not in the alpha region, we'd fail to reject the null hypothesis, providing no basis for us to support the research hypothesis.

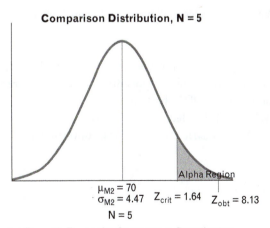

Comparison Distribution, N = 5

Alpha Region

$\mu_{M2} = 70$
$\sigma_{M2} = 4.47$ $Z_{crit} = 1.64$ $Z_{obt} = 8.13$
N = 5

FIGURE 8.7: Comparing the Z_{crit} with Z_{obt} on the Comparison Distribution.

CONFIDENCE INTERVALS

A common statistic that is based on the reasoning of the distribution of means pertains to *confidence intervals*. The basic idea here relates to how likely scores are to oscillate from a sample mean. Usually, people are interested in what's called the *5%* or *1%* confidence interval. The idea here is that if you have a sample mean based on a certain N, and you know the details of the distribution of means that it corresponds to, you can estimate how much your sample mean might vary from the population mean that you're trying to estimate. If you have a 5%-confidence interval, then you present your sample mean as well as the raw-score cutoff that has 2.5% of the distribution above it and the raw-score cutoff that has 2.5% of the distribution below it. With this statistic, you're essentially saying "our sample mean based on an N of thus-and-such is M, and based on our understanding of the population standard deviation and the size of our N, we can say with 95% certainty that the population mean we are trying to estimate is between this score and this other score."

For example, suppose that we're interested in the GPA for psychology majors. We know that the population standard deviation for GPA is .5 at the university. We sample 15 psychology majors and find their mean GPA to be 3.2. To compute the 95% confidence intervals, we'd do the following:

1. Compute σ_M as follows:

    $$\sigma = .5;$$
    $$\sigma^2 = .25;$$

    $$\sigma^2_M = \frac{\sigma^2}{N} = \frac{.25}{15} = .02$$

And

$$\sigma_M = \sqrt{\sigma^2_M} = \sqrt{.02} = .14$$

2. Figure out the z-score corresponding to cutting off 2.5% at the upper and lower end of the distribution.

If 2.5% of the distribution is above this point, then 47.5% of the distribution is between this point and the mean. The z-to-mean table (Appendix A) has this z-score as 1.96. So that cuts off the top 2.5%, and Z of −1.96 cuts off the bottom 2.5%.

Confidence intervals are represented in terms of raw scores, so we need to now convert these z-scores to raw scores. With a distribution of means, converting a z-score to a raw score is as follows:

$$M = Z(\sigma_M) + \mu_M$$

This translates to:

$$M = 1.96(.14) + 3.2 = 3.47$$

And

$$M = -1.96(.14) + 3.2 = 2.93$$

Note that the raw score is M—this is because a "raw score" in a distribution of means is a sample mean.

Our *95% confidence interval* is therefore between 2.93 and 3.47. This means simply that we're 95% certain that the real (population) mean for psych majors, based on our data, is between 2.93 and 3.47.

If we wanted to compute 99% confidence intervals, that means we'd follow this same process, but we'd use z-scores that cut off the top .5% and the lower .5%. To do so, we'd do the following:

1. Compute σ_M as we did in the prior computation ($\sigma_M = .14$).
2. Figure out the z-score corresponding to cutting off .5% at the upper and lower end of the distribution.

If .5% of the distribution is above this point, then 49.5% of the distribution is between this point and the mean. The z-to-mean table (Appendix A) has this z-score as 2.57. So that cuts off the top .5%, and Z of −2.57 cuts off the bottom .5%.

To compute raw-scores based on these z-scores, we'd use the following:

$$M = Z(\sigma_M) + \mu_M$$

This translates to:

$$M = 2.57(.14) + 3.2 = 3.56$$

And

$$M = -2.57(.14) + 3.2 = 2.84$$

So our *99% confidence interval* is between 2.84 and 3.56. This means simply that we're 99% certain that the real (population) mean for psych majors, based on our data, is between 2.84 and 3.56.

Based on what we know of distributions of means, we know that as the N increases, the standard deviation decreases. As such, with a larger N, our confidence intervals would improve— they would actually have smaller ranges as N increases. And if your goal is to best estimate population means, having a smaller range of error is a good thing. One more reason that larger Ns make for better statistics!

REAL RESEARCH EXAMPLE

Confidence intervals are often presented during political polls. During the 2012 Republican primary season, Romney and Santorum started out neck and neck. In March of 2012, the Marist

Poll showed Romney getting 32% of the votes and Santorum getting 34% of the votes. In the end, Romney won to emerge as the Republican presidential candidate. In any case, in this poll (presented here: http://americanresearchgroup.com/ratings/2012/ohrp/), the American Research Group made a point to indicate that the data represented a 95% Confidence Interval (with an "accuracy" of .08). In polling, this information signifies that the percentages presented are 95% likely to be between .08 percentage points from the percentages found in the sample. Of course, *95% certain* is never *100% certain*—but being *95% certain* has enormous advantages over having no sense of your certainty whatsoever.

SUMMARY

When we are dealing with situations in which N is greater than 1, our hypothesis-testing procedure needs to change slightly from situations in which N = 1. This is because the comparison distribution with an N > 1 needs to take into account the fact that it is a distribution of means, as opposed to a distribution of individual scores. A distribution of means is similar to distribution of individual scores (the means of these distributions are identical to one another), but they differ in terms of indices of variability. As N increases, the variability of scores in a distribution of means decreases.

A common and useful application of the distribution of means is found in *confidence intervals*, which are used to give a sense of how likely estimates of population means (and population-level percentages) are to be accurate. Political polling represents a very common field in which confidence intervals are utilized.

KEY TERMS

Confidence interval: The group of scores between an upper and lower score that is expected to contain the actual mean of the population.

Distribution of means: A conceptual distribution based on a population distribution as well as information about the population standard deviation and the sample size.

Standard error of the mean: Standard deviation of a distribution of means.

HOMEWORK SET A

1. You have a friend who thinks that people who take tons of pictures do so because they don't have very good memories, so they use pictures of an event less to document the event and more to help them remember it. You decide to collect data from 10 people you know who are always taking pictures, and you compare their mean score of 32 on the Memory Assessment Test to the population mean of 30 and standard deviation of 3. You use an alpha of .05.
    a. Articulate the research and null hypotheses.
    b. Determine the characteristics of the comparison distribution.
    c. Determine critical value.
    d. Compare Z_{obt} based on sample with Z_{crit}.
    e. Comment on the null hypothesis.
    f. Compute a 99% confidence interval.

2. You've listened to your father and his best friend call each other names as a form of greeting your whole life. The name calling is done in a good-natured fashion, and they both seem to thoroughly enjoy it. You also ponder the fact that you've never heard your mother and her friends call each other names. You wonder if name calling is a sign of strength of friendship in men. The Senior Center in your town just completed a study of friendship amongst its members, so you have population data to use for comparison. The Senior Center reports that among its male members, the mean friendship rating is 6.6 on a scale of 1–10, with a standard deviation of 2. You sit on a bench at the Senior Center on a group activity day, and listen as the men greet their friends. When you hear men good-naturedly calling each other names, you approach them and ask them to complete the Senior Center Friendship Rating. You survey 14 men, and calculate a mean on the Senior Center Friendship Rating of 8.1. You use an alpha level of .05.
    a. Articulate the research and null hypotheses.
    b. Determine the characteristics of the comparison distribution.
    c. Determine critical value.
    d. Compare Z_{obt} based on sample with Z_{crit}.
    e. Comment on the null hypothesis.
    f. Compute a 99% confidence interval.

3. Your friend who works at an animal shelter was telling you about some very unattractive animals who were recently adopted, much to the surprise of the shelter workers, who didn't think anyone would want such unattractive pets. This conversation gets you to wondering if people who adopt animals that are generally considered to be unattractive are more compassionate than the general population. You contact the ugly-pet adopters and ask them to complete an assessment of compassion, for which the population mean is 45 and the standard deviation is 4. The 8 people who adopted unattractive animals scored a mean of 47 on the compassion scale. You use an alpha level of .01.
    a. Articulate the research and null hypotheses.
    b. Determine the characteristics of the comparison distribution.
    c. Determine critical value.
    d. Compare Z_{obt} based on sample with Z_{crit}.
    e. Comment on the null hypothesis.
    f. Compute a 95% confidence interval.

HOMEWORK SET B

1. You've been spending your evenings watching the Olympics, and you realize that the more you watch the Olympics, the lower your assessment of your own physical prowess. For example, you participate in volleyball for recreation, and considered yourself a fairly good player, a solid 7 on a scale of 1 to 10. But now, after watching the Olympic volleyball players, you would rate your volleyball skills at a measly 4. You know from a recent study in your town that the population mean is 7.2 and the standard deviation is .5 on the Your Town Self-Assessment of Volleyball Skills (YTSAVS). You decide to see if other people who have just watched the Olympics tend to rate their skills lower on the YTSAVS. You gather 12 recreational volleyball players, show them an Olympic gold medal volleyball match, and then have them complete the YTSAVS. The mean of the group is 4.8 on the YTSAVS after watching Olympic volleyball. You use an alpha level of .01.

   a. Articulate the research and null hypotheses.
   b. Determine the characteristics of the comparison distribution.
   c. Determine critical value.
   d. Compare Z_{obt} based on sample with $Z_{crit.}$
   e. Comment on the null hypothesis.
   f. Compute a 99% confidence interval.

2. You've noticed that people who dress their pets in fancy clothes when they take them on walks garner a lot of attention. You wonder if people who dress their pets up for walks would score higher on a scale of attention-seeking behavior than people in general. You ask 10 dressed-pet walkers to complete a questionnaire of attention-seeking behavior, and find that their mean is 18 on the scale, which has a population mean of 15 and a standard deviation of 3. You use an alpha level of .05.

   a. Articulate the research and null hypotheses.
   b. Determine the characteristics of the comparison distribution.
   c. Determine critical value.
   d. Compare Z_{obt} based on sample with $Z_{crit.}$
   e. Comment on the null hypothesis.
   f. Compute a 95% confidence interval.

3. While waiting in line at the grocery store, you overhear the person in front of you in line talking on his cell phone about the merits of swimming lessons for children. He is very insistent that children who have not had formal swimming lessons are not safe in water. Later, you see on the news that the local swimming pool offered a water safety assessment for children, based on the Water Safety Skills Assessment Test (WSSAT). You learn that the WSSAT was recently used to compile data regarding water safety skills of children, and has a mean of 14, with a standard deviation of 2. You contact the local swimming pool, and they tell you that the 18 children who had not had formal swimming lessons had a mean of 13.5 on the WSSAT. You decide to see if the person in front of you in the grocery store was correct in stating that children who have not had formal swimming lessons are not safe in water. You use an alpha level of .05.

   a. Articulate the research and null hypotheses.
   b. Determine the characteristics of the comparison distribution.
   c. Determine critical value.
   d. Compare Z_{obt} based on sample with $Z_{crit.}$
   e. Comment on the null hypothesis.
   f. Compute a 95% confidence interval.

HOMEWORK SET A ANSWERS

1. a. $H_1: \mu_1 < \mu_2$

   $H_0: \mu_1 \geq \mu_2$

   b. $\sigma = 3$

   $\sigma^2 = 9$

   $\sigma^2_M = \dfrac{\sigma^2}{N} = \dfrac{9}{10} = .9$

   $\sigma_M = \sqrt{\sigma^2_M} = \sqrt{.9} = .95$

   c. $Z_{crit} = -1.64$ (Alpha level of .05, negative because the mean of the special population is predicted to be less than the mean for the general population.)

   d. $Z_{obt} = \dfrac{M - \mu_{M2}}{\sigma_{M2}}$

   $Z_{obt} = \dfrac{32 - 30}{.95} = 2.11$

   e. The Z_{obt} of 2.11 is not in the alpha region, so we fail to reject the null hypothesis. It appears that people who take a lot of photographs do not have worse memories than people in general.

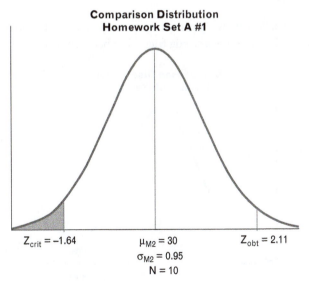

**Comparison Distribution
Homework Set A #1**

$Z_{crit} = -1.64$ $\mu_{M2} = 30$ $Z_{obt} = 2.11$
$\sigma_{M2} = 0.95$
$N = 10$

FIGURE 8.8: Homework Set A #1.

f. $M = Z(\sigma_M) + \mu_M$

$M = 2.57(.95) + 32 = 2.44 + 32 = 34.44$

And

$M = -2.57(.95) + 32 = -2.44 + 32 = 29.56$

The 99% confidence level is between 29.56 and 34.44. We are 99% certain, based on our data, that the population mean on the Memory Assessment Test for people who take a lot of pictures is between 29.56 and 34.44.

2. a. $H_1: \mu_1 > \mu_2$

$H_0: \mu_1 \leq \mu_2$

b. $\sigma = 2$
$\sigma^2 = 4$

$\sigma^2_M = \dfrac{\sigma^2}{N} = \dfrac{4}{14} = .29$

$\sigma_M = \sqrt{\sigma^2_M} = \sqrt{.29} = 54$

c. $Z_{crit} = 1.64$ (Alpha level of .05)

d. $Z_{obt} = \dfrac{M - \mu_{M2}}{\sigma_{M2}}$

$Z_{obt} = \dfrac{8.1 - 6.6}{.54} = 2.78$

e.   The Z_{obt} of 2.78 is in the alpha region, so we reject the null hypothesis. Name-calling may indeed be a sign of a strong friendship between men.

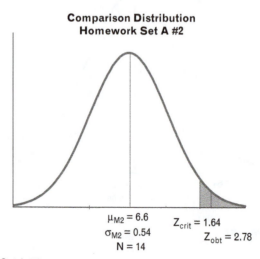

**Comparison Distribution
Homework Set A #2**

$\mu_{M2} = 6.6$
$\sigma_{M2} = 0.54$
$N = 14$

$Z_{crit} = 1.64$
$Z_{obt} = 2.78$

FIGURE 8.9: Homework Set A #2.

f. $M = Z(\sigma_M) + \mu_M$

$M = 2.57(.54) + 8.1 = 1.39 + 8.1 = 9.49$

And

$M = -2.57(.54) + 8.1 = -1.39 + 8.1 = 6.71$

The 99% confidence level is between 6.71 and 9.49. We are 99% certain, based on our data, that the population mean on the Senior Center Memory Assessment for men who call each other names is between 6.71 and 9.49.

3.   a. $H_1: \mu_1 > \mu_2$

$H_0: \mu_1 \leq \mu_2$

b. $\sigma = 4$

$\sigma^2 = 16$

$\sigma^2_M = \dfrac{\sigma^2}{N} = \dfrac{16}{8} = 2$

$\sigma_M = \sqrt{\sigma^2_M} = \sqrt{2} = 1.41$.

c. $Z_{crit} = 2.33$ (Alpha level of .01)

d. $Z_{obt} = \dfrac{M - \mu_{M2}}{\sigma_{M2}}$

$Z_{obt} = \dfrac{47 - 45}{1.41} = 1.42$

e.   The Z_{obt} of 1.42 is not in the alpha region, so we fail to reject the null hypothesis. Perhaps beauty is simply in the eye of the beholder.

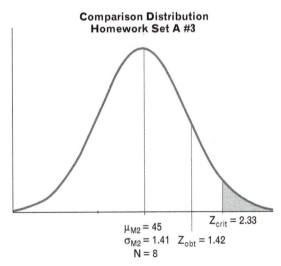

**Comparison Distribution
Homework Set A #3**

$\mu_{M2} = 45$
$\sigma_{M2} = 1.41$ $Z_{obt} = 1.42$
$N = 8$

$Z_{crit} = 2.33$

FIGURE 8.10: Homework Set A #3.

f. $M = Z(\sigma_M) + \mu_M$

$M = 1.96(1.41) + 47 = 2.76 + 47 = 49.76$

And

$M = -1.96(1.41) + 47 = -2.76 + 47 = 44.24$

The 95% confidence level is between 44.24 and 49.76. We are 95% certain, based on our data, that the population mean on the compassion scale for ugly-pet adopters is between 44.24 and 49.76.

REFERENCE

2012 Ohio Republican Presidential Primary Pollster Ratings. http://americanresearchgroup.com/ratings/2012/ohrp/ Retrieved July 28, 2012.

CHAPTER 9

STATISTICAL POWER

In chapter 7, we discussed the fact that hypothesis testing is an imperfect endeavor. In fact, a good lesson to come out of this course—along with most any other course you take in life—is that imperfection permeates the entirety of life. And, as a corollary, imperfection permeates any and all areas of academic inquiry.

Hypothesis testing, the core of modern-day statistics—which sits at the heart of so many scientific areas—is inherently imperfect. The best you can do is to reject the null hypothesis, supporting your a priori research hypothesis, and feeling reasonably confident that you have made the correct decision. As you recall, Type-I Error (rejecting the null hypothesis when, in fact, the null hypothesis is correct at the population level) and Type-II Error (failing to reject the null hypothesis, even though the null hypothesis is genuinely incorrect when examining things at the population level) are always possible outcomes of the hypothesis-testing procedure.

We do not want to come across as pessimists—a pessimistic life is not a very fun life. Rather, we're pointing out a problem with the process—but we also, in this chapter, focus on a solution to this problem. This solution revolves around the issue of *statistical power*. Simply and literally, statistical power is the probability of rejecting the null hypothesis when, in fact, the null hypothesis is false and the research hypothesis is true. So you may have a situation in which your research hypothesis is true, but this is a separate issue from how likely it is that the hypothesis-testing procedure will find that the research hypothesis is supported. See the difference? This nuance sits at the heart of the issue of statistical power.

With the concept of statistical power, instead of asking whether we're correct or not in our hypothesis-testing procedure, we, rather, ask how likely it is that we're able to find that we're correct (by rejecting the null hypothesis) if, in fact, our null hypothesis is false.

In short, with statistical power, instead of saying, "we're right—we rejected the null hypothesis—the research hypothesis is definitely right!," we can say something more like "not only did we reject the null hypothesis, but we can be very confident that we made the correct decision given the high amount of statistical power that we had in our design." This wording is slightly nuanced, but it's clear and strong—and it matches the best we can do in making the case that we've done well in working with our hypothesis-testing procedure.

WHAT IS STATISTICAL POWER?

Statistical power is often considered before you actually conduct a study. In terms of its definition, statistical power is *the probability of rejecting the null hypothesis if the research hypothesis is, at the population level, actually true.* It has less to do with whether the question you have is correct and more to do with your research design and how well that methodology is designed to uncover any effects that actually exist.

In lay terms, statistical power is essentially your likelihood of finding something if there's something there to be found.

AN EXAMPLE OF STATISTICAL POWER

Suppose that after you graduate with your degree in psychology, your university is so impressed with you that they want to offer you a job straight away. They then hire you in the Office of Institutional Research (an office commonly found on college campuses, which conducts research on issues related to the college, such as issues of grades, graduation rates, and so on; note that for people with interest and expertise in statistics, this is one of many options for solid career trajectories—there's a need in all kinds of industries for people who get this stuff!)

Your supervisor comes to you on your first day and says that she wants you to conduct a study to see if graduates from your college tend to score higher than the national average on a standardized test of job satisfaction (TMUJSI—The Made-Up Job Satisfaction Inventory). This test has been given to millions of Americans and the best estimates of the population mean (μ) and standard deviation (σ) are 25.00 and 5.00, respectively.

As you'll see in the real world (if you haven't seen already), money is tight all over—and, accordingly, your supervisor tells you that there's only enough in the budget for you to collect data from 20 randomly sampled graduates. You'd prefer to collect data from more, but you're new here, so you smile and say "Sure!" Your supervisor also asks you to use a standard alpha level (.05) and to assume a one-tailed test (with the research hypothesis being that graduates from your college score *higher* than the national average).

You quickly contact the office of Alumni Relations, get a list of email addresses of recent alumni, randomly select 20 to sample, and start emailing people, explaining who you are and what the research is generally about, and asking them to participate by completing the survey. After a few weeks, you have full data from 20 alumni and get started on your analysis. Before you get very far, you quickly compute the mean for your sample. It's 26. At this point, you hesitate. You're not sure exactly how your hypothesis test is going to go, but you know based on common sense that 26 is not much higher than 25 (recall that 25 is the national average). Does your hypothesis test even have a fighting chance? Suppose that the research hypothesis is even true— suppose that graduates from your school really do have higher scores (at the population level) than the national norm. With an N of 20 and a difference between the means of one unit (26 compared with 25), do you feel like your first task in this cool new position is going to succeed?

All this thinking pertains to the issue of estimating statistical power. Given all the information you have, *before you even conduct the hypothesis test*, you'd like to get a sense of how likely it is that you'll reject the null hypothesis. In other words, you'd like to estimate your statistical power.

Estimating statistical power is interesting for students in many ways. For one thing, there are no new mathematical concepts needed for this process. You'll discover that each of the steps involved includes information that you already know. Thus, this process is a large-scale instance of concept application and implementation. Additionally, we'll say this: Students don't always find this easy. So we suggest paying good attention, following specific details that we demarcate at each step, and doing multiple practice problems. Once you can master the mathematical process, you will necessarily have mastered an impressive ability to integrate and apply many high-level concepts—in a way that matters in the real world.

Here are the steps included in estimating power:

1. ARTICULATE THE NULL AND RESEARCH HYPOTHESES:

μ_1: The population mean for the special population (graduates of your great school) on TMUJSI

μ_2: The population mean for the general population of college graduates on TMUJSI

$$H_1: \mu_1 > \mu_2$$
$$H_0: \mu_1 \leq \mu_2$$

In other words, the population mean for the special population is predicted to be greater than the population mean for the general population.

2. DRAW A DISTRIBUTION CORRESPONDING TO THE COMPARISON DISTRIBUTION

You are not going to carry out the hypothesis test—that is not the point of estimating power. But if you *were* going to carry out the hypothesis test, what would be your comparison distribution? It would be a distribution corresponding to your general population. And, importantly, it would be a *distribution of means* corresponding to your general population. This is because your N is greater than 0! Remember the lessons from chapter 8—these lessons apply onward! Thus, the comparison distribution will be a distribution of means corresponding to your general population distribution—taking the N of the sample (20, in this case) into account. The mean for this distribution is represented by μ_{M2} ($\mu_{M2} = 25$) and the standard deviation is represented by σ_{M2} ($\sigma_{M2} = 1.12$).

In case you forgot from Chapter 8, here's how to derive σ_{M2}:

A. $\sigma^2 = \sigma * \sigma = 5 * 5 = 25$

B. $\sigma_{M2}^2 = \dfrac{\sigma^2}{N} = \dfrac{25}{20} = 1.25$

C. $\sigma_{M2} = \sqrt{(\sigma_{M2}^2)} = \sqrt{1.25} = 1.12$

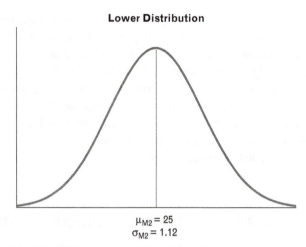

Lower Distribution

$\mu_{M2} = 25$
$\sigma_{M2} = 1.12$

FIGURE 9.1: Comparison Distribution (i.e., Lower Distribution).

Your comparison distribution will thus be a normal distribution (a distribution of means) with a mean (μ_{M2}) of 25 and a standard deviation (σ_{M2}) of 1.12. When you draw this distribution, give yourself lots of room—and, in particular, leave space for another distribution (and for some work) above it. In these problems, as the comparison distribution will be drawn on the lower part of the paper, we will often literally refer to this as *the lower distribution.*

3. DEMARCATE Z_{CRIT} ON THE COMPARISON DISTRIBUTION

You're not going to carry out the hypothesis test, but if you were, you'd need to demarcate Z_{crit}. Recall that this sets the alpha region (corresponding to the section of the distribution that you're defining as so low in probability that you'll reject the null hypothesis if a score lands in that region). Also recall that alpha = .05 and this is a one-tailed test. The mean for the special population is here predicted to be *greater than* the mean for the comparison distribution. These steps are all based on prior chapters, but, quickly, if alpha is 5% of the distribution, and is on the right of the mean of the comparison distribution (see Figure 9.2), then it refers to all points, in this case, that are to the right of Z_{crit}. Z_{crit} is based on alpha (and the fact that it's a one-tailed test). As 5% of the distribution is greater than this value, 45% is between this value and the mean of the distribution. We'll refer to our Mean-to-Z Table in the back of the book (Table 9.1). The particular Z corresponding to a "mean-to-z" of 45% is 1.64. So you should demarcate this Z_{crit} of 1.64 on your comparison distribution (see Figure 9.2).

4. SHADE THE ALPHA REGION

You're not going to carry out the hypothesis test, but if you were, you'd need the alpha region shaded. The alpha region is (in this case) the entire section to the right of Z_{crit} (see Figure 9.3).

Lower Distribution

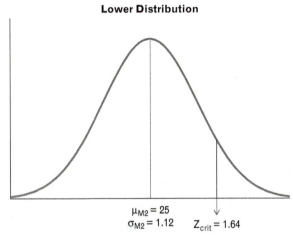

$\mu_{M2} = 25$
$\sigma_{M2} = 1.12$ $Z_{crit} = 1.64$

FIGURE 9.2: Comparison Distribution with Z_{crit} Demarcated.

5. DRAW THE UPPER DISTRIBUTION

The *upper distribution* is also the distribution that corresponds to the special population—with a mean represented by (μ_{M1}) and a standard deviation represented by (σ_{M1}). The mean for your upper distribution is an estimate—often this information is given in a problem (e.g., assume that the special population has a mean of…), or you can estimate, sometimes, based on a sample mean. In the current case, your sample mean for the special population of alumni from your institution is 26; given the information you have, this is your best estimate of μ_{M1}. Because this number is greater than the mean of the comparison distribution, the entire distribution (which you'll draw above the lower distribution) will be to the right of the lower distribution. Further, the shape will be the same. Here, we'll go with the *assumption of homogeneity of variance—* assuming that the variances and standard deviations for the two distributions are equal to one

Lower Distribution

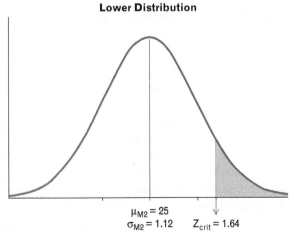

$\mu_{M2} = 25$
$\sigma_{M2} = 1.12$ $Z_{crit} = 1.64$

FIGURE 9.3: Comparison Distribution with Alpha Region Shaded.

Upper Distribution

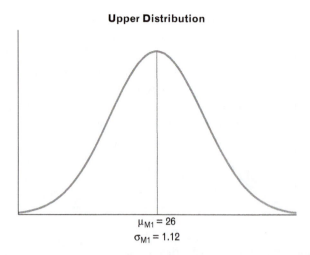

$\mu_{M1} = 26$
$\sigma_{M1} = 1.12$

Lower Distribution

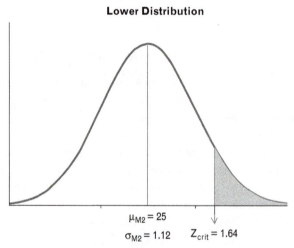

$\mu_{M2} = 25$
$\sigma_{M2} = 1.12$ $Z_{crit} = 1.64$

FIGURE 9.4: Upper Distribution Drawn Relative to Lower Distribution.

another. As this distribution is also a distribution of means, and we're assuming homogeneity of variance, $\sigma_{M1} = \sigma_{M2} = 1.12$. See Figure 9.4.

6. COMPUTE AND DEMARCATE M$_{CRIT}$

Ultimately, we'll need to see what percentage of the upper distribution overlaps with the alpha region in the lower distribution. In a strict, mechanical sense, that actually is power—the *percentage of the upper distribution that is extreme enough to reject the null hypothesis on the lower distribution*. We thus need a mechanism to compare across the two distributions. The critical value on the lower distribution needs to be understood in the context of the upper distribution. To this point, on the lower distribution, we know of this point in terms of Z_{crit}. But a z-score is always relative to a particular distribution. Z_{crit} is 1.64 standard deviations above the mean on the lower distribution, but that same score (whatever it is represented as a raw score) may well be a different number of standard deviations from the mean of the upper distribution.

We therefore need to figure out what Z_{crit} is as a raw score. In other words, regarding that point that is 1.64 standard deviations above the mean of the comparison distribution—what is that as a raw score? Here, we rely on our old friend—the equation to compute a z-score to a raw score. Generically, the formula is: $X = Z(SD) + M$. But here, we have a situation in which the raw score we are computing is not X but, rather, is M_{crit} (i.e., the Z_{crit} represented as a raw score). Further, Z is also modified to be more specific—Z_{crit}. Similarly, the standard deviation is now specific (it's σ_{M2}). Finally, the M is also now more specific (it's μ_{M2}).

To compute Z_{crit} into M_{crit}, the formula is as follows:

$$M_{crit} = Z_{crit}(\sigma_{M2}) + \mu_{M2}$$

In the current problem, this comes to $1.64(1.12) + 25 = 26.84$

Importantly, this is a specific version of the generic formula for converting a raw score to a z-score; it's the same as the formula we learned earlier on, just with each term specified for our particular situation at hand.

7. COMPUTE M_{UPPER}

We now need to think about that same point, which sets the alpha region on the lower distribution, in terms of the upper distribution. This may sound silly, but you'll find it useful; $M_{upper} = M_{crit}$. So $M_{upper} = 26.84$. We can now think of that same score (in this case, 26.84) in terms of both distributions. On the lower distribution, this point is M_{crit}; on the upper distribution, it's M_{upper}.

8. COMPUTE Z_{UPPER}

We're ultimately working toward figuring out what percentage of the upper distribution is extreme enough to reject the null hypothesis on the comparison distribution. To figure out percentages of sections in a normal distribution, we need to work with z-scores and use the Mean-to-Z table. Thus, we need to figure out what M_{upper} is as a z-score. Importantly, recall that z-scores are always only relevant to a particular distribution. Here, we're interested in how Z_{upper} is relative to the mean of the upper distribution. Thus, that same raw score of 26.84 will have a different Z value on the lower distribution than it will on the upper distribution—as it's a different number of standard deviations from the means of each distribution. Consequently, while this score corresponds to a Z of 1.64 on the lower distribution (i.e., Z_{crit}), it will have a different Z value (that we'll call Z_{upper}) on the upper distribution. And once we figure out that z-score, we can work toward computing power.

To compute Z_{upper}, we'll use a modified version of our standard Z formula,

$\left(Z = \dfrac{(X - M)}{SD} \right)$ Here, the particular formula we'll use, given our specific situation, is as follows:

$$Z_{upper} = \frac{(M_{upper} - \mu_{M1})}{\sigma_{M1}}$$

$$= \frac{(26.84 - 26)}{1.12}$$

$$= \frac{.84}{1.12} = .75$$

Note that $\mu_{M1} = 26$, as we'd previously concluded that the mean of the sample was our best estimate of the mean of the special population, and $\sigma_{M1} = 1.12$ because, as we'd concluded previously, given our assumption of homogeneity of variance, $\sigma_{M1} = \sigma_{M2}$.

9. CONNECT Z_{UPPER} AND Z_{CRIT} BETWEEN LOWER AND UPPER DISTRIBUTIONS

The question here ultimately pertains to what percentage of the upper distribution overlaps with the alpha region on the lower distribution. To address this, we'll need to place the distributions appropriately in space and draw a line connecting Z_{crit} on the lower distribution with Z_{upper} on the upper distribution (see Figure 9.5). This will allow us to see, visually, which sections of the upper distribution overlap with the alpha region of the lower distribution.

Refer to Figure 9.5 to see these two distributions connected and labeled appropriately.

Importantly, if you're working this stuff out by hand, as you are, note that getting things set up so that you have a perfect straight line is really difficult to make happen—and it's not actually necessary. The important thing here is that the line that connects the two distributions connects Z_{crit} and Z_{upper}. If you're drawing this all by hand, you may need to make a totally curved or squiggly line to make this happen. That's OK. Connecting the appropriate points is the goal here. Importantly, try for a straight line if you'd like, but note that getting a straight line is *not* the goal in this process (especially if you're doing this by hand). Students who see this (forcing a straight line) as the goal tend to get the problem incorrect. See Figure 9.6 for an example of what this would likely look like in a by-hand example.

10. SHADE POWER IN UPPER DISTRIBUTION

Power, mechanically speaking, is the percentage of the upper distribution that is extreme enough to reject the null hypothesis on the lower distribution. What percentage of the upper distribution overlaps with the alpha region? Looking at Figure 9.5, we can see that this corresponds to all of the upper distribution that's to the right of Z_{upper}. Importantly, we're interested in the section of the upper distribution that's to the *right* of Z_{upper} as the alpha region is on the right side of lower distribution (ultimately, as the research hypothesis predicts the mean of the upper distribution to be greater than the mean of the lower distribution).

Given that Z_{upper} (.75) is in the middle of the right half of the upper distribution, everything to the right of this point overlaps with the alpha region; *Power* is the entire part of the upper distribution that's to the right of Z_{upper}. We should now shade this area (see Figure 9.7).

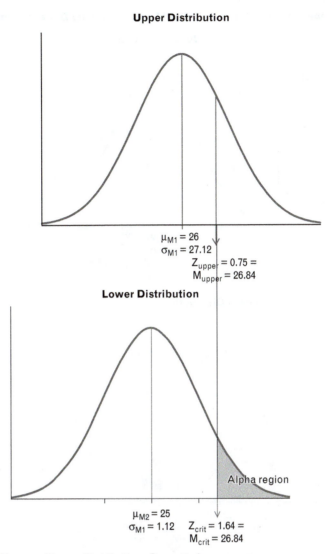

FIGURE 9.5: The Upper and Lower Distributions Connected.

11. COMPUTE POWER BASED ON SHADED SECTION OF UPPER DISTRIBUTION

To compute power, we'll use our Mean-to-Z Table. It's easy and it's something we've done throughout this book. If we divide the upper distribution into three sections, A, B, and C (see Figure 9.8), we discover that Z_{upper} divides up the right half of the distribution into sections B and C. Power is everything to the right of Z_{upper}; it's Section C. Recall that the Mean-to-Z Table only gives us Section B (the section between the particular z-score and the mean of the distribution). We therefore need to look up the z-score of interest (.75), which will give us Section B; we can then subtract that amount from 50%, and we'll have our answer—the percentage of the upper distribution that's in Section C.

Connecting Line Drawn as it Might Look if Correctly Done by Hand

Upper Distribution

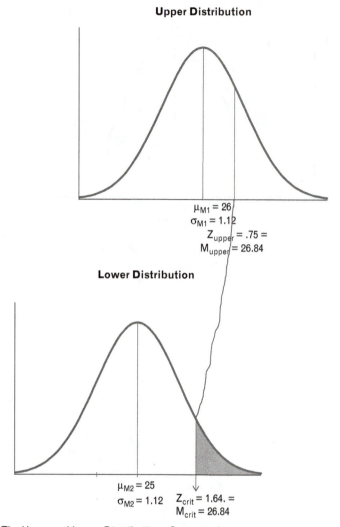

$\mu_{M1} = 26$
$\sigma_{M1} = 1.12$
$Z_{upper} = .75 =$
$M_{upper} = 26.84$

Lower Distribution

$\mu_{M2} = 25$
$\sigma_{M2} = 1.12$ $Z_{crit} = 1.64. =$
$M_{crit} = 26.84$

FIGURE 9.6: The Upper and Lower Distributions Connected.

According to the table, a z-score of .75 has 27.34% of the distribution between itself and the mean (this is Section B). To figure out what Section C is, we do 100%–(50% + 27.34%) = 22.66%.

Thus, power is equal to 22.66%—if you were going to conduct the hypothesis test, you'd have a 22.66% chance of rejecting the null hypothesis. Not really all that great, huh? Later in this chapter, we'll talk about factors that affect power, but, needless to say, the primary factor has to do with increasing your N; the larger the N, the greater your power. In the example delineated here, you'd probably want to go back to your supervisor and appeal for more time and resources for your project so you can increase your N and, thus, increase your power. If your odds of rejecting the null hypothesis are only 22.66%, then you're really setting yourself up for failure.

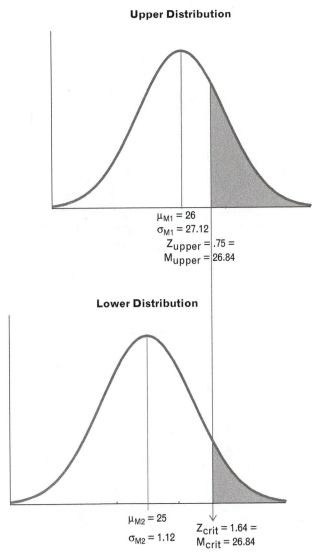

FIGURE 9.7: Upper Distribution with Power Shaded.

What is a sufficient level of power? Typically, as a rule of thumb, 80% is considered "sufficient." Honestly, the real rule is "the more power, the better." It really is something of a use-your-judgment situation.

Importantly, note that there's not a single equation, per se, to compute power—how to compute power using the Mean-to-Z Table will depend on the particulars of your situation. It'll depend on whether your alpha region is on the right side or the left side of the mean, if your Z_{upper} is on the right or left side, and so on. There are too many factors to be able to provide students with a single formula for this step. Instead of looking for a single formula, you'll need to understand the process and the goals you have in computing power.

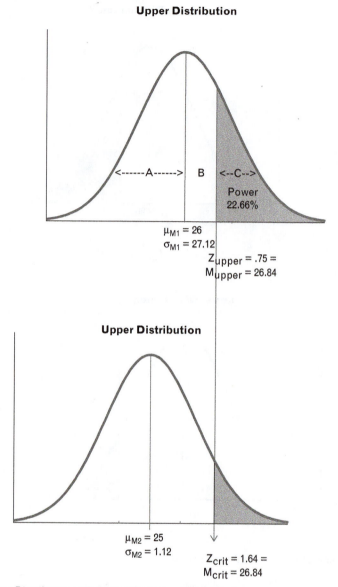

FIGURE 9.8: Upper Distribution with Power Shaded and Computed.

12. COMPUTE BETA

Beta is literally the probability of Type-II Error. But we can think about it very specifically in relation to power. If power is the probability of rejecting the null hypothesis (if the research hypothesis is correct), then Beta is the complement of power; computationally, 100%–Power (when power is expressed as a percentage). In this case:

$$Beta = 100-22.66 = 77.34\%$$

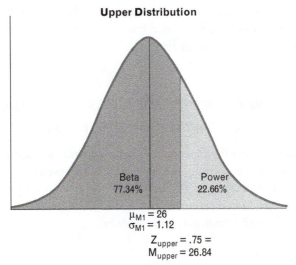

Upper Distribution

$\mu_{M1} = 26$
$\sigma_{M1} = 1.12$

$Z_{upper} = .75 =$
$M_{upper} = 26.84$

FIGURE 9.9: The Upper Distribution with Power and Beta Shaded.

So in this case, with low power, Beta tends to be high—even though the population mean for the special population is actually higher than the mean for the general population. Based on the assumptions of this problem, you're much more likely to fail to reject the null hypothesis (i.e., make Type-II Error) than to reject it. This is a bad situation! As a rule of thumb, you want power to be higher than Beta.

Now suppose you are an industrial psychologist with interests in the interface of health, behavior, and work productivity. You've come across a study suggesting that people who take daily vitamins miss less work than do others. You'd like to design a study to see if this pattern reflects how things are at your workplace. With the support of others in your workplace, you randomly select 20 people to be in the "vitamins" condition—these individuals agree to take multivitamins every day for the next year. The average number of sick days that an employee takes a year at your company is 4. The standard deviation for that population is 1. In your preliminary work, you find that the average number of sick days used by the vitamin-takers is 3. You assume this is your best estimate of the population mean for vitamin-takers based on the information you have.

The task now is this: Compute power. If you were going to conduct the hypothesis test, how likely would you be to reject the null hypothesis? You assume an alpha level of .01 (as your supervisor wants you to be very conservative and cautious with anything that has implications for changing health-related behaviors).

Let's walk through the same 12 steps to compute power for this example.

1. ARTICULATE THE NULL AND RESEARCH HYPOTHESES

μ_1: The entire population of workers who take multivitamins every day.
μ_2: The population mean for the general population of employees at the company.

H_1: $\mu_1 < \mu_2$
H_0: $\mu_1 \geq \mu_2$

In other words, the population mean for the special population is predicted to be less than the population mean for the general population (people who take vitamins will miss fewer days of work compared with the general population).

2. DRAW A DISTRIBUTION CORRESPONDING TO THE COMPARISON DISTRIBUTION

As N is 20 (and is, thus, greater than 1), our comparison distribution has a standard deviation that is a standard deviation of a distribution of means (σ_M). The comparison distribution will be the distribution of means corresponding to the general population with a mean represented by (μ_{M2}) and the standard deviation represented by σ_{M2}.

In case you forgot from chapter 8, here's how to derive σ_{M2}:

A. $\sigma^2 = \sigma * \sigma = 1 * 1 = 1$

B. $\sigma^2_{M2} = \dfrac{\sigma^2}{N} = \dfrac{1}{20} = .05$

C. $\sigma_{M2} = \sqrt{\sigma^2_{M2}} = \sqrt{.05} = .22$.

Thus, the comparison distribution (see Figure 9.10) has a mean (μ_{M2}) of 4 and standard deviation (σ_{M2}) of .22.

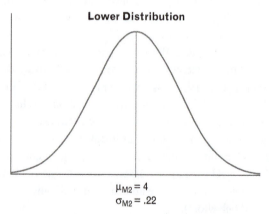

Lower Distribution

$\mu_{M2} = 4$
$\sigma_{M2} = .22$

FIGURE 9.10: Comparison Distribution (i.e., Lower Distribution).

3. DEMARCATE Z_{CRIT} ON THE COMPARISON DISTRIBUTION

Recall that Z_{crit} follows the research hypothesis. In this case, the mean of the special population is predicted to be *lower* than the mean for the general population. Thus, vitamin-takers are predicted to take fewer sick days than others. Consequently, the alpha region, demarcated by Z_{crit}, is to the left of the mean of the comparison distribution (see Figure 9.11). And 1% of the total distribution is to the left of this point (with 49% of the distribution between this point and

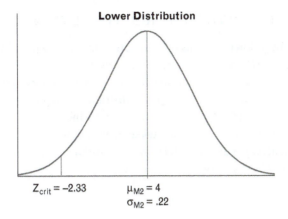

FIGURE 9.11: Comparison Distribution with Z_{crit} Demarcated.

the mean of the comparison distribution). To determine Z_{crit}, we need the Mean-to-Z Table. In this analysis, we must find the Z corresponding to having 49% of the distribution between that particular Z and the mean. Based on this table, we come to a Z of 2.33 (which corresponds to a percentage between the mean and Z of 49.01%—the closest in the table to 49%). The only additional point we need to consider is the fact that Z_{crit} is negative in sign (as it's on the left side of the comparison distribution). So $Z_{crit} = -2.33$ (see Figure 9.11).

4. SHADE THE ALPHA REGION

The alpha region is the entire section of the comparison distribution that is more extreme than the critical value—here, that's everything to the left of Z_{crit} (see Figure 9.12).

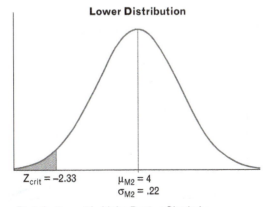

FIGURE 9.12: Comparison Distribution with Alpha Region Shaded.

5. DRAW THE UPPER DISTRIBUTION

Recall that the upper distribution represents our estimate of the special-population distribution (with the mean demarcated relative to the mean of the lower distribution). Here, the mean of the special population (vitamin-takers) is a distribution of means (as once N > 1, we're dealing with distributions of means). Further, the mean of this distribution (represented by μ_{M1}) is to the left of the mean of the lower distribution. Recall that $\mu_{M1} = 3$ while $\mu_{M2} = 4$. This is just another way of saying that the mean number of sick days taken by the population of vitamin-takers is 3, while the mean for the general population is 4. Drawn in two-dimensional space, relative to one another, these distributions look as shown in Figure 9.13.

6. COMPUTE AND DEMARCATE M_{CRIT}

Recall that M_{crit} is the raw-score version of Z_{crit}. And to compute a z-score to a raw score, we use the modified version of the standard Z-to-raw-score formula. As follows:

$$M_{crit} = Z_{crit}(\sigma_{M2}) + \mu_{M2}$$

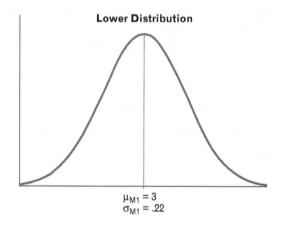

Lower Distribution

$\mu_{M1} = 3$
$\sigma_{M1} = .22$

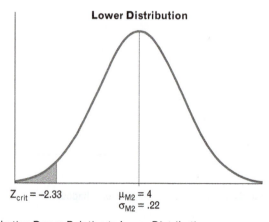

Lower Distribution

$Z_{crit} = -2.33$ $\mu_{M2} = 4$
$\sigma_{M2} = .22$

FIGURE 9.13: Upper Distribution Drawn Relative to Lower Distribution.

In the current problem, this comes to $-2.33(.22) + 4 = 3.49$

Thus, if you were going to complete the hypothesis test, the sample mean representing the special population of vitamin-takers would have to be less than 3.49 for you to reject the null hypothesis. This is important to consider here in order to put these details in light of the broader context of why 3.49 is important. All scores on the upper distribution that are more extreme than this score (i.e., less than 3.49) reflect "power"—or the section of the upper distribution that includes scores that are extreme enough to reject the null hypothesis on the comparison (lower) distribution.

7. COMPUTE M_{UPPER}

With this reasoning in mind, recall that $M_{upper} = M_{crit}$. These are the same score (3.49), but it is conceptualized differently on these different distributions. On the lower distribution, this score represents the critical value that sets off the alpha region. On the upper distribution, it demarcates the *power* section of that distribution. $M_{upper} = 3.49$.

8. COMPUTE Z_{UPPER}

As we'll need to ultimately figure out what percentage of that upper distribution is to the left of M_{upper}, we need to conceptualize this point as a z-score (Z_{upper}). To convert a raw score to a z-score, we use our modified version of the raw-to-Z formula, as follows:

$$Z_{upper} = \frac{M_{upper} - \mu_{M1}}{\sigma_{M1}}$$

$$= \frac{3.49 - 3}{.22}$$

$$= \frac{.49}{.22} = 2.23$$

Thus, this raw score of 3.49 is 2.23 standard deviations above the mean of the upper distribution. And everything to the left of this point in the upper distribution is *power*—i.e., is extreme enough to reject the null hypothesis on the lower distribution.

9. CONNECT Z_{UPPER} AND Z_{CRIT} BETWEEN LOWER AND UPPER DISTRIBUTIONS

Given that Z_{upper} and Z_{crit} correspond to the same raw score (3.49) and that we've created our graphs of the lower and upper distributions relative to one another, we can now draw a line connecting these points. Importantly, we'll do this with the understanding that everything to the left of this point on the lower distribution (Z_{crit}) represents *alpha* and everything to the left of this

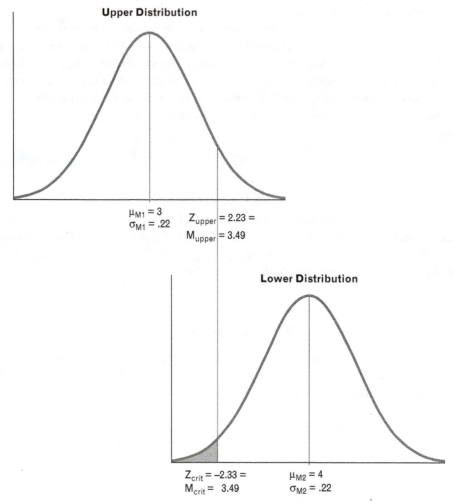

FIGURE 9.14: The Upper and Lower Distributions Connected.

point on the upper distribution (Z_{upper}) represents *power*. As mentioned before, try to get the line straight, but, most importantly, make sure they connect at the same raw-score point (3.49) (and don't worry if your connecting line is curved or squiggly. Refer to Figure 9.14 to see these two distributions connected and labeled appropriately.)

10. SHADE POWER IN UPPER DISTRIBUTION

To help calculate precisely what percentage of the upper distribution represents power, go ahead and shade the section of that distribution that represents power (the entire section of the distribution that is to the left of (Z_{upper}). See Figure 9.15.

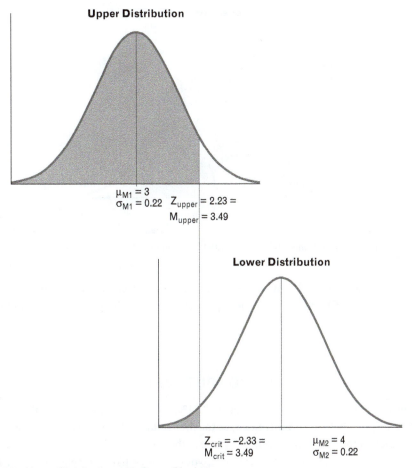

Upper Distribution

$\mu_{M1} = 3$
$\sigma_{M1} = 0.22$ $Z_{upper} = 2.23 =$
$M_{upper} = 3.49$

Lower Distribution

$Z_{crit} = -2.33 =$ $\mu_{M2} = 4$
$M_{crit} = 3.49$ $\sigma_{M2} = 0.22$

FIGURE 9.15: Upper Distribution with Power Shaded.

11. COMPUTE POWER BASED ON SHADED SECTION OF UPPER DISTRIBUTION

With this example, you should hopefully see that power represents all points to the left of Z_{upper} (as opposed to everything to the right of this point, which would be true in examples for which μ_1 is predicted to be greater than μ_2). Thus, if we look at the shaded area of the upper distribution and demarcate our standard sections of A, B, and C (to help us compute percentages of this distribution), we'll see that power is represented by sections A and B.

Section A is 50% (half) of the distribution. To determine Section B (the other part of the power area), we'll need to see what percentage of the distribution is between the relevant z-score (Z_{upper}) and the mean. Recall that $Z_{upper} = 2.23$. Based on our z-to-mean table, 48.71% of the distribution is in this section (Section B; see Figure 9.16). So 50% + 48.71% is 98.71%. Power = 98.71%.

Upper Distribution

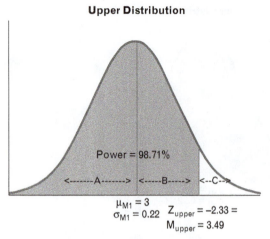

FIGURE 9.16: Upper Distribution with Power Shaded and Computed.

If you were going to test this hypothesis, your chances of rejecting the null hypothesis would be 98.71%. Not bad! Clearly, this is a more powerful research design than we had in our first example.

12. COMPUTE BETA

Beta is the complement of power. If Power = 98.71%, Beta = 1.29%. Recall that this is formally defined as the probability of Type-II Error, or the probability of failing to reject the null hypothesis (even though the research hypothesis is true at the population level).

With the research design in this example, you'd be very likely to reject the null hypothesis—and very unlikely to fail to reject the null hypothesis. If you were tasked with testing this vitamin/health-in-the-workplace hypothesis, you'd be in good shape!

Upper Distribution

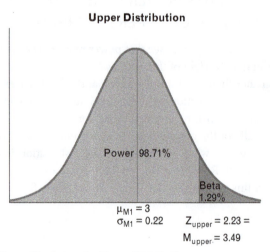

FIGURE 9.17: Beta and Power Shaded on the Upper Distribution.

FACTORS THAT AFFECT STATISTICAL POWER

ONE VERSUS TWO-TAILED TESTS

You'll notice that the two examples we used in this chapter each had one-tailed tests. There are a few points to note about why we structured it this way. First off, one-tailed tests are more power-ful than two-tailed tests. This point is simply due to the fact that the specific rejection regions are half as big with one-tailed rather than two-tailed tests (because a two-tailed test divides alpha across two rejection regions).

Also, it's worth noting that with a power example, a two-tailed test is actually logically inap-propriate—it's not something you'd really do. Think about it—with a power example, you're assuming that you know (or have a good, workable estimate of) the mean for the special popula-tion. As such, you're saying (a priori) that the upper distribution is either (a) shifted to the right of the mean of the lower distribution or (b) shifted to the left of the mean of the lower distribu-tion. You can't have it both ways.

For these reasons, we may, on one hand, think of one-tailed tests as being inherently more powerful than two-tailed tests or, more accurately, we may think of one-tailed tests as really being the only kind of appropriate tests in computing power problems.

See Table 9.1 for a summary of factors that affect power.

EFFECT SIZE (GENERALLY) AND COHEN'S D (IN PARTICULAR)

Recall from the prelude to this book that there are two primary ways to think of an outcome as statistically noteworthy. One pertains to *statistical significance*, which we've addressed in detail in the past few chapters. The other pertains to *effect size*—whether the effect is large, medium, or small in a practical sense.

When comparing two means, the appropriate test of effect size is *Cohen's d*, a test that simply compares two means relative to some estimate of population standard deviation. There are dif-ferent formulas for Cohen's d depending on the situation. But if you have population means and the population standard deviation (as we do in the examples in this chapter), the formula is as follows:

$$\text{Cohen's } d = \left| \frac{\mu_1 - \mu_2}{\sigma_2} \right|$$

Importantly, any and all effect size estimates rely on population-level information, not on information based on a distribution of means (and you'll see this point demarcated in the for-mula). This is because your estimate of the effect size is supposed to be based on your best guess as to how large the effect is in a general sense (not in any sense tied to a specific study or a spe-cific sample size). You're trying to estimate, essentially, *how big is the effect itself, separate from the details of any particular study per se.* Thus, all parameters in an effect size estimate, therefore, are free of information based on any particular sample size. For this reason, we use μ_1, μ_2, σ_2 as opposed to μ_{M1}, μ_{M2}, σ_{M2}. This formula is essentially asking "how different are the two popula-tion means from one another relative to the population standard deviation?"

In the current example, Cohen's $d = \left| \frac{3-4}{1} \right| = 1$.

Based on Cohen and Cohen's (1988) seminal work on the concept of effect size, effect sizes can be divided (roughly) into small, medium, and large based on the following conventions:

Small Cohen's d ~ .2
Medium Cohen's d ~ .5
Large Cohen's d ~ .8

In the current example, we have a Cohen's d of 1.0. Clearly, this is "larger than large"—so we can call this a *very large* effect size. Note that these conventions are sort of fuzzy—and are really broad benchmarks, as opposed to rules set in stone. That said, these conventions do provide a nice starting point to think about how large your effect is independent of your study design.

In relation to the issue of how Cohen's d relates to effect size, you'll see that the larger the effect size (all things equal), the more power you have. Note that, as a case in point, the second example in this chapter had a very large effect size and very high power (over 98%). Our first example had lower power (22.66%)—and this fact is not surprisingly coupled with the point that Cohen's d in this example would be as follows:

$\left|\dfrac{26-25}{5}\right| = .2$ (note that the numbers used for this calculation follow the generic formula

cohen's d $= \left|\dfrac{\mu_1 - \mu_2}{\sigma_2}\right|$ and use information from the first example in this chapter).

All things equal, a larger effect size corresponds to more power.
See Table 9.1 for a summary of factors that affect power.

POPULATION VARIABILITY

The formula for Cohen's d is very useful in helping us think about the relationship between population variability and power. Here's the formula again:

$$\text{Cohen's } d = \left|\frac{\mu_1 - \mu_2}{\sigma_2}\right|$$

In relation to this formula, population variability is reflected in the term σ_2. This is the population standard deviation for the general population (which is simply the square root of the population variance for the general population). Given this formula, we can easily see the relationship between Cohen's d and σ_2. As the standard deviation goes down (given that it's in the denominator), Cohen's d increases. So, simply:

Effect size increases as population variability decreases.

This point makes simple sense based on the elements of Cohen's d, but it also makes conceptual sense beyond the computational details. Consider, for instance, the second example in this chapter in which the number of sick days used by vitamin-takers was 3 and the number used by the general population was 4. That signifies one thing in light of a relatively small standard deviation (meaning that people don't vary much from 4 in the general population). But what if the amount of sick days in the general population varied wildly—so that the average was 4, but

Table 9.1: Factors that Affect Power

Factor	Effect on Power (All Things Being Equal)
Number of Tails in Test	One-Tailed tests are more powerful than Two-Tailed tests.
Effect Size	Larger effect sizes correspond to more power.
Population Variability	Lower levels of population variability correspond to more power.
Sample Size (N)	A higher N corresponds to more power.

some people had 35, some had 16, some had 0, and so on? This scenario would lead to a large population standard deviation—and it would also mean that a difference between 3 and 4 would be less clear as a "big effect" compared with looking at 3 versus 4 in a situation with a low level of population variability.

See Table 9.1 for a summary of factors that affect power.

SAMPLE SIZE (N)

An offshoot of the fact that power increases with lower population standard deviation (or variability) is the fact that power increases with increases in sample size (N).

If we were going to carry out the hypothesis test (as we did in chapter 8), we'd use the formula

$$Z = \frac{M - \mu_{M2}}{\sigma_{M2}}.$$

Recall that $\sigma_{M2} = \sqrt{\sigma_{M2}^2}$

and

$$\sigma_{M2}^2 = \frac{\sigma^2}{N}$$

and

$$\sigma^2 = \sigma * \sigma.$$

As an outcome of all this math, you'll see that as N increases, σ_{M2}^2 decreases $\left(\text{as } \sigma_{M2}^2 = \frac{\sigma^2}{N} \right)$

As such, as N increases, Z increases (and as Z increases, you're more likely to reject the null hypothesis).

We can also think of this a bit more conceptually—as your N increases, you're more likely to reject the null hypothesis (because the statistics become more biased, allowing you to reject the null hypothesis). This fact is a result of assuming that your sample mean is more likely to approximate the population mean it's estimating if that sample mean is based on a relatively large sample.

Simply: As sample size (N) increases, power increases.

See Table 9.1 for a summary of factors that affect power.

A REAL RESEARCH EXAMPLE

In a set of studies examining whether expressions of good luck (e.g., "break a leg!") improve performance, Damisch, Stoberock, and Mussweiler (2010) found interesting evidence for the usefulness of these kinds of comments. In one study, two groups of participants engaged in a golf-putting task. Participants in one group were given superstitious encouragement (e.g., they were told that they were using a "lucky ball"), while participants in the other group were not given this information. Results were clear, according to the authors:

As predicted, participants performed better when playing with an ostensibly lucky ball ($M = 6.42$, $SD = 1.88$) rather than a neutral ball ($M = 4.75$, $SD = 2.15$), $t(26) = 2.14$, $p < .05$, Cohen's d = 0.83 (Damish et al., 2010, p. 1015).

As you know, a Cohen's d of .83 is nothing to sneeze at (i.e., it's a *large* effect size). This fact helps explain why the hypothesis test was significant (explicated in the phrase *p <.05*). This is true in spite of the fact that the N was relatively small (as we'll see in future chapters, with this kind of t-test, the number in the parentheticals with *t* (in this case, 26) is 2 less than the total N for the study). Thus, the N for this study was 28—it was a relatively small study. However, with such a large effect size, the study had a lot of power—and this fact offset the adverse effects on power presented by the relatively low N.

SUMMARY

Power corresponds to the probability of rejecting the null hypothesis (if the research hypothesis is true). Computing power includes several steps—but these steps are all based on concepts related to z-scores, probability distributions, and hypothesis-testing that we've already covered.

Thus, if you want to increase your power in your research (and, hint-hint, you always do want to!), you should try to use a one-tailed test (when conceptually appropriate), try to have relatively low population variability (if you can somehow control this parameter; usually you can't!), try to have a large N (this one you can control!), and try to have a large effect size (if controllable).

KEY TERMS

Cohen's d: A test that compares two means relative to some estimate of population standard deviation to estimate, essentially, how big the effect itself is, separate from the details of any particular study. Cohen's d = $\left| \dfrac{\mu_{M1} - \mu_{M2}}{\sigma_2} \right|$.

Statistical power: The probability of rejecting the null hypothesis if the research hypothesis is, at the population level, actually true; the percentage of the upper distribution that is extreme enough to reject the null hypothesis on the lower distribution.

HOMEWORK SET A

1. You have been noticing wild bird feeders in the stores lately, and you always think that you just don't have the time to devote to the endeavor of feeding wild birds, which leads you to wonder if people who purchase wild bird feeders have shorter work weeks than those who don't purchase wild bird feeders. You ask a friend who works at a store that sells wild bird feeders to collect data for you regarding the number of hours a week people who purchase wild bird feeders work. On one day, 16 people purchase wild bird feeders, and the mean number of hours/week they work is 37. Before getting too far into this study, you decide to compute statistical power (by completing steps a-n), comparing your sample of wild bird feeder purchasers to the general population, with a mean number of hours worked per week of 40 and a standard deviation of 3. You use an alpha level of .05.
   a. Articulate the null and research hypotheses.
   b. Draw a distribution corresponding to the comparison distribution.
   c. Demarcate Z_{crit} on the comparison distribution.
   d. Shade the alpha region.
   e. Draw the upper distribution.
   f. Compute and demarcate M_{crit}
   g. Compute $M_{upper.}$
   h. Compute Z_{upper}.
   i. Connect Z_{upper} and Z_{crit} between lower and upper distributions.
   j. Shade power in the upper distribution.
   k. Compute power based on shaded section of upper distribution.
   l. Compute Beta.
   m. Calculate Cohen's d.
   n. Comment on the effect size and the power.

2. Donna, a local apartment building owner, noticed that the majority of people renting apartments in her building had young children, and became concerned that the children were not getting enough exercise, due to living in apartments with no yards in which to play. Trying to do her part to improve the lives of young children, Donna has a playground installed, and notices that people are bringing their children to play, but don't seem to be staying long. She believes that installing benches for parents to sit on will encourage people to stay longer. She calls you to help her determine if installing benches is, indeed, a logical step. You discover a recent study of apartment playgrounds with benches that gathered data from millions of apartments that reports that the mean number of minutes people stay at the playgrounds is 36 minutes, with a standard deviation of 4 minutes. You gather data from the first 12 people to bring children to play on Donna's playground, finding that the mean amount of time spent at Donna's playground is 30 minutes. You first compute statistical power (by completing steps a-n). You use an alpha level of .01.
   a. Articulate the null and research hypotheses.
   b. Draw a distribution corresponding to the comparison distribution.
   c. Demarcate Z_{crit} on the comparison distribution.
   d. Shade the alpha region.
   e. Draw the upper distribution.
   f. Compute and demarcate $M_{crit.}$
   g. Compute $M_{upper.}$

h.   Compute Z_{upper}.

i.   Connect Z_{upper} and Z_{crit} between lower and upper distributions.

j.   Shade power in the upper distribution.

k.   Compute power based on shaded section of upper distribution.

l.   Compute Beta.

m.   Calculate Cohen's d.

n.   Comment on the effect size and the power.

3.   Your boss has become interested in the happiness of her employees after reading an article that linked employee happiness with work production. She firmly believes that she has created a happy environment for her employees, and expects them to score above the mean on employee happiness. She gives you the task of determining the happiness level of her employees, using the Employee Happiness Scale, which has a mean of 50 and a standard deviation of 5. You collect data from 15 employees. You decide to compute the statistical power of your study (by completing steps a-n) once you determine that your sample has a mean of 52. You use an alpha level of .01.

a.   Articulate the null and research hypotheses.

b.   Draw a distribution corresponding to the comparison distribution.

c.   Demarcate Z_{crit} on the comparison distribution.

d.   Shade the alpha region.

e.   Draw the upper distribution.

f.   Compute and demarcate $M_{crit.}$

g.   Compute $M_{upper.}$

h.   Compute Z_{upper}.

i.   Connect Z_{upper} and Z_{crit} between lower and upper distributions.

j.   Shade power in the upper distribution.

k.   Compute power based on shaded section of upper distribution.

l.   Compute Beta.

m.   Calculate Cohen's d.

n.   Comment on the effect size and the power.

HOMEWORK SET B

1.   As a teacher's assistant, you've been given the task of organizing study groups before each major test. You've decided to try to increase the amount of participation amongst the attendees by tossing a Hershey's kiss to every person who contributes. You know, based on the National Study Group Participation Survey, the mean number of times a person in a typical study group contributes to the conversation in 1 hour is 6, with a standard deviation of 2. You calculate the mean number of times the 20 participants in your 1-hour study group contributed was 8. You decide to find the statistical power (by completing steps a-n). Use an alpha level of .01.

a.   Articulate the null and research hypotheses.

b.   Draw a distribution corresponding to the comparison distribution.

c.   Demarcate Z_{crit} on the comparison distribution.

d.   Shade the alpha region.

e.   Draw the upper distribution.

f.   Compute and demarcate $M_{crit.}$

g.   Compute $M_{upper.}$

    h.   Compute Z_{upper}.

    i.   Connect Z_{upper} and Z_{crit} between lower and upper distributions.

    j.   Shade power in the upper distribution.

    k.   Compute power based on shaded section of upper distribution.

    l.   Compute Beta.

    m.   Calculate Cohen's d.

    n.   Comment on the effect size and the power.

2.   Greta, the owner of Greta's Groceries, thinks that announcing that the store will be closing 10 minutes before closing time tends to cause people to select fewer items, reducing the dollar amount of the sales. Greta wants answers in a hurry so that she can determine whether to make the announcement 10 minutes before closing, or to simply announce closing at closing time to maximize store profit. Greta asks you to base your conclusion on one day of data collection without the 10-minute store closing announcement, and with the information that the mean amount of grocery store sales in the last 10 minutes before closing nationwide is \$19.60 with a standard deviation of \$1.20 when closing time is announced 10 minutes beforehand. On the day that you collect data from Greta's Groceries without the 10-minute store closing warning, there are 6 shoppers with a mean purchase amount of \$20 during the last 10 minutes. You begin by computing statistical power based on this data (by completing steps a-n). You use an alpha level of .05.

    a.   Articulate the null and research hypotheses.

    b.   Draw a distribution corresponding to the comparison distribution.

    c.   Demarcate Z_{crit} on the comparison distribution.

    d.   Shade the alpha region.

    e.   Draw the upper distribution.

    f.   Compute and demarcate $M_{crit.}$

    g.   Compute $M_{upper.}$

    h.   Compute Z_{upper}.

    i.   Connect Z_{upper} and Z_{crit} between lower and upper distributions.

    j.   Shade power in the upper distribution.

    k.   Compute power based on shaded section of upper distribution.

    l.   Compute Beta.

    m.   Calculate Cohen's d.

    n.   Comment on the effect size and the power.

3.   Your friend expresses the opinion that people who seek to adopt a cat have less satisfying social lives than the average person. Intrigued, you ask a local animal shelter to assist in data collection. People who apply to adopt a cat are asked to voluntarily complete the Social Satisfaction Scale in addition to the standard adoption application. You know that the mean for the Social Satisfaction Scale is 20 (with higher numbers corresponding to higher levels of social satisfaction) and the standard deviation is 2. Seeking to get answers as soon as possible, you compute statistical power (by completing steps a-n) after 10 potential cat adopters have completed the Social Satisfaction Scale, with a mean of 19. You use an alpha level of .05.

    a.   Articulate the null and research hypotheses.

    b.   Draw a distribution corresponding to the comparison distribution.

    c.   Demarcate Z_{crit} on the comparison distribution.

    d.   Shade the alpha region.

    e.   Draw the upper distribution.

    f.   Compute and demarcate $M_{crit.}$

    g.   Compute $M_{upper.}$

    h.   Compute $Z_{upper.}$

    i.   Connect Z_{upper} and Z_{crit} between lower and upper distributions.

    j.   Shade power in the upper distribution.

    k.   Compute power based on shaded section of upper distribution.

    l.   Compute Beta.

    m. Calculate Cohen's d.

    n.   Comment on the effect size and the power.

HOMEWORK SET A ANSWERS

1. $H_1: \mu_1 < \mu_2$

    $H_0: \mu_1 \geq \mu_2$

Computing standard deviation:

$$\sigma^2 = \sigma * \sigma = 3 * 3 = 9$$

$$\sigma^2_{M2} = \frac{\sigma^2}{N} = \frac{9}{16} = .56$$

$$\sigma_{M2} = \sqrt{(\sigma^2_{M2})} = \sqrt{.56} = .75$$

Computing M_{crit}:

$$M_{crit} = Z_{crit}(\sigma_{M2}) + \mu_{M2}$$
$$M_{crit} = -1.64(.75) + 40$$
$$M_{crit} = 38.77$$

Computing M_{upper}:

$$M_{crit} = M_{upper} = 38.77$$

Computing Z_{upper}:

$$Z_{upper} = \frac{M_{upper} - \mu_{M1}}{\sigma_{M1}} =$$

$$\frac{1.77}{.75} = 2.36$$

Computing Power:

   % Mean to Z of 2.36 = 49.09%

   Power = 50% + 49.09% = 99.09%

Computing Beta:

100%–99.09% = .91%

Calculation Cohen's d:

$$\text{Cohen's } d = \left| \frac{\mu_{M1} - \mu_{M2}}{\sigma_2} \right|$$

$$\text{Cohen's } d = \left| \frac{37 - 40}{3} \right| = -1$$

Comment on power and Cohen's d:

Effect size was very large in this study (the absolute value of Cohen's d = 1), and power was very high (99.09%).

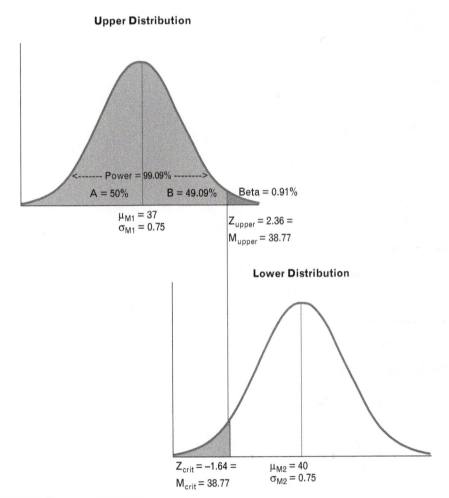

FIGURE 9.18: Homework Set A #1.

2. $H_1: \mu_1 < \mu_2$

$H_0: \mu_1 \geq \mu_2$

Computing standard deviation:

$$\sigma^2 = \sigma * \sigma = 4 * 4 = 16$$

$$\sigma^2_{M2} = \frac{\sigma^2}{N} = \frac{16}{12} = 1.33$$

$$\sigma_{M2} = \sqrt{(\sigma^2_{M2})} = \sqrt{1.33} = 1.15$$

Computing M_{crit}:

$$M_{crit} = Z_{crit}(\sigma_{M2}) + \mu_{M2}$$
$$M_{crit} = -2.33(1.15) + 36$$
$$M_{crit} = 33.32$$

Computing M_{upper}:

$$M_{crit} = M_{upper} = 33.32$$

Computing Z_{upper}:

$$Z_{upper} = \frac{M_{upper} - \mu_{M1}}{\sigma_{M1}}$$

$$\frac{33.32 - 30}{1.15} = 3.32$$

$$\frac{3.32}{1.15} = 2.89$$

Computing Power:

% Mean to Z of 2.89 = 49.81%
Power = 50% + 49.81% = 99.81%

Computing Beta:

100%–99.81% = .19%

Calculation Cohen's d:

$$\text{Cohen's } d = \left| \frac{\mu_{M1} - \mu_{M2}}{\sigma_2} \right|$$

$$\text{Cohen's } d = \left| \frac{30 - 36}{4} \right| = -1.5$$

Comment on power and Cohen's d:

Effect size was very large in this study (Cohen's d = 1.5), and power was very high (99.81%).

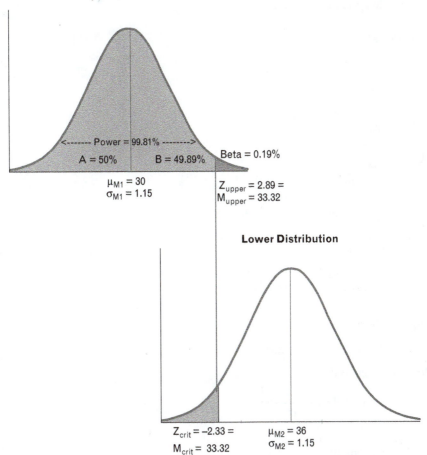

FIGURE 9.19:

3. $H_1: \mu_1 > \mu_2$

$H_0: \mu_1 \leq \mu_2$

Computing standard deviation:

$$\sigma^2 \ \sigma * \sigma = 5 * 5 = 25$$

$$\sigma^2_{M2} = \frac{\sigma^2}{N} = \frac{25}{15} = 1.67$$

$$\sigma_{M2} = \sqrt{(\sigma^2_{M2})} = \sqrt{1.67} = 1.29$$

Computing M_{crit}:

$$M_{crit} = Z_{crit}(\sigma_{M2}) + \mu_{M2}$$
$$M_{crit} = 2.33(1.29) + 50$$
$$M_{crit} = 3.01 + 50 = 53.01$$

Computing M_{upper}:

$$M_{crit} = M_{upper} = 53.01$$

Computing Z_{upper}:

$$Z_{upper} = \frac{M_{upper} - \mu_{M1}}{\sigma_{M1}}$$

$$\frac{53.01 - 52}{1.29} =$$

$$\frac{1.01}{1.29} = .78$$

Computing Power:

% Mean to Z of .78 = 28.23%
Power = 100%–(50% + 28.23%) = 21.77%

Computing Beta:

100%–21.77% = 78.23%

Calculation Cohen's d:

$$\text{Cohen's } d = \left| \frac{\mu_{M1} - \mu_{M2}}{\sigma_2} \right|.$$

$$\text{Cohen's } d = \left| \frac{52 - 50}{5} \right| = .4$$

Comment on power and Cohen's d:

Effect size was small in this study (Cohen's d = .4), and power was very low (21.77%).

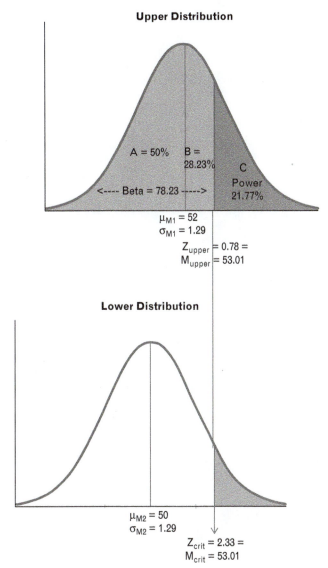

FIGURE 9.20: Homework Set A #3.

REFERENCES

Cohen, J. (1988). *Statistical power analysis for the behavioral sciences* (second edition). Hillsdale, New Jersey: Lawrence Erlbaum.

Damisch, L., Stoberock, B., & Mussweiler, T. (2010). Keep your fingers crossed! How superstition improves performance. *Psychological Science, 21,* 1014–1020.

t-TESTS (ONE-SAMPLE AND WITHIN-GROUPS)

To this point, our presentation of hypothesis-testing has been almost exclusively conceptual. That is, the statistics that we've gone over in chapters 6 through 9 are all conceptual building blocks that primarily serve the function of understanding the basics of hypothesis testing. There are many assumptions included in the statistics we've covered in these chapters—assumptions such as the idea that we know the population mean of the general population, that we know the standard deviation of the general population, and the idea of *homogeneity of variance*—that the population-level standard deviations are identical across multiple populations of interest.

In the real world, these assumptions and bits of given information do not always hold. In this chapter—and the subsequent chapters of this book, we enter the world of *real inferential statistics*—that is, we'll be learning about specific statistical processes that are commonly used by real statisticians to solve real problems.

The t-test is a basic kind of statistic that solves some important problems associated with the Z-tests that we've considered thus far. The fundamental feature of the t-test is that this test assumes that you do not have access to population-level variability information. In other words, this test assumes that you do not have the population standard deviation provided in a given problem. Rather, this test includes steps to estimate the population standard deviation. As you'll see, the simplest version of the t-test, the *one-sample t-test*, only assumes that you need to estimate the population standard deviation. The additional versions of the t-test that we'll encounter in this chapter and the next chapter (the *within-group* and *between-groups* t-tests) includes steps to estimate additional parameters such as the population means. But, true to the spirit of this book, we're progressing one step at a time. So to introduce the t-test concept, we'll start with the one-sample t-test.

ONE-SAMPLE t-TEST

The one-sample t-test includes situations that are essentially a hybrid of where we've been and where we're going. It's partly realistic, in that these situations do not include given information about population standard deviation. On the other hand, this kind of test requires the not-always-so-realistic aspect of including the mean of the general population. Again, we present this here as a step toward the more practical kinds of statistics that we'll run into in the remainder of this book.

To help explain the one-sample t-test, we need to consider an example in which we want to compare a sample mean with the mean of a population with an unknown population standard deviation. For instance, suppose that your friend is an engineering major—and she comes back to the dorm complaining about difficult classes and difficult grading—often insisting that the grading is more difficult in engineering classes than in other classes.

As a statistician, you're interested in this idea—and you decide on a simple way to test this hypothesis. You will examine if engineering majors have significantly lower GPAs than the general population of students at your school. The school newspaper recently reported that the average GPA at your school is 2.5. You call the reporter and ask for the population standard deviation, as you know that will help you with this problem. The reporter, who never took a statistics course, never returns your phone calls…

Well, you're not one to quit so easily. And, honestly, you can figure this one out (with a little help). To solve this problem, we'll need a bit more information. In addition to alpha (let's go with the standard of .05), we'll need actual scores (much as when we computed standard deviation from scratch earlier in this book).

The study would look about like this—you'd collect a random sample of scores (representing GPA) from a certain number of engineering majors. From these numbers, you'd compute a sample mean as well as an estimate of the population standard deviation. So, for this example (see Tables 10.1 and 10.2), let's assume the following scores from a random sample of 5 engineering majors:

Sure, these numbers are simple, but, consistent with our presentation of information in this book, we may as well use simple examples so that we can focus on the concepts at hand as opposed to computational complexities.

Computing our estimate of the population standard deviation includes a few points. First, note that we'll actually compute it via a nearly identical process as the one we used to compute standard deviation early on. Second, note that this estimate of the population standard deviation (represented by s, which is our best mathematical estimate of σ) is slightly different from SD (which we computed earlier on). The main difference is that, compared with SD, s is computed in a way to make it larger than SD—with the idea that population-level standard

Table 10.1: GPAs for Five Engineering Students

Engineering Student 1	2.0
Engineering Student 2	3.0
Engineering Student 3	1.0
Engineering Student 4	1.0
Engineering Student 5	3.0

deviations are similar to standard deviations found in samples, except, in general, there is more variability between scores in populations than in samples (simply because populations are, by definition, larger than samples). In short, computing s and derivative statistics (e.g., s^2) will follow a very familiar process. We'll go through the details of the process in the broader context of a hypothesis test.

STEPS FOR HYPOTHESIS TESTING WITH A ONE-SAMPLE t-TEST

1. ARTICULATE THE NULL AND RESEARCH HYPOTHESES

This step is identical to this same step in the comparable Z-test. We need to articulate the two populations of interest, along with the H_1 and H_0. In this example, the general population (with the mean represented by μ_2) includes all the students at your school and the special population (with the mean represented by μ_1) includes all the engineering students at your school. So we can articulate this as follows:

μ_2: General population of students at the school
μ_1: Population of engineering students at the school

And the research and null hypotheses are as follows:

$H_1: \mu_1 < \mu_2$

(signifying that the population mean GPA for engineers is predicted to be lower than the mean for the general population)

$H_0: \mu_1 \geq \mu_2$

(signifying that the population mean GPA for engineers is predicted to be equal to or greater than the mean for the general population)

2. DETERMINE THE CHARACTERISTICS OF THE COMPARISON DISTRIBUTION

The comparison distribution assumes that the *equal part* of the null hypothesis is true. That is, this distribution assumes that $\mu_1 = \mu_2$, or that there is no difference between the population means of interest. This distribution is quite similar to the distribution used for the Z-tests that we encountered in chapters 7 and 8. The primary difference here is that we're now using a *t-distribution* as opposed to a normal distribution (which is sometimes referred to as a *Z-distribution*).

A t-distribution is similar to a normal distribution, but it has an important additional feature. Essentially, as the number of participants in the study (N) approaches infinity, the t-distribution

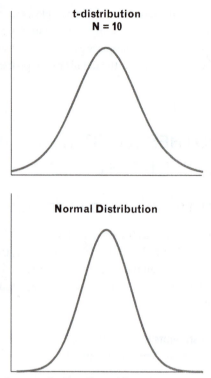

FIGURE 10.1: A t-Distribution Compared with a Normal Distribution.

approaches a normal distribution. So if the N is very large, a t-distribution essentially *is* a normal distribution. But as the N approaches zero, the t-distribution changes. And it changes in the following ways:

A. Compared with a normal distribution, a t-distribution tends to have "fatter tails" (See Figure 10.1), and
B. Compared with a normal distribution, a t-distribution tends to be flatter in the middle (See Figure 10.1).

As you can see in Figure 10.1, there are actually an infinite number of possible t-distributions as a function of N. For each possible N, there is a different t-distribution. And, as mentioned, as the N approaches infinity (i.e., as it increases), the t-distribution approaches the normal distribution. This point is made clear in Figure 10.2.

In our working example, N = 5. Remember, this simply means that we have 5 scores in our sample. Thus, our comparison distribution will be a t-distribution based on an N of 5 (See Figure 10.3).

You'll see from Figure 10.3 that, as with Z-distributions, t-distributions can be thought of in terms of raw scores or standardized scores. The main difference is that the standardized scores in a t-distribution are in t-units as opposed to in Z-units. So the mean of any t-distribution in t-units is 0, while the mean of the t-distribution in raw-score units varies as a function of both

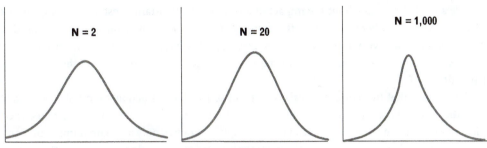

FIGURE 10.2: t-Distributions Based on Ns of 2, 20, and 1,000.

the raw-score scale as well as the type of t-test (which we'll see with additional kinds of t-tests from this chapter and chapter 11).

For the one-sample t-test, the mean in t-units is 0 and the mean in raw-score units is the mean of the general population (conceptualized as a mean of a distribution of means (μ_M), just like with a Z-test if N is greater than 0).

3. DETERMINE t-CRITICAL

With the one-sample t-test, t-critical (or t_{crit}) is very similar to Z_{crit}. It is determined by:

A. Whether the test is one-tailed or two-tailed,
B. The alpha level, and
C. The **degrees of freedom**.

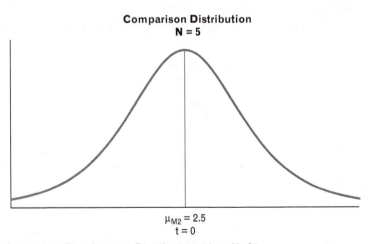

Comparison Distribution
N = 5

$\mu_{M2} = 2.5$
$t = 0$

FIGURE 10.3: Comparison Distribution; t-Distribution with an N of 5.

We already know all about the impact of a one- versus two-tailed test and the importance of alpha. What's new here pertains to the *degrees of freedom*. From here on, each of the statistics we encounter will have a *degrees of freedom term* (*df*). The specifics of df vary from statistic to statistic. It's always a function of N (or the number of scores in the sample). With the one-sample t-test, df = N−1.

The reason that this concept is called "degrees of freedom" is actually kind of esoteric and has little practical use. The short version is that with a sample of numbers, once a certain critical piece of information (such as the mean of the sample) is known, only a certain number of scores are "free to vary." So, for instance, if there are three scores in a sample and we know the mean is 5, two of the three scores can vary before we have enough information to determine the mean. If we know that one score is 5 and one is 7 (given that there are three total scores), the third score must be 3 (only two of the three scores are *free to vary*—thus making it so that there are *2 degrees of freedom* (N (of 3)−1 = 2). In other words, if we know that $\dfrac{5+7+X}{3} = 5$, X is not free to vary; it must be a score of 3 and only 3.

Honestly, while this is a technical explanation of the concept of df, this term is simply a way to describe relevant details of the study (such as the sample size). And the df terms are also used for the statistical tables that we'll encounter in the remainder of the book—which is why we describe this concept here in our discussion of t_{crit}.

To determine t_{crit}, we'll refer to Appendix B, which is a t-table. In this table, you'll see several columns. The first corresponds to degrees of freedom. In our current example, we have 5 scores, so df = N−1 = 5−1 = 4.

Next, we see two clusters of columns, those for one-tailed tests and those for two-tailed tests. As we have a prediction in a specific direction (that engineering students' GPAs are *lower* than the mean GPA of the general population), we're dealing with a one-tailed test—so we'll refer to the one-tailed cluster of columns. With a one-tailed test and an alpha of .05, and four degrees of freedom, we find a single score: 2.13. This is (just about) the t_{crit} for this example. We write "just about" for one reason. The t-table (like the Z-table) does not provide negative signs—we have to add negative signs ourselves when appropriate. With the current example, note that the mean for the special population (of engineering students) is predicted to be lower than the mean for the general population, so the rejection region will be to the left side of the comparison

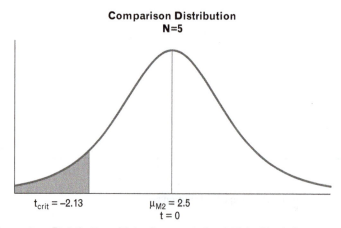

FIGURE 10.4: Comparison Distribution with t_{crit} Demarcated and Alpha Shaded.

distribution. Thus, t_{crit} = −2.13. All points to the left of this score are in the alpha region. See this point demarcated in Figure 10.4.

HERE ARE SOME SIMPLE RULES TO DETERMINE THE SIGN OF t_{CRIT} WITH A ONE-SAMPLE t-TEST

A.   In a one-tailed test, the sign of t_{crit} follows the research hypothesis;

if H_1: $\mu_1 > \mu_2$, t_{crit} is positive;
if H_1: $\mu_1 < \mu_2$, t_{crit} is negative.

B.   In a two-tailed test, there is always a positive version of t_{crit} along with a negative version of t_{crit}. So, for instance, if alpha = .01, df = 10, and we have a two-tailed test, based on information from the t-table, t_{crit} would be ± 3.17.

Note that with a two-tailed test, t_{crits} tend to be further from the mean of a t of 0. This is because a two-tailed test is more conservative than a one-tailed test, so the situation becomes biased to make it harder to reject the null hypothesis.

4. COMPUTE t

In a one-sample t-test, t (or $t_{obtained}$, or t_{obt}) is the t-score that corresponds to the sample mean that represents your special population. This statistic is computed in a way that's very similar to how a z-score is computed in our prior hypothesis-testing examples from chapter 8. The formula is as follows:

$$t = \frac{M - \mu_{M2}}{s_M}$$

The elements here are:

- M corresponds to the mean of your sample (representing your special population);
- μ_{M2} represents the mean (in raw-score units) of the comparison distribution (in a one-sample t-test, it's a mean of a distribution of means corresponding to the mean of the general population mean);
- s_M represents the standard deviation of this t-distribution (it's a standard deviation of a distribution of means and is, more specifically, our best mathematical estimate of σ_M).

To this point, we know μ_{M2} (which equals μ_2, which is just the mean of the general population, which was given information and is 2.5). We can thus easily compute M. We'll have to figure out s_M, determining M along the way.

To compute s_M, we'll use steps that are very familiar at this point. Along the way, we'll compute s. s is our best mathematical estimate of σ, which is our population-level standard deviation. Once we can estimate σ (and related parameters), we can move toward computing s_M.

To compute s and s_M, we will use the same process to extrapolate indices of variance from raw data as we used in earlier chapters in the book (with some minor differences that will be explained). The steps are explicated in Table 10.2.

Recall that these scores are based on GPAs of five randomly selected engineering students. (Computational explanation described in subsequent text.)

Importantly, in this process, we are estimating population variability (σ^2). In doing so, we compute s^2. This statistic is our best mathematical estimate of σ^2. You'll see here that we are following the same steps as when we computed SD^2 earlier in this course—with one important exception. SD^2 is the variance of a sample. s^2, on the other hand, is not just used to describe our sample's variability, but also to estimate the variance of the population from which it's drawn. For this reason, to get s^2, we divide SS not by N, but, rather, by N−1. The reasoning here is as follows: The amount that scores vary from one another in a population must be more than the amount that scores vary from one another within a sample. As such, SD^2 is probably a low estimate of population variability. But it's probably close. To compensate mathematically for this issue, we divide SS by N−1 instead of by N, thus coming up with an answer that's close to SD^2 but that's consistently slightly larger.

As shown in Table 10.2 (which includes the relevant formulas), once we compute s^2, we have the means to compute s, s^2_M, and s_M. These concepts are described briefly in turn as follows:

- s^2: The best estimate of the population-level variance based on the raw data from a sample (this estimate will be slightly higher than SD^2)

Table 10.2: Computing s_M and Other Indices of Variability in the One-Sample t-test

X	M	X−M	(X−M)²
2.0	2.0	0	0
3.0	2.0	1	1
1.0	2.0	−1	1
1.0	2.0	−1	1
3.0	2.0	1	1

$$M = \frac{\sum X}{N} ; \frac{10}{5} = 2$$

$$\Sigma (X-M)^2 = 4 = SS$$

$$s^2 = \frac{SS}{N-1} * = \frac{4}{4} = 1$$

$$s = \sqrt{s^2} = 1$$

$$s^2{}_M = \frac{s^2}{n} = \frac{1}{5} = .2$$

$$s_M = \sqrt{s^2_M} = \sqrt{.2} = .45$$

- s: The best estimate of the population-level standard deviation based on the raw data from a sample (importantly, note that this term is NOT used to compute either s^2_M or s_M! It will be used later in this chapter to compute Cohen's d, but, aside from that, it's a cool statistic because it's our best estimate of the population-level standard deviation, which is the most accessible and meaningful index of variability—it's conceptualized in terms of the units of the actual scale of whatever variable you're examining).
- s^2_M: This is your best estimate of the variance of the comparison distribution (which is a distribution of means).
- s_M: This is your best estimate of the standard deviation of the comparison distribution (which is a distribution of means). While s_M is not as interpretable as s in describing standard deviation of the population, it's the appropriate standard deviation term for the comparison distribution as that distribution is a distribution of means (because N is greater than 1).

Now let's get back to computing t! Now that we have computed M and s_M, we're good. t is as follows:

$$t = \frac{M - \mu_{M2}}{s_M}$$

$$\frac{2 - 2.5}{.45} = -1.11$$

5. COMMENT ON THE NULL HYPOTHESIS

Here, we follow the same general algorithm that we have for hypothesis-testing in general. t_{obt} is not in the alpha region, so, here, we fail to reject the null hypothesis. Based on our data, we cannot confidently conclude that the population mean for the GPAs of engineering students is lower than the population-level GPA for students in general. As usual, we're not saying that our research hypothesis is incorrect—rather, we're simply saying that we have not provided sufficient evidence to confidently reject the null hypothesis and to support the research hypothesis (see Figure 10.5).

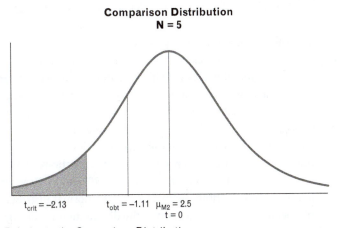

Comparison Distribution
N = 5

$t_{crit} = -2.13$ $t_{obt} = -1.11$ $\mu_{M2} = 2.5$
                                                $t = 0$

FIGURE 10.5: t_{obt} Relative to the Comparison Distribution.

As a note, if t_{obt} were in the rejection region (e.g., if $t_{obt} = -3.55$), we would then reject the null hypothesis and conclude that we could confidently support the research hypothesis (but, importantly, this was not the case in the current example).

COMPUTING EFFECT SIZE WITH A ONE-SAMPLE t-TEST

Effect size estimates for t-tests are all variants of the Cohen's d statistic that we were introduced to in chapter 9. Recall that Cohen's d is an estimate of how different two means are from one another in light of some index of population standard deviation. Population standard deviation is used instead of an index of standard deviation based on a distribution of means as effect size indices need to be computed in a way such that they are generalizable beyond the parameters of any particular sample size or study.

With a one-sample t-test, we don't have the actual population-level standard deviation (σ)—but we do have our best estimate of σ, which is represented by s. As such, with the one-sample t-test, we'll compute the effect size estimate as follows:

$$\text{Cohen's } d = \left| \frac{M - \mu_2}{S} \right|$$

With the current working example related to the GPAs of engineering students, Cohen's d would be as follows:

$$\text{Cohen's } d = \left| \frac{M - \mu_2}{S} \right| = \left| \frac{2 - 2.5}{1} \right| = .5$$

Based on the standard conventions for interpreting effect size (with the following approximations: small ~.2; medium ~.5; large ~.8), this is a solid medium effect size. Recall that we failed to reject the null hypothesis—in light of what we know about power, it may be that if we had a very large effect size, we might have ended up rejecting the null hypothesis (just to remind you of the relationship between power and effect size; as effect size increases, power increases).

HOW THE t-TEST IS BIASED AGAINST SMALL SAMPLES

A very smart feature of realistic inferential statistics is the fact that the statistics are highly skeptical of small samples. This makes sense, as the point of inferential statistics is to see if you can confidently infer that a pattern found in a sample likely represents the true pattern found at the population level. As such, the larger your sample is, the more likely it is that patterns in your sample mirror patterns at the population level. And, accordingly, as your N approaches the total number of individual scores in the population, you can be more and more confident that any pattern you have found represents the pattern at the population level.

With this said, think about the t-distribution as it changes as a function of N (as in Figure 10.2). Figure 10.2 includes three t-distributions—based on Ns of 2, 20, and 1,000 accordingly. As you can see, as the N increases, the t-distribution approaches the normal distributions—as the N increases, the tails thin out and the modal section of the distribution peaks higher. An artifact of this is the fact that t_{crit} will become further from the mean of the comparison distribution as the N is smaller. If the tails are very fat, t_{crit} needs to be further out in the tails to cut off a section of 5%; as the tails are thinner (as N increases), t_{crit} does not need to be as far out to cut off that same percentage.

One outcome associated with this reasoning is simple: With a relatively low N, it is more difficult to reject the null hypothesis. This fact, as you can see in light of this discussion, is no accident—the t-statistic is designed this way to bias the researcher against making strong claims based on data collected with a small N.

THE WITHIN-GROUP t-TEST

A very common kind of data situation is best examined with the within-group t-test. This test goes by many names, including the *within-group t-test, repeated-measures t-test, paired-samples t-test*, and probably others! This is a very common and important test with lots of practical value.

The within-group t-test is used when you have two continuous variables all from the same participants—and you want to see if the means of these variables differ significantly from one another. A common form of this is the *pre-test/post-test* situation. Here, we give participants a test (on some continuous variable), then some event or intervention, and then the same test. For instance, you might give students a math test, have them take a course in math, and then give them the same math test to see if the course had a positive effect on scores. Or you might weigh people before they start a diet, have them start a diet, and then weigh them after they are on the diet for a while.

The within-group t-test is not only used for pre-test/post-test situations. There are other situations in which you could be curious to see if two continuous variables from the same participants differ significantly. For instance, you might ask people to rate (on a 1–10 scale) their attitudes toward some movie (say *Harry Potter*, Episode 1) and then have them rate another movie (say *Harry Potter*, Episode 2). To see if people tend to (on average) like one movie over the other, we'd use the within-group t-test.

Mathematically, the basic thing we're doing with the within-group t-test is seeing if the mean difference score between scores on variable 1 and variable 2 is significantly different from 0. To understand the details, we'll use an example of whether a certain dietary regimen (let's say cutting out processed foods) helps people lose weight. The data (found in Table 10.3) are as follows:

Table 10.3: Weight in Pounds Before and After Implementation of Diet

Participant #	Weight Before Diet	Weight After Diet
1	180	160
2	200	200
3	190	180
4	135	120
5	150	145
6	220	200

Basically, we want to see if the average differences are substantial. Clearly, some participants lost weight (e.g., Participant #6 lost 20 pounds), but with this test, we want to see if overall the trend is for these differences to be indicative of weight loss. So, as with inferential statistics in general, we want to see if some general pattern found in a sample likely generalizes to the broader population. So here's how we do it.

STEPS IN COMPUTING THE WITHIN-GROUP t-TEST

1. ARTICULATE THE RESEARCH AND NULL HYPOTHESES

While this process is conceptually similar to how we've proceeded to this point, you'll see that there are some logistical differences as well. For these problems, we'll be thinking about $\bar{d}$ and $\hat{\bar{d}}$. $\bar{d}$ is the mean of the difference scores (or the ds). $\hat{\bar{d}}$ is the predicted $\bar{d}$ (you may recall from our chapter on regression that a cap over a statistic means a *predicted* (not real) version of that statistic).

With the current example, we have weight at time 1 followed by weight at time 2. If we put a column to the right of these and compute the difference in weight for each person (and label this column d for *difference*; as in Table 10.2), these differences will be either positive or negative (or zero if the scores for a particular participant are identical and there is no change). $\bar{d}$ is the average of the differences (the average of d) and $\hat{\bar{d}}$ is the *predicted* average of the differences. So one ($\bar{d}$) is *actual* while the other ($\hat{\bar{d}}$) is *predicted*. Importantly, as in the real world, predictions don't always match actuality. So it is perfectly possible for the signs of $\bar{d}$ and $\hat{\bar{d}}$ to mismatch.

The research hypothesis with the within-group t-test is based on the sign of $\bar{d}$ (i.e., the predicted sign of $\bar{d}$). You infer this from the setup of your data. If the second variable (here, weight at time 2) is predicted to be lower than the scores of the first variable, then the differences are predicted to be positive (e.g., 150–140 = +10). Importantly, this decision is independent of actual numbers. The research hypothesis is not about how things are—rather, it's about how things are predicted to be. So, importantly, make your determination about $\hat{\bar{d}}$ independent of your actual data.

The research hypothesis (H_1) is based on whether $\hat{\bar{d}}$ is predicted to be positive or negative. With the current example, we've predicted scores in variable 2 to be lower than in variable 1; we've predicted a drop in scores. Thus, $\hat{\bar{d}}$ is predicted to be positive in sign. We'll formulate this as such:

$$H_1: \hat{\bar{d}} > 0$$

And, as always, H_0 is the converse of H_1 and includes an equals sign, as such:

$$H_0: \hat{\bar{d}} \leq 0$$

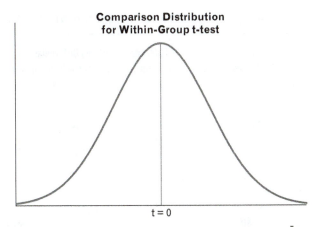

FIGURE 10.6: Comparison Distribution for Within-Group t-test (Distribution of $\bar{d}$.)

This all means, simply, that we are predicting (per our research hypothesis) that the scores in variable 2 are, on average, lower than the scores in variable 1 (at the population level).

(Note that if the scores in variable 2 are predicted to be higher than the scores in variable 1, $H_1 : \hat{\bar{d}} < 0$ and $H_0 : \hat{\bar{d}} \geq 0$; and if you have a two-tailed test (and you're just predicting an average difference (in no particular direction) between variable 1 and variable 2), $H_1 : \hat{\bar{d}} \neq 0$ and $H_0 : \hat{\bar{d}} = 0$).

2. COMPUTE THE DETAILS OF THE COMPARISON DISTRIBUTION

The comparison distribution with the within-groups t-test is a distribution of mean difference scores (or $\bar{d}$s). The idea is that with a single set of data (with two continuous variables from the same participants), you get a specific $\bar{d}$ based on the actual differences from the two scores of the two variables—but that particular $\bar{d}$ is one of an infinite number of possible $\bar{d}$s. If the zero-component of the null hypothesis is correct, the average of a normally distributed population of randomly generated $\bar{d}$s would be zero (but not all $\bar{d}$s in that distribution would be zero). So this comparison distribution is a normal distribution of $\bar{d}$s with a mean of zero (see Figure 10.6).

Technically, as with some other kinds of t-tests, the mean of this distribution as a raw score and as a standardized score is zero either way. In t-score units, any t-distribution has a mean of 0 with a score of 1.0 corresponding to 1 standard t-unit above the mean. And in raw-score units, since the $\bar{d}$ is based on variable 1–variable 2, with a null hypothesis predicting that these are the same on average and that the difference will be zero, the mean is zero when conceiving of this distribution in these raw-score units as well. This is all kinds of technical—the bottom line is that however you slice it, the mean of the comparison distribution for a within-group t-test is zero.

However, the standard deviation is different if you're looking at this in terms of raw or standardized (t) units. In t-units, the standard deviation is 1.0 (as is always the case with this kind of standardized distribution). However, in raw units, the standard deviation of the comparison

Table 10.4: Computing Indices of Variability for the Within-Group t-test

Variable 1 (pre-diet weight)	Variable 2 (post-diet weight)	(d) Difference	($\bar{d}$) Mean Difference	(d– $\bar{d}$) Difference between difference and mean difference	(d– $\bar{d}$)² Mean difference Squared
180	160	20	10	10	100
200	200	0	10	–10	100
190	180	–10	10	–20	400
135	120	15	10	5	25
150	145	15	10	5	25
220	200	20	10	10	100

$$\bar{d} = \frac{\sum d}{N}; \frac{60}{6} = 10$$

$$\sum(d-\bar{d})^2 = 750 = SS$$

$$s^2 = \frac{SS}{N-1} * = \frac{750}{5} = 150$$

$$s = \sqrt{s^2} = 12.45$$

$$s_M^2 = \frac{s^2}{N} = \frac{150}{6} = 25$$

$$s_M = \sqrt{s_M^2} = \sqrt{25} = 5$$

distribution, represented by s_M, is based on the raw scores, and is derived from a process that is very similar to the process for calculating s_M with the one-sample t-test. The steps involved in this process are found in Table 10.4.

3. DETERMINE THE CRITICAL VALUE AND ALPHA REGION

t_{crit} follows the nature of $\hat{\bar{d}}$ and the alpha region follows the research hypothesis (H₁). If $\hat{\bar{d}} > 0$, as in the current case, then t_{crit} is positive in sign. So for the current working example, t_{crit} will be a positive number. Further, as the prediction is directional (the diet will lead not just to weight change, but, specifically, to weight loss), this is a one-tailed test.

Note that if variable 2 were predicted to be higher than variable 1, $\hat{\bar{d}}$ would be negative in sign and alpha would be on the negative side of the comparison distribution—and if the prediction were two-tailed in nature (predicting weight change as opposed to weight decrease or increase), there would be two t_{crits}, one positive and one negative.

So here we have a single t_{crit} and it's positive. To compute the specifics of t_{crit}, we'll need an alpha level. Let's get silly and use an alpha of .01. We'll look this up in the t-table (Appendix B). In doing this, we'll need to know the degrees of freedom. In a within-group t-test, df = N–1. It's not about the number of scores, but the number of participants or cases. Here, we have 6 participants, so df = 5.

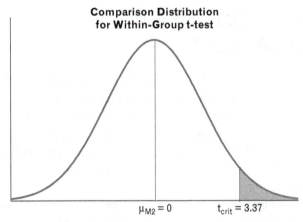

FIGURE 10.7: Comparison Distribution for Within-Group t-test with t_{crit} and Alpha Demarcated.

In our t-table, we see that for a one-tailed test with df of 5 and alpha of .01, t_{crit} = 3.37. And we know it's a positive number, so we keep it as is—we can demarcate it on the comparison distribution and shade the alpha region, as found in Figure 10.7.

4. COMPARE t OBTAINED WITH THE CRITICAL VALUE

To compute t_{obt}, we'll simply divide our mean difference score by the standard deviation of the comparison distribution—as follows:

$$t_{obt} = \frac{\overline{d}}{s_M}$$

This simply looks at the average of the differences found in our actual data relative to the raw-score version of the standard deviation of the comparison distribution. In this case, $t_{obt} = \frac{10}{5} = 2$.

As we can clearly see in Figure 10.7, t_{obt} (of 2) is not extreme enough to reject H_0, since it is not more extreme than the t_{crit} of 3.37.

5. COMMENT ON THE NULL HYPOTHESIS

By this point, this part of the process should be easy! Simply, t_{obt} was not in the alpha/rejection region. As such, we fail to reject the null hypothesis. Importantly, note that this finding does not imply that eating non-processed foods has no positive benefits regarding weight loss—it simply means that we have not provided sufficient evidence to make this case! As with other examples we've encountered, this may well pertain to the fact that we have a relatively small sample size. We also used a highly conservative alpha of .01 (had we used an alpha of .05, we would have been really close!). Separate from knowing if we've rejected the null hypothesis, it's often useful to be able to comment on the nature of effect size—a point we turn to next.

COMPUTING EFFECT SIZE WITH A WITHIN-GROUP t-TEST

Note that with a t-test, Cohen's d is always similar to computing the obtained t (or t_{obt}), except that you divide by an index of the population standard deviation as opposed to an index of the standard deviation of the comparison distribution. We do this because with effect size estimates, we want to make a comment about how big an effect likely is separate from details of a particular study (such as the N)—and the t_{obt} is always calculated as a function of N (recall that the beauty of the t-statistic is that it penalizes you for having a small N; so t is largely a function of N—whereas Cohen's d never is).

As such, the formula for Cohen's d with a within-group t-test is as follows:

$$\text{Cohen's } d = \left| \frac{\overline{d}}{s} \right|$$

Recall that while s_M is the standard deviation of your comparison distribution, s is your best mathematical estimate of the standard deviation of the population of d-bars based on the nature of your variables.

In the current case, $\text{Cohen's } d = \dfrac{10}{12.5} = .8$

This happens to work out as a solid "large" effect size. So while we failed to reject the null hypothesis, we did end up finding a large effect size. How did we fail to reject the null hypothesis even though our effect size was large? We had low power—largely due to our small N and our conservative alpha level (of .01).

A REAL RESEARCH EXAMPLE

In a recent study on the nature of evolution education, Glass, Wilson, and Geher (2012) found that experts on evolution in the behavioral sciences report that their educational backgrounds actually did not prepare them well for their work as evolutionists. In this study, the researchers administered a 10-point scale asking nearly 30 world-renowned experts in the field of evolutionary psychology how much general evolution training they received in their PhD education (with "1" meaning no training in this area and "10" meaning extensive training in this area). The following comes from this article:

> In terms of their own education, the majority of respondents reported that they received little training in general evolution. To explicate this point, we conducted a one-sample t-test, comparing the mean score for the authors (3.74, SD= 3.02, Mode = 1) with the midpoint of the scale (5). Higher scores on this scale indicate reporting having received strong training in evolution during graduate training. The mean for participants in this sample was significantly lower than the midpoint, $t(26) = 2.17, p < .05$, Cohen's $d = .42$.

Here, the authors used the one-sample t-test to make inferences about evolution training in higher education. The only sample mean the authors had to work with was derived from the sample of scholars who represented the field of evolutionary psychology—thus, to compare their mean (of 3.74) on this variable with something meaningful, the authors decided to compare with the mid-point of the scale (5). In spite of having a sample of less than 30 and a small-to-medium effect size (with Cohen's d at .42), the authors rejected the null hypothesis (this point is represented by the phrase $p < .05$). Thus, these authors provide strong evidence, using a one-sample t-test, suggesting that evolution education is lacking at the graduate level in modern academia—at least in the behavioral sciences.

SUMMARY

In real-world statistics, t-tests are very common and helpful. A primary feature of the t-test is the fact that it includes an estimate of population-level variability (when information on such variability is not available). t-tests are also designed in a way that is biased against small samples—with t-tests, it is relatively difficult to reject the null hypothesis with a small sample—and it becomes easier to reject the null hypothesis with a larger sample (a feature that makes it hard to generalize findings from a small sample to a large population).

In this chapter, we learned about the one-sample t-test, in which you compare a sample mean with some other mean, only having raw data from one sample (but means representing two populations). This situation emerges when you have data from one sample (with which you can compute a sample mean), but only a mean to represent the other population.

The within-group t-test is one of the most commonly used statistics. It is utilized in cases in which the same participants provide scores for two continuous variables, and you seek to see if the means on these two variables are significantly different from one another.

KEY TERMS

Degrees of freedom: The number of scores free to vary.
One sample t-test: Type of t-test used when you want to compare a single sample mean with the mean of a population with an unknown population standard deviation.
Within-group t-test: Type of t-test used when you have two continuous variables from the same participants, and you want to see if the means of the variables differ significantly from one another. Also known as repeated-measures t-test and paired-samples t-test.

HOMEWORK SET A

1. The biggest change you've noticed since moving out of the dorms is that you no longer have friends knocking on your door all the time, inviting you to do things that sound like more fun than studying. You now study more, and your test scores have improved. You wonder if other people who have recently moved out of the dorms are scoring higher than the mean on tests. In your statistics class, 5 people recently moved out of the dorms, and you ask them what they scored on the latest test. Their scores were 87, 84, 83, 86, and 90. You know that the mean on the last test was 86. Using the steps for hypothesis testing, you conduct a one-sample t-test with an alpha level of .05.
   a. Articulate the null and research hypotheses.
   b. Determine the characteristics of the comparison distribution.
   c. Determine t_{crit}.
   d. Compute t.
   e. Comment on the null hypothesis.
   f. Compute effect size and comment on the effect size.

2. After weeks and weeks of dreary winter days, you feel a bit down. You stop to buy a coffee, and drop your change into the box on the counter for a local charity. As you do so, you notice that the box seems rather empty, and you wonder if the lingering dark weather has resulted in people being less generous. You contact the owner of the coffee shop, who checks her records and tells you that in the last year, the average per day for the charity box is $14.00. Her records also indicate that during the last five dreary days of winter, the amounts in the box have been $12.00, $11.00, $10.00, $14.00, and $13.00. Using the steps for hypothesis testing, you conduct a one-sample t-test with an alpha of .01.
   a. Articulate the null and research hypotheses.
   b. Determine the characteristics of the comparison distribution.
   c. Determine t_{crit}.
   d. Compute t.
   e. Comment on the null hypothesis.
   f. Compute effect size and comment on the effect size.

3. You have never been a huge fan of stories of magic and wizardry. Your younger brother has been reading the *Harry Potter* series, and bugs you until you agree to read the first book. Having read the book, you find that your attitudes toward magic and wizardry have changed, and you even find yourself wishing that you had received an invitation to Hogwarts. You wonder if other people experience the same change in attitude after reading the book. You ask six of your friends to rate their attitudes toward magic and wizardry on a scale of 1 to 10, with 1 being not at all positive and 10 being very positive. You convince them to read the first *Harry Potter* book, then ask them to re-rate their attitudes toward magic and wizardry. Using the steps for hypothesis testing, you conduct a within-group t-test with an alpha level of .01.
   a. Articulate the null and research hypotheses.
   b. Compute the details of the comparison distribution.
   c. Determine the critical value and alpha region.
   d. Compare t_{obt} with the critical value.

Table 10.5: Attitudes about Wizardry Before and After Reading Harry Potter

Scores on attitudes toward magic/wizardry **before** reading the first *Harry Potter* book	Scores on attitudes toward magic/wizardry **after** reading the first *Harry Potter* book
2	9
5	7
2	9
3	10
4	9
1	6

    e.   Comment on the null hypothesis.

    f.   Compute effect size and comment on the effect size.

4.   Your friend, Staci, is a preschool teacher and also happens to be very thin. You ask Staci one day how she manages to stay so slender, and she jokingly replies that after seeing kids pick their noses all day, she doesn't have much of an appetite. This answer gets you thinking that perhaps watching kids pick their noses might, indeed, be an appetite suppressant. You have participants rate their hunger on a scale of 1 to 10, with 1 being not at all hungry and 10 being very hungry. You show the participants a video of a child picking his nose, then ask the participants to re-rate their hunger levels. Using the steps for hypothesis testing, you conduct a within-group t-test with an alpha level of .05.

    a.   Articulate the null and research hypotheses.

    b.   Compute the details of the comparison distribution.

    c.   Determine the critical value and alpha region.

    d.   Compare t_{obt} with the critical value.

    e.   Comment on the null hypothesis.

    f.   Compute effect size and comment on the effect size.

HOMEWORK SET B

1.   You have recently discovered that parakeets can learn to talk. You have never considered a parakeet as a pet before, but think it would be cool to have a little bird who can say a few words. You mention this to a friend who works at a pet store, who tells you that the owner of the store posted a sign next to the parakeets that said that some of

Table 10.6: Hunger Scores Before and After Watching Kids Pick Their Noses

Initial Hunger Score	Hunger Score after watching nose-picking video
6	4
5	2
2	1
8	1
4	3

the birds can learn to talk, in an attempt to increase the sale of parakeets. You ask your friend to find out the average monthly sales prior to the sign going up, and the number of parakeets sold for each of the 4 months since the sign has been up. Your friend tells you that the average prior to the sign was 3 birds per month, but the last 4 months' sales have totaled 7, 3, 3, and 7 parakeets. Using the steps for hypothesis testing, you conduct a one-sample t-test with an alpha of .01 to see if the sign significantly increased the sale of parakeets at the pet store.

a.   Articulate the null and research hypotheses.
b.   Determine the characteristics of the comparison distribution.
c.   Determine t_{crit}.
d.   Compute t.
e.   Comment on the null hypothesis.
f.   Compute effect size and comment on the effect size.

2.   It seems to you that a lot of football players get seriously injured during the season. Your friend, a football player, tells you that he doesn't worry too much about getting injured, because he has a theory that players who are injured playing football likely have a low level of fitness/strength. You decide to test his theory, using the formula that your college football team uses to assign a numeric value to the fitness and strength of each player. The team mean is 16, on a scale of 1–20. Of the players injured during the season, their fitness/strength levels are 19, 14, 16, 17, 17, and 19. Using the steps for hypothesis testing, you conduct a one-sample t-test with an alpha of .05 to test whether players who are injured have lower fitness/strength scores than the team average.

a.   Articulate the null and research hypotheses.
b.   Determine the characteristics of the comparison distribution.
c.   Determine t_{crit}.
d.   Compute t.
e.   Comment on the null hypothesis.
f.   Compute effect size and comment on the effect size.

3.   As a kid, you loved getting new school supplies at the beginning of a school year. A new backpack and new crayons, pencils, and notebooks made you feel excited for school to start again. Remembering how important new school supplies were to you, you become involved in a school supply drive for children who might not otherwise get new school supplies. As your group gives children a new backpack and school supplies, you ask a few of the children, before and after receiving their school supplies, if they are not excited, a little bit excited, or very excited for school to start. You assign these responses

Table 10.7: Excitement Scores Before and After Receiving School Supplies

Excitement Score Before Receiving Supplies	Excitement Score After Receiving Supplies
1	3
2	3
1	2
1	3
3	3

Table 10.8: Satisfaction Scores Before and After Policy Change

Satisfaction Score Before Policy Change	Satisfaction Score After Policy Change
6	5
7	5
10	10
9	7
9	8

number values of 1 (not excited), 2 (a little bit excited), and 3 (very excited). Using the steps for hypothesis testing, you then conduct a within-group t-test with an alpha level of .05 to see if the new school supplies made these kids excited for school to start.

a. Articulate the null and research hypotheses.
b. Compute the details of the comparison distribution.
c. Determine the critical value and alpha region.
d. Compare t_{obt} with the critical value.
e. Comment on the null hypothesis.
f. Compute effect size and comment on the effect size.

4. You read about a local company that has decided to institute a policy of ending every staff meeting by requiring each staff member to say something positive about another member of the staff. You wonder if forcing adults to say something nice might make the workers feel that they're being treated like elementary school children, thus decreasing morale and worker satisfaction. You contact the company, and management agrees to give you pre- and post-policy change data on the satisfaction rating of 5 random workers. Using the steps for hypothesis testing, you conduct a within-group t-test with an alpha level of .05.

a. Articulate the null and research hypotheses.
b. Compute the details of the comparison distribution.
c. Determine the critical value and alpha region.
d. Compare t_{obt} with the critical value.
e. Comment on the null hypothesis.
f. Compute effect size and comment on the effect size.

ANSWERS

HOMEWORK SET A

1. a. $H_1: \mu_1 > \mu_2$

    $H_0: \mu_1 \leq \mu_2$

    b. Comparison distribution is a t-distribution, N = 5.
    c. $t_{crit} = 2.13$

Table 10.9: Homework Set A #1 Calculations

X	M	X−M	(X−M)²
87	86	1	1
84	86	−2	4
83	86	−3	9
86	86	0	0
90	86	4	16

$$M = \frac{\sum X}{N} ; \frac{430}{5} = 86$$

$$S(X-M)^2 = 30 = SS$$

$$s^2 = \frac{SS}{N-1} * = \frac{30}{4} = 7.5$$

$$s = \sqrt{s^2} = 2.74$$

$$s^2_M = \frac{s^2}{n} = \frac{7.5}{5} = 1.5$$

$$s_M = \sqrt{s^2_M} = \sqrt{1.5} = 1.22$$

d.

$$t = \frac{M - \mu_{M2}}{s_M}$$

$$= \frac{86 - 86}{1.22} = 0$$

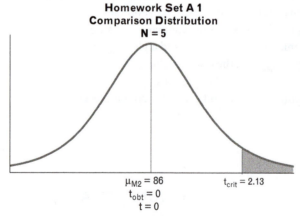

**Homework Set A 1
Comparison Distribution
N = 5**

$\mu_{M2} = 86$ $t_{crit} = 2.13$
$t_{obt} = 0$
$t = 0$

FIGURE 10.8: Homework Set A #1.

e. t_{obt} is not in the alpha region; therefore, we fail to reject the null hypothesis. Our results do not suggest that people who have recently moved out of the dorms score higher than the mean on tests.

f.   Cohen's $d = \left|\frac{M - \mu_2}{S}\right| = \left|\frac{86 - 86}{1.5}\right| = 0$

Cohen's d is 0, which is an extremely small effect size!

2. a. $H_1: \mu_1 < \mu_2$

    $H_0: \mu_1 \geq \mu_2$

    b. Comparison distribution is a t-distribution, N = 5.
    c. $t_{crit} = -3.75$
    d.

Table 10.10: Homework Set A #2 Calculations

X	M	X−M	(X−M)²
12	12	0	0
11	12	−1	1
10	12	−2	4
14	12	2	4
13	12	1	1

$$M = \frac{\Sigma X}{N}; \frac{60}{5} = 12$$

$$S(X-M)^2 = 10 = SS$$

$$s^2 = \frac{SS}{N-1}* = \frac{10}{4} = 2.5$$

$$s = \sqrt{s^2} = 1.58$$

$$s_M^2 = \frac{s^2}{n} = \frac{2.5}{5} = .5$$

$$s_M = \sqrt{s_M^2} = \sqrt{.54} = .71$$

$$t = \frac{M - \mu_{M2}}{s_M}$$

$$= \frac{12 - 14}{.71} = -2.82$$

e. t_{obt} is not in the alpha region; therefore, we fail to reject the null hypothesis. Our results do not indicate that people donate less to charity in the coffee shop on winter days.

f. Cohen's $d = \left|\frac{M - \mu_2}{S}\right| = \left|\frac{12 - 14}{1.58}\right| = -1.27$

The absolute value of Cohen's d is 1.27, which is a large effect size.

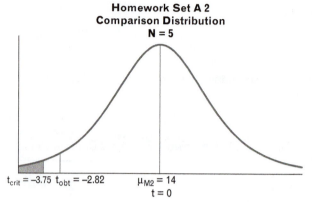

FIGURE 10.9: Homework Set A #2.

3. a. $H_1 : \hat{\bar{d}} < 0$

$H_0 : \hat{\bar{d}} \geq 0$

b. The comparison distribution is a normal distribution of $\bar{d}$s with a mean of zero.
c. $\hat{\bar{d}}$ is predicted to be less than 0, so t_{crit} is negative. There is a particular direction predicted, so the test is one-tailed, has an alpha of .01, and 5 degrees of freedom. $t_{crit} = -3.37$.
d.

Table 10.11: Homework Set A #3 Calculations

Variable 1 (pre-book rating)	Variable 2 (post-book rating)	(d) Difference	($\bar{d}$) Mean Difference	(d– $\bar{d}$) Difference between difference and mean difference	(d– $\bar{d}$)² Mean Difference Squared
2	9	−7	−5.5	−1.5	2.25
5	7	−2	−5.5	3.5	12.25
2	9	−7	−5.5	−1.5	2.25
3	10	−7	−5.5	−1.5	2.25
4	9	−5	−5.5	.5	.25
1	6	−5	−5.5	.5	.25

$$\bar{d} = \frac{\Sigma d}{N} ; \frac{-33}{6} = -5.5$$

$$\Sigma(d-\bar{d})^2 = 19.5 = SS$$

$$s^2 = \frac{SS}{N-1} * = \frac{19.5}{5} = 3.9$$

$$s = \sqrt{s^2} = 1.97$$

$$s_M^2 = \frac{s^2}{N} = \frac{3.9}{6} = .65$$

$$s_M = \sqrt{s_M^2} = \sqrt{.65} = .81$$

$$t_{obt} = \frac{\overline{d}}{s_M}$$

$$_{bt} = \frac{-5.5}{.81} = -6.79$$

e. t_{obt} is in the alpha region; therefore, we reject the null hypothesis. Our research suggests that people tend to embrace magic and wizardry more after reading *Harry Potter*.

f. Cohen's $d = \left| \frac{\overline{d}}{s} \right|$

Cohen's $d = \left| \frac{-5.5}{1.97} \right| = -2.79$

The absolute value of Cohen's d is 2.79, which is a large effect size.

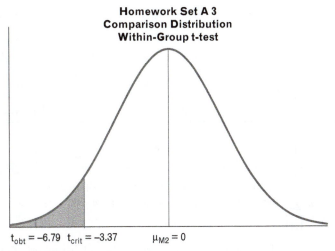

Homework Set A 3
Comparison Distribution
Within-Group t-test

$t_{obt} = -6.79$ $t_{crit} = -3.37$ $\mu_{M2} = 0$

FIGURE 10.10: Homework Set A #3.

4. a. $H_1 : \hat{\overline{d}} > 0$

$H_0 : \hat{\overline{d}} \leq 0$

b. The comparison distribution is a normal distribution of $\overline{d}_s$ with a mean of zero.

c. $\hat{\overline{d}}$ is predicted to be greater than 0, so t_{crit} is positive. There is a particular direction predicted, so the test is one-tailed, has an alpha of .05, and 4 degrees of freedom. $t_{crit} = 2.13$.

d.

Table 10.12: Homework Set A #4 Calculations

Variable 1 (pre-nose picking video hunger rating)	Variable 2 (post-nose picking video hunger rating)	(d) Difference	($\bar{d}$) Mean Difference	($d-\bar{d}$) Difference between difference and mean difference	($d-\bar{d}$)² Mean Difference Squared
6	4	2	2.8	−.8	.64
5	2	3	2.8	.2	.04
2	1	1	2.8	−1.8	3.24
8	1	7	2.8	4.2	17.64
4	3	1	2.8	−1.8	3.24

$$\bar{d} = \frac{\sum d}{N};$$

$$\frac{14}{5} = 2.8$$

$$\sum (d-\bar{d})^2 = 24.8 = SS$$

$$s^2 = \frac{SS}{N-1} * = \frac{24.8}{4} = 6.2$$

$$s = \sqrt{s^2} = 2.49$$

$$s_M^2 = \frac{s^2}{N} = \frac{6.2}{5} = 1.24$$

$$s_M = \sqrt{s_M^2} = \sqrt{1.24} = 1.11$$

$$t_{obt} = \frac{\bar{d}}{s_M}$$

$$t_{obt} = \frac{2.8}{1.11} = 2.52$$

e. t_{obt} is in the alpha region; therefore, we reject the null hypothesis. Our research suggests that watching kids pick their noses may, indeed, reduce hunger ratings.

f.   Cohen's d $= \left| \dfrac{\bar{d}}{s} \right|$

Cohen's d $= \left| \dfrac{6.2}{2.49} \right| = 2.49$

The absolute value of Cohen's d is 2.49, which is a large effect size.

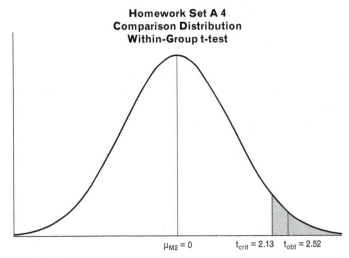

Homework Set A 4
Comparison Distribution
Within-Group t-test

$\mu_{M2} = 0$ $t_{crit} = 2.13$ $t_{obt} = 2.52$

FIGURE 10.11: Homework Set A #4.

REFERENCE

Glass, D. J., Wilson, D. S., & Geher, G. (2012). Evolutionary training in relation to human affairs is sorely lacking in higher education. EvoS Journal: The Journal of the Evolutionary Studies Consortium, 4, 16–22.

CHAPTER 11

THE BETWEEN-GROUPS t-TEST

The between-groups t-test is one of the most commonly employed of all statistics in the social sciences—and with good reason. This test fits perfectly with so many of the questions we have about our world. Consider the following questions you might ask yourself on any given day:

- Do girls read more than boys?
- Are cats (perhaps secretly) really smarter than dogs?
- Do people who go to private colleges end up with higher-paying jobs than those who go to state schools?
- Are the grades given out by my statistics professor significantly lower than those doled out by that other statistics professor?
- Are psychology professors any better-adjusted than biology professors?

The between-groups t-test allows us to address these kinds of inquiries. In each case, we have a *dichotomous categorical variable* and a single continuous variable. Recall from our earlier discussions of variable types that a categorical variable is one in which the different values represent differences in kind—different categories—such as gender (male or female). A *dichotomous* categorical variable is simply one with two possible categories. Note that in each of the examples presented above, there's a dichotomous categorical variable. These include gender (boys vs. girls), pet type (cats vs. dogs), school type (private vs. public), and so on. Note that you could add other levels to your categorical variable (e.g., cats, dogs, birds, and frogs for pets), but the variable would no longer be dichotomous; as such, the t-test would no longer be an appropriate choice.

Further, each of the above examples has a continuous variable being compared across the two categories (or levels) of the categorical variable. Take the example of whether psychology professors are better adjusted than biology professors. Here, the dichotomous categorical variable is professor type (psychology or biology) and the continuous variable being compared across the categories is psychological adjustment (which is often measured by self-report scales with scores that vary by degree).

For labeling purposes, it's important to know how researchers refer to these variables. Most typically, the dichotomous categorical variable is referred to as the *independent variable* and the continuous outcome variable is referred to as the *dependent variable*. In fact, as you learn more about scientific research methods, you'll discover that these labels should only be used when the categorical variable is carefully manipulated in an experimental manner—keep that point in the back of your mind. However, researchers often get lazy with their terminology—and it's very common for people to refer to these variables as the independent and dependent variables— even when the research is not experimental in nature (in other words, strict methodologists will have a problem with this terminology being used in situations that have no experimentally manipulated variable). To make matters somewhat more complex, you may recall from the chapter on correlation that researchers often refer to a predictor variable as an *independent variable* and to a criterion variable as a *dependent variable*—again, strict methodologists will shake their head at this use of these words (which should be reserved exclusively for variables included in true experiments)! Thus, these terms are useful for identifying the variables in your study and determining the appropriate tests, but they are not technically accurate unless the variable has been experimentally manipulated.

In its simplest form, the between-groups t-test allows us to assess whether the means from two samples (representing two categorically different populations) are significantly different from one another. For instance, suppose you gave out the Madeup Adjustment Test to samples of 50 psychology professors and 50 biology professors. Further, suppose the mean for the psychology professors is 8.3 while the mean for the biology professors is 6.2 (with higher scores corresponding to better adjustment). The between-groups t-test lets us know if this difference between means is *statistically significant*.

That's the simple version—which often works for explaining this test briefly. However, as we delve into the complexities of how the between-groups t-test is calculated, you'll see that this test is actually a bit more intricate. Formally, this test allows us to see if a difference between sample means is unlikely to have come from a distribution of differences in sample means with a mean of 0. I know—that's a mouthful. As we go through the process of how this statistic is calculated, however, you'll see that this interpretation corresponds to the true nature of the between-groups t-test.

THE ELEMENTS OF THE BETWEEN-GROUPS t-TEST

To understand the elements of the between-groups t-test, let's jump right in with an example. While everyone seems to be on the cell phone all the time nowadays, it seems that college students are particularly addicted to their cell phones. Suppose you were interested in whether college students are on their cell phones more than college professors are. To address this question, you'd compute a between-groups t-test. Your dichotomous categorical variable would be status (student or professor) and your continuous dependent variable would be number of hours spent a day on the cell phone.

First, you collect data on campus—asking five students and six professors how many hours a day they typically are on the cell phone. While this N is relatively small—and the methods of your research leave much to be desired—let's keep the example short and simple to allow a focus on the statistical concepts at hand. Here (see Table 11.1) are your data:

Table 11.1:

Students (N = 5)	Professors (N = 6)
2	0
3	1
4	2
4	2
2	1
	2

Consistent with the presentation of hypothesis-testing statistics throughout this book, we can use the same five steps of hypothesis-testing to implement a between-groups t-test—as follows:

1. State your research and null hypotheses in terms of population parameters.
2. Determine the characteristics of your comparison distribution.
3. Determine your critical value (used for defining the *rejection region*).
4. Compute your "obtained statistic" (here, your obtained t-score) and compare it with the critical value.
5. Comment on the null hypothesis.

Following, you'll find a description of the process of the between-groups t-test using the working example of whether students use cell phones significantly more than do professors.

1. State your research and null hypotheses in terms of population parameters.
    A. Define the two populations in terms of two different population means:
        μ_1 = the mean number of hours a day on the cell phone for **students** (for the entire population of college students)
        μ_2 = the mean number of hours a day on the cell phone for **professors** (for the entire population of college professors)
    B. Delineate research and null hypotheses:
        H_1: $\mu_1 > \mu_2$ (the population mean for college students is predicted to be greater than the population mean for professors)
        H_0: $\mu_1 \leq \mu_2$ (the population mean for college students is predicted to be less than or equal to the population mean for professors)

2. DETERMINE THE QUALITIES OF YOUR COMPARISON DISTRIBUTION

Recall that the comparison distribution is a distribution of scores from a world in which the "equal" part of the null hypothesis is true. In the case of the between-groups t-test, this distribution assumes that there is no difference between the population means of your two different populations. With the current example, this distribution assumes that the mean cell phone use for students = the mean cell phone use for professors. However, it actually gets a bit more complicated than that.

To understand the comparison distribution used for the between-groups t-test, we need to consider five different kinds of distributions. First, we have the two relevant population distributions of interest (here, that means the distribution of cell phone usage for the entire population of college students and the distribution of cell phone usage for the entire population of professors). In Figure 11.1, these distributions refer to the two population distributions.

However, as addressed in detail in our prior chapter on hypothesis testing if N > 1, once we have means of samples, we need to compare such means not with distributions of individual scores, but with distributions of means. Thus, for each theoretical population distribution, we need to conceptualize a corresponding distribution of means (that takes the N of the particular sample into account [recall from our prior chapter that the N of the sample drives the details of your particular distribution of means]). Recall that a distribution of means is similar to its corresponding population distribution—particularly in that the mean of the distribution of means

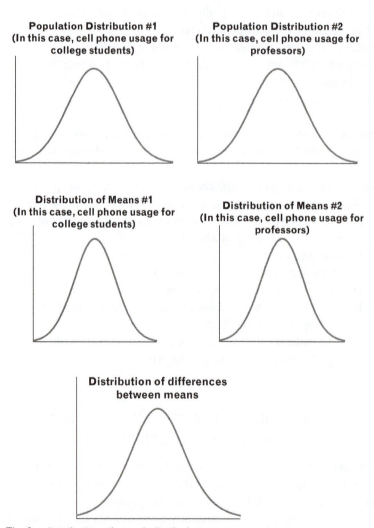

FIGURE 11.1: The five distributions that underlie the between-groups t-test.

(μ_M) equals the mean of the population distribution (μ). However, the variance (σ_M^2) and corresponding standard deviation (σ_M) for the distribution of means are reduced (as a function of N—recall that as N increases, the variance of the distribution of means decreases).

Thus, to determine the qualities of the comparison distribution for a between-groups t-test, we need to determine the qualities of the two distributions of means. In short, we need to compute s_{M1}^2 and s_{M2}^2. Here, s_{M1}^2 corresponds to our best estimate of the variance of the distribution of means corresponding to the population of students (based on an N of 5) and s_{M2}^2 is our best estimate of the variance of the distribution of means corresponding to the population of professors (based on an N of 6). Note that we use subscripts 1 and 2 to reflect whether we're talking about a statistical parameter based on the first sample (1) or the second sample (2).

Importantly, to keep our eye on the goal, note that once we compute our estimates of the variances of the distributions of means for our two populations, we're not quite done with figuring out the relevant features of our comparison distribution. In fact, our comparison distribution will ultimately be based on information from the two different distributions of means. The comparison distribution, referred to as a *distribution of differences between means*, is based on the population of differences between the means of the two different distributions of means. It's as if someone randomly pulled a score out of each of the two different distributions of means, computed a difference between these means (with an expected or most likely difference of 0), and then repeated this process a zillion more times to create the theoretical probability distribution of differences between means. The mean of this distribution is 0 if the equal part of the null hypothesis is true. The standard deviation of this distribution, s_{dif} (or the *standard deviation of the distribution of differences between means*), is what we ultimately need so as to be able to carry out the computations for our t-test. That standard deviation is derived from the variance estimates of the two distributions of means.

We therefore need to compute estimates of the variances of our distributions of means, ultimately, so we can compute the standard deviation of our comparison distribution. In computing these estimates of the variances of these different distributions of means, we will use the same process that we used to compute the variance of a distribution of means when we knew the standard deviation for the population (from chapter 8)—except that we are not given the population variance (σ^2) or standard deviation (σ). Thus, we need to estimate these parameters (the population variance and standard deviation)—as is always the case when conducting a t-test. Our estimate of the population variance will be represented by s^2 and our estimate of the population standard deviation will be the square root of the variance—represented by s. Note that while s is important conceptually (as it represents the estimate of the population standard deviation based on each sample), s^2 is actually more important in computing the between-groups t-test. The population variance estimates for each of the two samples (s_1^2 and s_2^2) are used in computing t, while the standard deviation estimates (s_1 and s_2) are **not** used for this process.

Here are the steps (with elaboration where appropriate) to compute s_{dif} (the standard deviation of our comparison distribution):

A.   Compute s_1^2 and s_2^2 (estimates of the variance of population for both populations)

B.   Compute s_{pooled}^2
       Compute s_{M1}^2 and s_{M2}^2
       Compute s_{dif}

A.   Computing s_1^2 and s_2^2

Table 11.2:

Group 1: Students

X_1	M_1	(X_1-M_1)	$(X_1-M_1)^2$
2	3	−1	1
3	3	0	0
4	3	1	1
4	3	1	1
2	3	−1	1

$\Sigma X_1 = 15$

$N_1 = 5$

$SS_1 = \Sigma(X_1-M_1)^2 = 4$

$s_1^2 = \dfrac{SS_1}{N_1-1} = 1$

$s_1 = \sqrt{s_1^2} = 1$

Importantly, note the following:

- $SS_1 = \Sigma(X-M)^2$; the sum of the squared deviation scores for sample 1; this is simply the sum of our rightmost column.
- $s_1^2 = \dfrac{SS_1}{N_1-1}$; as is always the case with t-tests, we divide by (N–1) instead of N to slightly increase our estimate of the variance (based on the assumption that population variances—which represent whole populations—are likely larger than variances of samples). s_1^2 represents the estimate of the population variance based on information obtained exclusively from sample 1.
- $s_1 = \sqrt{s_1^2}$; s_1 represents the estimate of the population standard deviation based on information obtained exclusively from sample 1.

Table 11.3:

Group 2: Professors

X_2	M_2	(X_2-M_2)	$(X_2-M_2)^2$
0	1.33	−1.33	1.77
1	1.33	−.33	.11
2	1.33	−.67	.45
2	1.33	−.67	.45
1	1.33	−.33	.11
2	1.33	−.67	.45

$\Sigma X_2 = 8$

$N_2 = 6$

$SS_2 = \Sigma(X_2-M_2)^2 = 3.34$

$s_2^2 = \dfrac{SS_2}{N_2-1} = .67$

$s_2 = \sqrt{s\dfrac{2}{2}} = .82$

Importantly, note the following:

- $SS_2 = \Sigma(X-M)^2$; the sum of the squared deviation scores for sample 2; this is simply the sum of our rightmost column.

- $s_2^2 = \dfrac{SS_2}{N_2 - 1}$; as is always the case with t-tests, we divide by (N–1) instead of N to slightly increase our estimate of the variance (based on the assumption that population variances—which represent whole populations—are likely larger than variances of samples). s_2^2 represents the estimate of the population variance based on information obtained exclusively from sample 2.

- $s_1 = \sqrt{s_2^2}$; s_2 represents the estimate of the population standard deviation based on information obtained exclusively from sample 2.

B.   Compute s_{pooled}^2

s_1^2 and s_2^2 represent our estimates of the population variances based on the data collected from the two samples. Ready for an important assumption and a mouthful? All things considered, an estimate of the population variance based on a larger N should be more valid compared with an estimate of the population variance based on a smaller N. With the between-groups t-test (and subsequent statistics that we'll run into in this book, such as the Analysis of Variance), we assume **homogeneity of variance**. That is, we assume that the nature of the population variance across the two groups is homogenous—or the same. While we are predicting that college students use cell phones more than professors do (in other words, we're predicting a difference between the population means), we have no predictions pertaining to the pattern of variance among scores being different across the two populations. In this case (and in most cases we run into in our research), it makes little sense to assume that the population variance differs across the groups. Thus, we assume homogeneity of variance—supposing that the population variance is the same across the two populations of interest.

In fact, there are times when this assumption is off the mark—there are advanced statistics designed to make judgments regarding whether homogeneity of variance truly exists and there are advanced statistics to deal with the problem of heterogeneity of variance (different variances across the two populations) when it exists. For now, it's important to know that statisticians usually assume that homogeneity of variance exists across groups (for the same variable)—and that this assumption is usually alright.

With that said, meet s_{pooled}^2. This statistic is an estimate of the population variance for both populations. Since we're assuming that the population variance is equal across the populations, we can then use information from both of our samples to come up with a pooled estimate of the variances. That's good news, because it allows us to estimate variances of populations based on a larger N (the combined N of both groups) compared with basing our estimates on either of the groups alone. Thus, s_{pooled}^2 represents our estimate of the population variance (for both populations). To compute s_{pooled}^2, we simply take an average of the variance estimates obtained from each sample in isolation (i.e., s_1^2 and s_2^2). However, if s_1^2 and s_2^2 are based on different Ns, we need to take a weighted average, essentially giving more weight to the variance estimate based on the larger N. In short, $s_{pooled}^2 = s_1^2 \left(\dfrac{df_1}{df_{total}} \right) + s_2^2 \left(\dfrac{df_2}{df_{total}} \right)$.

where $df_1 = N_1-1$, $df_2 = N_2-1$, and $df_{total} = df_1 + df_2$; we are essentially weighting these population estimates by the degrees of freedom that correspond to each sample (which is based on the N of each sample).

In terms of our working example,

$df_1 = 5-1 = 4;$

$df_2 = 6-1 = 5;$

$df_{total} = 4 + 5;$

$$s^2_{pooled} = \frac{4}{9}(1) + \frac{5}{9}(.67) = .44 + .37 = .81$$

C.   Compute s^2_{M1} and s^2_{M2}

Recall from chapters 7 and 8 that we compare single scores with comparison distributions of single scores and we compare means with distributions of means. In computing the between-groups t-test, we're working with means. In fact, while I hate to ruin the suspense, $t = \dfrac{M_1 - M_2}{s_{dif}}$. So actually, we're dealing with differences between means (as $M_1 M_2$ is a difference between means—which will ultimately be compared with a distribution of differences between means [our comparison distribution]). For this step, realize that we're dealing with means and, thus, that we need to compute estimates of the two different distributions of means that are relevant here. These distributions of means include the distribution of means for sample 1 (based on N_1) and the distribution of means for sample 2 (based on N_2). Recall that the variance of a distribution of means decreases as a function of N—so we need to figure out separate variances for samples 1 and 2—taking their particular Ns into account.

With that all said:

$$s^2_{M1} = \frac{s^2_{pooled}}{N_1}$$

and

$$s^2_{M2} = \frac{s^2_{pooled}}{N_2}.$$

In terms of our working example,

$$s^2_{M1} = \frac{.81}{5} = .16;$$

$$s^2_{M2} \frac{.81}{6} = .14;$$

D.   Compute S_{dif}

OK—we're getting there; honest! The comparison distribution for our t-test will be a distribution of differences between means. It's as if we randomly dip into the distribution of means for population 1 (students), then randomly dip into the distribution of means for population 2 (professors), compute the difference, put those means back, and then continue this process infinitely. This process will lead to a distribution of differences between means—assuming that the equal part of the null hypothesis is true. That is, the assumption of the comparison distribution is that there is no difference between the population means of interest—and that our expected difference between the means should be 0 (if the mean for professors and students are the same, their difference should be 0).

Thus, the mean of our comparison distribution—of the distribution of differences between means—is 0. That's actually true for t-distributions in general.

We also need to know the standard deviation of our comparison distribution. As usual, that means we first need to know the variance of our comparison distribution. That variance, represented by s^2_{dif} (or the variance of the differences between means) is the sum of s^2_{M1} and s^2_{M2}; both variance estimates contribute to the estimate of the variance of the comparison distribution—so we add them together. $s^2_{diff} = s^2_{M1} + s^2_{M2}$. In our working example, then, $s^2_{dif} = 14 + .16 = .30$.

Finally: the standard deviation is always the square root of the variance—in this case, $s_{dif} = \sqrt{s^2_{dif}} = .55$. That is the standard deviation of our comparison distribution in non-standardized units (in t units, as usual, the standard deviation is ± 1).

Our comparison distribution is a t-distribution. Further, it is a special kind of t-distribution—a distribution of differences between means with a mean of 0 and a standard deviation (in raw units) of .55. Done with Step #2—I know; it's a doozy!

3. DETERMINE YOUR CRITICAL VALUE (USED FOR DEFINING THE *REJECTION REGION*)

The process for determining your critical value is essentially the same as the process in the prior chapter on within-group and one-sample t-tests. The steps are as follows:

A. Determine your alpha level ahead of time. Let's stick with the standard .05 for this example.

B. Determine whether your test is "one-tailed" or "two-tailed." As in prior chapters, this decision is driven by our research hypothesis. In our example, we predict a difference in a specific direction (students to score higher than professors). Thus, we're only interested in one tail of the comparison distribution (the tail corresponding to the reality of students scoring higher than professors).

C. Use the t-table to determine the specific t-critical value based on the alpha level, the number of tails, and the degrees of freedom. For the between-groups t-test, we use the total degrees of freedom ($df_1 + df_2$) to drive this step.

Thus, here, we're looking for the t-critical corresponding to an alpha of .05, a one-tailed test, and 9 degrees of freedom.

Excerpt of t-table:

Table 11.4: Excerpt of t-Table

	ONE-TAILED		TWO-TAILED	
df	alpha of .05	alpha of .01	alpha of .05	alpha of .01
8	1.86	2.90	2.31	3.36
9	**1.83**	2.82	2.26	3.25
10	1.81	2.76	2.22	3.17

t_{crit} = 1.83. Thus, to reject our null hypothesis that professors use the cell phone either as much as or more than students, we'll have to obtain a t value of greater than 1.83. This outcome would support our research hypothesis, suggesting that the population mean for students is, in fact, greater than the population mean for professors.

Further, note that t-critical is positive in sign. That will be the case whenever the research hypothesis specifies that the mean of sample 1 should be **greater than** the mean of sample 2 (simply because that outcome should lead to a t that is positive in sign). If the research hypothesis specifies that the mean of sample 1 should be less than the mean of sample 2, t-critical will be negative in sign (you need to add the negative sign yourself, as the t-table has all positive numbers). Further, as has been the case, if you have a two-tailed test, t-critical will be both positive and negative in sign.

To reject the null hypothesis and, thus, provide support for the idea that students use their cell phones significantly more than professors, we'll have to obtain a t of greater than 1.83.

4. COMPUTE YOUR "OBTAINED STATISTIC" (HERE, YOUR OBTAINED t-SCORE) AND COMPARE IT WITH THE CRITICAL VALUE

Easy.

$$t = \frac{M_1 - M_2}{s_{dif}}.$$

$$t = \frac{3 - 1.33}{.55} = 3.04.$$

5. COMMENT ON THE NULL HYPOTHESIS

Here's a graphical representation of the relative positions of t_{obt} and t-critical:

Simply, when t is more extreme than t-critical and is in the rejection region (determined by our alpha level), we reject the null hypothesis—thus, providing some support for our research hypothesis. In this case, we conclude that when it comes to hours spent on the cell phone per day, the population mean for students is likely greater than the population mean for professors.

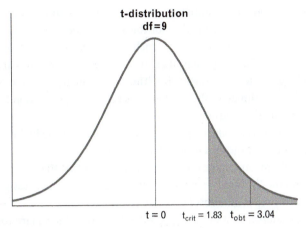

t-distribution
df = 9

t = 0 t_{crit} = 1.83 t_{obt} = 3.04

FIGURE 11.2: t-distribution with Critical Values and Obtained t Demarcated.

EFFECT SIZE WITH THE BETWEEN-GROUPS t-TEST

Recall that statistical significance and effect size are independent ways to comment on whether a particular finding is noteworthy. You may have a finding that is "statistically significant" (which corresponds to rejecting the null hypothesis), but that same finding may be very small and unimportant in the real world. Similarly, you may have a finding that is actually quite large, but that does not come out as "statistically significant" with the hypothesis-testing procedure (recall contexts in which this can happen from the prior chapter on statistical power). Thus, separate from commenting on whether a particular between-groups t is statistically significant, it's often useful to comment on whether there is a *large effect size*. In the case of a between-groups t-test, in which you're comparing two sample means with one another, a large effect size exists when your sample means are very different from one another—in light of the amount of variability at the population level. That is, relative to the amount that scores vary from one another in the population, are your means very different from one another? As was the case in our prior chapter on within-group and one-sample t-tests, we'll use Cohen's d to estimate effect size with the between-groups t-test.

Importantly, as was the case with Cohen's d in the prior chapter, and as is the case with effect-size estimates in general, we're interested in estimating the size of an effect independent of the particulars of the samples used in a specific study. We're not commenting on whether the difference between means was large in a particular study relative to the variability of scores in that study—rather, we're trying to say something bigger—that this effect is large in an absolute sense, regardless of the sample size in a particular study. To make that point, our equation needs to use parameters that are conceptually independent of the details of any particular study.

Thus, our equation for Cohen's d (for a between-groups t-test) is as follows:

$$\text{Cohen's } d = \left| \frac{M_1 - M_2}{s_{pooled}} \right|$$

Here, we're looking at the difference between the sample means in the context of our best estimate of the population-level standard deviation (s_{pooled}). Thus, while s_{pooled} is not used at all in the computation of our between-groups t-test, it is used in our computation of Cohen's d.

s_{pooled} is used because it's our best estimate of the population standard deviation—a conceptual statistical parameter that is independent of the sample size used in a particular study. If N = 11 or N = 1011, other variability estimates (such as s_{M2}^2) change wildly. However, in theory, s_{pooled} shouldn't change at all—conceptually, it's a universal estimate of the standard deviation at the population level—regardless of sample size. Thus, this equation allows us to comment on the size of an effect as an estimate of the "real effect size" at the population level (independent of the N used in any particular study).

The same effect-size conventions used in the prior chapter are used when talking about the size of Cohen's d for a between-groups t-test. That is, roughly:

.2 = small, .5 = medium, and .8 (or greater) = large. Recall that the sign of Cohen's d is generally irrelevant (as it's totally based on which population we arbitrarily assign as population 1 or 2)—thus, we generally report the absolute value of Cohen's d.

For our working example, recall that $s_{pooled}^2 = .81$. If we take the square root of that, we get s_{pooled}, which is .9. This is, in effect, our best estimate of the population-level standard deviation (for both populations). Thus, Cohen's $d = \left| \dfrac{3-1.33}{.9} \right| = 1.86$. Of course, if .8 is large, 1.86 is **very large**. Not only do students use their cell phones significantly more than professors—but this difference (relative to the amount of variability between individuals in the population) is huge!

ANOTHER EXAMPLE

Going deep into human pre-history, cat lovers and dog lovers have quarreled about the relative merits of their favored four-legged friends. Dogs can jump through hoops while cats (of course) just seem smart. What's the deal? For the current example, suppose that psychologists at Middle American University have just unveiled their animal IQ measure—with the wonderful quality of being applicable across all animal species! For your psychology research project, you and the other members of your group (half of whom are dog lovers, half of whom are cat lovers) decide to determine, once and for all, which kind of beast is intellectually superior.

To be fair to both sides, you decide to run a two-tailed between-groups t-test. It's two-tailed because you don't want your research hypothesis biased toward one animal or the other (as half your group essentially predicts that cats will score higher while the other half predicts that dogs will). In looking for subjects for your research, you find five cats and seven dogs. You then carefully implement the animal IQ test (which is on a scale of 0–4) to each of these beasts.

Here's what you find:

Table 11.5:

Cats	Dogs
3	1
2	0
4	4
4	3
2	0
	4
	2

In computing a between-groups t-test to see which beast is smarter, we'll follow our five standard hypothesis-testing steps as follows (assume an alpha level of .01):

1. State your research and null hypotheses in terms of population parameters.
2. Determine the characteristics of your comparison distribution.
3. Determine your critical value (used for defining the *rejection region*).
4. Compute your "obtained statistic" (here, your obtained t score) and compare it with the critical value.
5. Comment on the null hypothesis.

1. STATE YOUR RESEARCH AND NULL HYPOTHESES IN TERMS OF POPULATION PARAMETERS

A. Define the two populations in terms of two different population means:
   μ_1 = mean IQ score for the entire population of domesticated cats
   μ_2 = mean IQ score for the entire population of domesticated dogs
B. Delineate research and null hypotheses:
   H_1: $\mu_1 \neq \mu_2$ (the population mean for cats is predicted to be different from [either greater or less than] the population mean for dogs)
   H_0: $\mu_1 = \mu_2$ (the population mean for cats is predicted to be equal to the population mean for dogs)

2. DETERMINE THE CHARACTERISTICS OF YOUR COMPARISON DISTRIBUTION

The comparison distribution will be a t-distribution (representing a distribution of differences between means) with a mean of 0 and a standard deviation (in raw units) represented by s_{dif}. We need to compute s_{dif}. To do so, we must do the following:

A. Compute s_1^2 and s_2^2 (estimates of the variance of population for both populations)
B. Compute s_{pooled}^2
C. Compute s_{M1}^2 and s_{M2}^2
D. Compute s_{dif}

Table 11.6: Cats

Group 1: Cats

X_1	M_1	(X_1-M_1)	$(X_1-M_1)^2$
3	3	0	0
2	3	−1	1
4	3	1	1
4	3	1	1
2	3	−1	1
$\Sigma X_1 = 15$			$SS_1 = \Sigma(X-M)^2 = 4$
			$s_1^2 = \dfrac{SS_1}{N_1-1} = 1$
$N_1 = 5$			$s_1 = \sqrt{s_1^2} = 1$

Note the following:

- $SS_1 = \Sigma(X-M)^2$; the sum of the squared deviation scores for sample 1; this is simply the sum of our rightmost column
- $s_1^2 = \dfrac{SS_1}{N_1-1}$; as is always the case with t-tests, we divide by (N–1) instead of N to slightly increase our estimate of the variance (based on the assumption that population variances—which represent whole populations—are likely larger than variances of samples). s_1^2 represents the estimate of the population variance based on information obtained exclusively from sample 1.
- $s_1 = \sqrt{s_1^2}$; represents the estimate of the population standard deviation based on information obtained exclusively from sample 1.

Table 11.7: Dogs

Group 2: Dogs

X_2	M_2	$(X_2–M_2)$	$(X_2–M_2)^2$
1	2	–1	1
0	2	–2	4
4	2	2	4
3	2	1	1
0	2	–2	4
4	2	2	4
2	2	0	0
$\Sigma X_2 = 14$			$SS_2 = \Sigma(X_2–M_2)^2 = 18$
$N_2 = 7$			$s_2^2 = \dfrac{SS_2}{N_2-1} = 3$
			$s_2^2 = \sqrt{s_2^2} = 1.73$

Also note the following:

- $SS_2 = \Sigma(X-M)^2$; the sum of the squared deviation scores for sample 2; this is simply the sum of our rightmost column
- $s_2^2 = \dfrac{SS_2}{N_2-1}$; as is always the case with t-tests, we divide by (N–1) instead of N to slightly increase our estimate of the variance (based on the assumption that population variances—which represent whole populations—are likely larger than variances of samples). s_2^2 represents the estimate of the population variance based on information obtained exclusively from sample 2.
- $s_2 = \sqrt{s_2^2}$; s_2 represents the estimate of the population standard deviation based on information obtained exclusively from sample 2.

B. Compute s^2_{pooled}

$$s^2_{pooled} = s^2_1 \left(\frac{df_1}{df_{total}} \right) + s^2_2 \left(\frac{df_2}{df_{total}} \right) ;$$

In terms of our working example,

$df_1 = 5 - 1 = 4$;
$df_2 = 7 - 1 = 6$;
$df_{total} = 4 + 6 = 10$;

$$s^2_{pooled} = \frac{4}{10}(1) + \frac{6}{10}(3) = .4 + 1.8 = 2.2$$

C. Compute s^2_{M1} and s^2_{M2}

$$s^2_{M1} = \frac{s^2_{pooled}}{N_1}$$

and

$$s^2_{M2} = \frac{s^2_{pooled}}{N_2}.$$

In terms of our working example,

$$s^2_{M1} = \frac{2.2}{5} = .44 ;$$

$$s^2_{M2} = \frac{2.2}{7} = .31$$

D. Compute S_{dif}

$$s^2_{dif} = s^2_{M1} + s^2_{M2}$$

$$s^2_{dif} = .44 + .31 = .75$$

$$s_{dif} = \sqrt{s^2_{dif}} = .87$$

3. DETERMINE YOUR CRITICAL VALUE (USED FOR DEFINING THE *REJECTION REGION*)

Our given information is that **alpha = .01** and, based on our research hypothesis, we have a **two-tailed** test. Further, our total degrees of freedom (df_{total}) = **10**.

Here's a relevant excerpt of the t-table:

Table 11.8:

| df | ONE-TAILED | | TWO-TAILED | |
	alpha of .05	alpha of .01	alpha of .05	alpha of .01
8	1.86	2.90	2.31	3.36
9	1.83	2.82	2.26	3.25
10	1.81	2.76	2.22	**3.17**

As you can see, 3.17 corresponds to a two-tailed test with an alpha of .01 and 10 degrees of freedom. Further, as is true with all two-tailed tests, our critical value is both positive and negative (thus, our critical value is ±3.17—displayed in Figure 11.3).

4. COMPUTE YOUR "OBTAINED STATISTIC" (HERE, YOUR OBTAINED T SCORE) AND COMPARE IT WITH THE CRITICAL VALUE

$$t = \frac{M_1 - M_2}{s_{dif}}$$

$$t = \frac{3-2}{.87} = 1.15$$

5. COMMENT ON THE NULL HYPOTHESIS

As you can see clearly in Figure 11.4, your obtained t is not close to your rejection regions. It is not more extreme than either of our t-critical values. Thus, we **fail to reject the null hypothesis**.

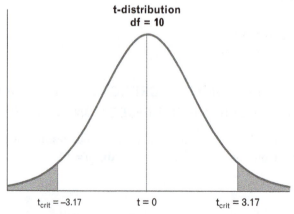

FIGURE 11.3: t-distribution with Critical Values Demarcated.

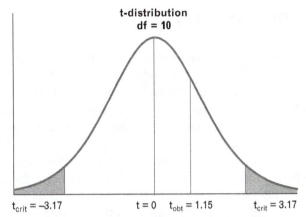

FIGURE 11.4: Comparing our Obtained t with our t-critical Values.

In other words, we have failed to find any evidence suggesting that cats and dogs differ in their overall intelligence. This eternal question remains unanswered!

Recall that separate from whether a finding is statistically significant, we can assess the size of an effect obtained from our research. With our between-groups t-test, we use the Cohen's d statistic to make this judgment. With our cats and dogs example, we have the following:

In terms of the value ranges presented for Cohen's d, .68 falls between "medium" and "large." Thus, in fact, while we have not provided evidence that cats are smarter than dogs, the mean for cats (3) is higher than the mean for dogs (2) and the effect corresponding to this difference is pretty big.

What's going on here? How can we say that there is no significant difference between cats and dogs (based on our failing to reject the null hypothesis) and at the same time say that there is a big effect consistent with the idea that cats are smarter than dogs? The answer partly lies in the content of chapter 9 dealing with power and effect size. Recall that even if you have a large effect size, you may well have low power and, thus, have a small chance of rejecting the null hypothesis (even if the null hypothesis is, in fact, false). Recall also that a major contributor to low power is a relatively small N. In the example study here, we have an N of 12. That's small! In the real world, you want larger numbers of subjects in your research—largely for this reason. We turn to a real-world example next.

#104 03-02-2017 6:47PM
Item(s) checked out to p12306915.

TITLE: Straightforward statistics : unde
BARCODE: 31220010891775
DUE DATE: 03-23-17

REAL RESEARCH EXAMPLE

In a study of sex differences in the reasons for having friends of the opposite sex, April Bleske-Rechek and David Buss (2001) asked nearly 100 male and 100 female heterosexual college students to complete a survey reporting on their reasons for having opposite-sex friends who are, in fact, *just friends*. Interestingly, males and females differed significantly in terms of many of their responses. For instance, one question asked all subjects to use a 5-point scale to rate how much they initiated a current friendship with an opposite-sex individual because of initial sexual attraction. On this scale, low numbers (such as 1 and 2) meant that this was not a reason for forming the friendship, whereas higher numbers meant that the subject did, in fact, think that sexual attraction was a cause of the development of the friendship. In their published report on these findings, Bleske-Rechek and Buss assert the following:

For males, the mean on this rating scale was 3.56 (with a standard deviation of 1.98), whereas for females, the mean was 2.49 (with a standard deviation of 1.61). Further, the between-groups t-test designed to see if this difference was significant revealed a significant effect: $t(196) = 3.05$, $p < .05$. This phrase means, essentially, that the obtained t (which corresponded to 196 total degrees of freedom) was 3.05. Further, the fact that the authors tell you "$p > .05$" means that this t was in the rejection region (with an alpha level of .05). This t was, in other words, more extreme than the t-critical on the comparison distribution.

Finally, the authors also report Cohen's d as .30. Thus, the authors are telling us that this effect, which was statistically significant, was small/medium in size. Thus, here, we have a case in which a finding was statistically significant, but the effect it corresponds to is not huge.

To sum this all up for a layperson, you could say that in this study, males rated sexual attraction as significantly more important in their decisions to have friendships with females (compared with females' ratings). Simply put: men seem to think that they are friends with women partly because they are sexually attracted to these women. Women, on the other hand, don't seem to report that they are friends with men because of sexual attraction. The only saving grace of all this is that the effect size is somewhat small.

SUMMARY

The between-groups t-test allows us to address a very basic question—do two groups differ on some continuous variable? In computing this t-test, we are essentially seeing if the difference between two sample means (thought to represent two different populations) are different enough so as to allow us to conclude that the population means they represent are likely different from one another. Thus, the between-groups t-test allows us to see if two sample means are "significantly different." In addition to this issue of statistical significance, we can compute Cohen's d to estimate the effect size—roughly corresponding to the difference between the sample means (taking the population-level standard deviation into account). As is always the case, statistical significance and effect size are distinct concepts and, accordingly, a finding that corresponds to a small effect size can be statistically significant, while a finding corresponding to a large effect size may not be found to be statistically significant. Coupled with the Cohen's d statistics, the between-groups t-test provides a clear mechanism for addressing differences between sample means that represent two discrete populations.

KEY TERMS

Dichotomous categorical variable: Variable in which the different values represent one of two different categories

Distribution of Differences between Means: The comparison distribution used for the between-groups t-test –it is theoretically comprised of an infinite sample of differences between two populations (whose means are assumed to be equal)

Heterogeneity of variance: Assumption that the nature of the population variance across groups is different

Homogeneity of variance: Assumption that the nature of the population variance across groups is the same

Pooled Variance Estimate: A single of the population variance for two different populations based on information collected from multiple samples

SYMBOLS

M = mean (M_1 = mean of sample 1; M_2 = mean of sample 2)

N = number of scores (N_1 = number of scores for sample 1; N_2 = number of scores for sample 2)

μ = mean of the population distribution (μ_1 mean of population distribution for sample 1; μ_2 mean of population distribution for sample 2)

μ_M = mean of the distribution of means

σ = standard deviation of the population

σ_M = standard deviation of the distribution of means

σ^2 = variance of the population

σ_M^2 = variance of the distribution of means

df = N–1; degrees of freedom (df_1 = degrees of freedom for sample 1; df_2 = degrees of freedom for sample 2)

df_{total} = total degrees of freedom (e.g., $df_1 + df_2 = df_{total}$)

$SS = \Sigma(X - M)^2$; the sum of the squared deviation scores (SS_1 = sum of the squared deviation scores for sample 1; SS_2 = sum of the squared deviation scores for sample 2)

$s = \sqrt{s^2}$ estimate of the population standard deviation

$s^2 = \dfrac{SS}{N-1}$ estimate of the population variance (s^2_1 = estimate of the population variance for sample 1; s^2_2 estimate of the population variance for sample 2)

s_M^2 estimate of the variance of the distribution of means corresponding to the population (s_{M1}^2 = estimate of the variance of the distribution of means corresponding to the population of sample 1; s_{M2}^2 = estimate of the variance of the distribution of means corresponding to the population of sample 2)

$s^2_{pooled} = s_1^2 \left(\dfrac{df_1}{df_{total}} \right) + s_2^2 \left(\dfrac{df_2}{df_{total}} \right)$; pooled estimate of the population variance deviation; estimate of the population variance for both populations

s_{dif} = standard deviation of the distribution of differences between means

HOMEWORK SET A

For each of the problems A-C, complete 1–5.

1. State your research and null hypotheses in terms of population parameters.
2. Determine the characteristics of your comparison distribution.
3. Determine your critical value (used for defining the *rejection region*).
4. Compute your "obtained statistic" (here, your obtained t score) and compare it with the critical value.
5. Comment on the null hypothesis (include effect size).
   A. A former 1st-grade teacher is now teaching 10th grade, and tells you that the first graders are better at making friends than the 10th graders. You decide to test this hypothesis, and gather data, using 5 1st graders and 6 10th graders who complete a scale measuring how easily each person makes friends, with scores ranging from 1–10. Assume an alpha of .05. The data are as follows:

Table 11.9: Homework Set A, B Data

1st Graders	10th Graders
8	3
7	5
9	7
5	6
6	6
	5

   B. You and a friend disagree on whether dentists take better care of their teeth than people who work in candy shops. Are dentists better or worse at oral health practices than people who work in candy shops? You and your friend decide to collect data. You obtain scores for five dentists and six candy shop workers on a measurement of oral health, with a range of 0–8. Assume an alpha of .01. Here are your data:

Table 11.10: Homework Set A, B Data

Dentists	Candy shop workers
3	8
5	6
8	6
7	4
4	3
	5

C. You have an acquaintance who always claims that if she didn't work full-time, she would bake cookies and cakes all the time. So you wonder, do people who work part-time make more baked goods than people who work full-time? You ask people who work full-time and people who work part-time how many baked goods they make in a month. Assume an alpha level of .05. Here are the data:

Table 11.11: Homework Set A, C Data

Part-Time	Full-Time
3	5
1	3
1	1
2	0
4	2
3	
2	

HOMEWORK SET B

For each of the problems A-C, complete 1–5.

1. State your research and null hypotheses in terms of population parameters.
2. Determine the characteristics of your comparison distribution.
3. Determine your critical value (used for defining the *rejection region*).
4. Compute your "obtained statistic" (here, your obtained t score) and compare it with the critical value.
5. Comment on the null hypothesis (include effect size).
    A. You have a few friends who are very introverted, and they rarely go on dates. However, a friend of yours claims that her introverted friends go on *more* dates than her extroverted friends. To see if introverts go on more or fewer dates, you collect data from five introverts and five extroverts regarding the number of dates they went on in the last month. Assume an alpha level of .05. Here are the data:

Table 11.12: Homework Set B, A Data

Introverts	Extroverts
3	1
1	3
1	2
2	4
4	3

B. You know a family that has an in-home nanny for the children rather than having the children attending daycare, and you've noticed that these children have exceptional manners, never failing to say "please" or "thank you." You think that perhaps in-home nannies have more time to work with the children on manners than do daycare providers, and therefore, children with nannies may have better manners than children who attend daycare. You find nine participants; four children who have nannies and five children who attend daycare. As a measure of manners, you offer each child ten objects, and record how many times the child says "thank you." Assume an alpha level of .01. Your data are as follows:

Table 11.13: Homework Set B, B Data

Nannies	Daycare
9	2
3	8
4	6
6	3
	5

C. You have noticed that people who seem to be risk takers tend to dress in skimpier clothes than people who do not seem to be risk takers. You decide to test this hypothesis and find out if risk takers do, indeed, dress in more revealing clothes than non-risk takers. You give 10 people a survey assessing risk-taking behavior, and find that four are risk-takers and six are not. You then set up an appointment with each of them, and weigh their clothes (in pounds) when they show up for the appointment, as skimpier, more revealing clothes likely have less bulk and weigh less than clothes that offer more coverage. You use this data to determine if risk-takers wear skimpier clothing than non-risk takers. Assume an alpha level of .05. The raw data, in pounds, are as follows:

Table 11.14: Homework Set B, C Data

Non-risk takers	Risk takers
1.5	1.7
2.2	1.2
1.6	.8
1.92	1.3
2.5	
2.3	

HOMEWORK SET A ANSWERS

A

1. State your research and null hypotheses in terms of population parameters.
   A. Define the two populations in terms of two different population means:
   μ_1 = mean friendship score for the entire population of 1st graders
   μ_2 = mean friendship score for the entire population of 10th graders

B. Delineate the research and null hypotheses:

$H_1 = \mu_1 > \mu_2$ (the population mean for 1st graders is predicted to be greater than the population mean for 10th graders)

$H_0 = \mu_1 \leq \mu_2$ (the population mean for 1st graders is predicted to be less than or equal to the population mean for 10th graders)

2. Determine the characteristics of your comparison distribution.

A. Compute s_1^2 and s_2^2

Table 11.15: Computing s_1^2

Group 1: 1st Graders

X_1	M_1	(X_1-M_1)	$(X_1-M_1)^2$
8	7	1	1
7	7	0	0
9	7	2	4
5	7	-2	4
6	7	-1	1
$\Sigma X_1 = 35$			$SS_1 = \Sigma(X_1-M_1)^2 = 10$
			$s_1^2 = \dfrac{SS_1}{N_1 - 1} = 2.5$
$N_1 = 5$			
			$s_1 = \sqrt{s_1^2} = 1.58$

Table 11.16: Computing s_2^2

Group 2: 10th Graders

X_2	M_2	(X_2-M_2)	$(X_2-M_2)^2$
3	5.33	-2.33	5.43
5	5.33	-.33	.11
7	5.33	1.67	2.79
6	5.33	.67	.45
6	5.33	.67	.45
5	5.33	-.33	.11
$\Sigma X_2 = 32$			$SS_2 = \Sigma(X_2-M_2)^2 = 9.34$
			$s_2^2 = \dfrac{SS_2}{N_2 - 1} = 1.87$
$N_2 = 6$			
			$s_2 = \sqrt{s_2^2} = 1.37$

B. Compute s_{pooled}^2.

$$s_{pooled}^2 = s_1^2\left(\frac{df_1}{df_{total}}\right) + s_2^2\left(\frac{df_2}{df_{total}}\right);$$

$df_1 = 5-1 = 4;$

$$df_2 = 6 - 1 = 5;$$
$$df_{total} = 4 + 5 = 9;$$

$$s^2_{pooled} = \frac{4}{9}(2.5) + \frac{5}{9}(1.87) = 1.1 + 1.05 = 2.15$$

C. Compute s^2_{M1} and s^2_{M2}

$$s^2_{M1} = \frac{s^2_{pooled}}{N_1} = \frac{2.15}{5} = .43$$

$$s_M = \frac{s_{pooled}}{N} = \frac{}{} = 36$$

D. Compute s_{dif}

$$s^2_{dif} = s^2_{M1} + s^2_{M2}$$

$$s^2_{dif} = .43 + .36 = .79$$

$$s^2_{dif} = \sqrt{s^2_{dif}} = .89$$

3. Determine your critical value (used for defining the *rejection region*).

The alpha is .05 and the total degrees of freedom = 9. We have a one-tailed test. According to the chart, our critical value is 1.83.

4. Compute your "obtained statistic" (here, your obtained t-score) and compare it with the critical value.

$$t_{obt} = \frac{M_1 - M_2}{s_{dif}} = \frac{7 - 5.33}{.89} = 1.88$$

The t-score of 1.88 is more extreme than the critical value of 1.83, and thus does fall into the rejection region.

5. Comment on the null hypothesis (include effect size).

The null hypothesis is rejected because t_{obt} is more extreme than t_{crit}. Our t value is in the rejection region. Therefore, when it comes to making friends, the population mean for 1st graders is likely greater than the population mean for 10th graders—1st graders likely are better at making friends than 10th graders.

$$\text{Cohen's } d = \left| \frac{M_1 - M_2}{s_{pooled}} \right| = \left| \frac{7 - 5.33}{\sqrt{2.15}} \right| = \left| \frac{1.67}{1.47} \right| = 1.14$$

Cohen's d is 1.14, which indicates that the effect size of the difference is very large. 1st graders are not only likely better at making friends than 10th graders, but they are likely *much* better at making friends than 10th graders.

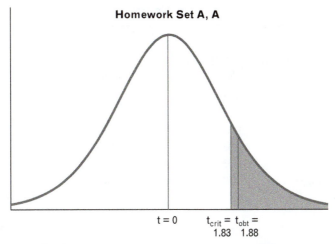

FIGURE 11.5: Homework Set A, A.

B

1. State your research and null hypotheses in terms of population parameters.
    A. Define the two populations in terms of two different population means:
    μ_1 = mean oral health score for the entire population of dentists
    μ_2 = mean oral health score for the entire population of candy shop workers

    B. Delineate research and null hypotheses:
    $H_1 = \mu_1 \neq \mu_2$ (the population mean for dentists is predicted to be different from [either greater than or less than] the population mean for candy shop workers)
    $H_0 = \mu_1 = \mu_2$ (the population mean for dentists is predicted to be equal to the population mean for candy shop workers)

2. Determine the characteristics of your comparison distribution.
    A. Compute s_1^2 and s_2^2

Table 11.17: Computing s_1^2

Group 1: Dentists

X_1	M_1	$(X_1 - M_1)$	$(X_1 - M_1)^2$
3	5.4	−2.4	5.76
5	5.4	−.4	.16
8	5.4	2.6	6.76
7	5.4	1.6	2.56
4	5.4	−1.4	1.96
$\Sigma X_1 = 27$			$SS_1 = \Sigma(X_1 - M_1)^2 = 17.2$
$N_1 = 5$			$s_1^2 = \dfrac{SS_1}{N_1 - 1} = 4.3$
			$s_1 = \sqrt{s_1^2} = 2.07$

Table 11.18: Computing s_2^2

Group 2: Candy shop workers

X_2	M_2	(X_2-M_2)	$(X_2-M_2)^2$
8	5.33	2.67	7.13
6	5.33	.67	.45
6	5.33	.67	.45
4	5.33	−1.33	1.77
3	5.33	−2.33	5.43
5	5.33	−.33	.11

$\Sigma X_2 = 32$

$N_2 = 6$

$SS_2 = \Sigma(X_2-M_2)^2 = 15.34$

$s_2^2 = \dfrac{SS_2}{N_2-1} = 3.07$

$s_2 = \sqrt{s_2^2} = 2.65$

B. Compute s_{pooled}^2

$$s_{pooled}^2 = s_1^2\left(\frac{df_1}{df_{total}}\right) + s_2^2\left(\frac{df_2}{df_{total}}\right);$$

$df_1 = 5-1 = 4;$
$df_2 = 6-1 = 5;$
$df_{total} = 4 + 5 = 9;$

$$s_{pooled}^2 = \frac{4}{9}(4.3) + \frac{5}{9}(3.07) = 1.89 + 1.72 = 3.61$$

C. Compute s_{M1}^2 and s_{M2}^2

$$s_{M1}^2 = \frac{s_{pooled}^2}{N_1} = \frac{3.61}{5} = .72$$

$$s_{M2}^2 = \frac{s_{pooled}^2}{N_2} = \frac{3.61}{6} = .60$$

D. Compute s_{dif}

$$s_{diff}^2 = s_{M1}^2 + s_{M2}^2$$

$$s_{diff}^2 = .72 + .60 = 1.32$$

$$s_{diff}^2 = \sqrt{s_{dif}^2} = 1.15$$

3.   Determine your critical value (used for defining the *rejection region*)

The alpha is .01 and the total degrees of freedom = 9. We have a two-tailed test. According to the chart, our critical value is ±3.25.

4. **Compute your "obtained statistic" (here, your obtained t score) and compare it with the critical value.**

$$t_{obt} = \frac{M_1 - M_1}{s_{dif}} = \frac{5.4 - 5.33}{1.15} = .06$$

The t score of .06 is not more extreme than the critical value of ±3.25, and thus does not fall into the rejection region.

5. Comment on the null hypothesis (include effect size).

The null hypothesis is not rejected because t_{obt} does not fall into the rejection region. Therefore, when it comes to oral health, the population mean for dentists is not likely greater than, nor less than, the population mean for candy shop workers—dentists are not likely better or worse at oral health practices than are candy shop workers.

$$\text{Cohen's } d = \left| \frac{M_1 - M_2}{s_{pooled}} \right| = \left| \frac{5.4 - 5.33}{\sqrt{3.61}} \right| = \left| \frac{.07}{1.90} \right| = .04$$

Cohen's d is .04, which indicates that the effect size of the difference is very small. There is likely no difference between dentists and candy shop workers in the matter of oral health.

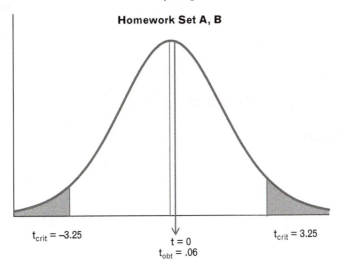

Homework Set A, B

$t_{crit} = -3.25$ $t = 0$ $t_{crit} = 3.25$
                           $t_{obt} = .06$

FIGURE 11.6: Homework Set A, B.

C

1. State your research and null hypotheses in terms of population parameters.
    A. Define the two populations in terms of two different population means:
    μ_1 = mean number of baked goods for the entire population of part-time workers
    μ_2 = mean number of baked goods for the entire population of full-time workers

B. Delineate research and null hypotheses:

$H_1 = \mu_1 > \mu_2$ (the population mean for part-time workers is predicted to be greater than the population mean for full-time workers)

$H_0 = \mu_1 \leq \mu_2$ (the population mean for part-time workers is predicted to be less than or equal to the population mean for full-time workers)

2. Determine the characteristics of your comparison distribution.

A. Compute s_1^2 and s_1^2

Table 11.19: Computing $s_1{}^2$

Group 1: Part-time Workers

X_1	M_1	(X_1-M_1)	$(X_1-M_1)^2$
3	2.29	.71	.50
1	2.29	−1.29	1.66
1	2.29	−1.29	1.66
2	2.29	−.29	.08
4	2.29	1.71	2.92
3	2.29	.71	.50
2	2.29	−.29	.08
$\Sigma X_1 = 16$			$SS_1 = \Sigma(X_1-M_1)^2 = 7.4$
$N_1 = 7$			$s_1^2 = \dfrac{SS_1}{N_1-1} = 1.23$
			$s_1 = \sqrt{s_1^2} = 1.11$

Table 11.20: Computing $s_2{}^2$

Group 2: Full-time Workers

X_2	M_2	(X_2-M_2)	$(X_2-M_2)^2$
5	2.2	2.8	7.84
3	2.2	.8	.64
1	2.2	−1.2	1.44
0	2.2	−2.2	4.84
2	2.2	−.2	.04
$\Sigma X_2 = 11$			$SS_2 = \Sigma(X_2-M_2)^2 = 14.8$
$N_2 = 5$			$s_2^2 = \dfrac{SS_2}{N_2-1} = 3.7$
			$s_2 = \sqrt{s_2^2} = 1.92$

B. Compute s_{pooled}^2

$$s_{pooled}^2 = s_1^2\left(\frac{df_1}{df_{total}}\right) + s_2^2\left(\frac{df_2}{df_{total}}\right);$$

$df_1 = 7 - 1 = 6;$

$$\mathbf{df}_2 = 5 - 1 = 4;$$

$$\mathbf{df}_{total} = 6 + 4 = 10;$$

$$s^2_{pooled} = \frac{6}{10}(1.23) + \frac{4}{10}(3.7) = .74 + 1.48 = 2.22$$

C. Compute s^2_{M1} and s^2_{M2}

$$s_M = \frac{s_{pooled}}{N} = \underline{\quad\quad} = \mathbf{32}$$

$$s^2_{M2} = \frac{s^2_{pooled}}{N_2} = \frac{2.22}{5} = \mathbf{.44}$$

D. Compute s_{dif}

$$s^2_{dif} = s^2_{M1} + s^2_{M2}$$

$$s^2_{dif} = .32 + .44 = .76$$

$$S_{dif} = \sqrt{s^2_{dif}} = .87$$

3. Determine your critical value (used for defining the *rejection region*)

The alpha is .05 and the total degrees of freedom = 10. We have a one-tailed test. According to the chart, our critical value is 1.81.

4. Compute your "obtained statistic" (here, your obtained t score) and compare it with the critical value.

$$t_{obt} = \frac{M_1 - M_2}{s_{dif}} = \frac{2.29 - 2.2}{.87} = .10$$

The t score of .10 is not more extreme than the critical value of 1.81, and thus does not fall into the rejection region.

5. Comment on the null hypothesis (include effect size).

The null hypothesis is not rejected because t_{obt} is not more extreme than t-critical. Our t value is not in the rejection region. Therefore, when it comes to making baked goods, the population mean for part-time workers is not likely greater than the population mean for full-time workers. There is likely no difference in the amount of baked goods made by part-time and full-time workers.

$$\text{Cohen's } d = \left| \frac{M_1 - M_2}{s_{pooled}} \right| = \left| \frac{2.29 - 2.2}{\sqrt{2.22}} \right| = \left| \frac{.09}{1.49} \right| = .06$$

Cohen's d is .06, which indicates that the effect size of the difference is very, very small. According to our findings, there is no evidence that part-time workers make more baked goods than full-time workers.

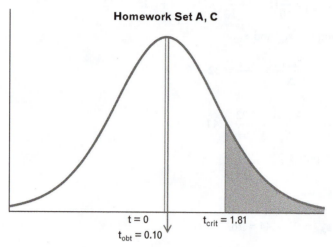

FIGURE 11.7: Homework Set A, C.

REFERENCE

Bleske, A. L., & Buss, D. M. (2001). Opposite sex friendship: Sex differences and similarities in initiation, selection, and dissolution. Personality and Social Psychology Bulletin, 27, 1310–1323.

ANALYSIS OF VARIANCE

O ur prior two chapters dealt with various kinds of t-tests, which are all designed to compare two means with one another. In many instances, however, you're actually interested in comparing more than two means with one another. For instance, do Canada, Mexico, and the United States differ from one another in terms of the mean number of children families have? Do students who major in business, art, psychology, or theater differ from one another in terms of their self-esteem? Do people who were raised in single-family homes, two-parent homes, or by grandparents differ from one another in terms of how positively they rate the concept of marriage? And so forth. Under many realistic research conditions, you are interested in comparing more than two means in a shot.

The analysis of variance (ANOVA) is designed to address this situation. As you'll see in our section on advanced statistics (Appendix E), there are many different forms of ANOVA—each designed to address specific research situations. All forms of ANOVA follow a general concept. The basic reasoning of ANOVA, which we'll present in detail here, pertains to exactly what the name of this statistic purports to do—analyzing variance. More specifically, the ANOVA analyzes some form of variance between different means relative to what is sometimes called *error variance*—or variance that is not accounted for by differences between means but that is, rather, accounted for simply as a function of differences between individuals.

The ANOVA is encapsulated in the F statistic. Analyzing the formula for F helps explicate the reasoning of the basic principles of ANOVA. As such, we start here with this formula:

$$F = \frac{MS_B}{MS_W}.$$

MS_B is an index of between-group variability (how much the means of different groups vary from one another), while MS_W is an index of within-group variability (synonymous with *error variance* or *error variability*). MS_W speaks to how much variability there is between scores of individuals within the different groups. More specific, computation-based definitions of these concepts are forthcoming—but for now, we can think of these concepts in the generic to help us best understand what the F statistic is all about.

ANOVA AS A SIGNAL-DETECTION STATISTIC

Imagine that you're deep in the jungles of the heart of Africa. As a behavioral biologist who studies courtship behaviors in various bird species, you're hoping to record and document, for the first time ever, the mating call of a recently discovered species—the African Red-Headed Fluffball (yes, in reality, this is a yet-to-be discovered species!). The original biologists who took photographs of this bird believe that they heard the males making an intensive staccato call during mating season that lasted over a full minute and included at least six specific verses. But that was really just their first impression—and they're not the courtship call expert, you are!

You head deep into the jungle, with your recorder, your bug spray, and a smile. The first thing you notice is that there are tons of noises. Leaves of thousands of kinds of plants and trees rustling in the wind; waterfalls and streams a-plenty; swarms of insects numbering into the thousands; and all kinds of reptiles, mammals, and birds—doing all kinds of things—making all kinds of noises.

To even discern the call of the Red-Headed Fluffball, you're going to have to auditorily sift through an awful lot of background noise. And, to make things more difficult, you've never heard the call that you're listening for—you've only heard a vague description of it. This is not an easy task.

The aforementioned undertaking can be thought of as a *signal-detection task*. In trying to discern the Red-Headed Fluffball's call against the backdrop of the many noises that constantly permeate the African jungle, you'll need to detect a particular signal (the call of the Red-Headed Fluffball) among the background noise. You'll be hard-pressed to find a situation in which you happen to hear only the Fluffball's call. In the best-case scenario, you'll likely be able to barely make out the Fluffball's call among a sea of competing noises. So you'll need all your skills and equipment—and some luck—to be able to detect the signal (i.e., the Fluffball's call) among the background noise.

The ANOVA is a sort of signal-detection task. With an ANOVA, you're essentially looking to see if some signal (differences between means of groups) is statistically discernible in light of background noise (individual variability within groups).

Suppose, for instance, that you're interested in whether students who read one of three statistics books differ, on average, from one another on a national exam of statistical knowledge. The scale of the exam is from 0 to 100. You randomly assign 15 statistics students to the following textbook conditions (with the scores on the national test included in the information below; Table 12.1):

Table 12.1: Hypothetical Scores and Means for Students Assigned One of Three Statistical Textbooks

Textbook: Geher & Hall	Textbook: Schmedley and Pickles*	Textbook: Freud and Jung*
85	80	77
80	92	86
95	55	59
77	67	90
80	87	84
M = 83.4	M = 76.2	M = 79.2

*No, this is not a real textbook!

Based on the data from Table 12.1, is there strong evidence that students who read Geher and Hall are superior to others in their statistical knowledge? Clearly, the mean for that group (at 83.4) is higher than in the other groups. But not everyone in the first group did great. For instance, one student in the first group got a 77, while a student in the second group (who all read Schmedley and Pickles's renowned book) got a 92. And a student of Freud and Jung's got a 90. Have we provided evidence that Geher and Hall's book is significantly more effective than the others (and that the population means, if we were going to somehow obtain them, would show that the mean on this test for students who took Geher and Hall was greater than the mean for the other two groups)?

The answer is that we can't quite yet answer this question! But here's something to add to this thought exercise. One thing about the data in Table 12.1 pertains to "noise" in the data. There is a good bit of individual variability within each group. This fact makes it harder to detect "the signal" (or differences between means) as separate from the "noise"—or the within-group variability. With all the within-group variability that's going on, it's hard to tell if our differences between means represent a true "signal" that can be generalized to the broader populations. When there's a lot of background noise in the jungle, it's hard to tell if what you're hearing is the mating call of the male Red-Headed Fluffball!

To further extend the signal-detection metaphor, consider trying to discern the call of the Fluffball under totally silent conditions. You're not likely to find that in the deep jungle of Africa any time of day, but we can imagine. So you happen upon a fully silent moment in the jungle, and suddenly, clear as day, you hear the long melodic staccato that you'd only dreamed of to this point. Against the backdrop of pure silence, you now are assured—and you record it and upload the file. You're the first person in history to ever record the courtship call of the African Red-Headed Fluffball.

When there is zero background noise, it's easy—signals that you are looking for emerge distinctly and clearly. The same goes for the ANOVA.

Imagine now that you've randomly assigned 15 students to read one of the three statistics textbooks that you've got (as before). However, now, imagine that the effect of the textbook is so profound that there is zero within-group variability (see Table 12.2):

In this case, when you ask if "83.4 is sufficiently higher than 79.2 or 76.2," you likely come up with a different response than you may have based on the first example. The data are very clear. First, the mean is higher (83.4 is higher than the other two means). Additionally, the fact that there is zero variability simply makes 83.4 *look* even higher. There is no within-group

Table 12.2: Hypothetical Scores and Means for Students Assigned One of Three Statistical Textbooks (with Zero Variability Within Groups)

Textbook: Geher & Hall	Textbook: Schmedley and Pickles*	Textbook: Freud and Jung*
83.4	76.2	79.2
83.4	76.2	79.2
83.4	76.2	79.2
83.4	76.2	79.2
83.4	76.2	79.2
M = 83.4	M = 76.2	M = 79.2

*No, this is not a real textbook!

variability. Our naïve understanding of such a table must tell us—any differences between the means are likely not due to random differences between individuals but, rather, to difference between the conditions (in this case, differences in effectiveness among the three statistics textbooks).

Ultimately, ANOVA is a signal-detection task—in which you're trying to detect whether the differences between means are clearly the effect of some condition, group, or treatment above and beyond the "noise" of within-group variability.

AN EXAMPLE OF THE ONE-WAY ANOVA

As you'll see, the one-way ANOVA is very similar in scope to the between-groups t-test. The main thing this statistic is doing is comparing whether the differences between means of groups are unlikely to simply be due to within-group variability. To understand the nuances of the one-way ANOVA, consider the following example. You are interested in the effects of different forms of media on the attention spans of children. You assign a group of nine 10-year-olds to one of three conditions: (a) 20 hours of TV a week, (b) 20 hours of video games a week, or (C) no electronic media per week. After the week is up, you administer an index of attention span to all participants. Scores on the attention-span index vary from 1 to 10. Scores for the individuals in each group are as follows (in Table 12.3):

Table 12.3: Attention Span Scores for Students in Three Media Conditions

TV	Video Games	No Media
6	2	10
4	6	5
5	4	6
$M_1 = 5$; $N_1 = 3$; $df_1 = 2$	$M_2 = 4$; $N_2 = 3$; $df_2 = 2$	$M_3 = 7$; $N_3 = 3$; $df_3 = 2$

To help us anticipate the steps of the problem, we've included the sample means, Ns for each group, and df terms for each group as well (we'll ultimately need all this in solving this problem). Note here, off the bat, that it looks like the attention span for the non-media group is higher than the mean for the TV group, which is higher than the mean for the video game group (but, of course, at this point we're just eyeballing the data, and a formal hypothesis test awaits).

The steps in hypothesis-testing for the one-way ANOVA are as follows:

1. ARTICULATING THE RESEARCH AND NULL HYPOTHESES

The research and null hypotheses are different with the one-way ANOVA than with other tests we've done—with the primary distinction being the fact that we're now predicting differences among a number of means beyond just two. As a result, we're really only interested in whether any of the means is different, statistically, from any of the other means. As such, it is actually most useful, here, to first articulate our null hypothesis, which assumes equality among all the population means of interest, as follows:

μ_1 = Population mean for students who watch TV
μ_2 = Population mean for students who play video games
μ_3 = Population mean for students who do not use electronic media
H_0: $\mu_1 = \mu_2 = \mu_3$

And if we had more groups (e.g., four or five), the reasoning here would extend out—that all population means are equal to one another.

The null hypothesis, then, simply assumes that there are no population differences among the means—and any deviation from this fact would lead to rejecting the null hypothesis. The research hypothesis, thus, is literally as follows:

H_1: NOT H_0

So with the ANOVA, this part is really simple enough.

2. THE COMPARISON DISTRIBUTION

F is a bit different from the other statistics we have run into. For one, consider the equation to determine F: $F = \dfrac{MS_B}{MS_W}$

Here, we have a variability parameter divided by another variability parameter. As all variability parameters are positive numbers (since they all include that squared term as part of the process), we here have a positive number divided by a positive number. So F is always positive (unless the numerator is 0, in which case F will be 0).

Also, note what happens if $MS_B = MS_W$. In this case, F = 1. And, in a sense, this is an alternative way to articulate the null hypothesis—that F = 1 (i.e., that the between-group variability is exactly equal to the within-group variability). Thus, an F distribution has a low point of 0, a peak of 1, and extends infinitely in the positive direction (See Figure 12.1).

The particular F distribution varies as a function of two degree of freedom (df) terms. One is called "Between-Groups df" (or df_B)—this is simply NG (Number of Groups)–1 or, in this case, 3–1 = 2.

The other (called df_w) is $df_{w1} + df_{w2} + df_{w3} + \cdots$, with $df_{w1} = N_1-1$, $df_{w2} = N_2-1$, $df_{w3} = N_3-1$, and so forth. This is also the sum of the df_{ws}. Here, $df_W = 6$.

Note that, importantly, the df terms change as a function of the number of groups and the number of individuals in each group. Also note that the number of individuals in each group need *not* be equal across groups. They happen to be in this case (each group has three individuals), but the ANOVA deals perfectly fine with situations with unequal Ns across groups.

The comparison distribution here, then, is an F distribution—but a specific F distribution corresponding to 2 df_B and 6 df_W. As such (as you'll see in Figure 12.1), the df terms for specific F distributions are demarcated in parentheses with the distribution itself. In Figure 12.1, this is represented with the (2, 6) in parentheses next to the distribution.

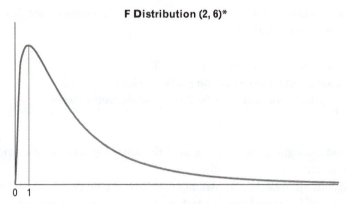

FIGURE 12.1: A Generic F Distribution.

*(2, 6) refers to the degrees of freedom corresponding to this particular distribution (2 between-group degrees of freedom and 6 within-group degrees of freedom).

3. DETERMINING THE CRITICAL VALUE AND ALPHA REGION

Based on our a priori alpha level (let's go with .05 in this case; the other standard option is .01; See Appendix C), we can determine F_{crit}, which will set the boundary for the alpha region. Note that alpha is always to the right side of the F distribution—there is no such thing as a negative F ratio (as F is always a ratio of one positive number to another). Also, particularly low F scores are actually not of interest (Fs between 0 and 1 simply mean "no effect"). So with an F distribution, we're only interested in defining extreme scores as being particularly high and positive.

We can use the F table (Appendix C) to cut off the alpha region. With this table, you'll see that the "numerator df" = df_B (or degrees of freedom between groups) and the "denominator df" = df_W (or degrees of freedom within groups). You'll zero-in on a cluster of values, based on different alphas. As you're going with an alpha of .05, your F_{crit} is 5.14. Here, we'd say F(2, 6) to demarcate our particular F distribution that corresponds to this particular F_{crit} of 5.14. You can see F_{crit} and the alpha region demarcated in Figure 12.2. Based on the standard algorithm for

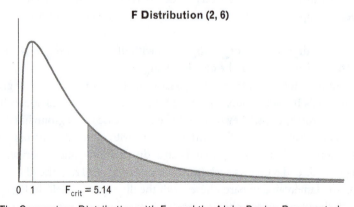

FIGURE 12.2: The Comparison Distribution with F_{crit} and the Alpha Region Demarcated.

hypothesis testing, you'll see that to reject the null hypothesis, we'll need to obtain an F that is greater than 5.14 to reject H_0.

4. COMPUTING THE F-STATISTIC

By this point, you should have a very clear sense of how things go with hypothesis testing. We've now got our comparison distribution (see Figure 12.2) all set up with our F_{crit} and alpha region demarcated. To reject H_0, we'll need to obtain an F (i.e., F_{obt}) that is in our alpha region (greater than 5.14). So we now need to calculate F.

Let's start with the equation for F and do some reverse engineering $F = \dfrac{MS_B}{MS_W}$. So to figure out F, we need to compute MS_B and MS_W. Let's start with MS_W since this process is very familiar (as you'll find).

$$MS_W = \frac{SS_W}{df_W}$$

Recall that MS_W is a marker of within-group variability. You can now see that it's a marker of within-group variability that is essentially corrected as a function of the size of the groups. SS_W is, rather, an index of within-group variability that does not take the sizes of the groups into account. So we first need to compute SS_W after which we can compute MS_W.

$$SS_W = SS_{W1} + SS_{W2} + SS_{W3} + \cdots.$$

You are now probably thinking "well, how do I figure out SS_{W1}, etc.?!" You'll see that it's easy and that it makes sense.

Any particular SS_W (e.g., SS_{W1}) is the same as our old friend SS (sum of squared deviation scores). It simply refers to the sum of the squared deviation scores for a particular group of scores. So we can figure out SS_{W1}, SS_{W2}, and SS_{W3} as found in Tables 12.4, 12.5, and 12.6.

With all this information in hand, SS_W (or the total sum of the squared deviation scores for the within-groups term) is as follows:

$$SS_W = SS_{W1} + SS_{W2} + SS_{W3} = 2 + 8 + 14 = 24.$$

$$\text{Recall that } MS_W = \frac{SS_W}{df_W} = \frac{24}{6} = 4.$$

Table 12.4: Computing SS_{W1} for Attention Span Scores for Students in the TV Condition

X_1	M_1	$(X_1 - M_1)$	$(X_1 - M_1)^2$
6	5	1	1
4	5	−1	1
5	5	0	0
$M_1 = 5$; $N_1 = 3$; $df_1 = 2$			$SS_1 = SS_{W1} = 2$

*note that the subscripts of 1 in terms such as X_1 and M_1 refer to "group" or "sample" 1

Table 12.5: Computing SS_{W2} for Attention Span Scores for Students in the Video Games Condition

X_2	M_2	(X_2-M_2)	$(X_2-M_2)^2$
2	4	−2	4
6	4	2	4
4	4	0	0
$M_2 = 4$; $N_2 = 3$; $df_2 = 2$			$SS_2 = SS_{W2} = 8$

*note that the subscripts of 2 in terms such as X_2 and M_2 refer to "group" or "sample" 2

Table 12.6: Computing SS_{W3} for Attention Span Scores for Students in the No Media

X_3	M_3	(X_3-M_3)	$(X_3-M_3)^2$
10	7	3	9
5	7	−2	4
6	7	−1	1
$M_3 = 7$; $N_3 = 3$; $df_3 = 2$			$SS_3 = SS_{W3} = 14$

*note that the subscripts of 3 in terms such as X_3 and M_3 refer to "group" or "sample" 3

So now we've got much of F_{obt} figured out. $F = \dfrac{MS_B}{4}$. Let us now figure out MS_B.

The entire way that the F statistic is set up is such that if the null hypothesis is correct, $MS_B = MS_W$. This is an assumption that essentially says that any differences found between the means of groups are fully accountable as a function of variability within the groups. With this reasoning in mind, the F statistic is set up so that computing MS_B is a very similar process to computing MS_W; it has to be, as it ultimately seeks to compute indices of similar phenomena (variability between different scores) on the same scale as one another. You'll thus see that the process for computing MS_B is parallel to the process for computing MS_W. The details of the process are found in the text below and in Tables 12.7–12.9.

$$MS_B = \frac{SS_B}{df_B}$$

$$SS_B = SS_{B1} + SS_{B2} + SS_{B3} + \cdots.$$

We now need to compute SS_{B1}, SS_{B2}, and SS_{B3}, as found in Tables 12.7–12.9. Before we progress, you will need to understand one more statistic: GM (which stands for "Grand Mean"). GM is the mean of all the scores (regardless of group)—which is the sum of all scores (across groups) divided by the total number of scores. Thus,

$$GM = \frac{\sum X_1 + \sum X_2 + \sum X_3 + \cdots}{\sum (N_1 + N_2 + N_3 + \cdots)}.$$

$$= \frac{15 + 12 + 21}{3 + 3 + 3} = \frac{48}{9} = 5.33$$

In the process of computing SS_B, we need to determine how much each sample mean deviates from the grand mean (from GM). And we'll need to compute this once for each score in each sample to make sure that we're keeping the numbers for computing SS_B on the same scale as we used for SS_W. As you'll see, this process will seem very familiar. This process is demarcated in Tables 12.7, 12.8, and 12.9.

Table 12.7: Computing SS_{B1} for Attention Span Scores for Students in the TV Condition

M_1	GM	(M_1-GM)	$(M_1-GM)^2$
5	5.33	−.33	.11
5	5.33	−.33	.11
5	5.33	−.33	.11
$M_1 = 5$; $N_1 = 3$; $df_1 = 2$			$SS_{B1} = .33$

*note that the subscripts of 1 in terms such as M_1 refer to "group" or "sample" 1

Table 12.8: Computing SS_{B2} for Attention Span Scores for Students in the Video Games Condition

M_2	GM	(M_2-GM)	$(M_2-GM)^2$
4	5.33	−1.33	1.77
4	5.33	−1.33	1.77
4	5.33	−1.33	1.77
$M_2 = 4$; $N_2 = 3$; $df_2 = 2$			$SS_{B2} = 5.31$

*note that the subscripts of 2 in terms such as M_2 refer to "group" or "sample" 2

Table 12.9: Computing SS_{B3} for Attention Span Scores for Students in the No Media

M_3	GM	(X_3-M_3)	$(X_3-M_3)^2$
7	5.33	1.67	2.79
7	5.33	1.67	2.79
7	5.33	1.67	2.79
$M_3 = 7$; $N_3 = 3$; $df_3 = 2$			$SS_{B3} = 8.37$

OK—we're done with the busy work. We've now got the following:

$SS_{B1} = .33$
$SS_{B2} = 5.31$
$SS_{B3} = 8.37$
Recall that $SS_B = SS_{B1} + SS_{B2} + SS_{B3} + \cdots$.
Thus, $SS_B = .33 + 5.31 + 8.37 = 14.01$

Finally, recall that SS terms are not corrected for size of samples (or numbers of groups), but MS terms are. And the F ratio uses MS terms. So we'll now compute MS_B as follows:

$$MS_B = \frac{SS_B}{df_B} = \frac{14.01}{2} = 7$$

We can now compute F, as follows:

$$F = \frac{MS_B}{MS_W} = \frac{7}{4} = 1.75$$

So $F_{obt} = 1.75$ while $F_{crit} = 5.14$.
As we can see from Figure 12.3, F_{obt} is not extreme enough to allow us to reject H_0.

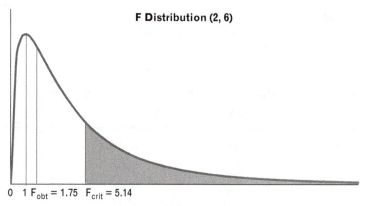

F Distribution (2, 6)

0   1 $F_{obt} = 1.75$ $F_{crit} = 5.14$

FIGURE 12.3: Comparing F_{obt} with F_{crit} on the Comparison Distribution.

5. COMMENTING ON THE NULL HYPOTHESIS

On one hand, this step is easy (especially at this point in the book). If your obtained statistic is not in your alpha region, you fail to reject the null hypothesis. You have not provided sufficient evidence to support the research hypothesis.

On the other hand, it's up to you to make a bit more out of what this means in any particular circumstance. In this particular case, we have failed to reject the null hypothesis. Recall that the null hypothesis is as follows:

$$H_0: \mu_1 = \mu_2 = \mu_3$$

Given that:

μ_1 = Population mean for students who watch TV
μ_2 = Population mean for students who play video games
μ_3 = Population mean for students who do not use electronic media

We have therefore failed to find evidence that the attention spans of kids in these different groups differ at all from one another—and we've failed, specifically, to provide strong evidence that these means likely are unequal to one another at the population level.

Importantly, as has been true throughout this book, this null finding does not mean that we were wrong in our research hypothesis—rather, it simply means that we have failed to provide strong evidence to support this hypothesis. We may have an instance of Type-II Error on our hands. Recall that Type-II Error exists when your research hypothesis is true at the population level, but you fail to reject the null hypothesis. One common reason for committing Type-II Error is low power—and the most common cause of low power is a small sample size. In our study presented here, we have only 9 total subjects, with three in each condition. That seems like a pretty small sample size, doesn't it?!

These issues of factors that affect power and factors that affect the ability to reject the null hypothesis are thus crucial and need to be considered with pretty much any statistical projects that you run into. Always.

WHAT CAN AND CANNOT BE INFERRED FROM ANOVA (THE IMPORTANCE OF FOLLOW-UP TESTS)

In the example used in this chapter, we failed to reject the null hypothesis. However, you shouldn't feel so bad! In fact, if you had rejected the null hypothesis, you'd still know very little! That is because the null hypothesis (H_0: $\mu_1 = \mu_2 = \mu_3$) is saying very little. In rejecting this hypothesis, you are simply saying that something in H_0 is probably not true. But if F is significant, you're not saying anything more than that. It may be significant because $\mu_1 < \mu_2$, or perhaps $\mu_3 < \mu_2$, or perhaps some other contrast between two specific means is significant. The fact is that when F_{obt} is greater than F_{crit}, you know that you have rejected H_0, but you don't know which specific means are different from which other specific means. For this reason, the F test is a particularly non-specific test.

In this way, the F test is almost like a medical test that says "something's wrong, but we don't know what it is." For instance, when you get blood drawn, you may have an inflated white-blood-cell count. This tells the doctors something, but not really too much. This could mean there is some bacterial infection, virus, cancer, immunological problem, and so on. When a physician receives an "increased white-blood-cell count report," he or she immediately starts thinking about follow-up tests to zero-in on the specifics.

The same is true of the F test. When a statistician receives a significant F test, he or she immediately knows to start thinking about "follow-up tests"—tests that hone in on which specific means are significantly different from which other specific means. In the current example, if the F were significant (which it was not—but if it were…), you might conduct a test, for instance, to see if the mean attention score for participants in the no-media condition is significantly higher than the score in the video-game condition. Or you might test whether two other specific means are significantly different from one another.

At this point, you actually have a tool in your statistical toolbox to help you with this sort of issue. If you did find a significant F and you wanted to test if two specific means were significantly different from one another at that point, you could use the between-groups t-test. For instance, you could use the between-groups t-test to see if the attention scores for participants in the no-media group was significantly higher than scores in the video-game group.

Thus, a significant ANOVA is much like a positive white-blood-cell count found by a physician. It tells you that something is going on, but you need to conduct follow-up tests to get to the bottom of it.

This may get you wondering why we would do an ANOVA in the first place—especially since the results are always in need of follow-up tests that perhaps could have been conducted in the first place. The main reasons usually given pertain to reducing Type-I Error. All things equal, the more statistical analyses you conduct, the more likely you are to run into Type-I Error—a finding that comes out as a significant finding but that is really just an error—a false positive. The more tests you conduct, the more likely you are to encounter a false positive. With this reasoning in mind, then, the idea is that you should do tests like ANOVAs that examine lots of effects in a single analysis and let the findings of the ANOVA guide whether follow-up tests seem appropriate.

ESTIMATING EFFECT SIZE WITH THE ONE-WAY ANOVA

As with many statistics, there are multiple ways to determine how large an effect of an ANOVA is. One straightforward way that follows on the presentation of variance estimates in this book is computing R^2. This statistic, which is conceptually identical to the statistic by the same name encountered in our chapter on regression, is an index of how much of the total variability in scores is the result of variability between means. So, for instance, in the example in this chapter, the first person in the video games data (see Table 12.5) scored a 2 on the attention measure—and the mean of that group was 4. The grand mean (GM) was 5.33. The question here is essentially how much of the individual's score we can attribute to simple variability between individuals versus how much we can attribute to the importance of the differences between means. It's actually interpreted as a percentage. This person scored a 2. What percentage of this fact can we estimate to be due to the fact that this person was in the video game group and what percentage can we estimate to be due simply to the fact that individual scores, regardless of group (or condition), vary from one another?

To address this point, we'll set up a very simple ratio—and we'll use SS estimates of variance instead of MS estimates, as SS estimates are independent of sample size—and effect size estimates are always independent of sample size (so they can be broadly applied beyond the parameters of a particular study).

This all said, $R^2 = \dfrac{SS_B}{SS_B + SS_W}$ or $\dfrac{SS_B}{SS_{Tot}}$.

In other words, we're looking at how much of the total variability between scores (thus the phrase SS_{Tot}) is the result of between-group variability (or SS_B). And the idea here is that the total amount of variability in scores (i.e., SS_{Tot}) is a combination of variability due to differences between groups (SS_B) and variability due to differences between individuals within groups (SS_W).

In the current case, then, R^2 is as follows:

$$R^2 = \frac{SS_B}{SS_B + SS_W} = \frac{14.01}{14.01 + 24} = .37, \text{ or } 37\%.$$ Thus, we can say that even though the ANOVA was not significant (largely due to low power), a good-sized amount of the variability in scores (37%) can be attributed to differences between the means of the groups.

Unlike with Cohen's d, there are no real conventions for effect size for this statistic. People typically use their judgment and consider the particulars of the situation at hand when assessing whether this kind of effect size (which estimates a percentage of the variability that is due to some effect) is "large" or not.

REAL RESEARCH EXAMPLE

In a study of parent/offspring relationships and mating behaviors, Dubbs and Buunk (2010) write, "a one-way ANOVA between people who belong to an organized religion (Protestant, Catholic, Muslim, etc.) versus people who do not (non-religious, agnostic, atheist, spiritual, etc.) was conducted on... the mean of (an index)... indicating a lack of parental investment/cooperation" (p. 591). Note that these authors used a one-way ANOVA comparing two groups (religious versus non-religious individuals)—which is perfectly acceptable (although in this chapter we discuss examples of ANOVA with more than two groups). In any case, the authors then write,

> The one-way ANOVA conducted on parents who identify themselves as belonging to an organized religion (Catholic, Christian, Muslim, etc.) versus those who do not (nonreligious, agonistic, atheist, spiritual, etc.) produced a significant main effect. People who identify themselves as belonging to an organized religion, compared to those who do not, have a significantly lower mean for the six traits indicating parental investment/cooperation, $F(1, 473) = 6.719$, $p = .01$, (organized religion $M = 3.75$, does not $M = 3.95$). This indicates that parents who belong to an organized religion view negative traits reflecting a lack of parental investment and cooperation with the ingroup as being more unacceptable in a child's romantic partner than parents who do not belong to an organized religion (p. 593).

Being a member of an organized religion corresponds to wanting one's grown children to seek partners who are parental-investment-minded. And it was a solid one-way ANOVA that was used to make this point!

SUMMARY

The ANOVA is one of the core statistics used to address a number of research questions. Generally, an ANOVA compares variability in scores that results from differences between means with variability in scores that results from differences between individuals (also known as *error variance* or *error variability*). The one-way ANOVA, presented in detail in this chapter, seeks to determine if means between groups are significantly different from one another in light of variability within groups.

The F ratio is the primary statistic for an ANOVA. This statistic compares between-group variability with within-group variability. The F distribution is used to see if any particular F is significant, or is more extreme than an F_{crit} that is based on an a priori alpha level. An accessible and interpretable effect-size estimate for the ANOVA is R^2, which estimates the percentage of variability between scores that is due to variability between means of groups.

KEY TERMS

ANOVA: Analysis of variance; statistical process that compares variability in scores that results from differences between means with variability in scores that results from error variance or error variability (differences between individuals).

Error variance: Differences between individuals, independent from differences between groups. Also known as error variability.

HOMEWORK SET A

1. You are helping to coach a youth basketball team, and you are curious if kids who start playing basketball sooner have better skills than those who start later. You are coaching 4th grade, so at the beginning of the season, you ask the kids if they started playing basketball in 2nd, 3rd, or 4th grade. You then rate the kids' skills on a scale of 1–5, with 5 being the highest skill level. You follow the steps of hypothesis testing for the one-way ANOVA with an alpha level of .05.

Table 12.10: Homework Set A #1 Data

Started playing in 2nd grade	Started playing in 3rd grade	Started playing in 4th grade
1	3	5
4	3	4
3	4	2
4	2	5

a. Articulate the research and null hypothesis
b. Determine the characteristics of the comparison distribution
c. Determine the critical value and alpha region
d. Compute the F statistic
e. Comment on the null hypothesis
f. Compute the effect size and comment on how much of the variability in the data can be attributed to differences between the means of the groups

2. You have a friend who signs her children up for multiple activities at all times. Her children participate in dance, taekwondo, soccer, basketball, 4H, and local parades and talent shows, and your friend and her husband rarely spend any time together. You wonder if she has a happy marriage; perhaps involving her children in so many activities is a way to avoid spending time with her husband. You gather marital satisfaction data from people whose children are involved in no activities, 1–2 activities at a time, and 3 or more activities at a time. The marital satisfaction scale produces a score of 1–10, with higher scores indicating more satisfaction. You follow the steps of hypothesis testing for the one-way ANOVA with an alpha level of .05.

a. Articulate the research and null hypothesis
b. Determine the characteristics of the comparison distribution
c. Determine the critical value and alpha region

Table 12.11: Homework Set A #2 Data

No activities	1–2 activities	3+ activities
10	9	6
4	5	4
7	6	3
8	4	4
6		8

    d.   Compute the F statistic

    e.   Comment on the null hypothesis

    f.   Compute the effect size and comment on how much of the variability in the data can be attributed to differences between the means of the groups

3.   One of your 6th-grade teachers told the class that people who use swear words are not smart enough to think of alternative words to express themselves. You wonder if this is true, and collect IQ scores from people who use swear words all the time, people who use swear words sometimes, and people who never use swear words. You follow the steps of hypothesis testing for the one-way ANOVA with an alpha level of .01.

Table 12.12: Homework Set A #3 Data

Never swear	Sometimes swear	Swear all the time
97	120	104
100	109	96
99	102	93
104	100	100
90	99	97

    a.   Articulate the research and null hypothesis

    b.   Determine the characteristics of the comparison distribution

    c.   Determine the critical value and alpha region

    d.   Compute the F statistic

    e.   Comment on the null hypothesis

    f.   Compute the effect size and comment on how much of the variability in the data can be attributed to differences between the means of the groups

HOMEWORK SET B

1.   We've all heard the term "crazy cat lady." You wonder if there may be a grain of truth in the saying, and collect mental stability scores for women with no indoor cats, 1–3 indoor cats, and 4 or more indoor cats. The mental stability index consists of scores from 1 to 20, with higher scores corresponding to higher mental stability. You follow the steps of hypothesis testing for the one-way ANOVA with an alpha level of .05.

Table 12.13: Homework Set B #1 Data

No cats	1–3 cats	4+ cats
20	19	16
16	19	16
18	16	13
18		15

    a.   Articulate the research and null hypothesis

    b.   Determine the characteristics of the comparison distribution

c. Determine the critical value and alpha region
d. Compute the F statistic
e. Comment on the null hypothesis
f. Compute the effect size and comment on how much of the variability in the data can be attributed to differences between the means of the groups

2. You have known Dave since elementary school. Dave has always been a bit immature, but you were friends, and sometimes his immaturity was fun. However, the older you get, the more Dave's immaturity annoys you. It was fun to try to walk through the drive through at a fast food restaurant at 14 years old, but not so much fun at 25 years old. You wonder if immature people are rated as less socially acceptable the older they get. You collect data for people who are immature, asking friends of immature people to complete the social acceptability index, considering their immature friend at age 15, 20, and 25. Scores on the social acceptability index vary from 1-10. You follow the steps of hypothesis testing for the one-way ANOVA with an alpha level of .05.

Table 12.14: Homework Set B #2 Data

Age 15	Age 20	Age 25
9	7	4
8	6	7
7	5	5
8	6	4

a. Articulate the research and null hypothesis
b. Determine the characteristics of the comparison distribution
c. Determine the critical value and alpha region
d. Compute the F statistic
e. Comment on the null hypothesis
f. Compute the effect size and comment on how much of the variability in the data can be attributed to differences between the means of the groups

3. You are talking with some of your friends about in-laws. One of your friends, who tends to be very jealous, does not get along with her in-laws at all. Another friend, who does not tend to be jealous at all, has a wonderful relationship with her in-laws. This gets you to wondering if people who are jealous tend to have more strained relationships with their in-laws. Curious, you collect data regarding in-law relationship satisfaction, with possible scores ranging from 1–10. You follow the steps of hypothesis testing for the one-way ANOVA with an alpha level of .05.

Table 12.15: Homework Set B #3 Data

People who score high in jealousy	People who score neutral in jealousy	People who score low in jealousy
8	5	6
9	6	5
9	7	4
8	7	5
6	10	5

a.   Articulate the research and null hypothesis
b.   Determine the characteristics of the comparison distribution
c.   Determine the critical value and alpha region
d.   Compute the F statistic
e.   Comment on the null hypothesis
f.   Compute the effect size and comment on how much of the variability in the data can be attributed to differences between the means of the groups

ANSWERS

HOMEWORK SET A

1.

Table 12.16: Homework Set A #1

Started playing in 2nd grade	Started playing in 3rd grade	Started playing in 4th grade
1	3	5
4	3	4
3	4	2
4	2	5
$\Sigma X_1 = 12$, $M_1 = 3$, $N_1 = 4$, $df_1 = 3$	$\Sigma X_2 = 12$, $M_2 = 3$, $N_2 = 4$, $df_2 = 3$	$\Sigma X_3 = 16$, $M_3 = 4$, $N_3 = 4$, $df_3 = 3$

a. H_1: NOT H_0

H_0: $\mu_{10} = \mu_2 = \mu_3$

b.   The comparison distribution is F(2, 9)
c.   The alpha level is .05, numerator degrees of freedom = 2, and denominator degrees of freedom = 9, so $F_{crit} = 4.26$

d. $F = \dfrac{MS_B}{MS_W}$

$MS_W = \dfrac{SS_W}{df_W}$

$SS_W = SS_{W1} + SS_{W2} + SS_{W3} + \cdots.$

Table 12.17: Skill scores for kids who started playing in 2nd grade (X_1)

X_1	M_1	(X_1-M_1)	$(X_1-M_1)^2$
1	3	−2	4
4	3	1	1
3	3	0	0
4	3	1	1
$M_1 = 3$; $N_1 = 4$; $df_1 = 3$			$SS_1 = SS_{W1} = 6$

Table 12.18: Skill scores for kids who started playing in 3rd grade (X_2)

X_2	M_2	(X_2-M_2)	$(X_2-M_2)^2$
3	3	0	0
3	3	0	0
4	3	1	1
2	3	−1	1
$M_2 = 3$; $N_2 = 4$; $df_2 = 3$			$SS_2 = SS_{W2} = 2$

Table 12.19: Skill scores for kids who started playing in 4th grade (X_3)

X_3	M_3	(X_3-M_3)	$(X_3-M_3)^2$
5	4	1	1
4	4	0	0
2	4	−2	4
5	4	1	1
$M_3 = 4$; $N_3 = 4$; $df_3 = 3$			$SS_3 = SS_{W3} = 6$

$$SS_W = SS_{W1} + SS_{W2} + SS_{W3} = 6 + 2 + 6 = 14$$

$$MS_W = \frac{SS_W}{df_W} = \frac{14}{9} = 1.56$$

$$F = \frac{MS_B}{1.56}$$

$$MS_B = \frac{SS_B}{df_B}$$

$$SS_B = SS_{B1} + SS_{B2} + SS_{B3} + \cdots.$$

$$= \frac{\sum X_1 + \sum X_2 + \sum X_3 + \cdots}{\sum (N_1 + N_2 + N_3 + \cdots)}.$$

$$= \frac{12+12+16}{4+4+4} = \frac{40}{12} = 3.33$$

Table 12.20: Computing SS_{B1} for skill scores for kids starting in 2nd grade (X_1)

M_1	GM	(M_1-GM)	$(M_1-GM)^2$
3	3.33	−.33	.11
3	3.33	−.33	.11
3	3.33	−.33	.11
3	3.33	−.33	.11
$M_1 = 3; N_1 = 4; df_1 = 3$			$SS_{B1} = .44$

Table 12.21: Computing SS_{B2} for skill scores for kids starting in 3rd grade (X_2)

M_2	GM	(M_2-GM)	$(M_2-GM)^2$
3	3.33	−.33	.11
3	3.33	−.33	.11
3	3.33	−.33	.11
3	3.33	−.33	.11
$M_2 = 3; N_2 = 4; df_2 = 3$			$SS_{B2} = .44$

Table 12.22: Computing SS_{B3} for skill scores for kids starting in 4th grade (X_3)

M_3	GM	(M_3-GM)	$(M_3-GM)^2$
4	3.33	.67	.45
4	3.33	.67	.45
4	3.33	.67	.45
4	3.33	.67	.45
$M_3 = 4; N_3 = 4; df_3 = 3$			$SS_{B3} = 1.8$

$SS_{B1} = .44$
$SS_{B2} = .44$
$SS_{B3} = 1.8$
$SS_B = SS_{B1} + SS_{B2} + SS_{B3} + \cdots.$
$SS_B = .44 + .44 + 1.8 = 2.68$

$$MS_B = \frac{SS_B}{df_B} = \frac{2.68}{2} = 1.34$$

$$F = \frac{MS_B}{MS_W} = \frac{1.34}{1.56} = .86$$

e. $F_{obt} = .86$, while $F_{crit} = 4.26$; therefore, we fail to reject the null hypothesis. We have not found evidence that skill levels of 4th-grade basketball players vary by whether they started playing basketball in 2nd, 3rd, or 4th grade.

f. $R^2 = \frac{SS_B}{SS_B + SS_W} = \frac{2.68}{2.68 + 14} = .16$, or 16%. Not much of the variability in scores (16%) can be attributed to differences between the means of the groups.

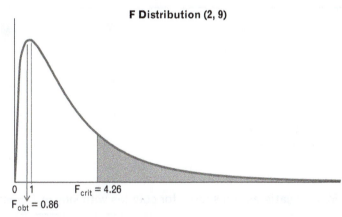

FIGURE 12.4: F Distribution for Homework Set A #1.

2.

Table 12.23: Homework Set A #2

No activities	1–2 activities	3+ activities
10	9	6
4	5	4
7	6	3
8	4	4
6		8
$\Sigma X_1 = 35$, $M_1 = 7$, $N_1 = 5$, $df_1 = 4$	$\Sigma X_2 = 24$, $M_2 = 6$, $N_2 = 4$, $df_2 = 3$	$\Sigma X_3 = 25$, $M_3 = 5$, $N_3 = 5$, $df_3 = 4$

a. H_1: NOT H_0

H_0: $\mu_1 = \mu_2 = \mu_3$

    b.   The comparison distribution is F(2, 11)

    c.   The alpha level is .05, numerator degrees of freedom = 2, and denominator degrees of freedom = 11, so F_{crit} = 3.98

    d. $F = \dfrac{MS_B}{MS_W}$

$$MS_W = \dfrac{SS_W}{df_W}$$

$$SS_W = SS_{W1} + SS_{W2} + SS_{W3} + \cdots.$$

Table 12.24: Marital satisfaction scores for couples with kids in no activities (X_1)

X_1	M_1	(X_1-M_1)	$(X_1-M_1)^2$
10	7	3	9
4	7	−3	9
7	7	0	0
8	7	1	1
6	7	−1	1
M_1 = 7; N_1 = 5; df_1 = 4			$SS_1 = SS_{W1} = 20$

Table 12.25: Marital satisfaction scores for couples with kids in 1–2 activities (X_2)

X_2	M_2	(X_2-M_2)	$(X_2-M_2)^2$
9	6	3	9
5	6	−1	1
6	6	0	0
4	6	−2	4
M_2 = 6; N_2 = 4; df_2 = 3			$SS_2 = SS_{W2} = 14$

Table 12.26: Marital satisfaction scores for couples with kids in 3+ activities (X_3)

X_3	M_3	(X_3-M_3)	$(X_3-M_3)^2$
6	5	1	1
4	5	−1	1
3	5	−2	4
4	5	−1	1
8	5	3	9
M_3 = 5; N_3 = 5; df_3 = 4			$SS_3 = SS_{W3} = 16$

$$SS_W = SS_{W1} + SS_{W2} + SS_{W3} = 20 + 14 + 16 = 50$$

$$MS_W = \frac{SS_W}{df_W} = \frac{50}{11} = 4.55$$

$$F = \frac{MS_B}{4.55}$$

$$MS_B = \frac{SS_B}{df_B}$$

$$SS_B = SS_{B1} + SS_{B2} + SS_{B3} + \cdots$$

$$GM = \frac{\sum X_1 + \sum X_2 + \sum X_3 + \cdots}{\sum (N_1 + N_2 + N_3 + \cdots)}.$$

$$= \frac{35 + 24 + 25}{5 + 4 + 5} = \frac{84}{14} = 6$$

Table 12.27: Computing SS_{B1} for marital satisfaction scores for couples with kids in no activities

M_1	GM	(M_1-GM)	$(M_1-GM)^2$
7	6	1	1
7	6	1	1
7	6	1	1
7	6	1	1
7	6	1	1
$M_1 = 7$; $N_1 = 5$; $df_1 = 4$			$SS_{B1} = 5$

Table 12.28: Computing SS_{B2} for marital satisfaction scores for couples with kids in 1–2 activities

M_2	GM	(M_2-GM)	$(M_2-GM)^2$
6	6	0	0
6	6	0	0
6	6	0	0
6	6	0	0
$M_2 = 6$; $N_2 = 4$; $df_2 = 3$			$SS_{B2} = 0$

Table 12.29: Computing SS_{B3} for marital satisfaction scores for couples with kids in 3+ activities

M_3	GM	(M_3-GM)	$(M_3-GM)^2$
5	6	−1	1
5	6	−1	1
5	6	−1	1
5	6	−1	1
5	6	−1	1
$M_3 = 5$; $N_3 = 5$; $df_3 = 4$			$SS_{B3} = 5$

$SS_{B1} = 5$

$SS_{B2} = 0$

$SS_{B3} = 5$

$SS_B = SS_{B1} + SS_{B2} + SS_{B3} + \cdots$

$SS_B = 5 + 0 + 5 = 10$

$$MS_B = \frac{SS_B}{df_B} = \frac{10}{2} = 5$$

$$F = \frac{MS_B}{MS_W} = \frac{5}{4.55} = 1.10$$

e. $F_{obt} = 1.10$, while $F_{crit} = 3.98$; therefore, we fail to reject the null hypothesis. We have not found evidence that marital satisfaction scores vary by the number of activities the couple's children are involved in.

f. $R^2 = \dfrac{SS_B}{SS_B + SS_W} = \dfrac{10}{10 + 50} = .17$, or 17%. Not much of the variability in scores (17%) can be attributed to differences between the means of the groups.

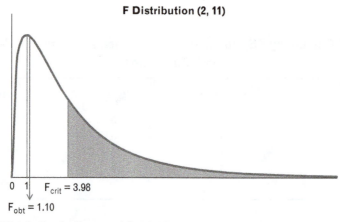

F Distribution (2, 11)

0 1 $F_{crit} = 3.98$

$F_{obt} = 1.10$

FIGURE 12.5: F Distribution for Homework Set A #2.

Table 12.30: Homework Set A #3

Never swear	Sometimes swear	Swear all the time
97	120	104
100	109	96
99	102	93
104	100	100
90	99	97
$\Sigma X_1 = 490, M_1 = 98, N_1 = 5, df_1 = 4$	$\Sigma X_2 = 530, M_2 = 106, N_2 = 5, df_2 = 4$	$\Sigma X_3 = 490, M_3 = 98, N_3 = 5, df_3 = 4$

3.

   a. H_1: NOT H_0

     H_0: $\mu_1 = \mu_2 = \mu_3$

   b. The comparison distribution is F(2, 12)

   c. The alpha level is .01, numerator degrees of freedom = 2, and denominator degrees of freedom = 12, so $F_{crit} = 6.93$

   d. $F = \dfrac{MS_B}{MS_W}$

$$MS_W = \frac{SS_W}{df_W}$$

$$SS_W = SS_{W1} + SS_{W2} + SS_{W3} + \cdots$$

Table 12.31: IQ Scores for people who never swear (X_1)

X_1	M_1	(X_1-M_1)	$(X_1-M_1)^2$
97	98	−1	1
100	98	2	4
99	98	1	1
104	98	6	36
90	98	−8	64
$M_1 = 98; N_1 = 5; df_1 = 4$			$SS_1 = SS_{W1} = 106$

Table 12.32: IQ scores for people who sometimes swear (X_2)

X_2	M_2	(X_2-M_2)	$(X_2-M_2)^2$
120	106	14	196
109	106	3	9
102	106	−4	16
100	106	−6	36
99	106	−7	49
$M_2 = 106; N_2 = 5; df_2 = 4$			$SS_2 = SS_{W2} = 306$

Table 12.33: IQ scores for people who swear all the time (X_3)

X_3	M_3	$(X_3 - M_3)$	$(X_3 - M_3)^2$
104	98	6	36
96	98	−2	4
93	98	−5	25
100	98	2	4
97	98	−1	1
$M_3 = 98$; $N_3 = 5$; $df_3 = 4$			$SS_3 = SS_{W3} = 70$

$$SS_W = SS_{W1} + SS_{W2} + SS_{W3} = 106 + 306 + 70 = 482$$

$$MS_W = \frac{SS_W}{df_W} = \frac{482}{12} = 40.17$$

$$F = \frac{MS_B}{40.17}$$

$$MS_B = \frac{SS_B}{df_B}$$

$$SS_B = SS_{B1} + SS_{B2} + SS_{B3} + \cdots.$$

$$GM = \frac{\sum X_1 + \sum X_2 + \sum X_3 + \cdots}{\sum (N_1 + N_2 + N_3 + \cdots)}.$$

$$GM = \frac{490 + 530 + 490}{5 + 5 + 5} = \frac{1510}{15} = 100.67$$

Table 12.34: Computing SS_{B1} for people who never swear (X_1)

M_1	GM	$(M_1 - GM)$	$(M_1 - GM)^2$
98	100.67	−2.67	7.13
98	100.67	−2.67	7.13
98	100.67	−2.67	7.13
98	100.67	−2.67	7.13
98	100.67	−2.67	7.13
$M_1 = 98$; $N_1 = 5$; $df_1 = 4$			$SS_{B1} = 35.65$

Table 12.35: Computing SS_{B2} for people who sometimes swear (X_2)

M_2	GM	(M_2–GM)	(M_2–GM)^2
106	100.67	5.33	28.41
106	100.67	5.33	28.41
106	100.67	5.33	28.41
106	100.67	5.33	28.41
106	100.67	5.33	28.41
M_2 = 106; N_2 = 5; df_2 = 4			SS_{B2} = 142.05

Table 12.36: Computing SS_{B3} for people who swear all the time (X_3)

M_3	GM	(M_3–GM)	(M_3–GM)^2
98	100.67	−2.67	7.13
98	100.67	−2.67	7.13
98	100.67	−2.67	7.13
98	100.67	−2.67	7.13
98	100.67	−2.67	7.13
M_3 = 98; N_3 = 5; df_3 = 4			SS_{B3} = 35.65

$SS_{B1} = 35.65$
$SS_{B2} = 142.05$
$SS_{B3} = 35.65$
$SS_B = SS_{B1} + SS_{B2} + SS_{B3} + \cdots.$
$SS_B = 35.65 + 142.05 + 35.65 = 213.35$

$$MS_B = \frac{SS_B}{df_B} = \frac{213.35}{2} = 106.68$$

$$F = \frac{MS_B}{MS_W} = \frac{106.68}{40.17} = 2.66$$

e. F_{obt} = 2.66, while F_{crit} = 6.93; therefore, we fail to reject the null hypothesis. We have not found evidence that people who swear a lot are less intelligent than people who do not swear a lot.

f. $R^2 = \frac{SS_B}{SS_B + SS_W} = \frac{213.35}{213.35 + 482} = .31$, or 31%. A good deal of the variability in scores (31%) can be attributed to differences between the means of the groups.

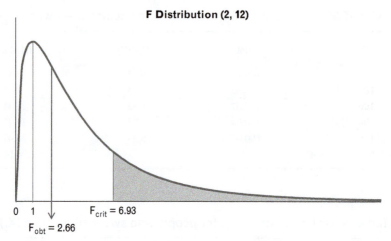

FIGURE 12.6: F Distribution for Homework Set B #3.

REFERENCE

Dubbs, S. L., & Buunk, A. P. (2010). Parents just don't understand: Parent-offspring conflict over mate choice. *Evolutionary Psychology*, 8, 586–598.

CHI SQUARE AND HYPOTHESIS-TESTING WITH CATEGORICAL VARIABLES

To this point, we've gone through the main elements of hypothesis testing, including the basic rationale of this process as well as issues that need to be considered (such as Type-I and Type-II Error). We've also covered several of the most commonly employed and important forms of hypothesis-testing statistics used in the behavioral sciences (such as the within-group t-test and the one-way ANOVA).

The hypothesis-testing statistics that we've covered so far generally include at least one continuous variable. For instance, the within-group t-test includes two continuous variables (it's a comparison of whether the means of two continuous variables differ significantly from one another). The between-groups t-test has one categorical variable (whether people are in "group 1" or "group 2" (whatever those groups may be)) and one continuous variable (to see if the mean on the continuous variable differs significantly across the groups). And so forth.

The content of this chapter deals with a different kind of situation. Specifically, this chapter deals with the situation in which you have only categorical variables—and no continuous variables to speak of. Often, these kinds of research questions are framed in terms of differences in proportions. Such questions would include, for instance:

(a) Is the proportion of males-to-females at my university different from the proportion at the national level?

(b) Is the proportion of people who own a bicycle different in Portland, Oregon, than it is in Portland, Maine?

(c) Are some of the major world religions represented disproportionately in the United States?

With these kinds of questions, we're not looking at means of continuous variables. With the religion question, for instance, we're not aiming to determine whether people in the United States differ from other places in the world in terms of their degree of religiosity. That would be a question regarding *degree*. And most hypothesis-testing questions we've encountered to this point are of that variety. Rather, here, we're asking questions regarding *kind* (or *quality*). Is the religious composition in the United States qualitatively different from the religious composition worldwide?

One way to think about this kind of scenario pertains to the concept of *frequency*. With the religion question, for instance, we're examining if the frequency of people with different religious beliefs is somehow disproportionate from the frequencies that would be expected based on the numbers at the world level.

CHI SQUARE TEST OF GOODNESS OF FIT

The Chi Square statistic is designed to examine hypothesis-testing issues when you've only got categorical variables on your hands. The most basic kind of Chi Square test is the "Goodness of Fit" test—which seeks to determine if some pattern of frequencies is significantly different than would be expected based on some criteria. If the test is "not significant," that means that the *observed frequencies* "fit" the pattern of the *expected frequencies* well. If the test is "significant," that means that the "fit is not good" or that the observed frequencies do not fit the pattern of the expected frequencies. Or, more simply, if the test is significant, that means that your observed (or actual) frequencies are significantly different from the expected frequencies.

The test itself is easy and follows the same reasoning we've used all along. Let's walk through the steps in conducting the Chi Square Goodness of Fit with an example. You're curious. You've heard that the ratio of females to males at your college is 65/35—mostly females. But as a psychology major, you could swear that the proportion is even more biased in your major— at least it seems to you there is an even higher proportion of females to males relative to the university-wide numbers. You're currently taking a course in evolutionary psychology (and you just love it!). In this class of 40, you know that there are 32 females and 8 males. Is this ratio significantly more female-biased than the ratio at the university in general? Here's how you'd find out:

STEPS IN HYPOTHESIS TESTING WITH CHI SQUARE GOODNESS OF FIT

1. ARTICULATE THE RESEARCH AND NULL HYPOTHESES

As with the ANOVA, your research hypothesis here is non-directional, and is simply that the null hypothesis is incorrect. The best way to spell out the hypotheses has to do with the relationship between E and Ó (or O-prime).

E corresponds to the *expected frequencies*. And you'll see that how to compute E varies very much as a function of your situation. In the current situation, E for females and E for males is based on the university-wide ratio of 65 to 35. So if you have a sample of, say, 200 students and you want to see how many females and males you would expect in that pool of 200 students, you'd multiply 200 by .65 (to get 130) for females and you'd multiple that total N of 200 by .35 (to get 70) for males. As you can see, the current N is actually 40, so we'll be working with this N as we move forward on this example (we used an N of 200 here just to show you how to compute E across more than one specific situation).

Thus, E is equal to the total N (total number of individuals included in the sample or pool) multiplied by *the appropriate weight*. And *the appropriate weight* is determined by the information given in the question itself—so you'll need to derive that on a case-by-case basis. In a formula, E = N(appropriate weight).

Ó (or O-prime) represents the observed frequencies *at the full population level*—compared with O (which we'll work with soon), which corresponds to the observed frequencies in your sample. In the current working case, Ó would represent what you observe in terms of the frequencies of males and females at the full population of psychology students at your school. O is essentially an inference, or estimate of Ó. And as is usual with our null and research hypotheses, we articulate these in terms of population parameters.

This all said, the null hypothesis is as follows:

$$H_0: \acute{O} = E$$

And the research hypothesis is similar to the research hypothesis found in ANOVA—as follows:

$$H_1: \text{not } H_0 \text{ (or } \acute{O} \neq E)$$

2. DETERMINE THE CHARACTERISTICS OF THE COMPARISON DISTRIBUTION

As with the F in ANOVA, the Chi Square statistic (as you'll soon see) is always a positive number. As such, the comparison distribution is like the F distribution—it starts at 0 (at the Y axis), typically peaks soon to the right, and then moves toward the X axis as the scores increase. Also as with the F distribution, the Chi Square distribution itself varies as a function of degrees of freedom (df)—so there is a different Chi Square distribution based on the df of a particular problem. With a Chi Square Goodness of Fit, df = NC-1 (with *NC* corresponding to *Number of Categories*). In the current case, we're dealing with the Chi Square distribution based on 1 df (as there are 2 categories (female and male)). See Figure 13.1.

3. DETERMINE THE CRITICAL VALUE

The algorithm here is the same as we've been using generally for hypothesis testing. We'll start with an a priori alpha level (let's go with the standard .05) and we'll mark the point X^2_{crit} on the comparison distribution. To help with this process, we'll refer to the Chi Square table (Appendix D). You'll see that it's very straightforward. With an alpha of .05 and a df of 1,

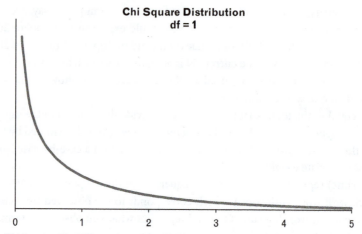

FIGURE 13.1: Chi Square Distribution based on df = 1.

$X^2_{crit} = 3.84$. So to reject the null hypothesis, we'll need an obtained X^2 of greater than 3.84 (See Figure 13.2).

4. COMPUTING CHI SQUARE X^2_{obt}

Computing Chi Square follows a process that is very similar to what we've done all along. We're essentially looking to see if the observed frequencies differ significantly from the expected frequencies. We'll examine this question for each category and then come up with a general summary of whether, overall, the pattern suggests that the observed frequencies (across categories) are significantly different from the expected frequencies. Along the way, we square these

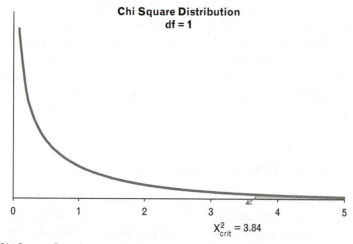

FIGURE 13.2: Chi Square Distribution with X^2_{crit} and Alpha Demarcated.

Table 13.1: Computing x^2_{obt} or the Goodness of Fit Test

Category	E (expected frequency)	0 (observed frequency)	(0 − E)	(0 − E)²	$\frac{(0 - E)^2}{E}$
Female	26	32	−6	36	1.38
Male	14	8	6	36	2.57

$$X^2_{obt} = \Sigma \frac{(O - E)^2}{E} = 3.95$$

discrepancies (to ameliorate the issue of summing to zero; an issue we've dealt with throughout) and divide this squared product by the expected value for each category (to get a sense of how much the observed and expected scores deviate from one another in light of the magnitude of the expected score). X^2_{obt} is the sum of this final product across categories. Specifically, the formula for X^2_{obt} is as follows:

$$X^2_{obt} = \frac{(O - E)^2}{E}$$

To complete this problem, we need both the observed frequencies for the different categories and the expected frequencies. The two categories are female and male—and the observed frequencies are 32 and 8, respectively. The expected frequencies are based on the ratio of females to males (65:35) at the university level. Based on this expected ratio, the expected frequency for females is 40 * .65 (or 26) and the expected frequency for males is 40 * .35 (or 14).

The full process for computing X^2_{obt} or the Goodness of Fit test is found in Table 13.1.

5. COMMENT ON NULL HYPOTHESIS

As is always the case with hypothesis testing, this decision is dichotomous. Here, $X^2_{crit} = 3.84$ and $X^2_{obt} = 3.95$. As you can see in Figure 13.3, X^2_{obt} is in the alpha region, so we reject the null hypothesis. We can thus conclude that the proportion of females to males majoring in psych at our school is likely significantly different from this gender ratio at the university level.

This said, our ability to make inferences based on whether we have rejected the null hypothesis is limited. In fact, the situation is actually quite similar to the situation with ANOVA. Knowing that we reject the null hypothesis tells us something—but certainly not all we need to know…

WHAT CAN AND CANNOT BE INFERRED FROM A SIGNIFICANT CHI SQUARE

In the working example, we've shown that the proportion of female to male students in your psychology program department is likely different than the proportion at the university writ

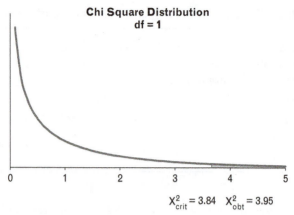

FIGURE 13.3: X^2_{obt} Relative to X^2_{crit}.

large. But that's all you know! Based on the Chi Square test, you don't have any additional information. The test, like ANOVA, is inherently non-directional—so you don't know based simply on the Chi Square if the effect is due to a relatively high number of male students *or* a relatively high number of female students.

To make this more specific inference, you need to examine the actual data. Here, with two categories and a significant Chi Square, the situation is actually pretty straightforward—the Chi Square is significant (so the observed frequencies are significantly different from the expected frequencies) and the number of observed female students is greater than the expected number of female students. Concurrently, the number of observed male students is less than the expected number of male students. With this information combined with the significant Chi Square, we now know the full story—the observed frequencies are significantly different from the expected frequencies *such that* the ratio of females to males in the psychology program is more female-biased than the gender ratio at the university in general.

With two categories, this kind of decision is not too difficult. With more categories, a significant Chi Square becomes less interpretable—and an examination of the specific frequencies becomes more important in allowing you to tell the full story. Sometimes, you need to follow up a Chi Square on a large number of categories with a smaller Chi Square based on a subset of two of the categories just to be able to make inferences regarding whether specific categories show significant effects.

CHI SQUARE GOODNESS OF FIT TESTING FOR EQUALITY ACROSS CATEGORIES

A common situation for the Chi Square Goodness of Fit examines the situation in which you're testing if the observed frequencies in different categories are statistically equal (or unequal) to one another. Is the number of Jets fans in New York State significantly different from the number of Giants fans? Do strawberry, chocolate, and vanilla ice cream cones sell in equal proportions? Are foreign students at your school equally representative of Africa, Asia, Australia, Europe, and South America? And so forth.

In fact, this kind of question is the same general kind of question that we addressed in our first example (of whether the proportion of females to males in the psychology program differs from the gender rate in the school at large). The difference is that in the current discussion, we're talking about situations in which the test is against whether the frequencies across categories are equal to one another (in the prior example, the test was against a situation in which the ratio was unequal (65:35)).

Therefore, in this section, we're really just dealing with a specific case of the more general process we learned in the prior section.

As an example, let's consider popularity of sports teams. In California, are fans of the Angels, Athletics, Dodgers, Giants, and Padres equally as frequent? Are these four baseball teams represented evenly in popularity among baseball fans in the Golden State? To address this question fairly, you randomly sample 1,000 baseball fans equally representing all regions of California. You ask each person to name their favorite Major League team from California. Your results are as follows (see Table 13.2):

Table 13.2: Frequencies of Number of Fans
for Five California Sports Teams

Team	Number of Fans
Angels	200
Athletics	50
Dodgers	400
Giants	150
Padres	200

To test the hypothesis of whether the fans of the teams are represented unequally across these fans, we'll follow the standard five steps of hypothesis testing, as such:

1. ARTICULATE THE NULL AND RESEARCH HYPOTHESES

In words, the null hypothesis is that the number of fans of each of these five teams is equally represented at the population level (i.e., there are as many Angels fans as Athletics fans as Dodgers fans as Giants fans as Padres fans). In words, the research hypothesis is essentially that some teams are more popular than others and that the number of fans rooting for each team is not equal at the population level. In symbols, these hypotheses are as follows:

H_0: Ó = E
H_1: not H_0 (or Ó ≠ E)

2. DETERMINE THE CHARACTERISTICS OF THE COMPARISON DISTRIBUTION

The comparison distribution is a Chi Square distribution. There are five categories, so $df = 5 - 1 = 4$. The comparison distribution is a Chi Square distribution based on a df of 4. See Figure 13.4.

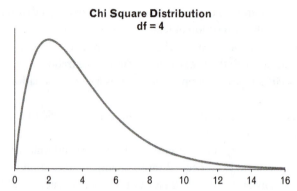

FIGURE 13.4: Chi Square Distribution based on df = 4.

3. DETERMINE THE CRITICAL VALUE

For variety, let's use an alpha of .01. With this information and the knowledge that df = 4, we'll refer to the Chi Square table (Appendix D). In this case, $X^2_{crit} = 13.23$. So to reject the null hypothesis, we'll need an obtained X^2 of greater than 13.23 (See Figure 13.5).

Figure 13.5: Chi Square Distribution with X^2_{crit} and Alpha Demarcated

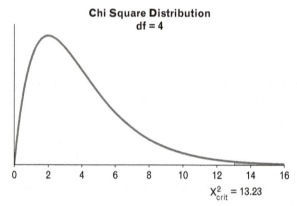

FIGURE 13.5: Chi Square Distribution with X_{crit}^2 and Alpha Demarcated.

4. COMPUTING CHI SQUARE X^2_{obt}

When we're testing the specific question of whether the observed frequencies representing different categories are significantly different from one another, we can still use the same algorithm that we've been using to compute the expected frequencies (E). That is, E = N(appropriate weight). In this case, we have five categories—and we're testing the idea of equality across the categories. As such, the null hypothesis assumes the same number of individuals in each of the five categories; the null hypothesis predicts that $\frac{1}{5}$ of all participants are in each category. Thus, .2 ($\frac{1}{5}$ as a weighted decimal) of all participants are predicted to be in each category. As such, E

Table 13.3: Computing X^2_{obt} or the Goodness of Fit Test for Baseball Team Preference

Category	E (expected frequency)	O (observed frequency)	(O – E)	(O – E)²	$\dfrac{(O-E)^2}{E}$
Angels	200	200	0	0	0
Athletics	200	50	150	22,500	112.5
Dodgers	200	400	–200	40,000	200
Giants	200	150	50	2,500	12.5
Padres	200	200	0	0	0

$$X^2_{obt} = \Sigma \frac{(O-E)^2}{E} = 325$$

for each category is 1,000 * .2, or 200. N divided by NC (number of categories) would work just as well. In any case, this information comes into play as we work out X^2_{obt} in Table 13.3):

5. COMMENT ON NULL HYPOTHESIS

Here, $X^2_{crit} = 13.23$ and $X^2_{obt} = 325$. As you can see in Figure 13.6, X^2_{obt} is in the alpha region (by a lot!) so we reject the null hypothesis. Apparently, not all California baseball teams are loved equally.

Based on what we can and cannot infer from a significant Chi Square, we can only make a general comment at this point. We can say that preferences for these five teams are not equally distributed across fans. However, we cannot at this point make more specific comments on this situation. We cannot say that there are significantly more Angels fans than Athletics fans, for instance.

If we did want to make finer-grained distinctions, we'd need to do Chi Squares that are subsets of the analysis we just conducted. For instance, if we wanted to see if there are significantly

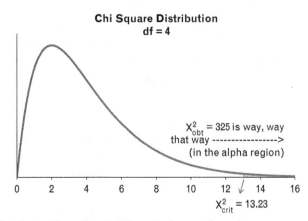

Chi Square Distribution
df = 4

$X^2_{obt} = 325$ is way, way
that way ------------------>
(in the alpha region)

0   2   4   6   8   10   12   14   16

$X^2_{crit} = 13.23$

FIGURE 13.6: X^2_{obt} Relative to X^2_{crit} or Baseball Team Preference Example.

more Angels fans than Athletics fans, we could do a Chi Square Goodness of Fit test examining just the frequencies for those two teams' fan memberships.

CHI SQUARE TEST OF INDEPENDENCE

The other primary kind of Chi Square test is referred to as the *Chi Square Test of Independence*. Here, we're seeing if two categorical variables are dependent on (or related to) one another. For instance:

(a)   Is academic major related to one's ice cream flavor preference?
(b)   Is political orientation related to geographical region?
(c)   Is preference for certain kinds of music related to preferences for certain kind of foods?

These questions are all about the relationships between two variables—but, in each case, unlike with correlation (which includes two continuous variables), each question corresponds to the relationship between two categorical variables. With such a test, a significant Chi Square essentially says that the variables are significantly related (or dependent on one another); a non-significant Chi Square essentially says that you have provided no evidence that these variables are dependent.

As an example, let's consider whether political orientation relates to academic major. Are some academic majors likely to overrepresent (or underrepresent) certain political orientations? To test this question, you survey 150 students at your school—50 business majors, 50 psychology majors, and 50 sociology majors. You then simply ask them to indicate which political party (Democrat or Republican) they primarily identify with.

With a Chi Square test of independence, we'll collect data and organize them into a tabular format, as found in Table 13.4.

Here, we have the data organized as a function of the two categorical variables—academic major and political affiliation. The hypothesis-testing steps are as follows:

1. ARTICULATING THE NULL AND RESEARCH HYPOTHESES

In the generic, the null and research hypotheses are the same as with the Goodness of Fit test. The main difference is that the null hypothesis now is that the two variables are unrelated to one another at the population level, with the research hypothesis indicating that the two variables are related to one another. More specifically, the null hypothesis here says that academic major is

Table 13.4: Data Examining Academic Major Related to Political Affiliation

	Business	Psychology	Sociology
Democrat	10	30	40
Republican	40	20	10

unrelated to political affiliation, while the research hypothesis states that one's political affiliation depends on one's academic major.

As you'll see, computing the Chi Square is ultimately the same as with the Goodness of Fit, and formally, the null and research hypotheses will remain the same, as follows:

$H_0: \acute{O} = E$

$H_1:$ not H_0 (or $\acute{O} \neq E$)

2. DETERMINE THE CHARACTERISTICS OF THE COMPARISON DISTRIBUTION

The comparison distribution is a Chi Square distribution. With a Test of Independence, the df is a function of NC (number of categories) for the rows and the NC for the columns. Specifically, df = $(NC_{row} - 1)$ * $(NC_{column} - 1)$. In this case, there are two rows and three columns, so df = (2−1) * (3−1) = 1 * 2 = 2. The comparison distribution is a Chi Square distribution based on df = 2 (see Figure 13.7).

3. DETERMINING CRITICAL VALUE

The determination of the critical value follows the same reasoning as for the Goodness of Fit test. Let's go with a standard alpha level of .05. Based on the Chi Square table (in Appendix D), with a df of 2, $X^2_{crit} = 5.99$. See Figure 13.8.

4. COMPUTING CHI SQUARE

With a Chi Square Test of Independence, the computational process is a bit more involved than with the Goodness of Fit test. The first step involves computing the expected values (one for each observed value). For each observed value, $E = \dfrac{\sum R}{N} * \sum C$, with $\sum R$ corresponding to the sum of a particular row and $\sum C$ corresponding to the sum of a particular column (See Table 13.5).

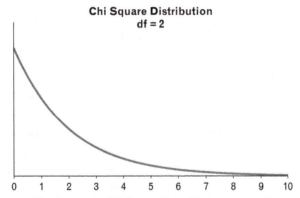

Chi Square Distribution
df = 2

FIGURE 13.7: Comparison Distribution for Chi Square Test of Independence Example.

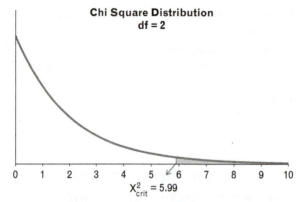

FIGURE 13.8: Comparison Distribution with and X^2_{crit} Alpha Demarcated.

Expected values (E) are in parentheses next to O (or observed values).

These expected values assume that there is no relationship between the two variables. So our test is essentially seeing how much our observed frequencies differ from these expected frequencies.

Given the complexities of the Test for Independence, it is simplest to do the actual calculation in sentence (as opposed to table) format.

The formula for Chi Square is as follows:

$$X^2_{obt} = \Sigma \frac{(O - E)^2}{E}$$

Thus, we need to compute a product for each observed frequency. In this case, with three categories in one variable and two in the other, we have six total observed frequencies—so in computing X^2_{obt}, we'll sum six products. Note that each product is an index of how much a particular observed frequency deviates from the expected frequency (which assumes no relationship between the two variables). In the current case, we compute Chi Square as follows:

$$X^2_{obt} = \frac{(10 - 26.67)^2}{26.67} + \frac{(30 - 26.67)^2}{26.67} + \frac{(40 - 26.67)^2}{26.67} + \frac{(40 - 23.33)^2}{23.33}$$
$$+ \frac{(20 - 23.33)^2}{23.33} + \frac{(10 - 23.23)^2}{23.33}$$

$10.42 + .42 + 6.66 + 11.91 + .48 + 7.62$

$= 37.51$

Table 13.5: Computing Expected Values for Chi Square for Test of Independence

		Business	Psychology	Sociology	SIGMA R
Democrat		10(26.67)	30(26.67)	40(26.67)	80
Republican		40(23.33)	20(23.33)	10(23.33)	70
	SIGMA	50	50	50	N = 150

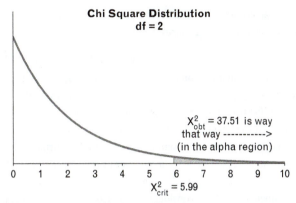

Chi Square Distribution
df = 2

$X^2_{obt} = 37.51$ is way
that way ----------->
(in the alpha region)

0   1   2   3   4   5   6   7   8   9   10
$X^2_{crit} = 5.99$

FIGURE 13.9: Comparing X^2_{crit} with X^2_{obt} or Chi Square Test of Independence.

Clearly, 37.51 is greater than 5.99, so X^2_{crit} is more extreme than X^2_{obt} and is in the alpha region (See Figure 13.9).

We've thus got a significant Chi Square. With a Test of Independence, this essentially means that the two variables are *dependent* on one another—or are related to one another. The result is parallel to finding a correlation between two continuous variables. Based on the findings in this example, political orientation is related to one's academic major.

As with the Goodness of Fit test, the Test of Independence still lacks a bit in the way of specificity. We now know that academic major and political orientation are related at beyond-chance levels, but we don't have specific data speaking to the details of the pattern. For instance, are business majors significantly more likely to be Republicans as compared with psychology majors? As with the Goodness of Fit test, we'd need to design and implement sub-tests (smaller versions of this same general Chi Square) to zero-in on such specific details. Often, examining the pattern of data dovetailed with information on whether the Chi Square is significant is sufficiently informative—and whether you conduct follow-up tests often depends on whether you have specific questions regarding the nuances. For instance, with the current example, while we can't state for certain if business majors are more likely to be Republicans than are psychology majors, we can state confidently that there is a relationship between academic major and political orientation, and we can state that based on the observed frequencies, business majors are the most likely to be Republican and sociology majors are the most likely to be Democrat. The issue of follow-up therefore really depends on the nature of your research goals and the precise questions you're looking to answer.

REAL RESEARCH EXAMPLE

In a recent study examining the issue of interdisciplinarity, Garcia, Geher, Crosier, Saad, Johnsen, and Pranckitas (2011) examined whether journals that focus on evolutionary approaches to human behavior draw on more disciplines than psychology journals in general (based on the idea that evolutionary approaches to human behavior are broad in their reach across academic areas). To examine this, Garcia et al. (2011) compared the number of disciplines represented by top journals in the field of evolutionary psychology (*Evolutionary Psychology* and *Evolution and Human Behavior*) with top journals in several other fields of psychology. In this work, the researchers examined if the number of different academic areas (such as anthropology, biology, philosophy, etc.) cited varied across the different journals. The researchers used a Chi Square Goodness of Fit test to examine this question, as follows:

> this analysis addresses if the number of non-psychology fields differed across the journals. Thus, if a journal included articles first-authored only by psychologists, sociologists, and anthropologists, the frequency of non-psychology fields would be two. This analysis was conducted to gauge the number of different fields represented across the journals. Again, a chi-square goodness-of-fit test was implemented. This test had a null hypothesis that the frequency of number of academic fields outside psychology would not differ significantly across the journals. As such, the expected number, vis a`vis this null hypothesis, was the number of non-psychology fields represented by each journal, summed and divided by 10–this came to 4.5. To the extent that some journals have actual (observed) frequencies that are considerably lower or greater than this expected number, the chi-square statistics will increase. The analysis was significant ($X^2(9) = 18.33$, $p < .05$), offering additional support for the general hypothesis regarding the greater interdisciplinarity of EP. A greater number of academic disciplines was represented within evolution-themed journals compared to the non-evolution-themed journals. (p. 756).

SUMMARY

When we are asking analytical questions based on categorical variables, we cannot rely on statistics that require a mean and standard deviation. Under such conditions, we can use different forms of the Chi Square statistic. Chi Square tests assume that you have only categorical variables—and they compare observed frequencies (how frequent different categories are) with some expected frequencies (how frequently different categories are expected to be, based on some existing criterion or hypothesis). Ultimately, Chi Square tests examine if there is a significant discrepancy between observed frequencies and expected frequencies—allowing us to carry out hypothesis testing using categorical data.

KEY TERMS

Chi Square. Statistic designed to examine hypothesis-testing issues when you only have categorical variables.

Chi Square "Goodness of Fit" Test. Type of Chi Square test which seeks to see if some pattern of frequencies is significantly different than would be expected based on some criteria.

Chi Square Goodness of Fit Testing for Equality across Categories. Chi Square test which seeks to see if the observed frequencies in different categories are statistically equal (or unequal) to one another.

Chi Square Test of Independence. Chi Square test which seeks to see if two categorical variables are dependent on (or related to) one another.

REFERENCE

Garcia, J. R., Geher, G., Crosier, B., Saad, G., Gambacorta, D., Johnsen, L., & Pranckitas, E. (2011). The interdisciplinary context of evolutionary approaches to human behavior: a key to survival in the ivory archipelago. *Futures*, 43, 749–761.

HOMEWORK SET A

1. A lingerie company typically directs its advertising to women. However, with Valentine's Day approaching, the company asks you to collect data, expecting the ratio of female to male customers to differ from the typical 85/15 ratio. You find that on a single day the week before Valentine's Day, there were 1,000 purchases made, 300 of them by men. You conduct a Chi Square Goodness of Fit test with an alpha of .01, using the steps for hypothesis testing.
    a. Articulate the null and research hypothesis
    b. Determine the characteristics of the comparison distribution
    c. Determine the critical value
    d. Compute the Chi Square
    e. Comment on the null hypothesis

2. You volunteer to assist with a community recreation preschool craft project, and are interested in whether the preschool boys choose all paper colors equally, or whether they shy away from the pink paper selection. The children are all allowed to choose freely, and you take note of the color selection for boys. You then conduct a Chi Square Goodness of Fit Equality Across Categories test with an alpha of .05, using the steps for hypothesis testing. See data in Table 13.6.

Table 13.6: Homework Set A #2

Color	# of Times Chosen
Blue	52
Red	54
Yellow	52
Pink	42

    a. Articulate the null and research hypothesis
    b. Determine the characteristics of the comparison distribution
    c. Determine the critical value
    d. Compute the Chi Square
    e. Comment on the null hypothesis

3. You know from recent studies that many teenagers are engaging in "sexting" behavior, sending sexual messages and nude pictures via text messaging. You poll 400 teenagers to gather information on whether the education level of the parents has any relationship to a teen's sexting behavior. You conduct a Chi Square Test of Independence with an alpha of .05, using the steps for hypothesis testing. See Table 13.7 for data.

Table 13.7: Homework Set A #3

	Less than High School Education	High School Diploma	College Degree
Has engaged in sexting	50	70	70
Has not engaged in sexting	40	80	90

a. Articulate the null and research hypothesis
b. Determine the characteristics of the comparison distribution
c. Determine the critical value
d. Compute the Chi Square
e. Comment on the null hypothesis

HOMEWORK SET B

1. You are visiting your friend, who lives in a town near the beach. Your friend tells you that he hardly ever goes to the beach, and that most people who live in the town rarely go to the beach. You look at the town's website, and see that at any given time, only 30% of the people on the beach are town residents. You arrive on the beach on a very nice, sunny day, and decide to collect some data while you're there, to see if the sunny weather brought more than the average number of town residents to the beach. Of the 100 people you talked to, 40 of them were town residents. You conduct a Chi Square Goodness of Fit test with an alpha of .01, using the steps for hypothesis testing.
   a. Articulate the null and research hypothesis
   b. Determine the characteristics of the comparison distribution
   c. Determine the critical value
   d. Compute the Chi Square
   e. Comment on the null hypothesis

2. You have a friend who is very involved with art. She shows you an abstract painting that has been the source of a great deal of excitement in the art community. You are not very interested in abstract art in general, and do not see anything particularly exciting in the painting. You are curious, however, whether you are just missing something special in this painting that others can see. You provide your eight-year-old niece and two of her friends with the same colors of paint used in the painting, show her the acclaimed painting, and ask them to paint something similar. You show the paintings to 100 random people, and ask them to identify which painting they believe is an acclaimed work of art. You then conduct a Chi Square Goodness of Fit Equality Across Categories test with an alpha of .05, using the steps for hypothesis testing. See Table 13.8 for data.

Table 13.8: Homework Set B #2

Painting	Number of Times Selected
"Acclaimed" painting	29
8-year-old painting #1	25
8-year-old painting #2	23
8-year-old painting #3	23

    a.   Articulate the null and research hypothesis

    b.   Determine the characteristics of the comparison distribution

    c.   Determine the critical value

    d.   Compute the Chi Square

    e.   Comment on the null hypothesis

3.   Activity buses, which typically run an hour and a half after regular school buses for students participating in after-school sports and clubs, were once common in middle and high schools. Due to budget cuts, schools in your area no longer offer activity buses. Many people in your community are pushing to bring back activity buses, hoping to keep students more involved in sports and clubs and reduce non-supervised time for teenagers. You wonder if the people who are the strongest supporters of activity buses were involved in after-school sports and clubs as teenagers. You collect data and conduct a Chi Square Test of Independence with an alpha level of .05. See Table 13.9 for data.

Table 13.9: Homework Set B #3

	In favor of having activity buses	Against having activity buses	No opinion on activity buses
Participated in sports/clubs	80	5	0
Did not participate in sports/clubs	30	40	5

    a.   Articulate the null and research hypothesis

    b.   Determine the characteristics of the comparison distribution

    c.   Determine the critical value

    d.   Compute the Chi Square

    e.   Comment on the null hypothesis

HOMEWORK SET A ANSWERS

1. a. H_0: Ó $=$ E

      H_1: not H_0 (or Ó $\neq$ E)

    b. The comparison distribution is a Chi Square distribution with df=1 (because we have 2 categories—female and male)

    c. The critical value X^2_{crit} of a Chi Square distribution with 1 df and an alpha level of .01 is 6.63.

d.

Table 13.10: Homework Set A Answers #1d

Category	E (expected frequency)	O (observed frequency)	$(O-E)$	$(O-E)^2$	$\dfrac{(O-E)^2}{E}$
Female	850	700	−150	22,500	26.47
Male	150	300	150	22,500	150

$$X^2_{obt} = \Sigma \frac{(O-E)^2}{E} = 176.47$$

e. We reject the null hypothesis. The results indicate that the ratio of females to males purchasing lingerie the week before Valentine's Day may vary significantly from the typical ratio.

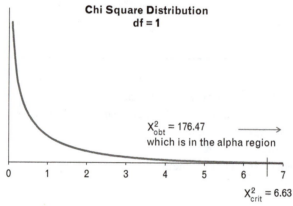

$X^2_{obt} = 176.47$ which is in the alpha region

$X^2_{crit} = 6.63$

FIGURE 13.10: Homework Set A #1.

2. a. $H_0: \acute{O} = E$

$H_1:$ not H_0 (or $\acute{O} \ne E$)

b. The comparison distribution is a Chi Square distribution with df = 3 (because there are 4 categories and df = 4−1)

c. The critical value X^2_{crit} of a Chi Square distribution with 3 df and an alpha level of .05 is 7.81

d.

Table 13.11: Homework Set A Answers #2d

Category	E (expected frequency)	O (observed frequency)	$(O-E)$	$(O-E)^2$	$\dfrac{(O-E)^2}{E}$
Blue	50	52	2	4	.08
Red	50	54	4	16	.32
Yellow	50	52	2	4	.08
Pink	50	42	−8	64	1.28

$$X^2_{obt} = \Sigma \frac{(O-E)^2}{E} = 1.76$$

e.   We fail to reject the null hypothesis. The results indicate that preschool boys appear to choose equally amongst the colors offered for craft projects.

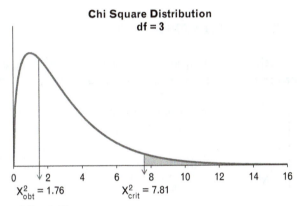

FIGURE 13.11: Homework Set A #2.

3.   a. $H_0: \acute{O} = E$

H$_1$: not H_0 (or $\acute{O} \neq E$)

b.   The comparison distribution is a Chi Square distribution with df = 2 (because we have two rows and three columns, so df = $(2-1)*(3-1) = 2$)

c.   The critical value X^2_{crit} of a Chi Square distribution with 2 df and an alpha level of .05 is 5.99.

d.

Table 13.12: Homework Set A Answers #3d

	Less than high school education	High school diploma	College Degree	ΣR
Has engaged in sexting	50 (42.75)	70 (71.25)	70 (76)	190
Has not engaged in sexting	40 (47.25)	80 (78.75)	90 (84)	210
ΣC	90	150	160	N = 400

Expected values (E) are in parentheses next to O (or observed values)

$$X^2_{obt} = \frac{(50-42.75)^2}{42.75} + \frac{(70-71.25)^2}{71.25} + \frac{(70-76)^2}{76} + \frac{(40-47.25)^2}{47.25}$$
$$+ \frac{(80-78.75)^2}{78.75} + \frac{(90-84)^2}{84}$$

$$1.23 + .02 + .47 + 1.11 + .02 + .43 = 2.81$$

e.   We fail to reject the null hypothesis. It does not appear that a teenager's sexting behavior, or lack thereof, is related to the education level of the parents.

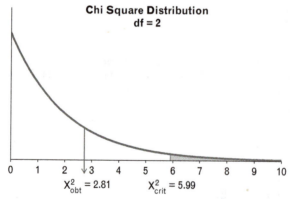

FIGURE 13.12: Homework Set A #3.

REFERENCE

Garcia, J. G., Geher, G., Crosier, B., Saad, G., Gambacorta, D., Johnsen, L., & Pranckitas, E. (2011). The interdisciplinary context of evolutionary approaches to human behavior: a key to survival in the ivory archipelago. *Futures*, 43, 749–761.

APPENDIX A

Cumulative Standardized Normal Distribution

Table A: Normal Curve Areas: Percentage of the Normal Curve Between the Mean and the Z-Scores Shown

Z	% Mean-to-Z	Z	% Mean-to-Z	Z	% Mean-to-Z
.00	.00	.24	9.48	.48	18.44
.01	.40	.25	9.87	.49	18.79
.02	.80	.26	10.26	.50	19.15
.03	1.20	.27	10.64	.51	19.50
.04	1.60	.28	11.03	.52	19.85
.05	1.99	.29	11.41	.53	20.19
.06	2.39	.30	11.79	.54	20.54
.07	2.79	.31	12.17	.55	20.88
.08	3.19	.32	12.55	.56	21.23
.09	3.59	.33	12.93	.57	21.57
.10	3.98	.34	13.31	.58	21.90
.11	4.38	.35	13.68	.59	22.24
.12	4.78	.36	14.06	.60	22.57
.13	5.17	.37	14.43	.61	22.91
.14	5.57	.38	14.80	.62	23.24
.15	5.96	.39	15.17	.63	23.57
.16	6.36	.40	15.54	.64	23.89
.17	6.75	.41	15.91	.65	24.22

(continued)

Table A: Continued

Z	% Mean-to-Z	Z	% Mean-to-Z	Z	% Mean-to-Z
.18	7.14	.42	16.28	.66	24.54
.19	7.53	.43	16.64	.67	24.86
.20	7.93	.44	17.00	.68	25.17
.21	8.32	.45	17.36	.69	25.49
.22	8.71	.46	17.72	.70	25.80
.23	9.10	.47	18.08	.71	26.11
.72	26.42	1.19	38.30	1.66	45.15
.73	26.73	1.20	38.49	1.67	45.25
.74	27.04	1.21	38.69	1.68	45.35
.75	27.34	1.22	38.88	1.69	45.45
.76	27.64	1.23	39.07	1.70	45.54
.77	27.94	1.24	39.25	1.71	45.64
.78	28.23	1.25	39.44	1.72	45.73
.79	28.52	1.26	39.62	1.73	45.82
.80	28.81	1.27	39.80	1.74	45.91
.81	29.10	1.28	39.97	1.75	45.99
.82	29.39	1.29	40.15	1.76	46.08
.83	29.67	1.30	40.32	1.77	46.16
.84	29.95	1.31	40.49	1.78	46.25
.85	30.23	1.32	40.66	1.79	46.33
.86	30.51	1.33	40.82	1.80	46.41
.87	30.78	1.34	40.99	1.81	46.49
.88	31.06	1.35	41.15	1.82	46.56
.89	31.33	1.36	41.31	1.83	46.64
.90	31.59	1.37	41.47	1.84	46.71
.91	31.86	1.38	41.62	1.85	46.78
.92	32.12	1.39	41.77	1.86	46.86
.93	32.38	1.40	41.92	1.87	46.93
.94	32.64	1.41	42.07	1.88	46.99
.95	32.89	1.42	42.22	1.89	47.06
.96	33.15	1.43	42.36	1.90	47.13
.97	33.40	1.44	42.51	1.91	47.19
.98	33.65	1.45	42.65	1.92	47.26
.99	33.89	1.46	42.79	1.93	47.32
1.00	34.13	1.47	42.92	1.94	47.38
1.01	34.38	1.48	43.06	1.95	47.44
1.02	34.61	1.49	43.19	1.96	47.50
1.03	34.85	1.50	43.32	1.97	47.56
1.04	35.08	1.51	43.45	1.98	47.61
1.05	35.31	1.52	43.57	1.99	47.67
1.06	35.54	1.53	43.70	2.00	47.72
1.07	35.77	1.54	43.82	2.01	47.78
1.08	35.99	1.55	43.94	2.02	47.83

(continued)

Table A: Continued

Z	% Mean-to-Z	Z	% Mean-to-Z	Z	% Mean-to-Z
1.09	36.21	1.56	44.06	2.03	47.88
1.10	36.43	1.57	44.18	2.04	47.93
1.11	36.65	1.58	44.29	2.05	47.98
1.12	36.86	1.59	44.41	2.06	48.03
1.13	37.08	1.60	44.52	2.07	48.08
1.14	37.29	1.61	44.63	2.08	48.12
1.15	37.49	1.62	44.74	2.09	48.17
1.16	37.70	1.63	44.84	2.10	48.21
1.17	37.90	1.64	44.95	2.11	48.26
1.18	38.10	1.65	45.05	2.12	48.30
2.13	48.34	2.44	49.27	2.75	49.70
2.14	48.38	2.45	49.29	2.76	49.71
2.15	48.42	2.46	49.31	2.77	49.72
2.16	48.46	2.47	49.32	2.78	49.73
2.17	48.50	2.48	49.34	2.79	49.74
2.18	48.54	2.49	49.36	2.80	49.74
2.19	48.57	2.50	49.38	2.81	49.75
2.20	48.61	2.51	49.40	2.82	49.76
2.21	48.64	2.52	49.41	2.83	49.77
2.22	48.68	2.53	49.43	2.84	49.77
2.23	48.71	2.54	49.45	2.85	49.78
2.24	48.75	2.55	49.46	2.86	49.79
2.25	48.78	2.56	49.48	2.87	49.79
2.26	48.81	2.57	49.49	2.88	49.80
2.27	48.84	2.58	49.51	2.89	49.81
2.28	48.87	2.59	49.52	2.90	49.81
2.29	48.90	2.60	49.53	2.91	49.82
2.30	48.93	2.61	49.55	2.92	49.82
2.31	48.96	2.62	49.56	2.93	49.83
2.32	48.98	2.63	49.57	2.94	49.84
2.33	49.01	2.64	49.59	2.95	49.84
2.34	49.04	2.65	49.60	2.96	49.85
2.35	49.06	2.66	49.61	2.97	49.85
2.36	49.09	2.67	49.62	2.98	49.86
2.37	49.11	2.68	49.63	2.99	49.86
2.38	49.13	2.69	49.64	3.00	49.87
2.39	49.16	2.70	49.65	3.50	49.98
2.40	49.18	2.71	49.66	4.00	50.00
2.41	49.20	2.72	49.67	4.50	50.00
2.42	49.22	2.73	49.68		
2.43	49.25	2.74	49.69		

APPENDIX B

t Distribution: Critical Values of t

Table B: Cutoff Scores for the *t* Distribution

df	One-Tailed Tests			Two-Tailed Tests		
	.10	.05	.01	.10	.05	.01
1	3.078	6.314	31.821	6.314	12.706	63.657
2	1.886	2.920	6.965	2.920	4.303	9.925
3	1.638	2.353	4.541	2.353	3.182	5.841
4	1.533	2.132	3.747	2.132	2.776	4.604
5	1.476	2.015	3.365	2.015	2.571	4.032
6	1.440	1.943	3.143	1.943	2.447	3.708
7	1.415	1.895	2.998	1.895	2.365	3.500
8	1.397	1.860	2.897	1.860	2.306	3.356
9	1.383	1.833	2.822	1.833	2.262	3.250
10	1.372	1.813	2.764	1.813	2.228	3.170
11	1.364	1.796	2.718	1.796	2.201	3.106
12	1.356	1.783	2.681	1.783	2.179	3.055
13	1.350	1.771	2.651	1.771	2.161	3.013
14	1.345	1.762	2.625	1.762	2.145	2.977
15	1.341	1.753	2.603	1.753	2.132	2.947
16	1.337	1.746	2.584	1.746	2.120	2.921
17	1.334	1.740	2.567	1.740	2.110	2.898
18	1.331	1.734	2.553	1.734	2.101	2.879
19	1.328	1.729	2.540	1.729	2.093	2.861
20	1.326	1.725	2.528	1.725	2.086	2.846

(continued)

Table B: Continued

df	One-Tailed Tests			Two-Tailed Tests		
	.10	.05	.01	.10	.05	.01
21	1.323	1.721	2.518	1.721	2.080	2.832
22	1.321	1.717	2.509	1.717	2.074	2.819
23	1.320	1.714	2.500	1.714	2.069	2.808
24	1.318	1.711	2.492	1.711	2.064	2.797
25	1.317	1.708	2.485	1.708	2.060	2.788
26	1.315	1.706	2.479	1.706	2.056	2.779
27	1.314	1.704	2.473	1.704	2.052	2.771
28	1.313	1.701	2.467	1.701	2.049	2.764
29	1.312	1.699	2.462	1.699	2.045	2.757
30	1.311	1.698	2.458	1.698	2.043	2.750
35	1.306	1.690	2.438	1.690	2.030	2.724
40	1.303	1.684	2.424	1.684	2.021	2.705
45	1.301	1.680	2.412	1.680	2.014	2.690
50	1.299	1.676	2.404	1.676	2.009	2.678
55	1.297	1.673	2.396	1.673	2.004	2.668
60	1.296	1.671	2.390	1.671	2.001	2.661
65	1.295	1.669	2.385	1.669	1.997	2.654
70	1.294	1.667	2.381	1.667	1.995	2.648
75	1.293	1.666	2.377	1.666	1.992	2.643
80	1.292	1.664	2.374	1.664	1.990	2.639
85	1.292	1.663	2.371	1.663	1.989	2.635
90	1.291	1.662	2.369	1.662	1.987	2.632
95	1.291	1.661	2.366	1.661	1.986	2.629
100	1.290	1.660	2.364	1.660	1.984	2.626
∞	1.282	1.645	2.327	1.645	1.960	2.576

APPENDIX C

F Distribution: Critical Values of F

Table C: Cutoff Scores for the F Distribution

Denominator df	Significance Level	Numerator Degrees of Freedom					
		1	2	3	4	5	6
1	.01	4,052	5,000	5,404	5,625	5,764	5,859
	.05	162	200	216	225	230	234
	.10	39.9	49.5	53.6	55.8	57.2	58.2
2	.01	98.50	99.00	99.17	99.25	99.30	99.33
	.05	18.51	19.00	19.17	19.25	19.30	19.33
	.10	8.53	9.00	9.16	9.24	9.29	9.33
3	.01	34.12	30.82	29.46	28.71	28.24	27.91
	.05	10.13	9.55	9.28	9.12	9.01	8.94
	.10	5.54	5.46	5.39	5.34	5.31	5.28
4	.01	21.20	18.00	16.70	15.98	15.52	15.21
	.05	7.71	6.95	6.59	6.39	6.26	6.16
	.10	4.55	4.33	4.19	4.11	4.05	4.01
5	.01	16.26	13.27	12.06	11.39	10.97	10.67
	.05	6.61	5.79	5.41	5.19	5.05	4.95
	.10	4.06	3.78	3.62	3.52	3.45	3.41
6	.01	13.75	10.93	9.78	9.15	8.75	8.47
	.05	5.99	5.14	4.76	4.53	4.39	4.28
	.10	3.78	3.46	3.29	3.18	3.11	3.06
7	.01	12.25	9.55	8.45	7.85	7.46	7.19
	.05	5.59	4.74	4.35	4.12	3.97	3.87

(continued)

Table C: Continued

Denominator *df*	Significance Level	Numerator Degrees of Freedom					
		1	2	3	4	5	6
	.10	3.59	3.26	3.08	2.96	2.88	2.83
8	.01	11.26	8.65	7.59	7.01	6.63	6.37
	.05	5.32	4.46	4.07	3.84	3.69	3.58
	.10	3.46	3.11	2.92	2.81	2.73	2.67
9	.01	10.56	8.02	6.99	6.42	6.06	5.80
	.05	5.12	4.26	3.86	3.63	3.48	3.37
	.10	3.36	3.01	2.81	2.69	2.61	2.55
10	.01	10.05	7.56	6.55	6.00	5.64	5.39
	.05	4.97	4.10	3.71	3.48	3.33	3.22
	.10	3.29	2.93	2.73	2.61	2.52	2.46
11	.01	9.65	7.21	6.22	5.67	5.32	5.07
	.05	4.85	3.98	3.59	3.36	3.20	3.10
	.10	3.23	2.86	2.66	2.54	2.45	2.39
12	.01	9.33	6.93	5.95	5.41	5.07	4.82
	.05	4.75	3.89	3.49	3.26	3.11	3.00
	.10	3.18	2.81	2.61	2.48	2.40	2.33
13	.01	9.07	6.70	5.74	5.21	4.86	4.62
	.05	4.67	3.81	3.41	3.18	3.03	2.92
	.10	3.14	2.76	2.56	2.43	2.35	2.28
14	.01	8.86	6.52	5.56	5.04	4.70	4.46
	.05	4.60	3.74	3.34	3.11	2.96	2.85
	.10	3.10	2.73	2.52	2.40	2.31	2.24
15	.01	8.68	6.36	5.42	4.89	4.56	4.32
	.05	4.54	3.68	3.29	3.06	2.90	2.79
	.10	3.07	2.70	2.49	2.36	2.27	2.21
16	.01	8.53	6.23	5.29	4.77	4.44	4.20
	.05	4.49	3.63	3.24	3.01	2.85	2.74
	.10	3.05	2.67	2.46	2.33	2.24	2.18
17	.01	8.40	6.11	5.19	4.67	4.34	4.10
	.05	4.45	3.59	3.20	2.97	2.81	2.70
	.10	3.03	2.65	2.44	2.31	2.22	2.15
18	.01	8.29	6.01	5.09	4.58	4.25	4.02
	.05	4.41	3.56	3.16	2.93	2.77	2.66
	.10	3.01	2.62	2.42	2.29	2.20	2.13
19	.01	8.19	5.93	5.01	4.50	4.17	3.94
	.05	4.38	3.52	3.13	2.90	2.74	2.63
	.10	2.99	2.61	2.40	2.27	2.18	2.11
20	.01	8.10	5.85	4.94	4.43	4.10	3.87
	.05	4.35	3.49	3.10	2.87	2.71	2.60
	.10	2.98	2.59	2.38	2.25	2.16	2.09
21	.01	8.02	5.78	4.88	4.37	4.04	3.81
	.05	4.33	3.47	3.07	2.84	2.69	2.57
	.10	2.96	2.58	2.37	2.23	2.14	2.08

(continued)

Table C: Continued

Denominator *df*	Significance Level	1	2	3	4	5	6
		Numerator Degrees of Freedom					
22	.01	7.95	5.72	4.82	4.31	3.99	3.76
	.05	4.30	3.44	3.05	2.82	2.66	2.55
	.10	2.95	2.56	2.35	2.22	2.13	2.06
23	.01	7.88	5.66	4.77	4.26	3.94	3.71
	.05	4.28	3.42	3.03	2.80	2.64	2.53
	.10	2.94	2.55	2.34	2.21	2.12	2.05
24	.01	7.82	5.61	4.72	4.22	3.90	3.67
	.05	4.26	3.40	3.01	2.78	2.62	2.51
	.10	2.93	2.54	2.33	2.20	2.10	2.04
25	.01	7.77	5.57	4.68	4.18	3.86	3.63
	.05	4.24	3.39	2.99	2.76	2.60	2.49
	.10	2.92	2.53	2.32	2.19	2.09	2.03
26	.01	7.72	5.53	4.64	4.14	3.82	3.59
	.05	4.23	3.37	2.98	2.74	2.59	2.48
	.10	2.91	2.52	2.31	2.18	2.08	2.01
27	.01	7.68	5.49	4.60	4.11	3.79	3.56
	.05	4.21	3.36	2.96	2.73	2.57	2.46
	.10	2.90	2.51	2.30	2.17	2.07	2.01
28	.01	7.64	5.45	4.57	4.08	3.75	3.53
	.05	4.20	3.34	2.95	2.72	2.56	2.45
	.10	2.89	2.50	2.29	2.16	2.07	2.00
29	.01	7.60	5.42	4.54	4.05	3.73	3.50
	.05	4.18	3.33	2.94	2.70	2.55	2.43
	.10	2.89	2.50	2.28	2.15	2.06	1.99
30	.01	7.56	5.39	4.51	4.02	3.70	3.47
	.05	4.17	3.32	2.92	2.69	2.53	2.42
	.10	2.88	2.49	2.28	2.14	2.05	1.98
35	.01	7.42	5.27	4.40	3.91	3.59	3.37
	.05	4.12	3.27	2.88	2.64	2.49	2.37
	.10	2.86	2.46	2.25	2.11	2.02	1.95
40	.01	7.32	5.18	4.31	3.83	3.51	3.29
	.05	4.09	3.23	2.84	2.61	2.45	2.34
	.10	2.84	2.44	2.23	2.09	2.00	1.93
45	.01	7.23	5.11	4.25	3.77	3.46	3.23
	.05	4.06	3.21	2.81	2.58	2.42	2.31
	.10	2.82	2.43	2.21	2.08	1.98	1.91
50	.01	7.17	5.06	4.20	3.72	3.41	3.19
	.05	4.04	3.18	2.79	2.56	2.40	2.29
	.10	2.81	2.41	2.20	2.06	1.97	1.90
55	.01	7.12	5.01	4.16	3.68	3.37	3.15
	.05	4.02	3.17	2.77	2.54	2.38	2.27
	.10	2.80	2.40	2.19	2.05	1.96	1.89

(continued)

Table C: Continued

Denominator *df*	Significance Level	Numerator Degrees of Freedom					
		1	2	3	4	5	6
60	.01	7.08	4.98	4.13	3.65	3.34	3.12
	.05	4.00	3.15	2.76	2.53	2.37	2.26
	.10	2.79	2.39	2.18	2.04	1.95	1.88
65	.01	7.04	4.95	4.10	3.62	3.31	3.09
	.05	3.99	3.14	2.75	2.51	2.36	2.24
	.10	2.79	2.39	2.17	2.03	1.94	1.87
70	.01	7.01	4.92	4.08	3.60	3.29	3.07
	.05	3.98	3.13	2.74	2.50	2.35	2.23
	.10	2.78	2.38	2.16	2.03	1.93	1.86
75	.01	6.99	4.90	4.06	3.58	3.27	3.05
	.05	3.97	3.12	2.73	2.49	2.34	2.22
	.10	2.77	2.38	2.16	2.02	1.93	1.86
80	.01	6.96	4.88	4.04	3.56	3.26	3.04
	.05	3.96	3.11	2.72	2.49	2.33	2.22
	.10	2.77	2.37	2.15	2.02	1.92	1.85
85	.01	6.94	4.86	4.02	3.55	3.24	3.02
	.05	3.95	3.10	2.71	2.48	2.32	2.21
	.10	2.77	2.37	2.15	2.01	1.92	1.85
90	.01	6.93	4.85	4.01	3.54	3.23	3.01
	.05	3.95	3.10	2.71	2.47	2.32	2.20
	.10	2.76	2.36	2.15	2.01	1.91	1.84
95	.01	6.91	4.84	4.00	3.52	3.22	3.00
	.05	3.94	3.09	2.70	2.47	2.31	2.20
	.10	2.76	2.36	2.14	2.01	1.91	1.84
100	.01	6.90	4.82	3.98	3.51	3.21	2.99
	.05	3.94	3.09	2.70	2.46	2.31	2.19
	.10	2.76	2.36	2.14	2.00	1.91	1.83
∞	.01	6.64	4.61	3.78	3.32	3.02	2.80
	.05	3.84	3.00	2.61	2.37	2.22	2.10
	.10	2.71	2.30	2.08	1.95	1.85	1.78

APPENDIX D

Chi Square Distribution: Critical Values of χ^2 (Chi Squared) Distribution: Critical Values of χ^2

Table D: Cutoff Scores for the Chi-Square Distribution

df	Significance Level		
	.10	.05	.01
1	2.706	3.841	6.635
2	4.605	5.992	9.211
3	6.252	7.815	11.345
4	7.780	9.488	13.277
5	9.237	11.071	15.087
6	10.645	12.592	16.812
7	12.017	14.067	18.475
8	13.362	15.507	20.090
9	14.684	16.919	21.666
10	15.987	18.307	23.209

APPENDIX E

Advanced Statistics to Be Aware of

This book is designed as an introduction to basic statistics for an undergraduate audience. If you master the materials from this book, you should have a strong foundation for understanding the basics of the statistical processes used in the behavioral sciences. You should understand why statistics are used to help support ideas and theories along with the basics of both descriptive and inferential statistics. You should understand the differences between *statistical significance* and *effect size*—and you should have a strong understanding of how many of the basic statistical processes (e.g., the between-groups t-test) operate. This book is meant to be a strong and clear introduction to the basics of the statistics used by modern behavioral and social scientists.

This said, this book was not intended to introduce students to relatively advanced statistics. While many of the statistics presented in this book are used by real researchers in the field, modern scientists who use statistics often use a variety of advanced statistics as well—many such statistics are not covered in this book. However, we have two pieces of good news on that front. First, when you go to graduate school, you will likely get to learn all about the details of lots of advanced statistics! Secondly, in this appendix, we present many of the advanced statistics that you're likely to run into in reading primary scientific literature in the behavioral sciences. Here, we present these statistics at a summary level, so that you can have a basic understanding of what these statistical procedures are and what kinds of questions they seek to address.

ADVANCED FORMS OF ANOVA

The ANOVA is a very common form of statistical process. In this book, we learned the basic idea of ANOVA—comparing some estimate of variance due to some effect with some index of "error variance." The one-way ANOVA introduced in chapter 12 provides a backbone for understanding this statistic in general. However, depending on your research design, there are several variants of ANOVA that are implemented by researchers.

FACTORIAL ANOVA

The factorial ANOVA is used when multiple categorical independent variables are included in a study concurrently—and one continuous dependent variable is employed. For instance, you might want to see if both region of upbringing (the East Coast versus the West Coast) and gender (Male or Female) affect attitudes about alternative fashions (with the dependent variable being how positively people rate various alternative fashions on some continuous scale). Here, with a factorial ANOVA, we can examine the effect of each independent variable (do males and females differ from one another; do East versus West Coasters differ from one another?) and we can also examine the interaction between these variables. For instance, perhaps being from the East versus West Coast affects attitudes about alternative fashions differently for males and females. Perhaps everyone on the West Coast has a positive attitude (generally) about alternative fashions, while only females on the East Coast do. Such a different pattern across levels of an independent variable would be an *interaction*—and the factorial ANOVA allows for an examination of such interactions. So with a factorial ANOVA, you can see the effects of specific independent variables (i.e., *main effects*) while you can also see the effects of interactions between these variables.

WITHIN-GROUP ANOVA

The within-group ANOVA is comparable to a within-group t-test, but it may include more than two variables. Recall that the within-group t-test seeks to determine if two continuous variables collected from the same sample are significantly different from one another. With a within-group ANOVA, you apply the same reasoning—but you can examine as many variables as you'd like. For instance, suppose that you wanted to see if people's moods vary after four distinct dietary interventions. In this study, you have people's moods (on a continuous measure, with higher scores meaning a more positive mood) measured on four occasions. On one occasion, you measure them at baseline, before the study starts. You then have them spend a month on the Atkins diet, a month on the Paleolithic diet, and a month on a vegan diet, measuring their mood at the end of each month. In this study, you would seek to determine whether the means for the moods at these four times differed significantly. This design would allow for a within-group ANOVA.

MIXED ANOVA

On some occasions, you have a between-group variable and a within-group variable. For such a situation, you would conduct a *mixed ANOVA*. This kind of analysis examines the effect of each of the between-groups variables (or factors) and the within-group variable (or factor), along with possible interactions between them. Suppose, for instance, that you wanted to see if males and females (between-groups factor) differed in terms of how much they liked movies—but you also had all participants rate both romance and action movies (within-group factor). Here, you could see the overall effects of each factor on liking movies (do males rate overall liking of the movies higher than females, for instance)—and you can examine the overall effect of the kind of movie, as well as the interaction (does the kind of movie one likes depend on his or her gender?). Mixed ANOVAs allow you to examine main effects of between-groups and within-group variables concurrently—and they let you examine the interaction between them as well.

MANOVA

The "M" in MANOVA stands for "Multiple Dependent Variables." So if you're conducting an ANOVA but you have more than one dependent variable you're interested in examining, this statistic is for you. Suppose, for instance, that you are interested in whether being a member of the baseball team versus the swim team versus the football team has effects on academic and emotional outcomes. You sample participants from each of these three groups and measure (a) their GPA and (b) their emotional state (using some continuous mood scale). Here, you have two dependent variables. The MANOVA allows you to examine the effects of the independent variable (sports team membership) on both dependent variables simultaneously.

As with most statistical processes, things can get even more complex very quickly. With a MANOVA (as with most forms of ANOVA), you can add other variables. You can add more between-groups independent variables. You can add within-group variables. You can add more dependent variables. You can add one or more *covariates* (which are variables that you think covary with the dependent variable and that you'd like to control for in your analysis).

As you see, it doesn't take much to come up with highly complex statistical designs. For this reason, we urge you to keep in mind the basics of statistics delineated in this book—and when thinking about advanced statistics, you may want to ask yourself if the research questions at hand are best addressed by advanced versus more basic statistics. All things equal, in life, simplicity is not a bad way to go (complexity tends to emerge anyway!).

MULTIPLE AND HIERARCHICAL REGRESSION

In our chapter on regression, we examine its simplest form—bivariate regression, in which you seek to determine if one predictor variable is significantly predictive of scores on one dependent variable. In advanced statistics, we often run into *multiple regression*—in which we seek to determine if a set of predictor variables is predictive of some dependent variable. For instance, if you're trying to predict success in college, you may be interested in whether high school GPA, SAT scores, and number of extracurricular activities predict college GPA. With multiple regression, you can ask to see if this set of predictor variables is significantly predictive of college GPA (with a statistic called R^2) or you can ask if each specific predictor variable is significantly predictive of the dependent variable (with a statistic called β, the same statistic we ran into in our chapter on bivariate regression).

A variant of the multiple regression analysis is the *hierarchical regression* analysis. In this analysis, you look to see if some predictor variable is significantly predictive of some dependent variable after having controlled for scores on some set of other predictor variables. You may be interested, for instance, in whether the number of extracurricular activities in high school is significantly predictive of college GPA above and beyond high school GPA and SAT scores. Sure, you figure that these academically oriented predictor variables have some predictive utility, but you're trying to see if this extracurricular variable increases our ability to predict college GPA, beyond what's predicted by these other two variables. In such a case, you'd use hierarchical regression, putting different clusters of predictor variables on different *steps*. The first step would, in this case, include high school GPA and SAT scores. Once you had the analysis figure out how much these variables accounted for in terms of variability in college GPA, you would then be able to control for these effects to see, above and beyond, how much variability in college GPA is accounted for by participation in extracurricular activities in high school.

STRUCTURAL EQUATION MODELING

Structural Equation Modeling (SEM)—also often referred to as *path analysis*—is very similar to multiple regression. However, SEM allows you to observe the relationships between multiple variables in one shot in order to examine bidirectional influence of variables. So with SEM, instead of just looking to see if high school GPA, SAT scores, and extracurricular activities predict college GPA, you'd be able to see how each of these variables interrelates to one another—and you could make an assessment on whether the *paths* between variables are significant and are likely *causal*. Thus, you could see, for instance, if high school GPA is not only significantly related to college GPA, but the SEM allows you to make an inference as to whether high school GPA likely is a *cause* of one's college GPA. With SEM, researchers typically produce *path diagrams* that place all the different variables in the model in two-dimensional space and include arrows that show which variables are significantly related to which other variables and which variables (or sets of variables) are likely causally related to other variables. Along the way, an SEM typically presents a Chi Square or similar statistic speaking to the overall *fit* of the model, letting the reader know if the overall model that demarcates which variables are related to which other variables—and how they are related—is a significantly effective way of describing the raw data (or if the model is really no better than chance at describing the relationships among the variables).

NON-PARAMETRIC STATISTICS

This book is heavily biased toward "parametric tests," which include statistics on continuous variables. There are, however, instances in which you have non-continuous variables. For example, you may be interested in the relationship between high school rank and college rank. In such a situation, you've got two ordinal variables on your hands—you cannot (appropriately) compute a standard correlation (also referred to as the Pearson correlation). In this case, you have *non-parametric data* (due to non-continuous variables), so you need to conduct analyses designed for such situations. There are various non-parametric tests out there. To correlate two ordinal variables, you'd use something called *Spearman's Rho* statistic. Other non-parametric tests exist as well. In the modern behavioral sciences, such tests are typically strayed from—as good researchers usually make sure to utilize continuous variables—which allow you to use more powerful parametric statistics.

FACTOR ANALYSIS

Factor analysis is a statistical process for essentially reducing data. Suppose that you have created a bunch of questions designed to measure intelligence. Some of your questions are straight-out vocabulary questions (Define *hyper-vigilant*), some are math questions (What is the square root of 81?), some are word questions (What is the maximum number of clowns in a clown car if everyone is to buckle in and the clown car has four rows, each with two seats?), and so forth. Suppose you come up with 100 questions in total, and administer this test to all 8,000 students at your college (great way to make friends, by the way!).

Once you receive your data, the best analysis to perform right off the bat would likely be the factor analysis. This analysis essentially correlates every variable with each and every other variable. It then determines statistical clusters—it asks if there are some groups of items with scores that tend to be intercorrelated with one another (and not-so-correlated with other items). The analysis will compute a *factor loading table*, which will tell you how intercorrelated all variables are. And it will *extract factors*—which is a way of providing clusters of items that statistically hang together. It also gives you a sense of how strong each factor is in producing an *eigenvalue*, which is a statistic that tells you how robust a factor is. If a factor has a large eigenvalue, this means that not only does it have a bunch of items that are intercorrelated, but the nature of the intercorrelation is pretty high.

When you have a factor with a high eigenvalue, it is useful to interpret the items that *load onto* that factor. This simply means looking at the content of the variables that are strongly related to that factor and seeing if they share a common theme or set of content. If, for instance, all the math items were strongly intercorrelated and comprised "factor 1" with

Table E.1: Brief Summary of the Details of Several Advanced Statistics

Advanced Statistic	Basic Summary	When to Use It
Factorial ANOVA	An ANOVA that includes more than one independent variable at a time	When you are interested in the effects of more than one categorical independent variable on some continuous dependent variable
Within-Group ANOVA	An ANOVA that examines if means from multiple continuous variables collected from same participants differ significantly from one another.	When you want to compare multiple means on continuous variables from the same participants in the same data set
Mixed ANOVA	An ANOVA that includes at least one between-groups variable and one within-group variable concurrently	When you are interested in the concurrent effects of within-group and between-groups variables on some continuous dependent variable
MANOVA	An ANOVA that includes at least one independent variable and multiple dependent variables	When you want to see whether a categorical independent variable (or set of independent variables) has significant effects on multiple continuous dependent variables

(continued)

Table E1: Continued

Advanced Statistic	Basic Summary	When to Use It
Multiple Regression	A regression with one continuous dependent variable and multiple continuous predictor variables	When you are interested in whether a set of predictor variables significantly predicts scores on some continuous dependent variable
Hierarchical Regression	A regression in which you separate analyses out by steps—examining the effects of certain variables (in terms of predicting the dependent variable) on earlier steps and putting other variables on subsequent steps	When you want to see if some variables (that are put on later steps) predict scores on a continuous dependent variable, controlling for the possibly significant effects of other variables that may also relate to the same dependent variable
Structural Equation Modeling	A regression-like analysis that examines the interrelationship among multiple variables concurrently—allowing for an examining of not only whether relationships between variables are significant, but also which variables likely cause changes in which other variables	When you have multiple variables included in a large model and are interested in (a) the utility of the model as well as (b) the nature of the interrelationships among the variables on the model
Non-Parametric Tests	A variety of statistics used when you are not using continuous variables (such as Spearman's rho, which is a correlation on two ordinal variables).	When your variables do not lend themselves to the use of standard, parametric tests
Factor Analysis	A statistic used to examine how interrelated several variables are to one another. This statistic sees if several variables form into clusters (or factors) of highly interrelated variables that may share common meaning or content	When you have many continuous variables and are interested in whether there are some common themes (or superordinate variables) that characterize the data

an eigenvalue of 5.4 (as a rule of thumb, eigenvalues greater than 1.0 are considered worth examining), you'd probably say that the analysis uncovered a *math factor* as a distinct ability measured by your test.

As with all advanced statistics, factor analysis comes in many flavors. There are variants of *exploratory factor analysis*, which examine the data with no guidance from the researcher—other than to "see what items are related to what other items"—and there are variants of *confirmatory factor analysis*, which proceed based on an a priori set of rules (such as "Assume that there are 3 specific factors, and assume that these items load onto Factor 1, these items load onto Factor 2, and these load onto Factor 3. How good are these assumptions? Do they match the data? Can the analysis confirm this a priori conceptualization of the data that the researcher has?").

SUMMARY

This book presents the basic ideas underlying statistics in the behavioral sciences in detail—and it covers the nuts and bolts associated with how to compute and interpret the primary fundamental statistics that are used in our field. Beyond the statistics presented in this book, there are several forms of advanced statistics that are used by researchers in the behavior sciences. This section gives a taste of some of the more commonly used advanced statistics, to give the reader, who is on a path of lifelong learning (as we all are) an idea of what kinds of statistics are on the horizon!

KEY TERMS

Confirmatory factor analysis: Factor analysis that proceeds based on an a priori set of rules.
Covariates: Variables that need to be controlled for in analysis, as they may covary with the dependent variable.
Eigenvalue: Statistic that tells you how robust a factor is.
Exploratory factor analysis. Means of examining data with no guidance from the researcher.
Factor analysis: A statistic to examine how interrelated several variables are to one another. This statistic sees if several variables form into clusters (or factors) of highly interrelated variables that may share common meaning or content. Factor analysis is used when you have many continuous variables and are interested in whether there are some common themes (or superordinate variables) that characterize the data.
Factorial ANOVA: An ANOVA that includes more than one independent variable at a time, used when you are interested in the effects of more than one categorical independent variable on some continuous dependent variable.
Factor extraction: A means of revealing clusters of items that statistically hang together in factor analysis.
Factor loading table: Table produced in factor analysis that tells you how intercorrelated all variables are.
Hierarchical regression: A regression in which you separate analyses out by steps—examining the effects of certain variables (in terms of predicting the dependent variable) on earlier steps and putting other variables on subsequent steps. Hierarchical regression is used when you want to see if some variables (that are put on later steps) predict scores on a continuous dependent variable, controlling for the possibly significant effects of other variables that may also relate to the same dependent variable.
Interaction: When the combination of variables produces an effect not produced by the variables independently.
Main effect: The effect of specific independent, individual variables.
MANOVA: An ANOVA that includes at least one independent variable and multiple dependent variables, used when you want to see if a categorical independent variable (or set of independent variables) has significant effects on multiple continuous dependent variables.
Mixed ANOVA: An ANOVA that includes at least one between-groups variable and one within-group variable concurrently, used when you are interested in the concurrent effects of within-group and between-groups variables on some continuous dependent variable.

Multiple regression: A regression with one continuous dependent variable and multiple continuous predictor variables, used when you are interested in whether a set of predictor variables significantly predicts scores on some continuous dependent variable.

Non-parametric data: Data with non-continuous variables.

Non-parametric tests: A variety of statistics used when you are not employing continuous variables (such as Spearman's rho, which is a correlation on two ordinal variables), and therefore, your variables do not lend themselves to the use of standard, parametric tests.

Path analysis: Another name for structural equation modeling.

Path diagram: Diagram typically produced in structural equation modeling, which places all variables in the model in two-dimensional space and includes arrows that show which variables are significantly related to which other variables and which variables or sets of variables are likely causally related to other variables.

Parametric tests: Statistics used with continuous variables.

Spearman's rho: Statistic used to correlate two ordinal variables.

Structural equation modeling: (Also known as path analysis) A regression-like analysis that examines the interrelationship among multiple variables concurrently—allowing for an examining of not only whether relationships between variables are significant, but also which variables likely cause changes in which other variables. Structural equation modeling is used when you have multiple variables included in a large model and are interested in (a) the utility of the model as well as (b) the nature of the interrelationships among the variables on the model.

Within-Group ANOVA: An ANOVA that examines whether means from multiple continuous variables collected from same participants differ significantly from one another, used when you want to compare multiple means on continuous variables from the same participants in the same data set.

APPENDIX F

Using SPSS

SPSS has become the primary software package used in the social and behavioral sciences. This software is up to V .20 (as of 2013). This appendix includes several SPSS lab assignments, each designed to help you understand how to use important elements of SPSS. SPSS is very powerful and you'll see that what's included in this appendix is the tip of the iceberg. That said, the activities included in this section provide a clear and helpful introduction to the basics of SPSS.

Note that in many cases, the activities point you toward certain sample data sets. These data sets can be accessed from http://faculty.newpaltz.edu/glenngeher/index.php/glenns-spss-lab-pages/, and are labeled with the same names used in this appendix.

Note that the following tasks are presented as activities, numbered 1–10. Each activity is designed to be fully autonomous—so you can simply go through each activity (or as much of it as you'd like) to learn the process being presented.

ACTIVITY 1: SPSS DATA ENTRY LAB

Goal: This activity is designed to help you become familiar with the basics of dealing with data entry using SPSS.

SPSS DATA ENTRY BASICS

- Start by clicking the SPSS icon on the desktop
- In the opening window, you are asked, "What would you like to do?"
- "Open an existing file" is checked. Click "Cancel."
- The DATA VIEW window will pop up. There are 2 ways of viewing the spreadsheet:

1. DATA VIEW, which is used for working with data after variables have been entered already.
2. VARIABLE VIEW, which is used for entering the names and characteristics of all variables that will be included.

- Click on the VARIABLE VIEW tab that is located at the bottom of the screen.
- When in VARIABLE VIEW, the rows correspond to variables and the columns correspond to characteristics of variables. These characteristics include:
  - Name—this is where you create names for your variables (Default allows up to 8 characters)
  - Type—this refers to different types of variables such as text, numeric, string, and so on. (For your purposes, you will *always* use NUMERIC)
  - Width—this is the number of characters the variable name column allows; default is 8.
  - Decimals—the number of decimal places you will use.
  - Label—this is where you define your variable names.
  - Values—this is where you give numerical values to categorical data (e.g., 0 = males, 1 = females).
- Typically, the default settings for the different characteristics of each variable work fine—these settings assume you have a numerical variable that is continuous in nature. Usually, this is true, but sometimes you want to change the settings for a particular characteristic.
  - To change default settings for a particular characteristic of a variable, put the cursor in the rightmost side of the appropriate box and double click. For example, if you have the categorical variable of "gender," you would want to change the settings in the "value" column for this variable.
  - When in the row corresponding to "gender," click on the rightmost side of the box corresponding to the "value" column. A "value label" dialog box will appear. Choose what label you want to represent each number (e.g., 0 may represent male, 1 may represent female).
  - *IMPORTANT*—"Add" each label before hitting OK!
- You must define your variables by creating names for each. For each variable that will exist in the research, you must type in a name for that variable in a row in the VARIABLE VIEW mode by clicking on "Edit," then "Insert Variable," then typing a name for your variable.
- While entering the variable names, make a "data map," using one of your blank surveys.
- This "data map" is a hard (i.e., paper) copy of one of your surveys that has notes corresponding to how the variables in the survey are named and coded in your DATA VIEW part of the.sav file (a.sav file is a data file in SPSS).
- After all variables are named, switch to DATA VIEW by clicking the DATA VIEW tab on the bottom of the screen.
- In DATA VIEW, rows always represent cases (or participants) and columns always represent variables. Place the cursor on row 1, column 1 and click. Enter the data in DATA VIEW in the order you want.
- After all data are entered, save your file.
- Click File→Save. The "Save Data As" dialog box will appear. Name your file something meaningful to you (noting that it will have a.sav extension).

ACTIVITY 2: WORKING WITH SPSS SYNTAX FILES

Goal: Use SPSS syntax files to recode reverse-scored items, to compute new composite variables, and to compute the mean and standard deviation of these new composite variables. Syntax files are files that include code used to compute statistics and to work with variables in SPSS. It is helpful to create syntax files and to save them for revisiting data. The current activity uses syntax files in the context of creating variables from multiple items (or multiple "little" variables).

We often need to create composite variables that include our individual variables to create scales. Before we do this part, we need to **recode** any reverse-scored items to make sure that all items in the composite variables are coded in the same direction. Next, we need to **compute** the new, composite variables. Finally, it is good to compute the mean and standard deviation for newly created composite variables.

SYNTAX FILES, RECODING VARIABLES, COMPUTE STATEMENTS, OUT FILES, AND THE COMPUTATION OF VARIABLES IN SPSS

- Opening the file
  - For this activity, you can refer to a data set related to jealousy that is found at this site: http://faculty.newpaltz.edu/glenngeher/index.php/glenns-spss-lab-pages/. It can be opened with SPSS.

RECODING VARIABLES

When we have multiple items in a psychological measure, several items are often worded in the opposite direction. To take this fact into account when we score our variables, we need to "recode" such items to make them in line with the other items. The best way to do this recoding is to use a SYNTAX (.sps) file.

In the example below, you will find syntax file statements made to recode the 'reverse-scored' items that exist in the jealousy data:

- To reproduce this file in SPSS, click on "File," then "New," then "Syntax." A blank page will appear.
- Type or paste in the commands from the example. In a syntax file, you use an asterisk (*) to indicate a comment to yourself (not something read by the computer).
- Save this file when you are done typing the recode statements.
- To recode variables, simply highlight the commands you want to execute—then go to the "run" command and click "selection."

COMPUTING NEW VARIABLES

- After you have recoded all reverse-scored items, you need to compute the composite variables. Create a new syntax file *or* add to your existing syntax file. See the example for this data set. Note how the syntax for creating these compute statements works.
- After you type all these commands in (it will be good for you!), run the compute statements. Once you have done this part, notice that you now have newly created variables in your data file. These variables are your composite variables.

OUTPUT FILES

- To get a sense of completing one simple SPSS command that produces an outfile, choose any of the composite variables you created.
- When in the Data file, click "Analyze," then "Descriptive Statistics," then "Descriptives."
- Now choose the variable you want to examine.
- The Descriptives command will give you the mean, standard deviation, N, and range of the variable of interest.
- After you choose your variable, hit "Paste" (not OK). After you hit "Paste," this command will go into an existing syntax file (at the bottom). You can then run the command from this syntax file by highlighting it and clicking "Run," then "Selection."

HAND IN

- A soft copy (e.g., emailed copy of disk) including the following files:
  - The modified data file (.sav) (with the composite variables computed)
  - Syntax file(s) (.sps) with recode, compute, and descriptives commands.
  - An Output file (.spv) with results from the descriptives command.

EXAMPLE: HOW TO RECODE ITEMS FOR THE JEALOUSY DATA AND COMPUTE COMPOSITE VARIABLES

- **Recode**: As an example of how to recode items in SPSS, we will recode the reverse-scored items from the mood scale across times A, B, and C
  - These items are all individual mood items (with the full scale found here: http://faculty.newpaltz.edu/glenngeher/index.php/glenns-spss-lab-pages/)
  - Type the following into your syntax file:
    RECODE
        mood_a1 mood_a7 mood_a12 mood_a17 mood_a21 mood_a24
        mood_b1 mood_b7 mood_b12 mood_b17 mood_b21 mood_b24
        mood_c1 mood_c7 mood_c12 mood_c17 mood_c21 mood_c24

(1=5) (2=4) (3=3) (4=2) (5=1).
   EXECUTE.
- **Compute** composite variables for jealousy data.
  - Type the following into your syntax file:
    * Computing variables for the jealousy data.
    * Computing composite variables for Mood Scales (higher scores mean more psychological discomfort)
    * Computing moodtot1

COMPUTE
moodtot1 = sum(mood_a1, mood_a2, mood_a3, mood_a4, mood_a5, mood_a6, mood_a7, mood_a8, mood_a9, mood_a10, mood_a11, mood_a12, mood_a13, mood_a14, mood_a15, mood_a16, mood_a17, mood_a18, mood_a19, mood_a20, mood_a21, mood_a22, mood_a23, mood_a24) .
Execute.
* Computing moodtot2

COMPUTE
moodtot2 = sum(mood_b1, mood_b2, mood_b3, mood_b4, mood_b5, mood_b6, mood_b7, mood_b8, mood_b9, mood_b10, mood_b11, mood_b12, mood_b13, mood_b14, mood_b15, mood_b16, mood_b17, mood_b18, mood_b19, mood_b20, mood_b21, mood_b22, mood_ b23, mood_b24) .
Execute.
* Computing moodtot3

COMPUTE
moodtot3 = sum(mood_c1, mood_c2, mood_c3, mood_c4, mood_c5, mood_c6, mood_c7, mood_c8, mood_c9, mood_c10, mood_c11, mood_c12, mood_c13, mood_c14, mood_c15, mood_c16, mood_c17, mood_c18, mood_c19, mood_c20, mood_c21, mood_c22, mood_c23, mood_c24) .
Execute.

ACTIVITY 3: DESCRIPTIVE STATISTICS

Goal: Learn to compute basic descriptive statistics, such as frequencies, range, mean, standard deviation, and number of cases, as well as to create histograms with SPSS.

SPSS makes computing basic descriptive statistics easy. The following activity helps you learn this process in a step-by-step manner.

FREQUENCIES, DESCRIPTIVES, AND HISTOGRAMS

In working with data, a typical first step is to compute frequencies for all categorical variables and to compute descriptive statistics for all continuous variables. Also, creating histograms for continuous variables is a nice first step. In this first section, where you're learning these skills, it might be helpful if you choose specific variables from your own data set to analyze. Now let's learn how to do all this fun stuff.

The "Frequencies" command in SPSS lets you know how common different values of a categorical variable are in the sample. For instance, you can use this command to determine how many males and females (in a variable, perhaps, called "gender") were included in your sample. To compute frequencies, do the following:

- Choose a categorical variable.
- When in data view, click on "Analyze," then "Descriptive Statistics," then "Frequencies."
- Choose the appropriate categorical variable to put in your variables list.
- Then click "Paste" to put the command in a syntax file.
- Run that part of the syntax file.

The "Descriptives" command provides information about continuous variables. For instance, you can obtain information about the range of scores, the mean of the variable, the standard deviation, and the number of cases. To compute this command, do as follows:

- Choose a continuous variable.
- When in data view, click on "Analyze," then "Descriptive Statistics," then "Descriptives."
- Choose the appropriate continuous variable to put in your variables list.
- Click "Paste" to put the command in a syntax file.
- Run that part of the syntax file.

The "Histogram" command provides a graph of how common each score is for a continuous variable. This graph can, for one, give you a sense of whether your variable is normally distributed. To run this command, do as follows:

- Choose a continuous variable.
- When in data view, click on "Graphs," then "Legacy Dialogs," then "Histogram."
- Choose the appropriate continuous variable to put in your variables list.
- Click "Paste" to put the command in a syntax file.
- Run that part of the syntax file.
- Look at your beautiful graph!

FREQUENCIES, DESCRIPTIVES, AND HISTOGRAMS FOR SAMPLE DATA

For this part, you need to collect data from the people in class on one continuous variable and one categorical variable. You will collect these data as a group (i.e., the whole class will agree on the variable to be measured). An example of the continuous variable could be height (in inches); an example of the categorical variable could be gender (male or female). Collect data from everyone in class. Next you will analyze these data and type up a brief lab report.

THE CONTINUOUS VARIABLE

For this variable, you will use SPSS to compute descriptive statistics. In your report, indicate the range, mean, standard deviation, and N for this variable.

Next, use SPSS to create a histogram for this variable. Briefly summarize this histogram and include the SPSS output (as an attachment) with both the summary of the descriptives and the histogram.

THE CATEGORICAL VARIABLE

For this variable, you will use SPSS to compute frequencies. Simply summarize the frequency of different values in your report. Also include the SPSS output for the frequencies command as an attachment. If you have anything interesting to say about these results, outline these points in your report.

HAND IN

- Your report summarizing (a) what variables were examined and (b) the results regarding these analyses.
- A printout of the syntax file(s) for all commands.
- A printout of the data file(s).
- A printout of the output file(s).

ACTIVITY 4: CORRELATIONS

Goal: Compute correlations with SPSS.

A primary analysis in any statistical toolbox is the correlation. Below is an activity designed to help you learn how to compute correlations with SPSS.

Generally, a *correlation* is an analysis computed to examine the relationship between two variables. The most common kind of correlation is the Pearson product correlation, which examines linear relationships between two continuous variables (e.g., years of education and income).

When SPSS computes a correlation, it ultimately provides two important statistics.

- First, it provides r, which is a *correlation coefficient*. This number varies between 1 and −1. Numbers near 1 indicate a strong positive correlation (e.g., the correlation between height and weight). Numbers near −1 indicate a strong negative correlation (e.g., the correlation between years of education and years of prison time served). Numbers near 0 indicate weak, negligible relationships (e.g., the correlation between SAT scores and number of rubber bands owned).
- Second, SPSS will provide you with a p value. This statistic refers to the probability that the obtained correlation (r) is due to chance alone. Traditionally, psychologists will say that a correlation is *significantly different from chance* if p is less than .05. Importantly, the p that

is provided is for a *two-tailed significance test*. This kind of test is for when you are looking for a relationship, but you have no hypothesis regarding the specific direction predicted. If you have a specific direction that is predicted for r ahead of time, then you are to divide the p value by 2. This new value is the p value for you.

Example: Suppose you hypothesize that outside temperature is negatively correlated with the number of students who attend class. To test this zany hypothesis, you measure (a) the temperature in degrees Fahrenheit and (b) the number of students who come to their favorite psychology class (Experimental Psychology). You collect these data over 5 days. Your data would look about like:

temp attend
30.00 25.00
80.00 3.00
50.00 15.00
25.00 25.00
75.00 7.00

To see if temperature and attendance are, indeed, negatively correlated, you would need to conduct a correlation, like so:

- Click on "Analyze" on toolbar
- Click on "Correlate"
- Click on "Bivariate"
- Variables would be "Attend" and "Temp"
- Click "Paste"
- Go to the.sps file and highlight the relevant commands
- Click on "Run"

SPSS will give you output that looks something like this:

Table F.1: SPSS Correlation Table Output

Correlations

		temp	attend
temp	Pearson Correlation	1	−.994**
	Sig. (2-tailed)		.001
	N	5	5
attend	Pearson Correlation	−.994**	1
	Sig. (2-tailed)	.001	
	N	5	5

**. Correlation is significant at the 0.01 level (2-tailed).

Notice that your prediction is clearly a one-tailed hypothesis. Thus, divide p (.001) by 2 to come up with .0005 (whoa!). This number refers to the probability that your correlation was due to chance alone. 5 out of 1,000 is pretty low odds!

Your report of the data would be similar to this:

"A strong and significant negative correlation was observed between temperature and attendance ($r(5) = -.99$, $p < .05$). As the temperature became warmer, students were less likely to attend class."

Note that the number "5" in the above parenthetical expression refers to the N, or the number of cases on which the correlation is based.

ASSIGNMENT

- **Part 1: Correlations Among Variables in the Jealousy Data**
  - Find two composite variables in the jealousy data that you think may be related to one another. Compute the correlation between the two variables. Report the correlation and briefly discuss what the result implies about the relationship between these two variables conceptually.
- **Hand in:**
  - A one-page summary including the hypothesis, a brief description of the variables of interest, a report of the correlation, and implications regarding the nature of the relationship between these two variables.
  - A printout of the.spv (output file).
- **Part 2: Correlations Among Variables in a Naturalistic College Setting**

For this part of the assignment, you will be collecting data by observing college students in a naturalistic setting. For example, you may want to collect data from people walking around in your environment (think college courtyard, main street, etc.)

Before you collect data, think of two variables that you would be able to measure that would lend themselves to a correlational analysis. For instance, you could go to the library and measure the correlation between the amount of time it takes someone to walk down a particular hallway and the number of books a person is carrying (fascinating data!).

- Get in groups of 3 or 4.
- Once you have come up with two variables that you could measure in such a setting, collect data from no less than 10 people (unobtrusively). Next, enter the data into an SPSS.sav file. Compute the correlation between the two variables. Report the correlation and briefly discuss what the result implies about the relationship between these two variables conceptually.
- **Hand in:**
  - A one-page summary including the hypothesis, a brief description of the variables of interest, a report of the correlation, and implications regarding the nature of the relationship between these two variables.
  - A printout of the.spv (output file).

ACTIVITY 5: REGRESSION

Goal: Conduct Multiple Regression Analysis with SPSS

Multiple regression is a statistical procedure that elaborates on the correlation coefficient (r), which corresponds to the degree to which two continuous variables are related. Multiple regression, more specifically, pertains to the situation in which you are trying to predict scores on some continuous outcome variable from multiple continuous predictor variables.

Multiple Regression Analysis provides an assessment of

- (a) how well your set of predictor variables account for variability in the outcome variable,
- (b) whether the overall amount of variability accounted for in the outcome variable is significantly greater than would be expected by chance,
- (c) how much unique contribution each predictor variable makes toward explaining variability in the outcome variable, and
- (d) whether the amount of unique variability accounted for by one predictor variable is significantly greater than would be expected by chance.

General steps involved in conducting a multiple regression analysis include first examining the (zero-order; i.e., regular) intercorrelations among all variables and then conducting the multiple regression analysis. Consider the following example:

Peter and Paul are roommates. Peter is a health nut—in addition to eating well, he lifts at the gym several times a week, runs 30 miles each week, and goes on long hikes in the mountains several times a month. Peter believes that his exercise regimen helps keep him happy and that he would be miserable if he did not exercise.

Paul, on the other hand, is something of a sloth. He never exercises and claims that exercise is a futile and ridiculous endeavor. Further, Paul has a nasty drug problem. Paul believes that illegal drugs make him happy, and that he would be unhappy if he stopped taking them. One semester, Peter and Paul find themselves taking Research Methods together (with the same really cool professor!). They decide to settle their differences once and for all empirically. Consequently, they design a study to address how related exercise and drug use are to overall happiness in life.

To conduct this research, they find 20 regular college students. Each participant reports (a) how many hours/week he or she exercises, (b) how many hours/week he or she is "high" on illegal drugs, and (c) how happy he or she is (on a 1–10 scale). You'll find those data in the file "regress.sav."

After collecting these data, Peter and Paul first compute zero-order correlations to examine the general intercorrelations among these three variables.

To compute such correlations, do the following:

- Click on "Analyze" on toolbar
- Click on "Correlate"
- Click on "Bivariate"
- Variables would be "exercise," "drugs," and "happy"
- Click "Paste"

- Go to the.sps file and highlight the relevant commands
- Click on "Run"
- Run selection

Your syntax file will look about like so:

CORRELATIONS
/VARIABLES=exercise drugs happy
/PRINT=TWOTAIL NOSIG
/MISSING=PAIRWISE.

You will then obtain output that looks like the following:

Table F.2: SPSS Correlation Table Output

Correlations

		exercise	drugs	happy
exercise	Pearson Correlation	1	−.922**	.855**
	Sig. (2-tailed)		.000	.000
	N	20	20	20
Drugs	Pearson Correlation	−.922**	1	−.795**
	Sig. (2-tailed)	.000		.000
	N	20	20	20
happy	Pearson Correlation	.855**	−.795**	1
	Sig. (2-tailed)	.000	.000	
	N	20	20	20

**. Correlation is significant at the 0.01 level (2-tailed).

Next, to examine the relationships between exercise and drugs with happiness concurrently, Peter and Paul go ahead and conduct the multiple regression. Here's how:

- Click on "Analyze" on the tool bar
- Click on "Regression"
- Click on "Linear"
- For Dependent variable choose Happy
- For Independent variables choose Exercise and Drugs
- Click on "Statistics"
- Toggle on "Part and Partial Correlations"
- Click "Continue"
- Click "Paste"
- Go to the.sps file and highlight the relevant commands
- Click on "Run"
- Run selection

Your syntax file will look about like so:

```
REGRESSION
/MISSING LISTWISE
/STATISTICS COEFF OUTS R ANOVA ZPP
/CRITERIA=PIN(.05) POUT(.10)
/NOORIGIN
/DEPENDENT happy
/METHOD=ENTER exercise drugs.
```

Here's the output created by that syntax file:

Table F.3: SPSS Regression Table (R^2)

Model Summary

Model		R	R Square	Adjusted R Square	Std. Error of the Estimate
dimension	1	.855[a]	.731	.700	1.34978

a. Predictors: (Constant), drugs, exercise

Table F.4: SPSS Regression Table (Summary of Model)

Variables Entered/Removed[b]

Model		Variables Entered	Variables Removed	Method
dimension	1	drugs, exercise[a]	.	Enter

a. All requested variables entered

b. Dependent Variable: happy

Table F.5: SPSS Regression Output (ANOVA Examining Significant Effects)

ANOVA[b]

	Model	Sum of Squares	df	Mean Square	F	Sig.
1	Regression	84.228	2	42.114	23.115	.000[a]
	Residual	30.972	17	1.822		
	Total	115.200	19			

a. Predictors: (Constant), drugs, exercise

b. Dependent Variable: happy

Table F.6: SPSS Regression Output (Effects of Individual Predictors)

Coefficients[a]

Model		Unstandardized Coefficients		Standardized Coefficients			Correlations		
		B	Std. Error	Beta	T	Sig.	Zero-order	Partial	Part
1	(Constant)	1.884	2.077		.907	.377			
	exercise	.596	.238	.813	2.500	.023	.855	.518	.314
	drugs	−.035	.246	−.046	−.140	.890	−.795	−.034	−.018

a. Dependent Variable: happy

Well, that's it—Peter and Paul have conducted the analysis. Here's how they would write it up:

RESULTS

To address whether exercise and drug use are related to dispositional happiness, zero-order correlations among these three variables were computed. Exercise was positively related to happiness ($r(20) = .86$, $p < .05$) and negatively related to drug use ($r(20) = −.92$, $p < .05$). Further, drug use was negatively related to happiness ($r(20) = −.80$, $p < .05$). These correlations are summarized in Table F.7.

To examine the overall amount of variability in happiness explained by drug use and exercise, and to examine the unique amount of variability explained by both drug use and exercise on happiness, a multiple regression was next conducted. A significant amount of variability was accounted for by the set of exercise and drug use ($R^2 = .73$, $F(2, 17) = 23.12$, $p < .05$). Thus, approximately 73% of variability in happiness can be accounted for by information regarding participants' exercise and drug use habits. Next, semi-squared partial correlations were computed to address the unique amount of variability in happiness accounted for, separately, by exercise and drug use. This information is summarized in Table F.8. As can be seen in the table, exercise uniquely accounts for a significant amount of variability in happiness ($sr^2 = .10$, $p < .05$), whereas drug use does not account for a significant amount of variability in happiness ($sr^2 = .00$, ns). These results suggest that drug use has such a strong zero-order correlation with happiness because of its overlap with exercise (drug use and exercise are very strongly negatively correlated). After controlling for the overlapping variance between drug use and exercise, it seems

Table F.7: Zero-Order Correlations among Exercise, Drug Use, and Happiness

	Exercise	Drug Use	Happiness
Exercise		−	
Drug Use		−.92*	−
Happiness		.86*	−.80*

* $p < .05$

Table F.8: Multiple Regression Predicting Happiness from Drug Use and Exercise

	Criterion Variable: Happiness		
	b	B	sr^2
Predictor Variables			
Exercise	.60	.81	.10
Drug Use	−.00	−.05	.00
$R^2 = .73*$			

* $p < .05$

that exercise is strongly and significantly predictive of happiness while drug use is not. Primarily, drug use seems to be negatively correlated with exercise—a fact that in effect makes drug use negatively correlated with happiness as well.

DISCUSSION

The current research sheds light on the debate between Peter and Paul—more specifically, these data speak to the differential patterns of relationships between exercise and drug use with happiness. Clearly, exercise is positively related to happiness. This fact was manifest in both the zero-order correlations and the regression. Drug use is negatively related to both exercise and happiness. In addition, drug use did not account for a significant amount of variability in happiness largely due to its overlap with exercise (as these variables were very strongly intercorrelated). In the end, these data imply that you should do laps, do reps, and don't do drugs! That guidance counselor from South Park, Mr. Mackey, was right when he said "Drugs are bad!"

ASSIGNMENT

- Get into groups of 3 or 4
- Come up with a study that will allow for a multiple regression analysis. Be sure to have one clear outcome (i.e., criterion, dependent) variable and at least two predictor variables. It would be nice if your study had some clear, meaningful rationale underlying it. Further, be sure that your variables are capable of being measured on a college campus easily and ethically within one hour.
- Collect data from at least 16 people on campus.
- Enter the data into SPSS.
- Run both the zero-order correlation and multiple regression analyses (as done in this lab).
- **Hand in:**
  - Each student needs to *independently* write up a report summarizing
  - (a) what the study was about,
  - (b) how data were collected,
  - (c) what the results were, and
  - (d) what the results imply.

ACTIVITY 6: t-TESTS

Goal: Compute t-tests with SPSS.

There are basically two kinds of t-tests.

- The between-groups (or independent means) t-test is a statistical test designed to examine whether means from two different samples are significantly different from one another.
- The within-groups (i.e., paired samples) t-test is designed to examine if the means of scores on two different variables for the same participants are significantly different from one another.

Independent Means t-test (Use if you expect the average score on some variable to differ between two *different* groups of participants)

Example: Suppose you think that men should score higher on the Emotional Sensitivity Scale (ESS) than women.

You would have two variables: gender (a categorical independent variable with two levels: 1 = Female; 2 = Male) and total scores on the ESS for each participant (a continuous dependent variable).

Your data would look something like this:

Gender	ESS
1.00	3.00
1.00	2.00
1.00	7.00
1.00	3.00
1.00	5.00
2.00	7.00
2.00	9.00
2.00	9.00
2.00	10.00
2.00	3.00

To see if the males' scores are significantly higher than the females' scores, you would need to conduct an independent means t-test, like so:

- Click on "Analyze" on toolbar
- Click on "Compare Means"
- Click "Independent Samples t-test"
- Test variable is going to be the DV (ESS in this case)
- Grouping variable is going to be the IV (gender in this case)
- Next, click on "Define groups"
- For Group 1, type "1"; for group 2, type "2"
- Click on "Continue"
- Click "Paste"
- Go to the.sps file and highlight the relevant commands
- Click on run

Here's what you'll see in the syntax file that you create:
    Syntax file:

T-TEST GROUPS=gender(1 2)
/MISSING=ANALYSIS
/VARIABLES=ess
/CRITERIA=CI(.95).

Output file:

Table F.9: Between-Groups t-Test Results in SPSS

	Group Statistics				
	gender		N	Mean	Std. Deviation	Std. Error Mean
Ess	dimension1	1.00	5	4.0000	2.00000	.89443
		2.00	5	7.6000	2.79285	1.24900

INDEPENDENT SAMPLES TEST

Notice that your prediction is clearly a one-tailed hypothesis. Thus, divide p (.047) by 2 to come up with .0235 (yipes!). This number refers to the probability that your correlation was due to chance alone. Pretty low odds! As long as this p value is below .05, it is considered significant.

Table F.10:

		Levene's Test for Equality of Variances							t-test for Equality of Means	
									95% Confidence Interval of the Difference	
		F	Sig.	t	df	Sig. (2-tailed)	Mean Difference	Std. Error Difference	Lower	Upper
ess	Equal variances assumed	.361	.565	−2.343	8	.047	−3.60000	1.53623	−7.14255	−.05745
	Equal variances not assumed			−2.343	7.248	.050	−3.60000	1.53623	−7.20753	.00753

Here's how to report it:

Males scored significantly higher (M = 7.6, SD = 2.79) than females (M = 4.0, SD = 2.0; t(8) = −2.34, p < .05).

Note that the 8 in the parenthetical expression refers to the degrees of freedom term (above, df, in printout).

Dependent Means t-test (Use if you expect THE SAME participants to have significantly different scores on two different variables).

Example: Does eating grapefruit raise people's IQs? (Assume you are using the Schmedley IQ test; you have five people that you measure before they eat a bunch of grapefruit; you then measure the same participants later).

Your data would look something like this:

pre	post
50.00	100.00
90.00	120.00
30.00	100.00
55.00	110.00
12.00	90.00

To see if eating grapefruit made people smarter, you would need to conduct a dependent means t-test like so:

- Click on "Analyze" on toolbar
- Click on "Compare Means"
- Click "Paired Samples t-test"
- Paired variables are post and pre
- Click "Paste"
- Go to the.sps file and highlight the relevant commands
- Click on "Run"

SPSS will give you something that looks like this:
Syntax:

T-TEST PAIRS=pre WITH post (PAIRED)
/CRITERIA=CI(.9500)
/MISSING=ANALYSIS.

Output:

Table F.11: Within-Participants t-Test

Paired Samples Statistics

		Mean	N	Std. Deviation	Std. Error Mean
Pair 1	Pre	47.4000	5	29.30529	13.10572
	Post	104.0000	5	11.40175	5.09902

Paired Samples Correlations

N	Correlation	Sig.		Pair 1	pre & post	5
.959		.010				

Table F.12: More SPSS Output on Within-Participants t-test

Paired Samples Test

Paired Differences

	Mean	Std. Deviation	Std. Error Mean	95% Confidence Interval of the Difference		t	df	Sig. (2-tailed)
				Lower	Upper			
Pair 1 pre— post	−56.60000	18.64940	8.34026	−79.75628	−33.44372	−6.786	4	.002

Again, notice that the default p value (under the heading 2-tail Sig) is for a two-tailed test.

You'd report your results like so:

IQ scores were significantly higher after participants ate grapefruit (M = 104.00, SD = 11.40) compared with IQ scores before participants ate grapefruit (M = 47.40, SD = 29.31; t(4) = 6.79, p < .05).

Note that the 4 in the parenthetical expression refers to the degrees of freedom term (above, df, in printout).

ASSIGNMENT

- Compute a within-groups (paired samples) t-test for the mood scores from the jealousy data. Recall that for this data set, mood was measured at three times. The first mood measurements comprised a baseline measure. The second measurements represent mood after imagining partners engaging in sexual infidelity. The third measurements represent mood after imagining partners engaging in emotional infidelity. Recall that higher scores on this measure indicate more psychological discomfort.
- Conduct **one** within-subjects t-test using two of these three composite mood variables.
- **Hand in:**
  - A brief (no more than one page) summary outlining the question being asked by this analysis, the nature of the analysis being conducted, the results, and the implications of these results.
  - The .spv file
- Compute a between-subjects (independent means) t-test to examine sex differences in variables from Monica's thesis data (you can obtain her data set at http://www.newpaltz.edu/~geherg/classes/spring08/methods/monicas.zip). In her thesis, Monica examined sex differences in variables pertaining to perceptions of body image. In her data, the variable "gender" refers to the gender of participants; a value of 1 stands for females, 2 stands for males. The variable in the rightmost column best refers to body esteem scale total scores. Higher scores here indicate more positive perceptions of one's body.

- Compute a between-groups t-test to examine whether males and females differ significantly on this variable.
- **Hand in:**
  - A brief (no more than one page) summary outlining the question being asked by this analysis, the nature of the analysis being conducted, the results, and the implications of these results.
  - The .spv file
- Compute a between-groups t-test examining sex differences among college students in campus behavior. As in the previous lab, you will need to collect naturalistic-behavior data from actual college students. Ultimately, you will be conducting a between-groups t-test to examine sex differences in some behavior.
  - Get in groups of 3 or 4.
  - Think of a continuous dependent variable that you can unobtrusively measure by observing male and female students on campus at this time. For instance, you could measure amount of time it takes to walk down a hallway alone, number of turns taken in a conversation within a group in a one-minute period, and so on.
  - Compute a between-groups t-test to examine whether males and females differ significantly on this variable.
- **Hand in:**
  - A brief (no more than one page) summary outlining the question being asked by this analysis, the nature of the analysis being conducted, the results, and the implications of these results.
  - The .spv file
- **Importantly, whenever you summarize the results from a t-test, you need to report the following statistics: t, df, p (or at least whether p is less than .05), Ms, and SDs.**
- **You are now done—go home and have fun!**

ACTIVITY 7: *ANOVA WITH SPSS*

Goal: Conduct ANOVA with SPSS

Analysis of Variance, or ANOVA, is a statistic designed to examine, basically, if variability between means of groups is significantly greater than variability of scores within groups. This lab assignment will address the simplest form of ANOVA: a one-way ANOVA. In a one-way ANOVA, you have two or more groups (usually 3 or more groups) that represent different levels of an IV. You perform the ANOVA to examine if the means of these groups differ on some continuous DV.

For instance, suppose I am interested in whether members of various majors differ from one another in terms of how "cool" they are. To address this question, I find five psychology majors, five engineering majors, and five sociology majors. I administer the coolness scale to each participant. The scores are entered in SPSS as follows:

group	cool
1	8
1	9
1	6
1	8
1	10
2	2
2	5
2	9
2	2
2	3
3	0
3	5
3	7
3	5
3	1

In this case, "group" corresponds to my categorical, independent variable. For this variable, 1 represents psychology major, 2 represents engineering major, and 3 represents sociology major. The continuous scores on the cool scale are such that higher scores represent cooler participants.

To conduct a one-way ANOVA on these data, I would do as follows:

- Click on Analyze on toolbar
- Click on "Compare Means"
- Click "One Way ANOVA'"
- Dependent variable is "cool"
- Factor is "group"
- Next, click on "POST HOC"
- Choose "Tukey" (the most common post-hoc test); hit "Continue"
- Go to "Options"
- Choose "Descriptive"; hit "Continue"
- Click "Paste"
- Go to the.sps file and highlight the relevant commands
- Click on "Run"

Here's what you'll see:
Syntax:

```
ONEWAY cool BY group
/STATISTICS DESCRIPTIVES
/MISSING ANALYSIS
/POSTHOC=TUKEY ALPHA(0.05).
```

Output:

Table F.13: SPSS Output for One-Way ANOVA

Descriptives

Cool

	N	Mean	Std. Deviation	Std. Error	95% Confidence Interval for Mean		Minimum	Maximum
					Lower Bound	Upper Bound		
1.00	5	8.2000	1.48324	.66332	6.3583	10.0417	6.00	10.00
2.00	5	4.2000	2.94958	1.31909	.5376	7.8624	2.00	9.00
3.00	5	3.6000	2.96648	1.32665	−.0834	7.2834	.00	7.00
Total	15	5.3333	3.17730	.82038	3.5738	7.0929	.00	10.00

Table F.14: More SPSS Output for One-Way ANOVA

ANOVA

Cool

	Sum of Squares	df	Mean Square	F	Sig.
Between Groups	62.533	2	31.267	4.761	.030
Within Groups	78.800	12	6.567		
Total	141.333	14			

POST HOC TESTS

Table F.15: More SPSS Output for One-Way ANOVA

Multiple Comparisons

Cool
Tukey HSD

(I) group		(J) group		Mean Difference (I–J)	Std. Error	Sig.	95% Confidence Interval	
							Lower Bound	Upper Bound
dimension2	1.00	dimension3	2.00	4.00000	1.62070	.071	−.3238	8.3238
			3.00	4.60000*	1.62070	.037	.2762	8.9238
	2.00	dimension3	1.00	−4.00000	1.62070	.071	−8.3238	.3238
			3.00	.60000	1.62070	.928	−3.7238	4.9238
	3.00	dimension3	1.00	−4.60000*	1.62070	.037	−8.9238	−.2762
			2.00	−.60000	1.62070	.928	−4.9238	3.7238

*. The mean difference is significant at the 0.05 level

HOMOGENEOUS SUBSETS

Table F.16: More SPSS Output for One-Way ANOVA

Cool

Tukey HSD[a]

group		N	Subset for alpha = 0.05	
			1	2
dimension1	3.00	5	3.6000	
	2.00	5	4.2000	4.2000
	1.00	5		8.2000
	Sig.		.928	.071

Means for groups in homogeneous subsets are displayed.

a. Uses Harmonic Mean Sample Size = 5.000.

When reporting results from an ANOVA, you typically report whether the overall F is significant in the text of your Results section. This information comes from the second component of the SPSS printout (above). For this example, that would look about like so:

The one-way ANOVA revealed that coolness scores differed significantly as a function of college major ($F(2, 12) = 4.76$, $p <.05$). For means, standard deviations, and specific contrasts between means that were significant, see Table F.17. The Tukey post-hoc test revealed that psychology students were significantly cooler than sociology majors. No other specific post-hoc contrasts were significant.

Note that in the text above, the numbers that follow F refer to the two different degree of freedom terms. The inclusion of this information gives the reader a sense of the number of groups and the number of participants in each group.

From the first part of the above SPSS printout, you are primarily interested in the means and standard deviations. I would make a table summarizing these numbers like so:

Table F.17: Means and Standard Deviations on Coolness Variable across Three College Majors

Major	Mean	Standard Deviation
Psychology	8.20$_a$	1.48
Engineering	4.20	2.95
Sociology	3.60$_b$	2.97

$N = 5$ for all groups; Means with different subscripts differ significantly from each other using the Tukey post-hoc test.

The subscripts from that table come from the output regarding post-hoc tests. If two particular means are significantly different from each other with the Tukey test, indicate so by using different subscripts to demarcate them.

ASSIGNMENT

- Open up Don's data (it can be found at http://faculty.newpaltz.edu/glenngeher/files/don_data.sav). Don was interested in the psychological effects of receiving ideal-self confirming versus ideal-self disconfirming feedback from a psychologist. To manipulate this variable, Don had several individuals complete a personality measure. He then had an "experimenter" provide them with feedback. The feedback was randomly assigned to fit one of three categories: confirming, neutral, or disconfirming. In Don's data file, the variable "group" corresponds to this independent variable. This variable is coded as such: 1 represents confirming feedback, 2 represents neutral feedback, and 3 represents disconfirming feedback.

  Don then measured several dependent variables, including their total mood scale (indicated as the variable "mood_tot" in his data file). This mood scale was the same one used in the jealousy study (higher scores mean more psychological discomfort).
  - Conduct a one-way ANOVA to determine if total mood scores differ significantly across the three conditions of the group variable. Be sure to obtain both descriptive statistics and post-hoc statistics (as in example above).
  - Write up a brief report summarizing
    - (a) the hypothesis being addressed,
    - (b) the nature of the data being examined,
    - (c) the analyses being conducted,
    - (d) the results (including text in the Results section and a table), and
    - (e) implications of the results.
- **Hand in:**
  - The report including the text and a separate table.
  - The output (.spv) file.
- ANOVA on data collected in class.
  - Get into groups of 3 or 4. Think of a hypothesis regarding naturalistic student behavior that would include at least three groups. For instance, you could measure speed of walking among different majors; simply measure walking speed of individuals in specified areas and then ask them their majors. You might even be able to think of something more interesting than that! It would be nice, but not mandatory, if you could come up with a study that was based on a specific hypothesis. Once you've got it, you should follow these steps (same steps as used in the example):
  - Conduct a one-way ANOVA to determine if total mood scores differ significantly across the three conditions of the group variable. Be sure to obtain both descriptive statistics and post-hoc statistics (as in example above).
  - Write up a brief report summarizing
    - (a) the hypothesis being addressed,
    - (b) the nature of the data being examined,
    - (c) the analyses being conducted,
    - (d) the results (including text in the Results section and a table), and
    - (e) implications of the results.
- **Hand in:**
  - The report including the text and a separate table
  - The output (.spv) file

ACTIVITY 8: FACTORIAL ANOVA

Goal: Conduct a Factorial ANOVA in SPSS

A factorial ANOVA examines the effects of multiple independent variables on one dependent variable concurrently.

For instance, suppose I am interested in the effects of Ritalin and how it relates to attentional problems in a classroom setting. There is some evidence that Ritalin actually makes kids with no attentional problems form attentional problems. If such is the case, and we had access to a large number of kids, half of whom have attentional problems and half of whom do not, we could randomly distribute Ritalin to half of the entire group, possibly finding that Ritalin appears to have no effect on attention (here, the dependent variable). However, if we separate the children into a second independent variable—tendency toward attentional problems—and examine, concurrently (at the same time), the effects of (IV1) Ritalin and (IV2) attentional problems on (DV) attention in the classroom, we may find that for kids with attentional problems, high doses of Ritalin increases attention, while for kids with no attentional problems, the opposite trend is observed: these kids have worse attention with the Ritalin.

Thus, a factorial ANOVA allows us to examine "interaction effects." Interaction effects exist when some independent variable has different effects on some dependent variable as a function of some other independent variable. Additionally, a factorial ANOVA allows us to examine more than just main effects (which are the effects of one IV on a DV, not taking other IVs into account).

Consider the following example (based on the made up data file two-way.sav or Factorial ANOVA Data at http://faculty.newpaltz.edu/glenngeher/index.php/glenns-spss-lab-pages/):

This data file is designed to address whether males and females vary in terms of how much they like movies as a function of whether the movies in question are action versus romance movies. To test this question, the data include information from 10 males and 10 females. Half the males watched an action movie whereas the other half watched a romance movie—and the same is true of the females. Note that the data have this information coded in the variables gender and movie. Each of these variables is an independent variable (each with two levels). The dependent variable in this study is called "like." It corresponds to how much each participant liked the movie that he or she saw (on a 1–10 scale—10 meaning "liked more").

To run a factorial ANOVA on these data, do the following:

- Click "Analyze" on the toolbar
- Click "General Linear Model"
- Click "Univariate"
- A dialog box will open. For "Dependent" enter "like"
- For "Fixed Factor" enter "Gender" (note that gender is a "fixed factor" because you do not manipulate it as the researcher)
- For "Random Factor" enter "movie" (note that movie is a "random factor" because you *do* manipulate it as the researcher)
- Click on "Options"
- Move overall, gender, movie, and gender*movie to "Display Means" box
- Toggle on the "Compare Main Effects" option

- Toggle on "Descriptive statistics" and "Estimates of effect size" options
- Click "Continue"
- Click on "Plots"
- Move "gender" to "Horizontal Axis" and "movie" to "Separate Lines"
- Click "Add"
- Click "Continue"
- Click "Paste"
- Highlight the paragraph that will now have been added to an SPSS syntax (.sps) file
- Click "Run"
- Click "Selection"
- You now should have output from this command

Your syntax file will now look about like so:

UNIANOVA like BY gender movie
/RANDOM=movie
/METHOD=SSTYPE(3)
/INTERCEPT=INCLUDE
/PLOT=PROFILE(gender*movie)
/EMMEANS=TABLES(OVERALL)
/EMMEANS=TABLES(gender) COMPARE ADJ(LSD)
/EMMEANS=TABLES(movie) COMPARE ADJ(LSD)
/EMMEANS=TABLES(gender*movie)
/PRINT=ETASQ DESCRIPTIVE
/CRITERIA=ALPHA(.05)
/DESIGN=gender movie gender*movie.

Next, you'll see that you obtain a significant interaction for this analysis. Once you have a significant interaction, you recompute your independent variables to make it as if you only have one IV with four levels. Once you have things configured that way, you can conduct a one-way ANOVA to see if the different means you have obtained are significantly different from one another. Sound fun?! Here's how to do it:

RECOMPUTING VARIABLES SO AS TO BE ABLE TO CONDUCT A ONE-WAY ANOVA TO EXAMINE SPECIFIC DIFFERENCES BETWEEN MEANS

Given that you have two IVs with two levels each, you really have four groups (males who watched action movie, males who watched romance, females who watched action movie, females who watched romance). You can create a new variable called "group" with four values to represent these four groups by doing the following:

- Create a new variable called "group" by clicking on "Edit," then "Insert Variable"
- When viewing the data file, click on "Transform" and then "Compute Variable"

- Click on "If"
- Toggle "Include if case satisfies condition"
- In the empty box, type in the following: "gender=1" and "movie=1"
- Click "Continue"
- Make sure to type "group" in space for Target Variable
- In box for numeric expression, type "1"
  - The "1" in the numeric expression box will make it so that all subjects who are males who saw the action movie will be in group 1.
- Click "Type&label" and label each group in a meaningful way (e.g., male action for group 1).
- Click "Paste" to paste the command into the syntax file.
- Repeat the process, starting with clicking on "Transform," to create the three other groups (males who watched the romance—group 2, females who watched the action movie—group 3, females who watched the romance—group 4). Be sure to change your "If" command each time to indicate the appropriate group (for example, "gender=2" and "movie=1" for group 3, females who watched the action movie).
- Highlight the "IF" commands that you added to the SPSS syntax (.sps) file during this process.
- Click "Run"
- Click "Selection"

Something like the following will be added to your syntax file:
  IF (gender=1 and movie=1) group=1.

VARIABLE LABELS group "maleaction."
EXECUTE.
IF (gender=1 and movie=2) group=2.
VARIABLE LABELS group "maleromance."
EXECUTE.
IF (gender=2 and movie=1) group=3.
VARIABLE LABELS group "femaleaction."
EXECUTE.
IF (gender=2 and movie=2) group=4.
VARIABLE LABELS group "femaleromance."
EXECUTE.

You now should have numbers in the column corresponding to "group" in your.sav file.

Once you have created your dandy new group variable, you can conduct the one-way ANOVA (to follow up on the significant interaction from your factorial ANOVA) as follows:

- Click on "Analyze" on toolbar
- Click on "Compare Means"
- Click "One Way ANOVA"
- Dependent variable is "like"
- Factor is "group"
- Click on "POST HOC"

- Choose "Tukey" (the most common post-hoc test); hit "Continue"
- Go to "Options"
- Choose "Descriptive"; hit "Continue"
- Click "Paste"
- Go to the.sps file and highlight the relevant commands.
- Click on "Run"

The syntax corresponding to this one-way ANOVA will look like so:

ONEWAY like BY group
/STATISTICS DESCRIPTIVES
/MISSING ANALYSIS
/POSTHOC=TUKEY ALPHA(0.05).

The output from this analysis is found following the output from the factorial ANOVA

UNIVARIATE ANALYSIS OF VARIANCE

Table F.18: SPSS Output for Factorial ANOVA

Between-Subjects Factors

		Value Label	N
Gender	1.00	male	10
	2.00	female	10
movie type	1.00	action	10
	2.00	romance	10

Table F.19: More SPSS Output for Factorial ANOVA

Descriptive Statistics

Dependent Variable:like

gender		movie type	Mean	Std. Deviation	N
male	dimension2	action	7.8000	1.92354	5
		romance	1.8000	.83666	5
		Total	4.8000	3.45768	10
female	dimension2	action	2.4000	1.67332	5
		romance	7.0000	2.12132	5
		Total	4.7000	3.02030	10
Total	dimension2	action	5.1000	3.31495	10
		romance	4.4000	3.13404	10
		Total	4.7500	3.16020	20

Table F.20: More SPSS Output for Factorial ANOVA

Tests of Between-Subjects Effects

Dependent Variable:like

Source		Type III Sum of Squares	df	Mean Square	F	Sig.	Partial Eta Squared
Intercept	Hypothesis	451.250	1	451.250	184.184	.047	.995
	Error	2.450	1	2.450[a]			
Gender	Hypothesis	.050	1	.050	.000	.988	.000
	Error	140.450	1	140.450[b]			
Movie	Hypothesis	2.450	1	2.450	.017	.916	.017
	Error	140.450	1	140.450[b]			
gender * movie	Hypothesis	140.450	1	140.450	48.017	.000	.750
	Error	46.800	16	2.925[c]			

a. MS(movie)
b. MS(gender * movie)
c. MS(Error)

Table F.21: More SPSS Output for Factorial ANOVA

Expected Mean Squares[a,b]

Source	Variance Component			
	Var(movie)	Var(gender * movie)	Var(Error)	Quadratic Term
Intercept	10.000	5.000	1.000	Intercept, gender
Gender	.000	5.000	1.000	gender
Movie	10.000	5.000	1.000	
gender * movie	.000	5.000	1.000	
Error	.000	.000	1.000	

a. For each source, the expected mean square equals the sum of the coefficients in the cells times the variance components, plus a quadratic term involving effects in the Quadratic Term cell.
b. Expected Mean Squares are based on the Type III Sums of Squares.

ESTIMATED MARGINAL MEANS

Table F.22: More SPSS Output for Factorial ANOVA

1. Grand Mean

Dependent Variable:like

		95% Confidence Interval	
Mean	Std. Error	Lower Bound	Upper Bound
4.750	.382	3.939	5.561

2. GENDER

Table F.23:

Estimates

Dependent Variable:like

	gender	Mean	Std. Error	95% Confidence Interval	
				Lower Bound	Upper Bound
dimension1	male	4.800	.541	3.653	5.947
	female	4.700	.541	3.553	5.847

Table F.24: More SPSS Output for Factorial ANOVA

Pairwise Comparisons

Dependent Variable:like

(I) gender		(J) gender		Mean Difference (I-J)	Std. Error	Sig.[a]	95% Confidence Interval for Difference[a]	
							Lower Bound	Upper Bound
dimension1 Male	dimension2	female		.100	.765	.898	−1.521	1.721
Female	dimension2	male		−.100	.765	.898	−1.721	1.521

Based on estimated marginal means
a. Adjustment for multiple comparisons: Least Significant Difference (equivalent to no adjustments).

Table F.25: More SPSS Output for Factorial ANOVA

Univariate Tests

Dependent Variable:like

	Sum of Squares	df	Mean Square	F	Sig.	Partial Eta Squared
Contrast	.050	1	.050	.017	.898	.001
Error	46.800	16	2.925			

The F tests the effect of gender. This test is based on the linearly independent pairwise comparisons among the estimated marginal means.

3. MOVIE TYPE

Table F.26: More SPSS Output for Factorial ANOVA

Estimates

Dependent Variable:like

	movie type	Mean	Std. Error	95% Confidence Interval	
				Lower Bound	Upper Bound
dimension1	Action	5.100	.541	3.953	6.247
	Romance	4.400	.541	3.253	5.547

Table F.27: More SPSS Output for Factorial ANOVA

Pairwise Comparisons

Dependent Variable:like

(I) movie type		(J) movie type		Mean Difference (I-J)	Std. Error	Sig.[a]	95% Confidence Interval for Difference[a]	
							Lower Bound	Upper Bound
dimension1	Action	dimension2	romance	.700	.765	.374	−.921	2.321
	Romance	dimension2	action	−.700	.765	.374	−2.321	.921

Based on estimated marginal means
a. Adjustment for multiple comparisons: Least Significant Difference (equivalent to no adjustments).

Table F.28: More SPSS Output for Factorial ANOVA

Univariate Tests

Dependent Variable:like

	Sum of Squares	df	Mean Square	F	Sig.	Partial Eta Squared
Contrast	2.450	1	2.450	.838	.374	.050
Error	46.800	16	2.925			

The F tests the effect of movie type. This test is based on the linearly independent pairwise comparisons among the estimated marginal means.

Table F.29: More SPSS Output for Factorial ANOVA

4. gender * movie type

Dependent Variable:like

	gender		movie type	Mean	Std. Error	95% Confidence Interval	
						Lower Bound	Upper Bound
dimension1	male	dimension2	action	7.800	.765	6.179	9.421
			romance	1.800	.765	.179	3.421
	female	dimension2	action	2.400	.765	.779	4.021
			romance	7.000	.765	5.379	8.621

PROFILE PLOTS

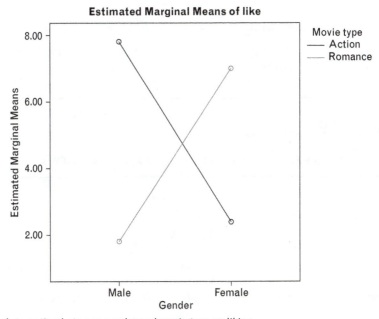

FIGURE F.1: Interaction between gender and movie type on liking.

ONE-WAY

Table F.30: More SPSS Output for Factorial ANOVA

Descriptives

Like

	N	Mean	Std. Deviation	Std. Error	95% Confidence Interval for Mean		Minimum	Maximum
					Lower Bound	Upper Bound		
1.00	5	7.8000	1.92354	.86023	5.4116	10.1884	5.00	10.00
2.00	5	1.8000	.83666	.37417	.7611	2.8389	1.00	3.00
3.00	5	2.4000	1.67332	.74833	.3223	4.4777	1.00	5.00
4.00	5	7.0000	2.12132	.94868	4.3660	9.6340	4.00	9.00
Total	20	4.7500	3.16020	.70664	3.2710	6.2290	1.00	10.00

Table F.31: More SPSS Output for Factorial ANOVA

ANOVA

Like

	Sum of Squares	df	Mean Square	F	Sig.
Between Groups	142.950	3	47.650	16.291	.000
Within Groups	46.800	16	2.925		
Total	189.750	19			

POST HOC TESTS

Table F.32: More SPSS Output for Factorial ANOVA

Multiple Comparisons

Like
Tukey HSD

(I) group		(J) group		Mean Difference (I-J)	Std. Error	Sig.	95% Confidence Interval	
							Lower Bound	Upper Bound
			2.00	6.00000*	1.08167	.000	2.9053	9.0947
			3.00	5.40000*	1.08167	.001	2.3053	8.4947
	1.00	dimension3	4.00	.80000	1.08167	.880	−2.2947	3.8947
			1.00	−6.00000*	1.08167	.000	−9.0947	−2.9053
			3.00	−.60000	1.08167	.944	−3.6947	2.4947
	2.00	dimension3	4.00	−5.20000*	1.08167	.001	−8.2947	−2.1053
			1.00	−5.40000*	1.08167	.001	−8.4947	−2.3053
			2.00	.60000	1.08167	.944	−2.4947	3.6947
dimension2	3.00	dimension3	4.00	−4.60000*	1.08167	.003	−7.6947	−1.5053

Table F.32: Continued

		1.00	−.80000	1.08167	.880	−3.8947	2.2947
		2.00	5.20000*	1.08167	.001	2.1053	8.2947
4.00	dimension3	3.00	4.60000*	1.08167	.003	1.5053	7.6947

*. The mean difference is significant at the 0.05 level.

HOMOGENEOUS SUBSETS

Table F.33: More SPSS Output for Factorial ANOVA

like

Tukey HSDª

			Subset for alpha = 0.05	
group		N	1	2
dimension1	2.00	5	1.8000	
	3.00	5	2.4000	
	4.00	5		7.0000
	1.00	5		7.8000
	Sig.		.944	.880

Means for groups in homogeneous subsets are displayed.
a. Uses Harmonic Mean Sample Size = 5.000.

Interpreting the results: As is almost always true with SPSS, much of the information produced is not needed for your purposes. Here is how I'd report the findings (note that I only use some of the information from the SPSS output):

Results: This analysis was designed to assess the effects of both gender and movie type on degree of liking for a movie. The analysis comprised a 2(gender: male vs. female) * 2(movie

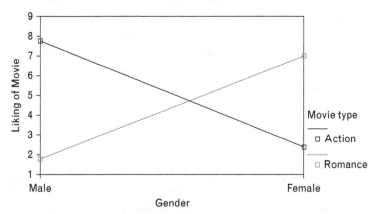

FIGURE F.2: Interaction between gender and movie type on liking.

type: action vs. romance) between-participants design, with the dependent variable being how much each participant liked the movie that he or she was randomly assigned to watch.

The ANOVA revealed no significant main effect for gender (F (1, 16) = 0.00, ns) or movie type (F (1, 16) = .02, ns). However, a significant interaction between these variables was observed (F (1, 16) = 48.02, $p < .05$). Further, this interaction accounted for a great deal of the variance in liking scores, as indicated by an h^2 of .75. Thus, 75% of liking scores were accounted for by this interaction. This interaction is clearly represented in Figure F.1.

As can be seen by this figure, males rated the romance movie low and the action movie high, whereas females showed the opposite pattern. The pattern of means in Table F.34 also speaks to the interaction obtained here.

Table F.34: Descriptive Statistics for Liking of Movie across Gender and Movie Type (Standard Deviations are in Parentheses)

Gender:	Male	Female	Total
MOVIE TYPE:			
Action	7.80 (1.92)a	2.40 (1.67)b	5.10 (3.31)
Romance	1.80 (.84)b	7.00 (2.12)a	4.40 (3.13)
Total	4.80 (3.46)	4.70 (3.02)	4.75 (3.16)

Means for liking of movie as a function of gender and movie type; means with different subscripts are significantly different from one another.

N = 5 for each cell; means with different subscripts are significantly different (based on the Tukey test) at the $p < .05$ level.

The factorial ANOVA conducted here does not provide information regarding whether specific means are significantly different from one another; it simply indicates that a significant interaction between the two IVs exists. To address whether these four means are significantly different from one another, a one-way ANOVA was computed. To conduct this ANOVA, four groups were created. These groups included males who watched the action movie, males who watched the romance, females who watched the action movie, and females who watched the romance. A one-way ANOVA was then computed to see if the means across those four groups differed. The analysis revealed a significant overall one-way effect (F(3, 16) = 16.29, $p < .05$). Post-hoc Tukey tests revealed that the males' action ratings and the females' romance ratings were both significantly greater than the females' action ratings and the males' romance ratings (See Table F. 34).

Regarding the figure and the table, note that I do not use exactly the information that I obtain from SPSS. For the figure, I edited the graph that SPSS provided; such editing is relatively simple— you can do it simply by clicking on the graph in the SPSS output file and changing words that you would like changed. Importantly, I put in names that match APA format for presenting figures.

Pretty much, I just made it meaningful to examine for the layperson. The table is based on the descriptive statistics that SPSS produced in the output file—but, again, I put this information into a readable format, keeping my audience (and APA format) in mind. Also, note that the subscripts from the table are based on the results of the "post hoc tests" from the SPSS output.

To create such subscripts, you need to determine, from the output, which groups are significantly different from which other groups (and, conversely, which are statistically the same)—and use some good old-fashioned logic!

So that is how to analyze data for a factorial ANOVA *and* how to report such an analysis. Now you are ready to do it on your own!

ASSIGNMENT:

- Get into groups of approximately three or four students. Come up with a factorial ANOVA all your own! In doing so, pick two independent variables that each have two levels. Further, pick a continuous dependent variable.
- The variables you choose should be parallel to the variables in the movie/gender example (above). Make sure the variables represent constructs that you can measure on this campus within an hour (within ethical boundaries!).
- Collect data from at least 16 people. It is not urgent that your cell sizes are equal (but it never hurts)!
- Enter the data into SPSS, analyze the data (creating a syntax file that is quite similar to the one in the example), and produce an output file. If you have a significant interaction, be sure to create a "group" variable as in the above example and conduct the appropriate follow-up (post hoc) analyses.
- Next, each student in your group must **independently** write a report summarizing the research question, the methods used to address the question, the nature of the data, the analysis, and the results.
- **Hand in (EACH STUDENT!):**
  - Your.sav (data) file (printed up)
  - Your.sps (syntax) file (printed up)
  - Your.spv (output) file (printed up)
  - Your **own** (independently written) report (in APA format, including a figure demonstrating any interaction (or lack thereof) and a table summarizing the descriptive statistics as in the above example).
- Have fun!

ACTIVITY 9: CHI SQUARE

Goal: Conduct a Chi Square with SPSS

The Chi Square (X^2) test of independence is designed to examine whether two categorical variables are related to each other in a way not expected by chance. For instance, suppose I wanted to see if males and females differ in terms of whether they prefer vanilla or chocolate ice cream. Assume that for gender, 1 = female and 2 = male, and for ice cream, 1 = vanilla and 2 = chocolate.

Here is the sample data set:

gender	ice cream
1.00	1.00
1.00	1.00
2.00	2.00
2.00	1.00
2.00	2.00
1.00	2.00
2.00	1.00
1.00	1.00
2.00	2.00
2.00	2.00

To compute the X^2 test for independence, follow these steps

- Click on "Analyze"
- Click on Descriptive statistics"
- Click on "Crosstabs"
- Click on "Statistics"
- Choose "Chi-square" and click "Continue"
- Choose one of your categorical variables for "row" and the other for "column"
- Click "Paste"
- Highlight the commands
- Click on "Run"
- Click on "Selection"

Your syntax will look like this:

```
CROSSTABS
/TABLES=gender BY icecream
/FORMAT=AVALUE TABLES
/STATISTICS=CHISQ
/CELLS=COUNT
/COUNT ROUND CELL.
```

Your output will look like so:

CROSSTABS

Here you are concerned with the Pearson Chi Square. In this case, the $X^2(1)$ is 1.67, *ns*. You would write it up accordingly—perhaps as follows:

This analysis was conducted to examine if males and females differ significantly in their preference for vanilla as opposed to chocolate ice cream. The X^2 test for independence suggested that there is no significant relationship between gender and ice cream choice ($X^2(1) = 1.67$, *ns*).

Table F.35: SPSS Cross-Tabs Output

Case Processing Summary

	Cases					
	Valid		Missing		Total	
	N	Percent	N	Percent	N	Percent
gender * ice cream	10	100.0%	0	.0%	10	100.0%

Table F.36: More SPSS Cross-Tabs Output

gender * ice cream Cross tabulation
Count

		Ice cream		Total
		1.00	2.00	
Gender	1.00	3	1	4
	2.00	2	4	6
Total		5	5	10

Table F.37: SPSS Output for Chi Square Test of Independence

Chi-Square Tests

	Value	df	Asymp. Sig. (2-sided)	Exact Sig. (2-sided)	Exact Sig. (1-sided)
Pearson Chi-Square	1.667[a]	1	.197		
Continuity Correction[b]	.417	1	.519		
Likelihood Ratio	1.726	1	.189		
Fisher's Exact Test				.524	.262
Linear-by-Linear Association	1.500	1	.221		
N of Valid Cases	10				

a. 4 cells (100.0%) have expected count less than 5. The minimum expected count is 2.00.

b. Computed only for a 2×2 table

ASSIGNMENT:

- X^2 on data collected in class
- Get into groups of 3 or 4. Think of a hypothesis that would include two categorical variables

- Create a.sav file
- Create two nominal variables—with at least 2 values each
- Make them variables that can actually be collected—either from other students in class or variables that can somehow be collected on the Web
- Conduct a X^2 test for independence
- **Hand in:**
  - Write up a brief report summarizing:
    - (a) the hypothesis being addressed,
    - (b) the nature of the data being examined,
    - (c) the analysis being conducted,
    - (d) the results (including text in the Results section and a table), and
    - (e) implications of the results.
- Give a brief report to the class that presents data from table and Chi Square results

GLOSSARY

CHAPTER ONE

CORRELATIONAL STATISTICS Statistics that address whether multiple variables are related to one another

DATA Quantified pieces of information (plural of the little-used and little-known *datum*)

DESCRIPTIVE STATISTICS Statistics that describe a pattern of data or the nature of the relationship among variables

EFFECT SIZE The magnitude of some statistical effect. It could correspond to the size of a relationship between variables, the size of a difference between means, or some other index of how big some statistical effect is.

INFERENTIAL STATISTICS Probability-based statistics that allow inferences to be made about populations based on data collected from samples

STATISTICAL SIGNIFICANCE An indication that an effect found (based on data collected from samples) is unlikely to have come about by chance, and likely accurately represents the pattern of data in the population

CHAPTER TWO

BIMODAL DISTRIBUTION A distribution in which two particular values are common.

CATEGORICAL VARIABLE A variable that has some number of categories, and someone "scores" by being in one category or another.

CENTRAL TENDENCY The typical score in a sample of scores.

CONSTANTS Attributes that do not vary.

CONTINUOUS VARIABLES Variables that include values that vary by degree.

DEVIATION SCORE How much any particular score deviates from the mean of the sample.

DISTRIBUTION OF SCORES A sample of scores.

FREQUENCY HISTOGRAM A bar graph used to represent frequency data, with a range of values across the x-axis and possible frequencies along the y-axis.

FREQUENCY POLYGON A line graph used to represent frequency data, with values of the variable along the x-axis and frequencies of values along the y-axis.

FREQUENCY TABLE A table that shows all the possible values in a range and how frequent each value is in the actual data.

GROUPED FREQUENCY TABLE A frequency table that uses intervals of values, rather than individual values.

INTERVAL-RATIO VARIABLE A true continuous variable, with differences between the values across the entire range of scores having similar interpretation across the scale.

KURTOSIS The extent that the primary peak of a distribution is peaked or flat.

KURTOTIC A distribution that has a particularly peaked or particularly flat primary peak, as compared to a normal distribution.

OPERATIONALIZED Mathematically measured.

ORDINAL VARIABLE A variable that corresponds to ranks, representing where a score is in the order of a sample of scores.

MEAN Arithmetic average. $M = \Sigma X/N$

MEDIAN The score that is in the middle of all other scores when scores are arranged sequentially.

MODALITY Relatively frequent clusters of values.

MODE The single most common score in a sample.

MULTIMODAL DISTRIBUTION A distribution in which more than one value is common.

NEGATIVELY SKEWED DISTRIBUTION A distribution with scores clustered on the right, or positive side of the distribution.

OUTLIER A score that is just off the scale, either much higher or much lower than other scores.

PATTERN OF VARIABILITY The manner in which scores differ from one another within a distribution of scores.

PILOT STUDY A small study done before a more formal, large-scale study.

POSITIVELY SKEWED DISTRIBUTION A distribution with scores clustered on the left, or negative, side of the distribution.

RANGE OF SCORES All the values between the lowest and highest scores in a distribution.

SCORE An actual data point on the measure of the variable; someone's actual score on the measure.

SKEWNESS The pattern of variability in a distribution.

SS Sum of the squared deviation scores.

STANDARD DEVIATION (SD) The average amount that scores in a distribution vary from one another.

UNIMODAL DISTRIBUTION A distribution in which a particular value in the middle is most common.

VALUE A possible score on some measure of a variable.

VARIABILITY How scores vary from one another within a distribution of scores.

VARIABLE An attribute for which there is some level of variability.

VARIANCE The average of the squared deviation scores.

CHAPTER THREE

ISOMORPHIC RELATIONSHIP A situation in which the items in one set correspond perfectly to specific items in another set. In terms of raw scores and z-scores, each raw score for a variable corresponds to a specific z-score for that same variable. The relationship between raw and z-scores is, thus, isomorphic.

RAW SCORE An unaltered number in the original units of measurement, a number that has not been transformed in any way

STANDARDIZED SCORE z-score

Z-SCORE A number that corresponds to the number of standard deviations a score is above or below the mean

CHAPTER FOUR

CONTINUOUS VARIABLE Variable for which values differ by degree

CORRELATION A relationship between two variables

CORRELATION DIRECTION Whether the correlation is positive (high X scores go with high Y scores and low X scores go with low Y scores) or negative (high X scores go with low Y scores, and vice versa)

CORRELATION STRENGTH Degree of scatter in a scatterplot; value of the r-coefficient on a scale of −1 to 1. Strong correlations are close to −1 or 1, whereas weak correlations are close to 0

CORRELATIONAL STATISTICS Statistics that address whether multiple variables are related

DEPENDENT VARIABLE (CRITERION OR OUTCOME VARIABLE) Variable that is thought to be predicted by the predictor variable; scores on the dependent variable follow from scores on the predictor variable

NEGATIVE CORRELATION Correlation in which high X scores go with low Y scores, and vice versa.

POSITIVE CORRELATION Correlation in which high X scores go with high Y scores and low X scores go with low Y scores

PREDICTOR VARIABLE The variable thought to precede, and perhaps cause, scores on the other variables

R-COEFFICIENT Also known as Pearson product-moment correlation coefficient. A number between −1 and 1 that indicates the direction and strength of a correlation

SCATTERPLOT A graph with the predictor variable along the horizontal (X) axis and the dependent variable along the vertical (Y) axis, with dots in two-dimensional space that each represent a particular case

CHAPTER FIVE

BETA WEIGHT Specific coefficient between −1.0 and +1.0 used in a regression equation to represent how much weight a particular variable should have in predicting an outcome variable

BIVARIATE REGRESSION Statistical analyses that allows for the prediction of scores on a dependent variable based on scores from a predictor variable

ERROR How different each Y is from each corresponding $\hat{y}$. $Y - \hat{Y} = $ Error

R SQUARED (R^2) The proportionate reduction of error in predicting Y relative to simply guessing the mean of Y, or the amount of variability in the Y variable that is accounted for by the relationship between X and Y

REGRESSION Statistics that predict outcomes

REGRESSION ANALYSES Analyses that allow the prediction of scores on one variable from other variables, given information about the correlations between the variables

STANDARDIZED REGRESSION ANALYSIS An analysis used to predict z-scores on the dependent (Y) variable from z-scores on the predictor (X) variable, given r_{xy} (the correlation between X and Y)

CHAPTER SIX

HYPOTHESIS TESTING Determining if some effect found in a sample is likely reflective of patterns in the population.

INFERENTIAL STATISTICS Statistics designed to allow us to infer whether some pattern found in a sample likely reflects a pattern found in the population; statistics designed to address whether statistical effects are beyond what would be expected by chance.

PROBABILITY The expected relative frequency of some outcome.

PROBABILITY DISTRIBUTION A distribution of possibilities; a mathematically derived function regarding how likely different values are expected to occur.

CHAPTER SEVEN

ALPHA REGION The portion of the comparison distribution that is determined to be so low in probability that the idea of a score landing in that region by chance alone is rejected.

CRITICAL VALUE (OR CUTOFF VALUE) A specific value that sits at the start of the alpha region, which, if reached or exceeded, results in the rejection of the null hypothesis.

HYPOTHESIS TESTING A process for determining if some effect found in a sample is likely reflective of patterns in the population.

NULL HYPOTHESIS The hypothesis that assumes there is no difference between populations; the hypothesis that assumes that your research hypothesis is wrong.

ONE-TAILED TEST (DIRECTIONAL TEST) Type of test used when the research hypothesis specifies that the special population mean differs from the general population mean in a particular direction; there is one alpha region at the tail of one end of the distribution.

TWO-TAILED TEST (NON-DIRECTIONAL TEST) Type of test used when the research hypothesis does not specify the direction in which the special population mean differs from the general population mean; there are two alpha regions, one at each tail of the distribution.

TYPE-I ERROR Rejecting the null hypothesis incorrectly; rejecting the null hypothesis when it is true.

TYPE-II ERROR Incorrectly failing to reject the null hypothesis; failing to reject the null hypothesis when it is false.

CHAPTER EIGHT

CONFIDENCE INTERVAL The group of scores between an upper and lower score that is expected to contain the actual mean of the population.

DISTRIBUTION OF MEANS A conceptual distribution based on a population distribution as well as information about the population standard deviation and the sample size.

STANDARD ERROR OF THE MEAN Standard deviation of a distribution of means.

CHAPTER NINE

COHEN'S D A test that compares two means relative to some estimate of population standard deviation to estimate, essentially, how big the effect itself is, separate from the details of any particular study. Cohen's d $= \left| \dfrac{\mu_1 - \mu_2}{\sigma_2} \right|$.

STATISTICAL POWER The probability of rejecting the null hypothesis if the research hypothesis is, at the population level, actually true; the percentage of the upper distribution that is extreme enough to reject the null hypothesis on the lower distribution.

CHAPTER TEN

DEGREES OF FREEDOM The number of scores free to vary.

ONE SAMPLE T-TEST Type of t-test used when you want to compare a single sample mean with the mean of a population having an unknown population standard deviation.

WITHIN-GROUP T-TEST Type of t-test used when you have two continuous variables from the same participants, and you want to see if the means of the variables differ significantly from one another. Also known as repeated-measures t-test and paired-samples t-test.

CHAPTER ELEVEN

DICHOTOMOUS CATEGORICAL VARIABLE Variable in which the different values represent one of two different categories

DISTRIBUTION OF DIFFERENCES BETWEEN MEANS The comparison distribution used for the between-groups t-test—it is theoretically comprised of an infinite sample of differences between two populations (whose means are assumed to be equal)

HETEROGENEITY OF VARIANCE Assumption that the nature of the population variance across groups is different

HOMOGENEITY OF VARIANCE Assumption that the nature of the population variance across groups is the same

POOLED VARIANCE ESTIMATE A single of the population variance for two different populations based on information collected from multiple samples.

CHAPTER TWELVE

ANOVA Analysis of variance; statistical process that compares variability in scores that results from differences between means with variability in scores that results from error variance or error variability (differences between individuals).

ERROR VARIANCE Differences between individuals, independent from differences between groups. Also known as error variability.

ANSWERS TO SET B HOMEWORK PROBLEMS

CHAPTER ONE

1. a. If the finding is statistically significant, then 6-year-old boys in the general population likely do enjoy climbing trees more than do 6-year-old girls, and the findings are likely accurate, rather than occurring by chance.
   b. If there is a big effect size, then there is a very large difference between how much the boys enjoy climbing trees and how much the girls enjoy climbing trees.
   c. If there is statistical significance and a big effect size, then there is a large difference between how much the boys enjoy climbing trees and how much the girls enjoy climbing trees, and this difference carries over beyond the study sample population into the general population of 6-year-old boys and girls.
   d. If there is neither statistical significance nor a big effect size, then there is little difference between the boys and the girls in term of enjoyment of climbing trees, and the results may just have occurred by chance—the sample population may not accurately reflect the general population.
   e. If there is statistical significance, but not a big effect size, then the findings are likely due to actual differences in the enjoyment levels of boys and girls climbing trees, and likely do represent the general population of 6-year-old children, but the difference between the boys and girls in terms of enjoyment of climbing trees was not very large.
   f. If there is no statistical significance, but a big effect size, then there was a large difference found between the enjoyment of boys and girls climbing trees, but the results are likely due to chance, and likely do not reflect the general population of 6-year-old children.
2. Correlational statistics are descriptive statistics that examine the relationships between multiple variables concurrently. This means that the statistics are able to determine whether variables are related to one another in some way.

3. a. descriptive and correlational because the research describes the relationship between participant beverage preferences and signs of hyperactivity. There is a correlation between a preference for juice and signs of hyperactivity.
    b. descriptive because the research describes the average age of people who chose to attend the matinee movie.
    c. inferential because the research involves statistical significance.
    d. descriptive and correlational because the research describes the relationship between the amount of reading people do and their scores on tests of vocabulary and spelling. There is a correlation between the amount of reading and the test scores of vocabulary and spelling.
    e. inferential because the research involves statistical significance.

CHAPTER TWO

1. a. height, weight—any variable that has values that vary by degree
    b. place in line, rank of finish in a race—any variable that corresponds to rank
    c. dog vs. cat, employed vs. unemployed—any variable that is scored by placement in a category
2. a. 22.54
    b. 3.29
    c. 53.99
    d. 78.00
    e. 13.01
    f. 211.91
3.

Table 2.25: Homework Set B #3 a–d

Not Physically Fit	Somewhat Physically Fit	Very Physically Fit
2	5	10
3	6	9
10	1	8
4	5	8
3	6	7
10	5	9
3	7	6
3	1	6
2	6	7
3	6	9
Mean $= M = \dfrac{\Sigma X}{N} = \dfrac{43}{10} = 4.3$	Mean $= M = \dfrac{\Sigma X}{N} = \dfrac{48}{10} = 4.8$	Mean $= M = \dfrac{\Sigma X}{N} = \dfrac{79}{10} = 7.9$
Median $= 3$	Median $= 5.5$	Median $= 8$
Mode $= 3$	Mode $= 6$	Mode $= 9$

(continued)

Table 2.25: Continued

Not Physically Fit	Somewhat Physically Fit	Very Physically Fit
Of the 10 scores, 2 of them are outliers, and very high for this data set, inflating the mean to 4.3. The median and mode, both 3, are better indexes of central tendency in this data set.	All but 2 of the 10 scores in this data set are between 5 & 7, yet the mean is 4.8 due to the 2 very low scores, which are outliers. Therefore, the median and mode, at 5.5 and 6, are better indexes of central tendency	The mean, median, and mode are all very close in this data set, in which all the scores fall between 6 & 10. All three indexes of central tendency are good measures of central tendency.

4. Casual Clothes:

Table 2.26: Homework Set B #4 Casual Clothing Group Calculations a–b

X	M	Deviation Score (X–M)	Squared Deviation Score (X–M)²
20	11.83	8.17	66.75
12	11.83	.17	.03
6	11.83	–5.83	33.99
3	11.83	–8.83	77.97
8	11.83	–3.83	14.67
22	11.83	10.17	103.43
$\Sigma = 71$			$\Sigma(X–M)^2 = 296.84$

$N = 6$

$M = 11.83$

$$SD^2 = \frac{(X-M)^2}{N} = 49.47$$

$$SD = \sqrt{(SD)^2} = 7.03$$

a. Deviation scores—see chart

b. Squared deviation scores—see chart

c. Sum of squared deviation scores $\Sigma(X-M)^2 = 296.84$

d. Variance $= SD^2 = \dfrac{(X-M)^2}{N} = 49.47$

e. Standard deviation $= SD = \sqrt{(SD)^2} = 7.03$

f. The statistical analyses of the people wearing casual clothes reveals a mean of 11.83 seconds of running before giving up on the bus stopping. The standard deviation is 7.03 seconds. Therefore, within this group, there is a great deal of variability in the amount of time that people run; there are people who run for a very short time as well as people who run for a very long time.

Business Attire:

Table 2.27: Homework Set B #4 Business Attire Group Calculations a–b

X	M	Deviation Score (X–M)	Squared Deviation Score (X–M)^2
6	7	−1	1
5	7	−2	4
8	7	1	1
8	7	1	1
9	7	2	4
6	7	−1	1

$\sum = 42$

$N = 6$

$M = 7$

$\sum(X–M)^2 = 12$

$$SD^2 = \frac{(X-M)^2}{N} = 2$$

$$SD = \sqrt{(SD)^2} = 1.41$$

a. Deviation scores—see chart

b. Squared deviation scores—see chart

c. Sum of squared deviation scores $\sum(X–M)^2 = 12$

d. Variance $= SD^2 = \dfrac{(X-M)^2}{N} = 2$

e. Standard deviation $= SD = \sqrt{(SD)^2} = 1.41$

f. The statistical analyses of the people wearing business attire reveals a mean of 7 seconds of running before giving up on the bus stopping. The standard deviation is 1.41 seconds. Therefore, there is little variation in the amount of time that people in business attire run for the bus before quitting.

5.

a. See Table 2.28.

Table 2.28: Homework Set B #5a

Number of Gadgets	Tick Marks	Frequency
4	||	2
5	|	1
6	||	2
7	|	1
8	|	1
9	|	1
10	|	1

b. See Figure 2.12.

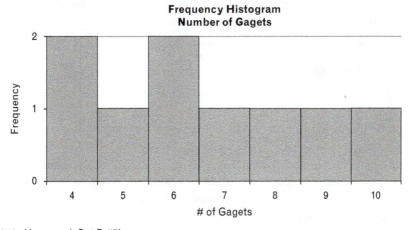

FIGURE 2.12: Homework Set B #5b.

c.

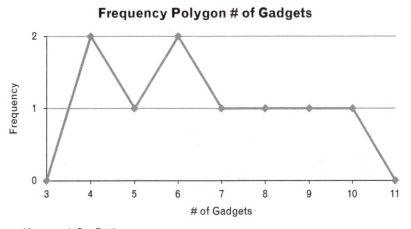

FIGURE 2.13: Homework Set B #5c.

d. The distribution of # of gadgets is bimodal, with modes of 4 and 6.
e. The distribution of # of gadgets is positively skewed, with more values on the left
    side of the distribution.

6. a. See Table 2.29.

Table 2.29: Homework Set B #6a

Value in Cents	Tick Marks	Frequency
0–9	JHT JHT IIII	14
10–19	III	3
20–29	II	2
30–39		0
40–49		0
50–59	I	1

b.   See Figure 2.14.c.   See Figure 2.15.

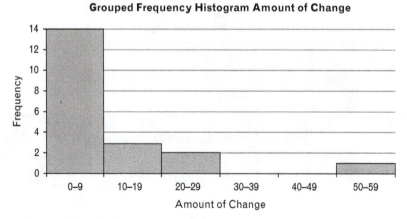

FIGURE 2.14: Homework Set B #6b.

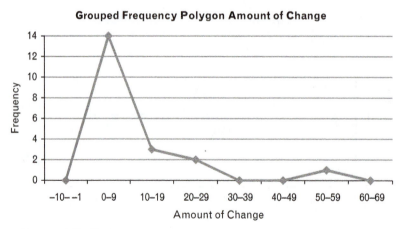

FIGURE 2.15: Homework Set B #6c.

d.   The distribution of amount of change is unimodal, with a mode of 0–9.
e.   This distribution is positively skewed, with the values clustered on the left side of the distribution.

7.   a   See Table 2.30.

Table 2.30: Homework Set B #7a

Category	Tick Marks	Frequency	Percentage
The Color Purple	ЖҬ ЖҬ ЖҬ III	18	90%
Uncle Tom's Cabin	II	2	10%

b.   See Figure 2.16.

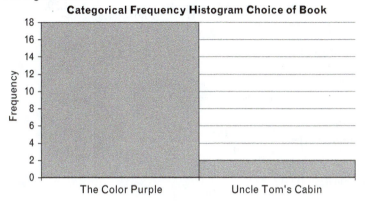

Categorical Frequency Histogram Choice of Book

FIGURE 2.16: Homework Set B #7b.

CHAPTER THREE

1. a. $Z = \dfrac{7.3 - 6}{.5} = \dfrac{1.3}{.5} = 2.6$. The raw score of 7.3 is 2.6 standard deviations above the mean.

   b. $Z = \dfrac{6.2 - 6}{.5} = \dfrac{.2}{.5} = .4$. The raw score of 6.2 is .4 standard deviations above the mean.

   c. $Z = \dfrac{5.4 - 6}{.5} = \dfrac{-.6}{.5} = -1.2$. The raw score of 5.4 is 1.2 standard deviations below the mean.

2. a. mean $(M) = -\dfrac{6 + 4 + 7 + 9}{4} = \dfrac{26}{4} = 6.5$

Standard deviation (SD) = 1.80

Table 3.10: Homework Set B #2a

X	M	X–M	(X–M)²	Z
6	6.5	−.5	.25	−.27
4	6.5	−2.5	6.25	−1.39
7	6.5	.5	.25	.28
9	6.5	2.5	6.25	1.39

$$\Sigma(X - M)^2 = 13$$

$$SD^2 = \left(\frac{\Sigma(X - M)^2}{N}\right) = \frac{13}{4} = 3.25$$

$$SD = \sqrt{SD^2} = \sqrt{3.25} = 1.80$$

$$z - \text{score of raw score } 6 = \frac{X - M}{SD} = \frac{6 - 6.5}{1.80} = \frac{-.5}{1.80} = -.28.$$

$$z - \text{score of raw score } 4 = \frac{X - M}{SD} = \frac{4 - 6.5}{1.80} = \frac{-2.5}{1.80} = -1.39.$$

$$z - \text{score of raw score } 7 = \frac{X - M}{SD} = \frac{7 - 6.5}{1.80} = \frac{.5}{1.80} = .28.$$

$$z - \text{score of raw score } 9 = \frac{X - M}{SD} = \frac{9 - 6.5}{1.80} = \frac{2.5}{1.80} = 1.39.$$

b.   mean $(M) = -\frac{41 + 39 + 46 + 43}{4} = \frac{169}{4} = 42.25$

Standard deviation (SD) = 2.59

Table 3.11: Homework Set B #2b

X	M	X–M	(X–M)²	Z
41	42.25	−1.25	1.56	−.48
39	42.25	−3.25	10.56	−1.25
46	42.25	3.75	14.06	1.45
43	42.25	.75	.56	.29

$$\Sigma(X - M)^2 = 26.74$$

$$SD^2 = \left(\frac{\Sigma(X - M)^2}{N}\right) = \frac{26.74}{4} = 6.69$$

$$SD = \sqrt{SD^2} = \sqrt{6.69} = 2.59$$

$$z - \text{score of raw score } 41 = \frac{X - M}{SD} = \frac{41 - 42.25}{2.59} = \frac{-1.25}{2.59} = -.48.$$

$$z - \text{score of raw score } 39 = \frac{X - M}{SD} = \frac{39 - 42.25}{2.59} = \frac{-3.25}{2.59} = -1.25.$$

$$z - \text{score of raw score } 46 = \frac{X - M}{SD} = \frac{46 - 42.25}{2.59} = \frac{3.75}{2.59} = 1.45.$$

$$z - \text{score of raw score } 43 = \frac{X - M}{SD} = \frac{43 - 42.25}{2.59} = \frac{.75}{2.59} = .29.$$

3. a.   X = M + (SD * Z) = 17 + (2.5 * −.65) = 17−1.63 = 15.37
    b.   X = M + (SD * Z) = 17 + (2.5 * 1.8) = 17 + 4.5 = 21.5
    c.   X = M + (SD * Z) = 17 + (2.5 * −2) = 17−5 = 12

4.   Computer—$Z = \dfrac{X - M}{SD} = \dfrac{300 - 699}{35} = \dfrac{-399}{35} = -11.4$

    Television—$Z = \dfrac{X - M}{SD} = \dfrac{275 - 589}{25} = \dfrac{-314}{25} = -12.56$

The television is a better deal, as it is 12.56 standard deviations below the mean, whereas the computer is only 11.4 standard deviations below the mean.

5. You—X = M + (SD * Z) = 52 + (3 * 1.11) = 52 + 3.33 = 55.33 sit-ups
    Your friend—X = M + (SD * Z) = 52 + (3 * 1.8) = 52 + 5.4 = 57.4 sit-ups

6. You need to compute your z-score. $Z = \dfrac{X - M}{SD} = \dfrac{215 - 196}{5} = \dfrac{19}{5} = 3.8$. Your fitness score is 3.8 standard deviations above the mean.

7. Yes, you can compare your performance on the history evaluation with your performance on the fitness evaluation. Just compute your z-score for the history evaluation—
    $Z = \dfrac{X - M}{SD} = \dfrac{520 - 410}{13} = \dfrac{110}{13} = 8.46$. Since your z-score for the fitness evaluation is 3.8, and your z-score for the American history test is 8.46, you can conclude that while you are well above average in fitness, your American history aptitude appears to be even more phenomenal. You are better at history than you are at fitness.

CHAPTER FOUR

1. a. moderate positive correlation
    b. strong negative correlation
    c. no correlation
2. a. moderate, positive correlation
    b. strong, negative correlation
    c. weak, negative correlation
    d. strong, positive correlation
3. a. The predictor variable is the number of dogs owned, because it is thought to predict the amount of time spent outside. The average number of minutes spent outside is the dependent variable because it is thought to be predicted by the number of dogs owned.

b & c.

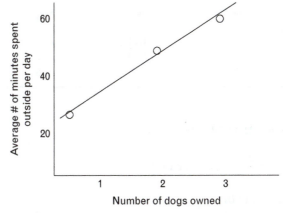

FIGURE 4.1: Simple Scatterplot.

d. The scatterplot shows a strong positive correlation; there is not much scatter. It appears that the more dogs a person owns, the more time s/he spends outside.

e.

Table 4.21: Homework Set B #3e

X (# of dogs owned)	M	X–M	(X–M)²	Zx
3	1.67	1.33	1.77	1.06
0	1.67	−1.67	2.79	−1.34
2	1.67	.33	.11	.26

$$M = \frac{5}{3} = 1.67 \qquad\qquad \Sigma(X-M)^2 = 4.67$$

$$SD^2 = \frac{2.33}{3} = 1.56$$

$$SD = 1.25$$

Table 4.22: Homework Set B #3e

Y (average # of minutes spent outside per day	M	Y–M	(Y–M)²	Zy
60	43.67	16.33	266.67	1.14
25	43.67	−18.67	348.57	−1.30
46	43.67	2.33	5.43	.16

$$M = \frac{131}{3} = 43.67 \qquad\qquad \Sigma(Y-M)^2 = 620.67$$

$$SD^2 = \frac{620.67}{3} = 206.89$$

$$SD = 14.38$$

Table 4.23: Homework Set B #3e

Zx	Zy	ZxZy
1.06	1.14	1.72
−1.34	−1.30	.99
.26	.16	.06

$$SZxZy = 1.21 + 1.74 + .04 = 2.99$$

$$\frac{\Sigma ZxZy}{N} = \frac{2.99}{3} = .997 \text{ (or } 1.00)$$

$$r = .997 \text{ (or } 1.00)$$

f. The correlation of .997 (or 1.00) is a strong positive correlation. The number of dogs owned is highly positively correlated with the number of minutes spent outside per day. It appears that the more dogs a person owns, the more time s/he spends outdoors. These findings are consistent with the scatterplot.

g. Causation cannot be determined.

h. The three possible explanations for the correlation are (1) owning more dogs causes people to spend more time outside, (2) spending more time outside causes people to own more dogs, or (3) something else entirely causes people to own more dogs and to spend more time outside.

4. a. The predictor variable is the number of classes, because the number of classes being taken is thought to predict the number of parties attended. The average number of parties attended in a month is the dependent variable because it is thought to be predicted by the number of classes being taken.

b & c.

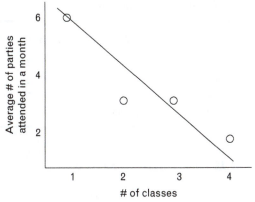

FIGURE 4.2: Simple Scatterplot with Estimated "Best Fit" Line.

d. The scatterplot shows a strong negative correlation. There is not much scatter. It appears that people who are taking more classes tend to attend fewer parties.

e.

Table 4.24: Homework Set B #4e

X (# of classes)	M	X–M	(X–M)²	Zx
4	2.5	1.5	2.25	1.34
1	2.5	−1.5	2.25	−1.34
2	2.5	−.5	.25	−.45
3	2.5	.5	.25	.45
	$M = \dfrac{10}{4} = 2.5$		$\Sigma(X–M)^2 = 5$	
			$SD^2 = \dfrac{5}{4} = 1.25$	
			$SD = 1.12$	

Table 4.25: Homework Set B #4e

Y (average # of parties attended in a month)	M	Y_M	(Y–M)²	Zy
2	3.5	–1.5	2.25	–1
6	3.5	2.5	6.25	1.67
3	3.5	–.5	.25	–.33
3	3.5	–.5	.25	–.33

$$M = \frac{14}{4} = 3.5$$

$$\Sigma(Y-M)^2 = 9$$

$$SD^2 = \frac{9}{4} = 2.25$$

$$SD = 1.5$$

Table 4.26: Homework Set B #4e

Zx	Zy	ZxZy
1.34	–1	–1.34
–1.34	1.67	–2.24
–.45	–.33	.15
.45	–.33	–.15

$$\Sigma ZxZy = -1.34 + -2.24 + .15 + -.15 = -3.58$$

$$\frac{\Sigma ZxZy}{N} = \frac{-3.58}{4} = -.90$$

$$r = -.90$$

f.   The correlation is strong and negative. The number of classes taken and the average number of parties attended in a month are highly negatively correlated. It appears that the more classes a person takes, the fewer parties s/he attends. These findings are consistent with the scatterplot.

g.   Causation cannot be determined from the findings.

h.   Three possible explanations for the correlation are (1) taking more classes causes people to attend fewer parties, (2) attending fewer parties causes people to take more classes, or (3) something else entirely causes people to take more classes and attend fewer parties.

CHAPTER FIVE

1.   #1–Number of people in the group
     #2–Roosters running loose in the dog park

#3–Number of people in the group with ankle injuries requiring crutches

#4–Number of boy scouts and girl scouts in the group

#5–Overall skill in canoeing within the group

#6–Number of people in the group who firmly believe in the paranormal

2.　a.　The best guess for stress level, with no other information available, is 20, which is the mean of the distribution.

　　b.　$Z\hat{y} = (\beta)(Zx)$

$$Z\hat{y} = (-.44)(2.2)$$
$$Z\hat{y} = -.97$$

　　c.　$Z\hat{y} = (\beta)(Zx)$

$$Z\hat{y} = (.35)(1.3)$$
$$Z\hat{y} = .46$$

　　d.　$Z\hat{y} = (\beta)(Zx)$

$$Z\hat{y} = (0)(3)$$
$$Z\hat{y} = 0$$

Teagan's $Z\hat{y}$ is 0, which corresponds to the mean of the distribution, which is 20.

3.　a.　$b = 1.00\left(\dfrac{14.38}{1.25}\right) = 1.00(11.50) = 11.50$

$a = 43.67 - 11.50(1.67) = 43.67 - 19.21 = 24.46$

$\hat{Y} = 24.46 + 11.50(x)$

　　b.　$\hat{Y} = 24.46 + 11.50(4) = 24.46 + 46.00 = 70.46$

$\hat{Y} = 70.46$ minutes

　　c.

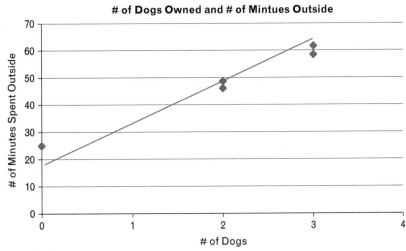

FIGURE 5.9: Homework Set B #3c.

pt. 1 = Ŷ = 24.46 + 11.50(2) = 24.46 + 23.00 = 47.46
pt. 1 = (2, 47.46)
pt. 2 = Ŷ = 24.46 + 11.50(3) = 24.46 + 34.5 = 58.96
pt. 1 = (3, 58.96)

d.

Table 5.14: Homework Set B # 3d Answers

X	Y	Ŷ	(Y–Ŷ) (Error)	(Y–Ŷ)² (Error)²
3	60	58.96	1.04	1.08
0	25	24.46	.54	.29
2	46	47.46	–1.46	2.13
				SSe = 3.50
				SSt = 620.67

$$r^2 = \frac{SSt - SSe}{SSt} = \frac{620.67 - 3.50}{620.67} = \frac{617.17}{620.67} = .99$$

$$r^2 = .99$$

e. 99% of the variability in the number of minutes spent outside can be accounted for by the relationship between the number of dogs owned and the number of minutes spent outside.

4. a. $b = -.90\left(\dfrac{1.5}{1.12}\right) = -.90(1.34) = -1.21$

   $a = 3.5 - (-1.21)(2.5) = 3.5 - (-3.03) = 6.53$
   $\hat{Y} = 6.53 + (-1.21)(x)$ or $\hat{Y} = 6.53 - 1.21(x)$

   b. $\hat{Y} = 6.53 + (-1.21)(5) = 6.53 + (-6.05) = .48$
   $\hat{Y} = .48$ parties

   c.

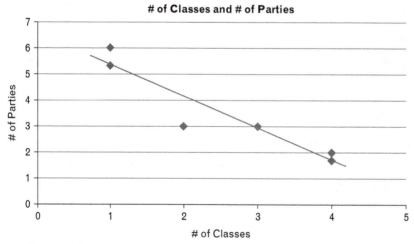

FIGURE 5.10: Homework Set B #4c.

pt. 1 = $\hat{Y}$ = 6.53 + (−1.21)(1) = 6.53 + (−1.21) = 5.32
pt. 1 = (1, 5.32)
pt. 2 = $\hat{Y}$ = 6.53 + (−1.21)(4) = 6.53 + (−4.84) = 1.69
pt. 1 = (4, 1.69)

d.

Table 5.15: Homework Set B # 4d Answers

X	Y	$\hat{Y}$	(Y−$\hat{Y}$) (Error)	(Y−$\hat{Y}$)² (Error)²
4	2	1.69	.31	.10
1	6	5.32	.68	.46
2	3	4.11	−1.11	1.23
3	3	2.90	.10	.01
				SSe = 1.8
				SSt = 9

$$r^2 = \frac{SSt - SSe}{SSt} = \frac{9 - 1.8}{9} = \frac{7.2}{9} = .80$$

$$r^2 = .80$$

e. 80% of the variability in the number of parties attended in this data set can be accounted for by the relationship between the number of classes taken and the number of parties attended.

CHAPTER SIX

1. a. 81%
   b. 23%
   c. 1%
2. a. p(.5)
   b. p(.5)
   c. p(.5)
   d. p(.125)
   e. p(.125)
3. a. X = Z(SD) + M
      X = 1.6(8) + 110
      X = 122.8 = your raw score

Homework Set B #3

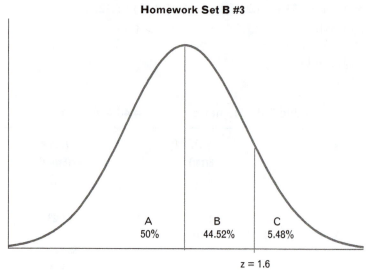

$z = 1.6$

FIGURE 6.19: Homework Set B #3.

    b.   50 + 44.52 = 94.52% of the test-takers scored lower than you

    c.   100–94.52 = 5.48% of the test-takers scored higher than you

4.   a.   X = Z(SD) + M

        X = −.69(4) + 85

        X = 82.24 = your raw score

Homework Set B #4

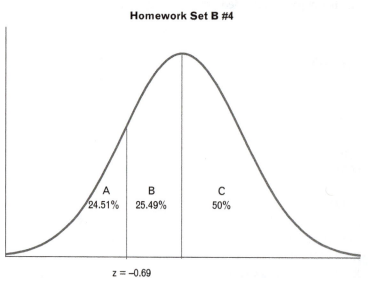

$z = -0.69$

FIGURE 6.20: Homework Set B #5.

b.   50 – 25.49 = 24.51% of the test-takers scored lower than you

c.   100 – 24.51 = 75.49% of the test-takers scored higher than you

5.   a.   Z = (X–M)/SD

Z = (56–60)/3

Z = –1.33

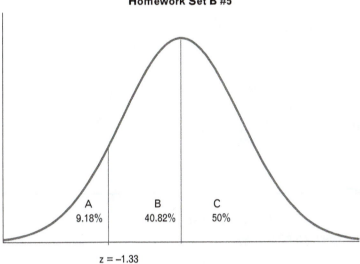

Homework Set B #5

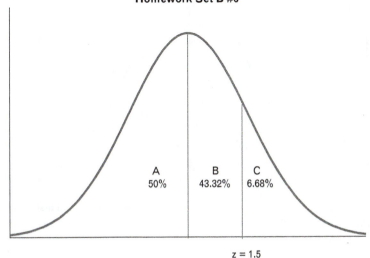

z = –1.33

FIGURE 6.21: Homework Set B #5.

b.   50–40.82 = 9.18% of the test-takers scored lower than you

c.   100–9.18% = 90.82% of the test-takers scored higher than you

6.   a.   Z = (X–M)/SD

Z = (115–100)/10

Z = 1.5

Homework Set B #6

z = 1.5

FIGURE 6.22: Homework Set B #6.

b.   50 + 43.32 = 93.32% of the test-takers scored lower than you
c.   100–93.32 = 6.68% scored higher than you

7.

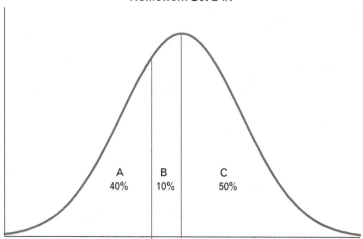

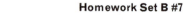

FIGURE 6.23: Homework Set B #7.

a.   His z-score is –.25 (9.87 on the % Mean-to-Z table)
b.   X = Z(SD) + M
     X = –.25(5) + 60 = 58.75 = His raw score on the first test

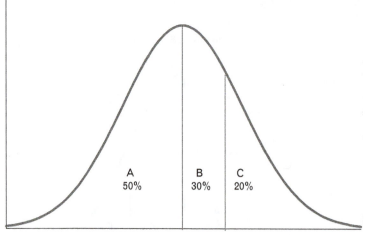

FIGURE 6.24: Homework Set B #7.

   c.   His z-score is .84 (29.95 on the % Mean-to-Z table)

   d.   X = Z(SD) + M

       X = .84(5) + 60 = 64.2 = His raw score on the second test

CHAPTER SEVEN

1. a. 1.   Research hypothesis: People who shower in the morning are more motivated than the general population.

$$H_1 : \mu_1 > \mu_2$$

Null hypothesis: People who shower in the morning are less motivated than, or as equally motivated as, the general population.

$$H_1 : \mu_1 \leq \mu_2$$

2.   The comparison distribution is the normal distribution of motivation in the general population.

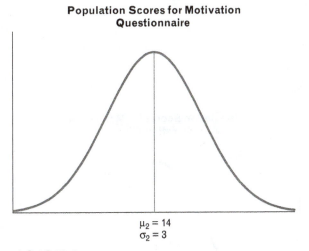

Population Scores for Motivation Questionnaire

$\mu_2 = 14$
$\sigma_2 = 3$

FIGURE 7.17: Homework Set B #1a2.

3. The alpha level is .01. The cutoff score is 2.33.

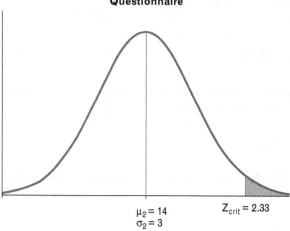

FIGURE 7.18: Homework Set B #1a3.

4. $Z = \dfrac{(X - \mu_2)}{\sigma_2}$

$Z = \dfrac{(15 - 14)}{3}$

$Z = .33 = Z_{obt}$

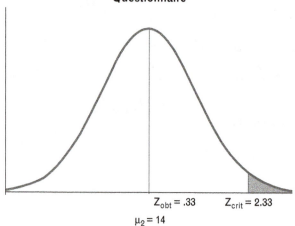

FIGURE 7.19: Homework Set B #1a4.

5. We failed to reject the null hypothesis. The sample is likely to have come from the population distribution.
b. The results are inconclusive, since we failed to reject the null hypothesis. The results do not prove or disprove anything, but they do not support the research hypothesis that showering in the morning increases motivation.
c. If an error were made in this research, it would be a Type-II error, failing to reject the null hypothesis when the research hypothesis was, in fact, true.

2. a. 1. Research Hypothesis: People who have been unemployed for more than 6 months will have higher social anxiety than the general population.

$$H_1 : \mu_1 > \mu_2$$

Null hypothesis: People who have been unemployed for more than 6 months will have levels of social anxiety less than, or equal to, the general population.

$$H_1 : \mu_1 \leq \mu_2$$

2. The comparison distribution is the normal distribution of scores on social anxiety.

Population Scores for Social Anxiety

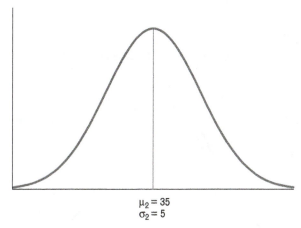

$$\mu_2 = 35$$
$$\sigma_2 = 5$$

FIGURE 7.20: Homework Set B #2a2.

3. The alpha level is .05, and the cutoff score is 1.64.

Population Scores for Social Anxiety

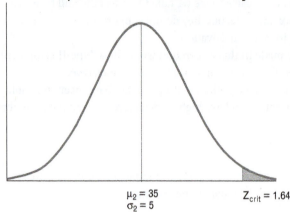

$\mu_2 = 35$
$\sigma_2 = 5$

$Z_{crit} = 1.64$

FIGURE 7.21: Homework Set B #2a3.

4. $Z = \dfrac{(X - \mu_2)}{\sigma_2}$

$Z = \dfrac{(44 - 35)}{5}$

$Z = 1.8 = Z_{obt}$

Population Scores for Social Anxiety

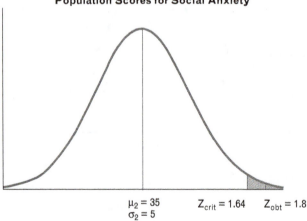

$\mu_2 = 35$
$\sigma_2 = 5$

$Z_{crit} = 1.64$ $Z_{obt} = 1.8$

FIGURE 7.22: Homework Set B #2a4.

5. We reject the null hypothesis. The sample is likely to come from a distribution other than the comparison distribution.

b. The results do not prove or disprove anything, but they do provide support for the research hypothesis that people who have been unemployed for more than 6 months may have higher social anxiety than the general population

c. If an error were made in this research, it would be Type-I error, rejecting the null hypothesis when the research hypothesis is false.

3.   a.   1.   Research Hypothesis: People who have low standards for romantic partners will have higher relationship satisfaction scores than the general population.

$$H_1 : \mu_1 > \mu_2$$

Null hypothesis: People who have low standards for romantic partners will have relationship satisfaction scores less than, or equal to, the general population.

$$H_1 : \mu_1 \leq \mu_2$$

2.   The comparison distribution is the normal distribution of relationship satisfaction scores in the general population.

**Population Scores for
Relationship Satisfaction**

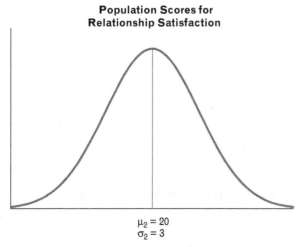

$\mu_2 = 20$
$\sigma_2 = 3$

FIGURE 7.23: Homework Set B #3a2.

3.   The alpha level is .01, which gives us a cutoff score of 2.33.

Population Scores for Relationship Satisfaction

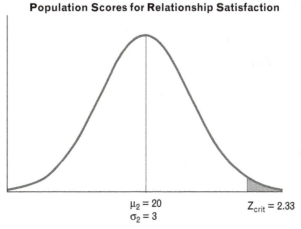

$\mu_2 = 20$ $Z_{crit} = 2.33$
$\sigma_2 = 3$

FIGURE 7.24: Homework Set B #3a3.

4. $Z = \dfrac{(X - \mu_2)}{\sigma_2}$

$Z = \dfrac{(28 - 20)}{3}$

$Z = 2.67 = Z_{obt}.$

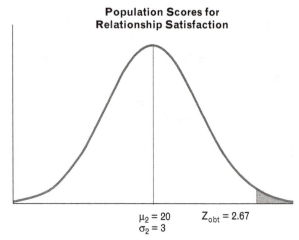

Population Scores for
Relationship Satisfaction

$\mu_2 = 20$ $Z_{obt} = 2.67$
$\sigma_2 = 3$

FIGURE 7.25: Homework Set B #3a4.

5. We will reject the null hypothesis because our Z_{obt} was more extreme than the Z_{crit}. The sample is likely to come from a distribution that is different than the population distribution for social anxiety.

b. The results do not prove or disprove anything, but they do provide support for the research hypothesis that people who have lower standards for romantic partners experience greater relationship satisfaction.

c. If an error were made in this research, it would be Type-I error, rejecting the null hypothesis when the research hypothesis is false.

CHAPTER EIGHT

1. a. $H_1: \mu_1 < \mu_2$

$H_0: \mu_1 \geq \mu_2$

b. $\sigma = .5$

$\sigma^2 = .25$

$\sigma^2_M = \dfrac{\sigma^2}{N} = \dfrac{.25}{12} = .02$

$\sigma_M = \sqrt{\sigma^2_M} = \sqrt{.02} = .14$

c. $Z_{crit} = -2.33$ (Alpha level of .01, negative because the mean of the special population is predicted to be less than the mean for the general population.)

d. $Z_{obt} \dfrac{M - \mu_{M2}}{\sigma_{M2}}$

$$Z_{obt} = \frac{4.8 - 7.2}{.14} = -17.14$$

e.   The Z_{obt} of -17.14 is in the alpha region, so we reject the null hypothesis. After watching Olympic athletes, people seem to lower their assessments of their own athletic skills.

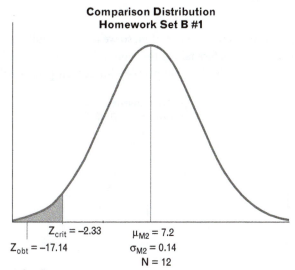

Comparison Distribution
Homework Set B #1

$Z_{crit} = -2.33$ $\mu_{M2} = 7.2$
$Z_{obt} = -17.14$ $\sigma_{M2} = 0.14$
                      $N = 12$

FIGURE 8.11: Homework Set B #1.

f. $M = Z(\sigma_M) + \mu_M$

$M = 2.57(.14) + 4.8 = .36 + 4.8 = 5.16$

And

$M = -2.57(.14) + 4.8 = -.36 + 4.8 = 4.44$

The 99% confidence level is between 4.44 and 5.16. We are 99% certain, based on our data, that the population mean on the YTSAVS for people who have recently watched an Olympic gold medal volleyball match is between 4.44 and 5.16.

2.   a. $H_1: \mu_1 > \mu_2$

$H_0: \mu_1 \leq \mu_2$

b. $\sigma = 3$

$\sigma^2 = 9$

$$\sigma^2_M = \frac{\sigma^2}{N} = \frac{9}{10} = .9$$

$$\sigma_M = \sqrt{\sigma^2_M} = \sqrt{.9} = .95$$

c. $Z_{crit} = 1.64$ (Alpha level of .05)

d. $Z_{obt} = \dfrac{M - \mu_{M2}}{\sigma_{M2}}$

$$Z_{obt} = \frac{18 - 15}{.95} = 3.16$$

e.   The Z_{obt} of 3.16 is in the alpha region, so we reject the null hypothesis. People who dress their pets up before taking them on walks seem to score higher on a scale of attention-seeking behavior than people who let their pets be naked on walks.

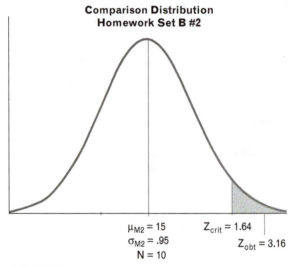

**Comparison Distribution
Homework Set B #2**

$\mu_{M2} = 15$
$\sigma_{M2} = .95$
$N = 10$

$Z_{crit} = 1.64$

$Z_{obt} = 3.16$

FIGURE 8.12: Homework Set B #2.

f. $M = Z(\sigma_M) + \mu_M$

$$M = 1.96(.95) + 18 = 1.86 + 18 = 19.86$$

And

$$M = -1.96(.95) + 18 = -1.86 + 18 = 16.14$$

The 95% confidence level is between 16.14 and 19.86. We are 95% certain, based on our data, that the population mean on the attention-seeking questionnaire for people who dress their pets up for walks is between 16.14 and 19.86.

3. a. $H_1: \mu_1 < \mu_2$

$H_0: \mu_1 \geq \mu_2$

b. $\sigma = 2$

$\sigma^2 = 4$

$\sigma^2_M = \dfrac{\sigma^2}{N} = \dfrac{4}{18} = .22$

$\sigma_M = \sqrt{\sigma^2_M} = \sqrt{.22} = .47$

c. $Z_{crit} = -1.64$ (Alpha level of .05, negative because the mean of the special population is predicted to be less than the mean for the general population.)

d. $Z_{obt} = \dfrac{M - \mu_{M2}}{\sigma_{M2}}$

$Z_{obt} = \dfrac{13.5 - 14}{.47} = -1.06$

e. The Z_{obt} of -1.06 is not in the alpha region, so we fail to reject the null hypothesis. Kids who learn to swim without swimming lessons are not less safe in water than are other kids.

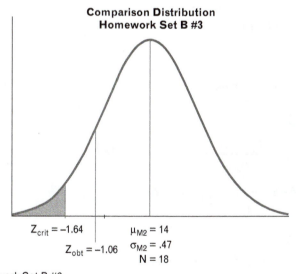

**Comparison Distribution
Homework Set B #3**

$Z_{crit} = -1.64$

$Z_{obt} = -1.06$

$\mu_{M2} = 14$

$\sigma_{M2} = .47$

$N = 18$

FIGURE 8.13: Homework Set B #3.

f. $M = Z(\sigma_M) + \mu_M$

$M = 1.96(.47) + 13.5 = .92 + 13.5 = 14.42$

And

$M = -1.96(.47) + 13.5 = -.92 + 13.5 = 12.58$

The 95% confidence level is between 12.58 and 14.42. We are 95% certain, based on our data, that the population mean on the WSSAT for children who have not had swimming lessons is between 12.58 and 14.42.

CHAPTER NINE

Homework Set B

1. $H_1: \mu_1 > \mu_2$

   $H_0: \mu_1 \leq \mu_2$

   Computing standard deviation:

   $$\sigma^2 = \sigma * \sigma = 2 * 2 = 4$$

   $$\sigma^2_{M2} = \frac{\sigma^2}{N} = \frac{4}{20} = .2$$

   $$\sigma_{M2} = \sqrt{\left(\sigma^2_{M2}\right)} = \sqrt{.2} = .45$$

   Computing M_{crit}:

   $$M_{crit} = Z_{crit}(\sigma_{M2}) + \mu_{M2}$$
   $$M_{crit} = 2.33(.45) + 6$$
   $$M_{crit} = 1.05 + 6 = 7.05$$

   Computing M_{upper}:

   $$M_{crit} = M_{upper} = 7.05$$

   Computing Z_{upper}:

   $$Z_{upper} = \frac{M_{upper} - \mu_{M1}}{\sigma_{M1}}$$

   $$\frac{7.05 - 8}{.45} = \frac{-.95}{.45} = -2.11$$

   Computing Power:

   % Mean to Z of –2.11 = 48.26%
   Power = 48.26% + 50% = 98.26%

   Computing Beta:

   100% – 98.26% = 1.74%

   Calculation Cohen's d:

   $$\text{Cohen's } d = \frac{\mu_{M1} - \mu_{M2}}{\sigma_2}$$

   $$\text{Cohen's } d = \frac{8 - 6}{2} = 1$$

Comment on power and Cohen's d:

Effect size was very large in this study (Cohen's d = 1), and power was very high (98.26%).

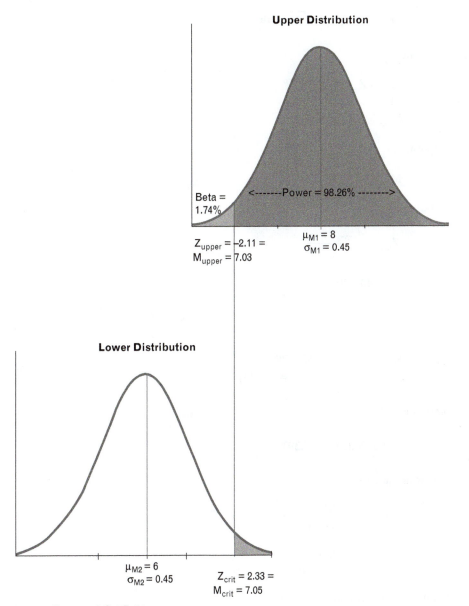

Upper Distribution

Beta = 1.74%

<-------Power = 98.26% -------->

$\mu_{M1} = 8$
$\sigma_{M1} = 0.45$

$Z_{upper} = -2.11 =$
$M_{upper} = 7.03$

Lower Distribution

$\mu_{M2} = 6$
$\sigma_{M2} = 0.45$

$Z_{crit} = 2.33 =$
$M_{crit} = 7.05$

FIGURE 9.21: Homework Set B #1.

2. $H_1: \mu_1 > \mu_2$

   $H_0: \mu_1 \leq \mu_2$

Computing standard deviation:

$$\sigma^2 = \sigma * \sigma = 1.2 * 1.2 = 1.44$$

$$\sigma^2_{M2} = \frac{\sigma^2}{N} = \frac{1.44}{6} = .24$$

$$\sigma_{M2} = \sqrt{(\sigma^2_{M2})} = \sqrt{.24} = .49$$

Computing M_{crit}:

$$M_{crit} = Z_{crit}(\sigma_{M2}) + \mu_{M2}$$
$$M_{crit} = 1.64(.49) + 19.6$$
$$M_{crit} = .80 + 19.6 = 20.40$$

Computing M_{upper}:

$$M_{crit} = M_{upper} = 20.40$$

Computing Z_{upper}:

$$Z_{upper} \frac{M_{upper} - \mu_{M1}}{\sigma_{M1}}$$

$$= \frac{20.40 - 20}{.49} = \frac{.40}{.49} = .82$$

Computing power:

% Mean-to-Z of .82 = 29.39%
Power = 50%–29.39% = 20.61%

Computing Beta:

100%–20.61% = 79.39%

Calculating Cohen's d:

$$\text{Cohen's } d = \left| \frac{\mu_{M1} - \mu_{M2}}{\sigma_2} \right|$$

$$\text{Cohen's } d = \left| \frac{20 - 19.6}{1.20} \right| = .33$$

Comment on power and Cohen's d:
    Effect size was small in this study (Cohen's d = .33), and power was low (20.61%).

Upper Distribution

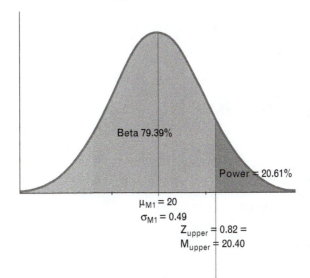

Beta 79.39%

Power = 20.61%

$\mu_{M1} = 20$
$\sigma_{M1} = 0.49$
$Z_{upper} = 0.82 =$
$M_{upper} = 20.40$

Lower Distribution

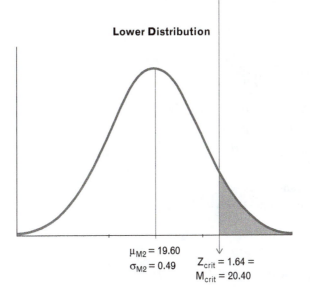

$\mu_{M2} = 19.60$
$\sigma_{M2} = 0.49$
$Z_{crit} = 1.64 =$
$M_{crit} = 20.40$

FIGURE 9.22: Homework Set B #2.

3. $H_1: \mu_1 < \mu_2$

   $H_0: \mu_1 \geq \mu_2$

Computing standard deviation:

$$\sigma^2 = \sigma * \sigma = 2 * 2 = 4$$

$$\sigma^2_{M2} = \frac{\sigma^2}{N} = \frac{4}{10} = .4$$

$$\sigma_{M2} = \sqrt{(\sigma^2_{M2})} = \sqrt{4} = .63$$

Computing M_{crit}:

$$M_{crit} = Z_{crit}(\sigma_{M2}) + \mu_{M2}$$
$$M_{crit} = -1.64(.63) + 20$$
$$M_{crit} = -1.03 + 20 = 18.97$$

Computing M_{upper}:

$$M_{crit} = M_{upper} = 18.97$$

Computing Z_{upper}:

$$z_{upper} = \frac{M_{upper} - \mu_{M1}}{\sigma_{M1}}$$

$$\frac{18.97 - 19}{.63} = \frac{-.03}{.63} = -.05$$

Computing power:

% Mean-to-Z of −.05 = 1.99%
Power = 50% −1.99% = 48.01%

Computing Beta:

100%−48.01% = 51.99%

Calculation Cohen's d:

$$\text{Cohen's } d = \left| \frac{\mu_{M1} - \mu_{M2}}{\sigma_2} \right|$$

$$\text{Cohen's } d = \left| \frac{19 - 20}{2} \right| = -.5$$

Comment on power and Cohen's d:

Effect size was medium in this study (the absolute value of Cohen's d = .5), and power was low (48.01%).

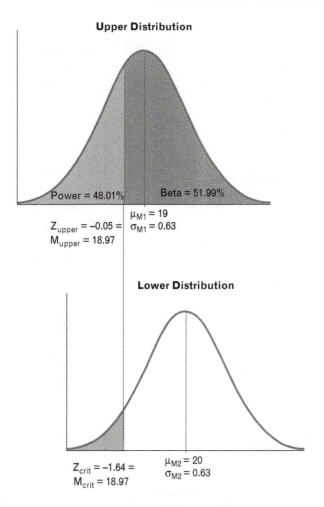

Upper Distribution

Power = 48.01%   Beta = 51.99%

$\mu_{M1} = 19$
$Z_{upper} = -0.05 =$ $\sigma_{M1} = 0.63$
$M_{upper} = 18.97$

Lower Distribution

$\mu_{M2} = 20$
$Z_{crit} = -1.64 =$ $\sigma_{M2} = 0.63$
$M_{crit} = 18.97$

FIGURE 9.23:

CHAPTER TEN

1. a. $H_1: \mu_1 > \mu_2$

   $H_0: \mu_1 \leq \mu_2$

   b. Comparison distribution is a t-distribution, N = 4.
   c. $t_{crit} = 4.54$

d.

Table 10.13: Homework Set B #1 Calculations

X	M	X−M	(X−M)²
7	5	2	4
3	5	0	0
3	5	0	0
7	5	2	4

$$M = \frac{\sum X}{N}; \frac{20}{4} = 5$$

$$\Sigma(X-M)^2 = 8 = SS$$

$$s^2 = \frac{SS}{N-1} * = \frac{8}{3} = 2.67$$

$$s = \sqrt{s^2} = 1.63$$

$$s^2{}_M = \frac{s^2}{n} = \frac{2.67}{4} = .67$$

$$s_M = \sqrt{s^2_M} = \sqrt{.67} = .82$$

$$t = \frac{M - \mu_{M2}}{s_M}$$

$$t = \frac{5-3}{.82} = 2.44$$

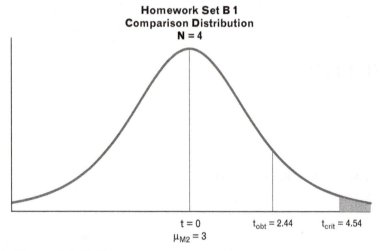

**Homework Set B 1
Comparison Distribution
N = 4**

t = 0 t_{obt} = 2.44 t_{crit} = 4.54
μ_{M2} = 3

FIGURE 10.12: Homework Set B #1.

e. t_{obt} is not in the alpha region; therefore, we fail to reject the null hypothesis. Our results indicate that putting up a sign informing people that parakeets can learn to talk does not increase parakeet sales at the pet store.

f.   Cohen's $d = \left| \dfrac{M - \mu_2}{S} \right| = \left| \dfrac{5-3}{1.63} \right| = 1.23$

Cohen's d is 1.23, which is a large effect size.

2. a. $H_1: \mu_1 < \mu_2$

$H_0: \mu_1 \geq \mu_2$

b.   Comparison distribution is a t-distribution, N = 6.

c. $t_{crit} = -2.02$

d.

Table 10.14: Homework Set B #2 Calculations

X	M	X−M	(X−M)²
19	17	2	4
14	17	−3	9
16	17	−1	1
17	17	0	0
17	17	0	0
19	17	2	4

$$M = \frac{\Sigma X}{N} ; \frac{102}{6} = 17 \qquad \Sigma(X-M)^2 = 18 = ss$$

$$s^2 = \frac{SS}{N-1} * = \frac{18}{5} = 3.6$$

$$s = \sqrt{s^2} = 1.90$$

$$s^2_{M} = \frac{s^2}{n} = \frac{3.6}{6} = .6$$

$$s_M = \sqrt{s^2_M} = \sqrt{.6} = .77$$

$$t = \frac{M - \mu_{M2}}{s_M}$$

$$t = \frac{17 - 16}{.77} = 1.30$$

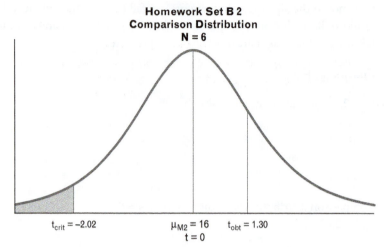

FIGURE 10.13: Homework Set B #2.

e. t_{obt} is not in the alpha region; therefore, we fail to reject the null hypothesis. We did not find evidence that injured players have low levels of fitness/strength.

f.   Cohen's $d = \dfrac{M - \mu_2}{S} = \dfrac{17 - 16}{1.90} = .53$

Cohen's d is .53, which is a medium effect size.

3.   a. $H_1 : \hat{\bar{d}} < 0$

$H_0 : \hat{\bar{d}} \geq 0$

b.   The comparison distribution is a normal distribution of $\bar{d}_s$ with a mean of zero.

c. $\hat{\bar{d}}$ is predicted to be less than 0, so t_{crit} is negative. There is a particular direction predicted, so the test is one-tailed, has an alpha of .05, and 4 degrees of freedom. $t_{crit} = -2.13$.

d.

Table 10.15: Homework Set B #3 Calculations

Variable 1 (rating before getting new school supplies)	Variable 2 (rating after getting new school supplies)	(d) Difference	($\bar{d}$) Mean Difference	(d– $\bar{d}$) Difference between difference and mean difference	(d– $\bar{d}$)² Mean Difference Squared
1	3	−2	−1.2	−.8	.64
2	3	−1	−1.2	.2	.04
1	2	−1	−1.2	.2	.04
1	3	−2	−1.2	−.8	.64
3	3	0	−1.2	1.2	1.44

$$\bar{d} = \frac{\sum d}{N}; \frac{-6}{5} = -1.2$$

$$\sum(d - \bar{d})^2 = 2.80 = SS$$

$$s^2 = \frac{SS}{N-1} * = \frac{2.80}{4} = .70$$

$$s = \sqrt{s^2} = .84$$

$$s^2{}_M = \frac{s^2}{N} = \frac{.64}{5} = .14$$

$$s_M = \sqrt{s^2_M} = \sqrt{.14} = .37$$

$$t_{obt} = \frac{\bar{d}}{s_M}$$

$$t_{obt} = \frac{-1.2}{.37} = -3.24$$

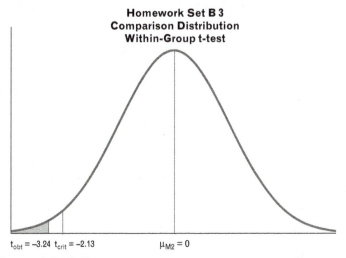

**Homework Set B 3
Comparison Distribution
Within-Group t-test**

$t_{obt} = -3.24$ $t_{crit} = -2.13$ $\mu_{M2} = 0$

FIGURE 10.14: Homework Set B #3.

e. t_{obt} is in the alpha region; therefore, we reject the null hypothesis. Our research indicates that giving kids new school supplies does seem to make them more excited for school to start.

f.   Cohen's $d = \left| \dfrac{-1.2}{.84} \right| = -1.43$

Cohen's d is –1.43, which is a large effect size.

4.

a. $H_1 : \hat{\bar{d}} > 0$

$H_0 : \hat{\bar{d}} \leq 0$

b.   The comparison distribution is a normal distribution of $\bar{d}_s$ with a mean of zero.

c. $\hat{\bar{d}}$ is predicted to be greater than 0, so t_{crit} is positive. There is a particular direction predicted, so the test is one-tailed, has an alpha of .05, and 4 degrees of freedom. $t_{crit} = 2.13$.

d.

Table 10.16: Homework Set B #4 Calculations

Variable 1 (pre-policy change satisfaction rating)	Variable 2 (post-policy change satisfaction rating)	(d) Difference	($\bar{d}$) Mean Difference	(d– $\bar{d}$) Difference between difference and mean difference	(d– $\bar{d}$)² Mean Difference Squared
6	5	1	1.2	–.2	.04
7	5	2	1.2	.8	.64
10	10	0	1.2	–1.2	1.44
9	7	2	1.2	.8	.64
9	8	1	1.2	–.2	.04

$$\bar{d} = \frac{\Sigma d}{N}; \frac{6}{5} = 1.2$$

$$\Sigma(d - \bar{d})^2 = 2.8 = SS$$

$$s^2 = \frac{SS}{N-1} * = \frac{2.8}{4} = .7$$

$$s = \sqrt{s^2} = .84$$

$$s^2_M = \frac{s^2}{N} = \frac{.7}{5} = .14$$

$$s_M = \sqrt{s^2_M} = \sqrt{.14} = .37$$

$$t_{obt} = \frac{\bar{d}}{s_M}$$

$$t_{obt} = \frac{1.2}{.37} = 3.24$$

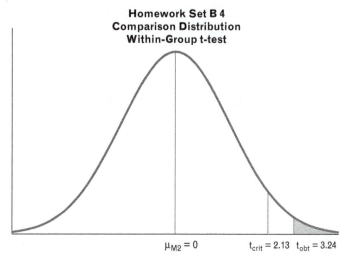

Homework Set B 4
Comparison Distribution
Within-Group t-test

$\mu_{M2} = 0$ $t_{crit} = 2.13$ $t_{obt} = 3.24$

FIGURE 10.15: Homework Set B #4.

e. t_{obt} is in the alpha region; therefore, we reject the null hypothesis. Our research suggests that forcing adults to say something nice at the end of staff meetings may decrease their job satisfaction.

f.   Cohen's $d = \left| \dfrac{\bar{d}}{s} \right|$

Cohen's $d = \left| \dfrac{1.2}{.84} \right| = 1.43$

Cohen's d is 1.43, which is a large effect size.

CHAPTER ELEVEN

A.   **1. State your research and null hypotheses in terms of population parameters.**
      A. Define the two populations in terms of two different population means:
      μ_1 = mean number of dates for the entire population of introverts
      μ_2 = mean number of dates for the entire population of extroverts
B.   Delineate research and null hypotheses:
      $H_1 = \mu_1 \neq \mu_2$ (the population mean for introverts is predicted to be different from [either greater than or less than] the population mean for extroverts)
      $H_0 = \mu_1 = \mu_2$ (the population mean for introverts is predicted to be equal to the population mean for extroverts)
2.   Determine the characteristics of your comparison distribution.
      A. Compute s_1^2 and s_2^2

Table 11.21: Computing s_1^2

Group 1: Introverts

X_1	M_1	(X_1-M_1)	$(X_1-M_1)^2$
3	2.2	.8	.64
1	2.2	−1.2	1.44
1	2.2	−1.2	1.44
2	2.2	−.2	.04
4	2.2	1.8	3.24

$\Sigma X_1 = 11$

$SS_1 = \Sigma(X_1-M_1)^2 = 6.8$

$N_1 = 5$

$$s_1^2 = \frac{SS_1}{N_1-1} = 1.7$$

$$s_1 = \sqrt{s_1^2} = 1.30$$

Table 11.22: Computing s_2^2

Group 2: Extroverts

X_2	M_2	(X_2-M_2)	$(X_2-M_2)^2$
1	2.6	−1.6	2.56
3	2.6	.4	.16
2	2.6	−.6	.36
4	2.6	1.4	1.96
3	2.6	.4	.16

$\Sigma X_2 = 13$

$SS_2 = \Sigma(X_2-M_2)^2 = 5.2$

$N_2 = 5$

$$s_2^2 = \frac{SS_2}{N_2-1} = 1.3$$

$$s_2 = \sqrt{s_2^2} = 1.14$$

B. Compute s_{pooled}^2

$$s_{pooled}^2 = s_1^2\left(\frac{df_1}{df_{total}}\right) + \left(\frac{df_2}{df_{total}}\right);$$

$df_1 = 5-1 = 4$;
$df_2 = 5-1 = 4$;
$df_{total} = 4+4 = 8$;

$$s_{pooled}^2 = \frac{4}{8}(1.7) + \frac{4}{8}(1.3) = .85 + .65 = 1.5$$

C. Compute s^2_{M1} and s^2_{M2}

$$s^2_{M1} = \frac{s^2_{pooled}}{N_1} = \frac{1.5}{5} = .3$$

$$s^2_{M2} = \frac{s^2_{pooled}}{N_2} = \frac{1.5}{5} = .3$$

D. Compute s_{dif}

$$s^2_{dif} = s^2_{M1} + s^2_{M2}$$

$$s^2_{dif} = .3 + .3 = .6$$

$$s_{dif} = \sqrt{s^2_{dif}} = .77$$

3. Determine your critical value (used for defining the *rejection region*)

The alpha is .05 and the total degrees of freedom = 8. We have a two-tailed test. According to the chart, t_{crit} is ± 2.31.

4. Compute your "obtained statistic" (here, your obtained t score) and compare it with the critical value.

$$t_{obt} = \frac{M_1 - M_2}{s_{dif}} = \frac{2.2 - 2.6}{.77} = -.52$$

The t score of −.52 is not more extreme than the critical value of 2.31, and thus does not fall into rejection region.

5. Comment on the null hypothesis (include effect size).

The null hypothesis is not rejected because t_{obt} does not fall into the rejection region. Therefore, when it comes to the number of dates, the population mean for introverts is not likely greater than, nor less than, the population mean for extroverts—based on these data, introverts are not likely to date any more or less frequently than extroverts.

$$\text{Cohens's } d = \left| \frac{M_1 - M_2}{s_{pooled}} \right| = \left| \frac{2.2 - 2.6}{\sqrt{1.5}} \right| = \left| \frac{-.4}{1.22} \right| = -.33$$

Recall that when it comes to Cohen's d, we take the absolute value (as the sign is totally a function of which population we arbitrarily assign to be population 1 and 2). In this case, a Cohen's d of −.33 (or just .33) indicates that the effect size of the difference is small to medium. There is likely no difference between introverts and extroverts when it comes to the amount of dating.

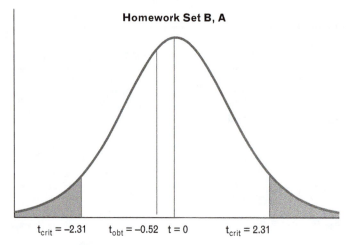

$t_{crit} = -2.31$ $t_{obt} = -0.52$ $t = 0$ $t_{crit} = 2.31$

FIGURE 11.8: Homework Set B, A.

B.   **1. State your research and null hypotheses in terms of population parameters.**
   A.   Define the two populations in terms of two different population means:
      μ_1 = mean number of thank-yous for the entire population of children with nannies
      μ_2 = mean number of thank-yous for the entire population of children in daycare
   B.   Delineate research and null hypotheses:
      $H_1 = \mu_1 > \mu_2$ (the population mean for children with nannies is predicted to be greater than the population mean for children in daycare)
      $H_0 = \mu_1 \leq \mu_2$ (the population mean for children with nannies is predicted to be less than or equal to the population mean for children in daycare)
2.   Determine the characteristics of your comparison distribution.
   A.   Compute s_1^2 and s_2^2

Table 11.23: Computing s_1^2

Group 1: Nanny children

X_1	M_1	(X_1-M_1)	$(X_1-M_1)^2$
9	5.5	3.5	12.25
3	5.5	-2.5	6.25
4	5.5	-1.5	2.25
6	5.5	.5	.25
$\Sigma X_1 = 22$			$SS_1 = \Sigma(X_1-M_1)^2 = 21$
			$s_1^2 = \dfrac{SS_1}{N_1-1} = 7$
$N_1 = 4$			
			$s_2 = \sqrt{s_2^2} = 2.65$

Table 11.24: Computing s_2^2

Group 2: Daycare children

X_2	M_2	(X_2-M_2)	$(X_2-M_2)^2$
2	4.8	-2.8	7.84
8	4.8	3.2	10.24
6	4.8	1.2	1.44
3	4.8	-1.8	3.24
5	4.8	.2	.04
$\Sigma X_2 = 24$			$SS_2 = \Sigma(X_2-M_2)^2 = 22.8$
			$s_2^2 = \dfrac{SS_2}{N_2-1} = 5.7$
$N_2 = 5$			$s_2 = \sqrt{s_2^2} = 2.39$

B.   Compute s_{pooled}^2

$$s_{pooled}^2 = s_1^2\left(\frac{df_1}{df_{total}}\right) + s_2^2\left(\frac{df_2}{df_{total}}\right);$$

$df_1 = 4-1 = 3;$
$df_2 = 5-1 = 4;$
$df_{total} = 3 + 4 = 7;$

$$s_{pooled}^2 = \frac{3}{7}(7) + \frac{4}{7}(5.7) = 3.01 + 3.25 = 6.27$$

C.   Compute s_{M1}^2 and s_{M2}^2 $\quad s_{M1}^2 = \dfrac{s_{pooled}^2}{N_1} = \dfrac{6.27}{4} = 1.57$

$$s_{M2}^2 = \frac{s_{pooled}^2}{N_2} = \frac{6.27}{5} = 1.25$$

D.   Compute s_{dif}

$$s_{dif}^2 = s_{M1}^2 + s_{M2}^2$$

$$s_{dif}^2 = 1.57 + 1.25 = 2.82$$

$$s_{dif} = \sqrt{s_{dif}^2} = 1.68$$

3.   Determine your critical value (used for defining the *rejection region*)

The alpha is .01 and the total degrees of freedom = 7. We have a one-tailed test. According to the chart, our critical value is 3.0.

4. Compute your "obtained statistic" (here, your obtained t-score) and compare it with the critical value.

$$t_{obt} = \frac{M_1 - M_2}{S_{dif}} = \frac{5.5 - 4.8}{1.68} = .42$$

The t score of .42 is not more extreme than the critical value of 3.0, and thus does not fall into rejection region.

5. Comment on the null hypothesis (include effect size).

The null hypothesis is not rejected. Therefore, when it comes to manners, the population mean for children with nannies is not likely greater than the population mean for children in daycare. There is likely no difference in the manners between children with nannies and children who attend daycare.

$$\text{Cohen's } d = \left|\frac{M_1 - M_2}{S_{pooled}}\right| = \left|\frac{5.5 - 4.8}{\sqrt{6.27}}\right| = \left|\frac{.7}{2.50}\right| = .28$$

Cohen's d is .28, which indicates that the effect size of the difference is small. According to our findings, there is no evidence that children who have nannies have better manners than children who attend daycare.

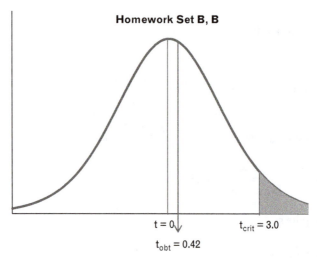

FIGURE 11.9: Homework Set B, B.

C. **1. State your research and null hypotheses in terms of population parameters.**
    A. Define the two populations in terms of two different population means:
        μ_1 = mean weight of clothes for the entire population of non-risk takers.
        μ_2 = mean weight of clothes for the entire population of risk takers
    B. Delineate research and null hypotheses:
        $H_1 = \mu_1 > \mu_2$ (the population mean for non-risk takers is predicted to be greater than the population mean for risk takers)
        $H_0 = \mu_1 \leq \mu_2$ (the population mean for non-risk takers is predicted to be less than or equal to the population mean for risk takers)

2. Determine the characteristics of your comparison distribution.
   A. Compute s_1^2 and s_2^2

Table 11.25: Computing s_1^2

Group 1: Non–risk takers

X_1	M_1	(X_1-M_1)	$(X_1-M_1)^2$
1.5	2.00	-.5	.25
2.2	2.00	.2	.04
1.6	2.00	-.4	.16
1.92	2.00	-.08	.01
2.5	2.00	.5	.25
2.3	2.00	.3	.09
$\Sigma X_1 = 12$			$SS_1 = \Sigma(X_1-M_1)^2 = .8$
			$s_1^2 = \dfrac{SS_1}{N_1-1} = .16$
$N_1 = 6$			$s_1 = \sqrt{s_1^2} = .4$

Table 11.26: Computing s_2^2

Group 2: Risk takers

X_2	M_2	(X_2-M_2)	$(X_2-M_2)^2$
1.7	1.25	.45	.20
1.2	1.25	-.05	.00
.8	1.25	-.45	.20
1.3	1.25	.05	.00
$\Sigma X_2 = 5$			$SS_2 = \Sigma(X_2-M_2)^2 = .40$
			$s_2^2 = \dfrac{SS_2}{N_2-1} = .13$
$N_2 = 4$			$s_2 = \sqrt{s_2^2} = .36$

B. Compute s_{pooled}^2

$$s_{pooled}^2 = s_1^2\left(\frac{df_1}{df_{total}}\right) + s_2^2\left(\frac{df_2}{df_{total}}\right);$$

$df_1 = 6-1 = 5;$

$$df_2 = 4-1 = 3;$$
$$df_{total} = 5 + 3 = 8;$$

$$s^2_{pooled} = \frac{5}{8}(.16) + \frac{3}{8}(.13) = .1 + .05 = .15$$

C. Compute s^2_{M1} and s^2_{M2}

$$s^2_{M1} = \frac{s^2_{pooled}}{N_1} = \frac{.15}{6} = .03$$

$$s^2_{M2} = \frac{s^2_{pooled}}{N_2} = \frac{.15}{4} = .04$$

D. Compute s_{dif}

$$s^2_{dif} = s^2_{M1} + s^2_{M2}$$

$$s^2_{dif} = .03 + .04 = .07$$

$$s_{dif} = \sqrt{s^2_{dif}} = .26$$

3. Determine your critical value (used for defining the *rejection region*)

The alpha is .05 and the total degrees of freedom = 8. We have a one-tailed test. According to the chart, our critical value is 1.86.

4. Compute your "obtained statistic" (here, your obtained t-score) and compare it with the critical value.

$$t_{obt} = \frac{M_1 - M_2}{s_{dif}} = \frac{2.00 - 1.25}{.26} = 2.88$$

The t score of 2.88 is more extreme than the critical value of 1.86, and thus does fall into the rejection region.

5. Comment on the null hypothesis (include effect size).

The null hypothesis is rejected because t is more extreme than t-critical. Our t value is in the rejection region. Therefore, when it comes to the amount of clothing worn, the population mean for non-risk takers is likely greater than the population mean for risk takers—risk takers likely wear skimpier clothing than non-risk takers.

$$\text{Cohen's d} = \left| \frac{M_1 - M_2}{s_{pooled}} \right| = \left| \frac{2.00 - 1.25}{\sqrt{.15}} \right| = \left| \frac{.75}{.39} \right| = 1.92$$

Cohen's d is 1.92, which indicates that the effect size of the difference is very, very large. Not only are risk takers wearing skimpier clothing, but it appears that the clothing is *much* skimpier than that of the non-risk takers.

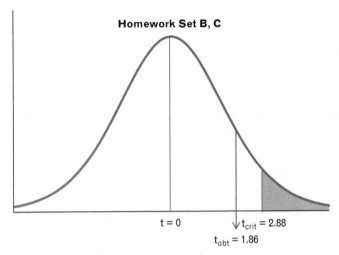

Homework Set B, C

$t = 0$

$t_{crit} = 2.88$

$t_{obt} = 1.86$

FIGURE 11.10: Homework Set B, C.

CHAPTER TWELVE

1.

Table 12.37: Homework Set B #1

No cats	1–3 cats	4+ cats
20	19	16
16	19	16
18	16	13
18		15
$\Sigma X_1 = 72$, $M_1 = 18$, $N_1 = 4$, $df_1 = 3$	$\Sigma X_2 = 54$, $M_2 = 18$, $N_2 = 3$, $df_2 = 2$	$\Sigma X_3 = 60$, $M_3 = 15$, $N_3 = 4$, $df_3 = 3$

   a. H_1: NOT H_0

       H_0: $\mu_1 = \mu_2 = \mu_3$

   b. The comparison distribution is F(2, 8)

   c. The alpha level is .05, numerator degrees of freedom = 2, and denominator degrees of freedom = 8, so $F_{crit} = 4.46$

d. $F = \dfrac{MS_B}{MS_W}$

$MS_W = \dfrac{SS_W}{df_W}$

$SS_W = SS_{W1} + SS_{W2} + SS_{W3} + \cdots$

Table 12.38: Mental stability scores for women with no cats (X_1)

X_1	M_1	(X_1-M_1)	$(X_1-M_1)^2$
20	18	2	4
16	18	−2	4
18	18	0	0
18	18	0	0
$M_1 = 18$; $N_1 = 4$; $df_1 = 3$			$SS_1 = SS_{W1} = 8$

Table 12.39: Mental stability scores for women with 1–3 cats (X_2)

X_2	M_2	(X_2-M_2)	$(X_2-M_2)^2$
19	18	1	1
19	18	1	1
16	18	−2	4
$M_2 = 18$; $N_2 = 3$; $df_2 = 2$			$SS_2 = SS_{W2} = 6$

Table 12.40 Mental stability scores for women with 4+ cats (X_3)

X_3	M_3	(X_3-M_3)	$(X_3-M_3)^2$
16	15	1	1
16	15	1	1
13	15	−2	4
15	15	0	0
$M_3 = 15$; $N_3 = 4$; $df_3 = 3$			$SS_3 = SS_{W3} = 6$

$SS_W = SS_{W1} + SS_{W2} + SS_{W3} = 8 + 6 + 6 = 20$

$MS_W = \dfrac{SS_W}{df_W} = \dfrac{20}{8} = 2.5$

$$F = \frac{MS_B}{2.5}$$

$$MS_B = \frac{SS_B}{df_B}$$

$$SS_B = SS_{B1} + SS_{B2} + SS_{B3} + \ldots$$

$$GM = \frac{\sum X_1 + \sum X_2 + \sum X_3 + \cdots}{\sum (N_1 + N_2 + N_3 + \cdots)}$$

$$GM = \frac{72 + 54 + 60}{4 + 3 + 4} = \frac{186}{11} = 16.91$$

Table 12.41: Computing SS_{B1} for women with no cats (X_1)

M_1	GM	$(M_1 - GM)$	$(M_1 - GM)^2$
18	16.91	1.09	1.19
18	16.91	1.09	1.19
18	16.91	1.09	1.19
18	16.91	1.09	1.19
$M_1 = 18$; $N_1 = 4$; $df_1 = 3$			$SS_{B1} = 4.76$

Table 12.42: Computing SS_{B2} for women with 1–3 cats (X_2)

M_2	GM	$(M_2 - GM)$	$(M_2 - GM)^2$
18	16.91	1.09	1.19
18	16.91	1.09	1.19
18	16.91	1.09	1.19
$M_2 = 18$; $N_2 = 3$; $df_2 = 2$			$SS_{B2} = 3.57$

Table 12.43: Computing SS_{B3} for women with 4+ cats (X_3)

M_3	GM	$(M_3 - GM)$	$(M_3 - GM)^2$
15	16.91	−1.91	3.65
15	16.91	−1.91	3.65
15	16.91	−1.91	3.65
15	16.91	−1.91	3.65
$M_3 = 15$; $N_3 = 4$; $df_3 = 3$			$SS_{B3} = 14.6$

$$SS_{B1} = 4.76$$
$$SS_{B2} = 3.57$$
$$SS_{B3} = 14.6$$
$$SS_B = SS_{B1} + SS_{B2} + SS_{B3} + \ldots$$
$$SS_B = 4.76 + 3.57 + 14.6 = 22.93$$

$$MS_B = \frac{SS_B}{df_B} = \frac{22.93}{2} = 11.47$$

$$F = \frac{MS_B}{MS_W} = \frac{11.47}{2.5} = 4.59$$

e. $F_{obt} = 4.59$, while $F_{crit} = 4.46$, therefore we reject the null hypothesis. The results suggest that women with many cats may, indeed, score lower on an index of mental stability.

f. $R^2 = \dfrac{SS_B}{SS_B + SS_W} = \dfrac{22.93}{22.93 + 20} = .53$ or 53%. A great deal of the variability in scores

(53%) can be attributed to differences between the means of the groups.

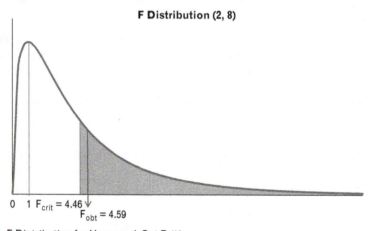

F Distribution (2, 8)

0   1 $F_{crit} = 4.46$
$F_{obt} = 4.59$

FIGURE 12.8: F Distribution for Homework Set B #1.

2.

Table 12.44: Homework Set B #2

Age 15	Age 20	Age 25
9	7	4
8	6	7
7	5	5
8	6	4
$\Sigma X_1 = 32$, $M_1 = 8$, $N_1 = 4$, $df_1 = 3$	$\Sigma X_2 = 24$, $M_2 = 6$, $N_2 = 4$, $df_2 = 3$	$\Sigma X_3 = 20$, $M_3 = 5$, $N_3 = 4$, $df_3 = 3$

a. H_1: NOT H_0

H_0: $\mu_1 = \mu_2 = \mu_3$

b. The comparison distribution is F(2, 9)
c. The alpha level is .05, numerator degrees of freedom = 2, and denominator degrees of freedom = 9, so $F_{crit} = 4.26$
d. $F = \dfrac{MS_B}{MS_W}$

$MS_W = \dfrac{SS_W}{df_W}$

$SS_W = SS_{W1} + SS_{W2} + SS_{W3} + \cdots$

Table 12.45: Social acceptability scores at 15 (X_1)

X_1	M_1	$(X_1 - M_1)$	$(X_1 - M_1)^2$
9	8	1	1
8	8	0	0
7	8	−1	1
8	8	0	0
$M_1 = 8; N_1 = 4; df_1 = 3$			$SS_1 = SS_{W1} = 2$

Table 12.46: Social acceptability scores at 20 (X_2)

X_2	M_2	$(X_2 - M_2)$	$(X_2 - M_2)^2$
7	6	1	1
6	6	0	0
5	6	−1	1
6	6	0	0
$M_2 = 6\ N_2 = 4; df_2 = 3$			$SS_2 = SS_{W2} = 2$

Table 12.47: Social acceptability scores for age 25 (X_3)

X_3	M_3	$(X_3 - M_3)$	$(X_3 - M_3)^2$
4	5	−1	1
7	5	2	4
5	5	0	0
4	5	−1	1
$M_3 = 5; N_3 = 4; df_3 = 3$			$SS_3 = SS_{W3} = 6$

$$SS_W = SS_{W1} + SS_{W2} + SS_{W3} = 2 + 2 + 6 = 10$$

$$MS_W = \frac{SS_W}{df_W} = \frac{10}{9} = 1.11$$

$$F = \frac{MS_B}{1.11}$$

$$MS_B = \frac{SS_B}{df_B}$$

$$SS_B = SS_{B1} + SS_{B2} + SS_{B3} + \cdots$$

$$GM = \frac{\sum X_1 + \sum X_2 + \sum X_3 + \cdots}{\sum(N_1 + N_2 + N_3 + \cdots)}.$$

$$GM = \frac{32 + 24 + 20}{4 + 4 + 4} = \frac{76}{12} = 6.33$$

Table 12.48: Computing SS_{B1} for social acceptability scores at 15 (X_1)

M_1	GM	(M_1-GM)	$(M_1-GM)^2$
8	6.33	1.67	2.79
8	6.33	1.67	2.79
8	6.33	1.67	2.79
8	6.33	1.67	2.79
$M_1 = 8$; $N_1 = 4$; $df_1 = 3$			$SS_{B1} = 11.16$

Table 12.49: Computing SS_{B2} for social acceptability scores for age 20 (X_2)

M_2	GM	(M_2-GM)	$(M_2-GM)^2$
6	6.33	−.33	.11
6	6.33	−.33	.11
6	6.33	−.33	.11
6	6.33	−.33	.11
$M_2 = 6$; $N_2 = 4$; $df_2 = 3$			$SS_{B2} = .44$

Table 12.50: Computing SS_{B3} for social acceptability scores for age 25 (X_3)

M_3	GM	(M_3–GM)	(M_3–GM)^2
5	6.33	−1.33	1.77
5	6.33	−1.33	1.77
5	6.33	−1.33	1.77
5	6.33	−1.33	1.77
$M_3 = 5$; $N_3 = 4$; $df_3 = 3$			$SS_{B3} = 7.08$

$$SS_{B1} = 11.16$$
$$SS_{B2} = .44$$
$$SS_{B3} = 7.08$$
$$SS_B = SS_{B1} + SS_{B2} + SS_{B3} + \cdots$$
$$SS_B = 11.16 + .44 + 7.08 = 18.68$$

$$MS_B = \frac{SS_B}{df_B} = \frac{18.68}{2} = 9.34$$

$$F = \frac{MS_B}{MS_W} = \frac{9.34}{1.11} = 8.41$$

e. $F_{obt} = 8.41$, while $F_{crit} = 4.26$; therefore, we reject the null hypothesis. Our research indicates that immature people are rated as less socially acceptable as they get older.

f. $R^2 = \dfrac{SS_B}{SS_B + SS_W} = \dfrac{18.68}{18.68 + 10} = .65$, or 65%. A large amount of the variability in

scores (65%) can be attributed to differences between the means of the groups.

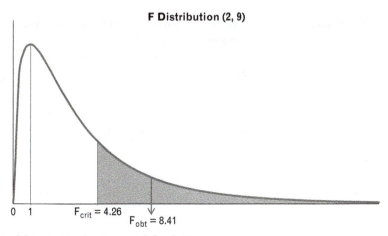

F Distribution (2, 9)

0 1 $F_{crit} = 4.26$ $F_{obt} = 8.41$

FIGURE 12.9: F Distribution for Homework Set B #2.

3.

Table 12.51: Homework Set B #3

People who score high in jealousy	People who score neutral in jealousy	People who score low in jealousy
6	5	8
5	6	9
4	7	9
5	7	8
5	10	6
$\Sigma X_1 = 25, M_1 = 5, N_1 = 5, df_1 = 4$	$\Sigma X_2 = 35, M_2 = 7, N_2 = 5, df_2 = 4$	$\Sigma X_3 = 40, M_3 = 8, N_3 = 5, df_3 = 4$

a. H_1: NOT H_0

   H_0: $\mu_1 = \mu_2 = \mu_3$

b.   The comparison distribution is F(2,12)

c.   The alpha level is .01, numerator degrees of freedom = 2, and denominator degrees of freedom = 12, so $F_{crit} = 6.93$

d. $F = \dfrac{MS_B}{MS_W}$

   $MS_W = \dfrac{SS_W}{df_W}$

   $SS_W = SS_{W1} + SS_{W2} + SS_{W3} + \ldots$

Table 12.52: In-law relationship satisfaction for people with high jealousy scores (X_1)

X_1	M_1	$(X_1 - M_1)$	$(X_1 - M_1)^2$
6	5	1	1
5	5	0	0
4	5	−1	1
5	5	0	0
5	5	0	0
$M_1 = 5; N_1 = 5; df_1 = 4$			$SS_1 = SS_{W1} = 2$

Table 12.53: In-law relationship satisfaction for people with neutral jealousy scores (X_2)

X_2	M_2	(X_2-M_2)	$(X_2-M_2)^2$
5	7	2	4
6	7	−1	1
7	7	0	0
7	7	0	0
10	7	3	9
$M_2 = 7$ $N_2 = 5$; $df_2 = 4$			$SS_2 = SS_{W2} = 14$

Table 12.54: In-law relationship satisfaction for people with low jealousy scores (X_3)

X_3	M_3	(X_3-M_3)	$(X_3-M_3)^2$
8	8	0	0
9	8	1	1
9	8	1	1
8	8	0	0
6	8	−2	4
$M_3 = 8$; $N_3 = 5$; $df_3 = 4$			$SS_3 = SS_{W3} = 6$

$$SS_W = SS_{W1} + SS_{W2} + SS_{W3} = 2 + 14 + 6 = 22$$

$$MS_W = \frac{SS_W}{df_W} = \frac{22}{12} = 1.83$$

$$F = \frac{MS_B}{1.83}$$

$$MS_B = \frac{SS_B}{df_B}$$

$$SS_B = SS_{B1} + SS_{B2} + SS_{B3} + \cdots$$

$$GM = \frac{\sum X_1 + \sum X_2 + \sum X_3 + \cdots}{\sum (N_1 + N_2 + N_3 + \cdots)}$$

$$GM = \frac{25 + 35 + 40}{5 + 5 + 5} = \frac{100}{15} = 6.67$$

Table 12.55: Computing SS_{B1} for in-law relationship satisfaction for people with high jealousy scores (X_1)

M_1	GM	(M_1-GM)	$(M_1-GM)^2$
5	6.67	−1.67	2.79
5	6.67	−1.67	2.79
5	6.67	−1.67	2.79
5	6.67	−1.67	2.79
5	6.67	−1.67	2.79
$M_1 = 5$; $N_1 = 5$; $df_1 = 4$			$SS_{B1} = 13.95$

Table 12.56: Computing SS_{B2} for in-law relationship satisfaction for people with neutral jealousy scores (X_2)

M_2	GM	(M_2-GM)	$(M_2-GM)^2$
7	6.67	.33	.11
7	6.67	.33	.11
7	6.67	.33	.11
7	6.67	.33	.11
7	6.67	.33	.11
$M_2 = 7$; $N_2 = 5$; $df_2 = 4$			$SS_{B2} = .55$

Table 12.57: Computing SS_{B3} for nn-law relationship satisfaction for people with low jealousy scores (X_3)

M_3	GM	(M_3-GM)	$(M_3-GM)^2$
8	6.67	1.33	1.77
8	6.67	1.33	1.77
8	6.67	1.33	1.77
8	6.67	1.33	1.77
8	6.67	1.33	1.77
$M_3 = 8$; $N_3 = 5$; $df_3 = 4$			$SS_{B3} = 8.85$

$SS_{B1} = 13.95$

$SS_{B2} = .55$

$SS_{B3} = 8.85$

$SS_B = SS_{B1} + SS_{B2} + SS_{B3} + \cdots$

$SS_B = 13.95 + .55 + 8.85 = 23.35$

$$MS_B = \frac{SS_B}{df_B} = \frac{23.35}{2} = 11.68$$

$$F = \frac{MS_B}{MS_W} = \frac{11.68}{1.83} = 6.38$$

e. F_{obt} = 6.38, while F_{crit} = 6.93. Although we were close, we fail to reject the null hypothesis. We have not found evidence that people who score low in jealousy have better relationships with their in-laws.

f. $R^2 = \dfrac{SS_B}{SS_B + SS_W} = \dfrac{23.34}{23.34 + 22} = .51$, or 51%. A large amount of the variability in scores (51%) can be attributed to differences between the means of the groups.

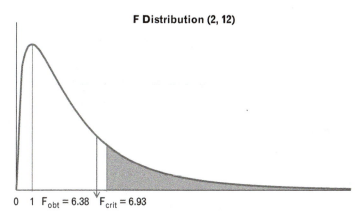

F Distribution (2, 12)

0   1 F_{obt} = 6.38 F_{crit} = 6.93

FIGURE 12.10: F Distribution for Homework Set B #3.

CHAPTER THIRTEEN

1. a. H_0: Ó = E

    H_1: not H_0 (or Ó ≠ E)

    b.   The comparison distribution is a Chi Square distribution with df = 1 (because we have 2 categories—resident and non-resident)

    c.   The critical value (X^2_{crit}) of a Chi Square distribution with 1 df and an alpha level of .01 is 6.63.

    d.

Table 13.13 Homework Set B #1d

Category	E (expected frequency)	O (observed frequency)	(O – E)	(O – E)²	$\dfrac{(O-E)^2}{E}$
Resident	30	40	10	100	3.33
Non-resident	70	60	–10	100	1.43

$$X^2_{obt} = \Sigma \frac{(O-E)^2}{E} = 4.76$$

e.   We fail to reject the null hypothesis. The results indicate that sunny weather does not bring significantly more than the expected number of residents to the beach.

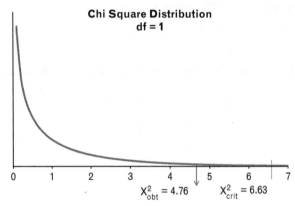

FIGURE 13.13: Homework Set B #1.

2.   a. H_0: Ó = E

     H_1: not H_0 (or Ó ≠ E)

     b.   The comparison distribution is a Chi Square distribution with df = 3 (because there are 4 categories and df = 4–1)
     c.   The critical value (X^2_{obt}) of a Chi Square distribution with 3 df and an alpha level of .05 is 7.81.
     d.

Table 13.14 Homework Set B #2d

Category	E (expected frequency)	0 (observed frequency)	(0 – E)	(0 – E)²	$\dfrac{(0-E)^2}{E}$
"Acclaimed Painting"	25	29	4	16	.64
8-year-old painting #1	25	25	0	0	0
8-year-old painting #2	25	23	−2	4	.16
8-year-old painting #3	25	23	−2	4	.16

$$X^2_{obt} = \Sigma \frac{(O-E)^2}{E} = .96$$

e.   We fail to reject the null hypothesis. The results indicate that you are not alone in not being able to identify an acclaimed painting as an extraordinary work of art amongst paintings.

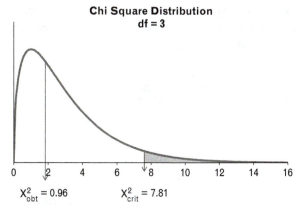

$X^2_{obt} = 0.96$ $X^2_{crit} = 7.81$

FIGURE 13.14: Homework Set B #2.

3. a. $H_0: Ó = E$

    $H_1:$ not H_0 (or $Ó \neq E$)

    b. The comparison distribution is a Chi Square distribution with df = 2 (because we have two rows and three columns, so df = (2−1) * (3−1) = 2)

    c. The critical value (X^2_{obt}) of a Chi Square distribution with 2 df and an alpha level of .05 is 5.99.

    d.

Expected values (E) are in parentheses next to O (or observed values)

Table 13.15 Homework Set B #3d

	In favor of activity buses	Against activity buses	No opinion on activity buses	ΣR
Participated in sports/clubs	80 (58.44)	5 (23.91)	0 (2.66)	85
Did not participate in sports/clubs	30 (51.56)	40 (21.09)	5 (2.34)	75
ΣC	110	45	5	N = 160

$$X^2_{obt} = \frac{(80-58.44)^2}{58.44} + \frac{(5-23.91)^2}{23.91} + \frac{(0-2.66)^2}{2.66}$$

$$+ \frac{(30-51.56)^2}{51.56} + \frac{(40-21.09)^2}{21.09} + \frac{(5-2.34)^2}{2.34}$$

$$= 7.95 + 14.96 + 2.66 + 9.02 + 16.96 + 3.02$$

$$= 54.57$$

e.   We reject the null hypothesis. How people feel about activity buses for middle and high schools appears to be related to whether they participated in after-school sports and/or clubs as teenagers.

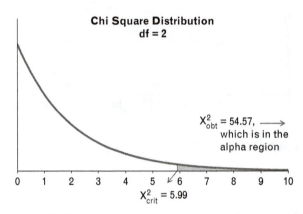

FIGURE 13.15: Homework Set B #3.

REFERENCES

2012 Ohio Republican Presidential Primary Pollster Ratings. http://americanresearchgroup.com/ratings/2012/ohrp/ Retrieved July 28, 2012.

Aron, A., & Aron, E.N. (1994). Statistics for Psychology. Upper Saddle River, NJ: Prentice-Hall.

Bleske, A. L., & Buss, D. M. (2001). Opposite sex friendship: Sex differences and similarities in initiation, selection, and dissolution. *Personality and Social Psychology Bulletin, 27*, 1310–1323.

Cohen, J. (1988). *Statistical power analysis for the behavioral sciences* (second edition). Hillsdale, New Jersey: Lawrence Erlbaum.

Damisch, L., Stoberock, B., & Mussweiler, T. (2010). Keep your fingers crossed! How superstition improves performance. *Psychological Science, 21*, 1014–1020.

Dubbs, S. L., & Buunk, A. P. (2010). Parents just don't understand: Parent-offspring conflict over mate choice. *Evolutionary Psychology, 8*, 586–598.

Gallant, S., Williams, L., Fisher, M., & Cox, A. (2011). Mating strategies and self-presentation in online personal advertisement photographs. *Journal of Social, Evolutionary and Cultural Psychology, 5*, 106–121.

Garcia, J. G., Geher, G., Crosier, B., Saad, G., Gambacorta, D., Johnsen, L., & Pranckitas, E. (2011). The interdisciplinary context of evolutionary approaches to human behavior: a key to survival in the ivory archipelago. *Futures, 43*, 749–761.

Glass, D. J., Wilson, D. S., & Geher, G. (2012). Evolutionary training in relation to human affairs is sorely lacking in higher education. *EvoS Journal: The Journal of the Evolutionary Studies Consortium, 4*, 16–22.

Mathews, A., Mackintosh, B., & Fulcher, E. P. (1997). Cognitive biases in anxiety and attention to threat. *Trends in Cognitive Sciences, 1*, 340–345.

McCrae, R. R., Terracciano, A., and 78 members of the Personality Profiles of Cultures Project. (2005). Universal Features of Personality Traits from the Observer's Perspective: Data from 50 Cultures. *Journal of Personality and Social Psychology, 88*, 547–561.

Nettle, D. (2006). The evolution of personality variation and humans and other animals. *The American Psychologist, 6*, 621–631.

Peterson, A., Geher, G., & Kaufman, S. B. (2011). Predicting preferences for sex acts: Which traits matter and why? *Evolutionary Psychology, 9*, 371–389.

Schmitt, D. P. (2005). Sociosexuality from Argentina to Zimbabwe: A 48-nation study of sex, culture, and strategies of human mating. *Behavioral and Brain Sciences, 28*, 247–311.

Zung, W. W. K. (1986). Zung self-rating depression scale and depression status inventory. In N. Sartorius & T. A. Ban (Eds.), *Assessment of depression* (pp. 221–231). Berlin: Springer Verlag.

INDEX

Bold locators indicate tables and *italics* locators indicate figures.

PORTLAND PUBLIC LIBRARY SYSTEM
5 MONUMENT SQUARE
PORTLAND, ME 04101

4/23/15

maner

WITHDRAWN